Evaluation and Treatment of Insomnia

Evaluation and Treatment of Insomnia

Anthony Kales, M.D.

Professor and Chairman, Department of Psychiatry
Pennsylvania State University College of Medicine

Joyce D. Kales, M.D.

Associate Professor of Psychiatry
Pennsylvania State University College of Medicine

New York   Oxford
OXFORD UNIVERSITY PRESS
1984

To our parents and children

Library of Congress Cataloging in Publication Data

Kales, Anthony, 1934–
  Evaluation and treatment of insomnia.

  Bibliography: p.
  Includes index.
  1. Insomnia.   I. Kales, Joyce D.   II. Title.   [DNLM:
1. Insomnia.   WM 188 K14e]
RC548.K35   1984   616.8′49   83–23637
ISBN 0–19–503434–1

Printing (last digit):   9 8 7 6 5 4 3

Printed in the United States of America

Preface

Insomnia is extremely prevalent and, in many cases, has a profound impact on an individual's life. As a consequence, physicians are confronted daily in their office practice with the problem of properly evaluating and treating insomnia in order to alleviate or prevent its many untoward consequences. In an effort to meet this need, this book discusses and answers important medical, psychiatric, and psychosocial questions pertaining to the overall management of insomnia.

The book begins with a brief history of sleep research and a description of normal sleep patterns and functions. Then we address the specific problem of insomnia in terms of its various epidemiologic, clinical, laboratory, and psychosocial dimensions. Subsequently, we focus on specific principles for the evaluation and treatment of this condition.

An overview of normal sleep patterns and their physiology, neuroendocrinology, and underlying mechanisms is included as a prerequisite for a better understanding of sleep pathology. In discussing the scope of the problem of insomnia, we report on the results of large-scale surveys of both the general population and physicians' practices which show a high prevalence of the symptom of insomnia and correlations between health risk and variations from optimal sleep quantity. Lending clinical validity to insomniacs' complaints is the finding that they can be successfully discriminated from controls on the basis of sleep difficulty, psychopathology, or both. We also provide data on a number of clinical characteristics and behavioral correlates of insomnia. The disorder may begin at any age and generally persists for many years. During the day patients with insomnia often have high levels of anxiety and at bedtime they have difficulty relaxing and demonstrate heightened physiologic activation.

Strong evidence is provided supporting the concept that the etiology of insomnia is multidimensional, including situational disruptions, medical and other pathophysiologic factors (aging, medical illness, and drug-related conditions), and psychologic disturbances. Stressful life events are commonly associated with the onset of sleep difficulty and appear to be mediated by certain predisposing personality factors. Additionally, psychologic testing and psychiatric diagnostic studies show high levels of psychopathology in patients with chronic insomnia; these patients' personality patterns are characterized by apprehensiveness, rumination, chronic anxiety and depression, inhibition of emotions and an inability to express anger.

Recommended components of the evaluation of patients with transient, short-term, or chronic insomnia include: taking a sleep history, drug history, and psychiatric history, as well as a general medical history and assessing for the presence of physical factors. For the management of insomnia, sleep hygiene and general health-promoting measures are often beneficial to some degree. When insomnia is intense and persistent, however, more vigorous multidimensional therapeutic endeavors are usually required. Counseling, stress management, psychotherapy, and behavioral therapy have an important role in the treatment of chronic insomnia. Guidelines are provided for the appropriate adjunctive use of hypnotic medication based on each hypnotic drug's pharmacologic and clinical profile, including initial efficacy, continued effectiveness, side effects during administration, and effects following withdrawal. Physicians also are offered recommendations for the use of antidepressant medication, which is indicated for those patients suffering from insomnia as a result of a major depression.

Each chapter of this book begins with a brief introduction stating its purpose. Then we present clinically relevant information drawn from epidemiologic surveys, clinical studies, sleep laboratory evaluations, drug trials, as well as from other research sources. Tables and figures are frequently used to present the data in a concise and practical manner. Further, case histories illustrate the applicability of the clinical findings and research data to the evaluation, diagnosis, and treatment of insomnia in the physician's office setting. Each chapter refers the physician to relevant material in other chapters in an effort to integrate different sections of the book. Finally, a detailed summary concludes each chapter, to provide both an overview and reinforce the information presented.

Because of a lack of extensive clinical experience and an inadequate scientific data base, sleep disturbances until recently have been surrounded by a great deal of mystique. Further, many scientific publications as well as articles in the popular media neglect a comprehensive discussion of the problem of insomnia. Accordingly, one of the goals of this book is to elucidate the multiple facets of insomnia and its treatment, drawing from data compiled in clinical and experimental studies.

We are indebted to Drs. Carmine D. Clemente, John D. French, Nathaniel Kleitman, and Richard D. Walter for their enthusiastic support in the development of our research interests at the Brain Research Institute of the University of California, Los Angeles. We are also especially grateful to Drs. Norman Q. Brill, George T. Harrell, Sherman M. Mellinkoff, and Louis Jolyon West for the opportunities they provided us to gain valuable clinical experience and to further our academic careers both at UCLA and the Pennsylvania State University.

We sincerely acknowledge the contributions of a number of colleagues who assisted in the collection and interpretation of bibliographic materials and preparation of the manuscript. Dr. Edward Bixler was tireless and creative in directing the Sleep Laboratory, while Dr. Roger Cadieux ably coordinated the many aspects of the Sleep Disorders Clinic. Drs. Constantin Soldatos and Antonio Vela-Bueno were of great help in critiquing chapters and making many insightful comments and constructive suggestions. With enthusiasm, Katherine Chamberlin expertly edited the book throughout all of its many stages. Judith Jacoby and Carol Nigh were painstakingly thorough in skillfully reviewing the final drafts. Mary Mack was diligent in typing the many versions of the manuscript, and Dolores Hudock and Miriam Myer provided support by operating an efficient office and typing parts of the manuscript when the need arose. Finally, we are indebted to our patients for providing us with the rich clinical experience without which this book would not have been possible.

Hershey, Pennsylvania A.K.
November 1983 J.D.K.

Preface to Second Printing

Since the first printing of *Evaluation and Treatment of Insomnia*, considerable new interest has developed in this field. A particularly important development has been the formation of a new section of the World Psychiatric Association (WPA) devoted to Psychiatry and Sleep/Wakefulness Disorders. This has proven to be most helpful in promoting research and exchanging information in an area too long neglected: emotional factors underlying or associated with disorders of sleep/wakefulness, particularly insomnia as discussed in Chapter 5 of this book. In October 1989, this new section sponsored two symposia at the VIIIth World Congress of Psychiatry in Athens, Greece. At the symposium called "Sleep Disorders Medicine" there was general consensus on the essential indications for sleep laboratory investigations of patients with sleep disorders; it was noted that the prevalence of sleep apnea and nocturnal myoclonus in insomniac patients is no different from that in the general population. Thus, there is now general agreement that sleep laboratory investigations usually are not indicated in the evaluation of insomnia (as discussed in Chapter 3). This is an important issue not only for developing countries, but also for industrialized countries striving to contain their rapidly escalating medical costs while utilizing available funds for diagnosis and treatment in a cost-effective manner.

The second symposium was called "Benzodiazepines: Efficacy/Side Effects and Pharmacokinetics/Dynamics." This session helped to dispel the notion that all benzodiazepines are alike in regard to their efficacy and safety, an issue discussed in Chapter 10. It is now widely recognized that certain pharmacokinetic (rapid elimination) and pharmacodynamic (high receptor affinity) properties are associated with frequent behavioral side effects that include amnesia, confusion, disorientation, hyperexcitability, delusions, hallucinations, rapid tolerance and withdrawal disturbances. In this regard, a review of adverse reactions to benzodiazepine hypnotics reported to the Food and Drug Administration (FDA)[1] and two recent, carefully controlled investigations[2,3] confirm and amplify the side effects discussed in Chapter 10.

Another important development since publication of this book has been that of a clinically useful diagnostic classification of sleep disorders. The Diagnostic and Statistical Manual, 3rd Edition (DSM-III) of the American Psychiatric Association (APA) did not contain an official classification of sleep disorders. In the development of such a classification for the next edition (DSM-III-R[4]), the APA rejected a proposed classification that consisted primarily of diagnoses with little clinical validity that relied heavily and unjustifiably on sleep laboratory recordings in favor of one that was clinically relevant, useful and understandable to the office-based practitioner. Furthermore, the DSM-III-R and forthcoming International Classification of Diseases, 10th Edition (ICD-10) classifications for sleep disorders are clinically applicable to patients with insomnia who are seen in primary care office practice as well as the minority of such patients referred for secondary or tertiary evaluation or treatment.

Finally, it is encouraging to note that increased attention and research are being devoted to insomnia. This augurs well for additional developments that will lead to the improved diagnosis and treatment of patients with this frequently occurring and often severe affliction.

Hershey, Pennsylvania   A. K.
January 1990   J. D. K.

1. Bixler, E. O., Kales, A., Brubaker, B. H., Kales, J. D.: Adverse Reactions to Benzodiazepine Hypnotics: Spontaneous Reporting System. *Pharmacology*, 35:286-300, 1987.

2. Adam, K., Oswald, I.: Can a Rapidly-eliminated Hypnotic Cause Daytime Anxiety? *Pharmacopsychiatry*, 22:115-119, 1989.

3. Bixler, E. O., Kales, A., Manfredi, R. L., Vgontzas, A. N.: Triazolam-induced Brain Impairment: Frequent Memory Disturbances. *European Journal of Clinical Pharmacology*, 3:A171, 1989.

4. American Psychiatric Association: *Diagnostic and Statistical Manual of Mental Disorders*, Third Edition, Revised. Washington, DC, American Psychiatric Association, 1987.

Contents

1. **The Study and Nature of Sleep, 3**
   Methods of Sleep Research, 3 / Normal Patterns of Sleep, 9
   Physiologic Correlates of Sleep, 12 / Role and Functions of Sleep, 17

2. **Insomnia: Scope of the Problem, 36**
   Prevalence of Insomnia, 36 / The Need for Sleep, 39
   Psychosocial Correlates of Insomnia, 43
   Physician Education on Insomnia, 50

3. **Sleep Laboratory Studies of Insomnia, 61**
   Methodologic Considerations, 61
   Nocturnal Sleep and Wakefulness in Normal Subjects, 62
   Nocturnal Sleep and Wakefulness in Insomniac Subjects, 67
   Sleep Stage Patterns, 72 / Physiologic Correlates of Insomnia, 73
   Sleep Apnea and Nocturnal Myoclonus, 75

4. **Onset, Clinical Characteristics, and Behavioral Correlates, 87**
   Demographics, 88 / Onset, Type, and Duration of Insomnia, 89
   Behavioral Correlates, 93 / General Health Correlates, 97
   Drug or Alcohol Treatment as a Factor, 102

5. **Psychiatric Factors in Insomnia, 111**
   Role of Predisposing Emotional Factors and Stressful Life Events, 111
   Psychologic Testing, 113 / Psychiatric Diagnoses, 122

6. **Medical and Other Pathophysiologic Factors in Insomnia, 134**
   Aging, 134 / Situational Disturbances, 136
   Medical Causes of Insomnia, 137
   Sleep Disruption in the Hospital Environment, 146
   Drug-Induced Insomnia, 148

7. **Evaluation of Insomnia, 162**
   Sleep History, 163 / Medical Assessment, 168 / Drug History, 169
   Psychiatric Assessment, 170 / Diagnosis of Insomnia, 174

Importance of Evaluation for Treatment Outcome, 175
Advantages of Assessment in the Office Setting, 176

8. **General Measures for Treating Insomnia, 186**
Obtaining an Optimal Amount of Sleep, 187
Establishing Regular Schedules, 188
Improving the Sleep Environment, 191 / Exercising Properly, 194
Regulating Nutrition, 196 / Managing Stress, 197
Avoiding Drug-Induced Sleep Disturbance, 201
Special Instructions for the Elderly, 202

9. **Psychotherapy and Behavior Therapy, 214**
General Psychotherapeutic Considerations, 215
Effectiveness of Psychotherapy, 218
Specific Psychotherapeutic Approaches, 219
Behavioral Treatment of Insomnia, 231

10. **Adjunctive Treatment of Insomnia with Hypnotic Drugs, 249**
Clinical Trials and Sleep Laboratory Evaluations, 250
Non-Benzodiazepine Hypnotic Drugs, 253
Benzodiazepine Hypnotic Drugs, 255
Guidelines for Prescribing Hypnotic Drugs, 267

11. **Use of Antidepressants in Treating Insomnia, 282**
Relation of Insomnia to Depression, 282
Tricyclic Antidepressants, 283
"Second Generation" Antidepressants, 287
Monoamine Oxidase Inhibitors (MAOIs), 290
Special Clinical Issues in Using Antidepressants for Insomnia, 291

Author Index, 309

Subject Index, 315

Evaluation and Treatment of Insomnia

1. The Study and Nature of Sleep

Sleep research is a relatively new discipline.[1-5] Yet in just a few decades, scientists have generated a wealth of information that is useful for physicians who evaluate and treat sleep problems.[6-12] In the case of chronic insomnia, it is often difficult for the clinician to decide when the information is applicable because of the complex array of medical, psychologic, and social factors associated with this symptom and condition.[10,13-15] Physicians must understand these complexities and be prepared to draw upon a wide range of clinical skills if they are to expect a successful treatment outcome with insomniac patients. To be most effective in managing transient or chronic insomnia, however, clinicians must first acquire a basic understanding of normal sleep. This chapter provides such introductory information.

First, a brief history of sleep research and its methodology is given from both sleep laboratory and clinical perspectives. Then, normal sleep is discussed, in terms of basic sleep patterns and their physiology, neuroendocrinology, and mechanisms. Finally, the functions of sleep are examined in light of experimental studies and the major theories advanced to explain the purpose of sleep.

Methods of Sleep Research

Pre-Modern Sleep Research Era

Electrophysiology, the technology that underlies modern sleep research, was introduced in the late eighteenth century when Galvani demonstrated the presence of electricity in animal tissues.[16] More than 100 years later (1929), Berger, who discovered the electroencephalogram, recorded the first brain waves in humans.[17] Soon afterward, in 1937, Loomis, Harvey, and Hobart described the electrophysiology of sleep and classified specific stages of sleep.[18]

Before the latter two developments took place, the scientific study of sleep had been limited to behavioral observations and reports of subjective experience. However, even without the aid of objective measures, many early speculations were made about the nature of sleep, particularly dreaming sleep, that subsequently would be proven accurate.[11] As early as 1868, for example, Griesinger speculated that dreaming was associated with periods of eye movements.[19] Another important observation was made by Freud, who noted that motor paralysis occurs during dreaming, and he hypothesized that this absence of motor discharge prevents the acting out of dreams.[20] This concept was substantiated many years later by electromyographic (EMG) recordings, which showed that muscle tonus decreases during rapid-eye-movement (REM) sleep,[21-23] the stage of sleep most frequently associated with dream recall.[1,4,5,24] Another discovery was made in 1897, when Howell, using plethysmographic methods, was able to describe the reduction in blood pressure that follows sleep onset, as well as the periodic elevations in blood pressure that occur throughout the night at intervals of 30 to 90 minutes.[25] Then, in 1923, MacWilliam observed that blood pressure, heart rate, and respiratory rate increased with "disturbed sleep" but did not change in "undisturbed sleep."[26] In 1942, Regelsberger observed changes in CO_2 respiratory output and skin resistance during sleep with a periodicity of 55 to 120[27] minutes. Shortly thereafter, Ohlmeyer and his associates reported on a periodic cycle of about 85 minutes in duration for penile erections during sleep.[28] A basic rest-activity cycle occurring during both sleep and wakefulness was later more clearly defined by Kleitman as more detailed electrophysiologic data became available.[29] In retrospect, it appears that many early investigators had observed the physiologic concomitants of REM sleep prior to its initial discovery.

Sleep research as we know it today began in the early 1950s, when Aserinsky and Kleitman observed that clusters of conjugate, rapid eye movements occurred periodically during sleep.[1,2] These bursts of eye movements were later found to be accompanied by a low-voltage, high-frequency EEG pattern.[3,4] Researchers also discovered that subjects recalled their dreams frequently when awakened from REM sleep but seldom had dream recall when aroused from non-rapid-eye-movement (NREM) sleep.[1,4,24] The modern sleep research laboratory has evolved from these discoveries. Its specialized and standardized electrophysiologic recording techniques[30] have enabled scientists to study sleep and dreaming in subjects whose sleep is normal and in those with sleep disorders.

Studies of Normal Sleep

Sleep laboratory studies have provided a comprehensive profile of normal sleep patterns—knowledge that is a prerequisite to understanding insomnia and other disorders of sleep. Indeed, during the first decade or two after the discovery of REMs and REM sleep, investigators concentrated on defining normal sleep and its variations. As a result, a great deal was learned about normal sleep, its physiologic characteristics, and its ontogenetic development.

The sleep laboratory provides an ideal setting for the evaluation and analysis of sleep, primarily because measurements are objective and experimental conditions can be rigorously controlled.[30-33] Because subjects sleep in sound-attenuated rooms that are also temperature- and humidity-controlled, they are not disturbed by environmental factors or by other individuals. Furthermore, because polygraphic recordings are continuous throughout the night, patterns of sleep and wakefulness are analyzed minute by minute. The data obtained from a single night's recording of eight hours is massive; stretched end-to-end the sleep recording extends about 1420 feet, or over one-quarter of a mile.

The use of standardized techniques contributes to precise data collection and a thorough evaluation of sleep.[30-33] In most studies, electroencephalographic (EEG), electro-oculographic (EOG), and electromyographic (EMG) tracings are recorded. Cup electrodes are filled with paste and then attached to the scalp to detect brain activity (EEG), taped above and below the outer canthus of each eye to record eye movements (EOG), and secured beneath the chin to monitor muscle tonus (EMG) (Fig. 1.1).[30]

The electrical potentials from the EEG, EOG, and EMG electrodes are transmitted to polygraph machines located in adjacent recording rooms. Detailed scoring of recordings for sleep stages and wakefulness is performed at a later time, usually on a "blind" basis, that is, by a technician who has no knowledge of the experimental conditions. In this manner, a subject's sleep profile may be objectively determined under any one of a variety of experimental conditions.

Many types of subjects have been evaluated in sleep laboratory studies, including persons of all ages with no sleep complaints, so-

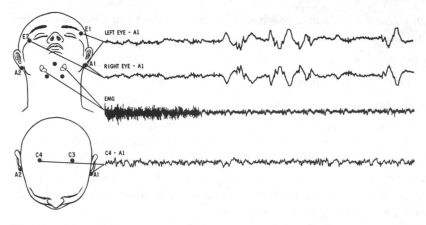

Fig. 1.1. Sleep laboratory recordings. The top two tracings show eye movements, the next tracing illustrates EMG or muscle tonus, and the lowest tracing shows brain waves (EEG). The recordings illustrate the onset of a REM sleep period. First, the EMG decreases sharply; then eye movements appear while the electroencephalographic waves change to low-amplitude, mixed-frequency. (From Rechtschaffen and Kales, eds[30])

called "normal" sleepers. Generally, subjects presumed to be "normal" sleepers are not included in studies if they have significant emotional or physical disorders or if they use drugs of any sort. Also excluded are any subjects, either normal or with sleep disorders, who appear to be unable to comply with the conditions of the study. Subjects are expected to maintain consistent levels of physical activity, to refrain from taking naps, and to abstain from alcoholic beverages and drugs that are not part of the study protocol. Adherence to these conditions is critical in studies of insomnia because slight changes in even one variable can significantly alter the sleep data.

Accuracy of data also depends upon recording a sufficient number of nights so that adaptation to the sleep laboratory is not a confounding factor.[34-37] Investigators have observed that patients take more time to fall asleep and awaken more often during their first night in the laboratory than they do on subsequent nights. Therefore, data from the first night in the sleep laboratory are not included in the sleep profile because subjects need to adapt to the new environment and to the encumbrance of the attached electrodes. By the third and fourth nights, subjects' customary sleep patterns are re-established.

Studies of Insomnia

Sleep Laboratory Studies   As noted earlier, studies in the sleep laboratory were at first devoted primarily to investigating sleep physiology. Clinically oriented studies in the sleep laboratory became more popular, however, as sleep researchers began to realize the laboratory's usefulness for evaluating sleep disorders as well as medical and psychiatric conditions in which sleep might be disrupted or altered.[6-12] Consequently, over the past few years the clinical aspects of sleep have been studied more extensively both in and out of the sleep laboratory.

In the case of insomnia, however, there have been few clinical studies in the sleep laboratory, even though such studies could contribute basic data on insomnia that would be objective and precise. For example, sleep laboratory studies can provide information on insomniac patients' "sleep efficiency," that is, how long it takes to fall asleep, how often they awaken during the night, and the total amount and percentage of sleep obtained. Sleep-stage patterns can also be accurately delineated in the sleep laboratory, as can other parameters, such as body movements, eye movements, heart rate, and respiratory rate. Additional research data can be obtained by determining the relationships between sleep stages and these other parameters.[30]

While few studies of insomnia have been systematically conducted in the sleep laboratory (see Chapter 3, Sleep Laboratory Studies of Insomnia), evaluations of hypnotic drugs have been numerous.[31-33] Such studies have been valuable for measuring the short-term efficacy of hypnotic drugs, determining whether efficacy is maintained with continued use, evaluating drugs' effects on sleep stages, and assessing any withdrawal effects.

Non-Laboratory Studies   Clinical studies of insomnia that do not use the sleep laboratory can accommodate a much larger sample size and enable investigators to assess other essential aspects of the disorder. Whereas sleep laboratory studies of insomnia focus on the electrophysiologic aspects of sleep difficulty, clinical studies can encompass a broader range of considerations: medical, psychologic, behavioral, and social. Because such factors can contribute to the development and persistence of insomnia, the research assessment of insomniac patients must be multidimensional. Furthermore, such an approach is needed to gather data on the disorder's clinical course and characteristics and to identify those treatment methods that will produce a favorable outcome.[10,13-15]

This multidimensional model for studying insomnia has a major impact on the physician's approach to managing insomniac patients. By taking a complete sleep history as a first step in evaluating sleep difficulty, the clinician obtains important information on the disorder's onset, progression, and clinical characteristics, as well as its effects on the patient's life.[38] Medical factors relating to insomnia can be evaluated with a physical examination and laboratory tests. Psychologic and behavioral factors can be assessed through psychometric testing and psychiatric interviews. Finally, any social dimensions of the insomnia can be identified through psychiatric interviews and information obtained from questionnaires.

In our clinical research studies, we integrate data from our Sleep Disorders Clinic and Sleep Laboratory, as illustrated in Figure 1.2. Findings that are clinically relevant are then made available to the

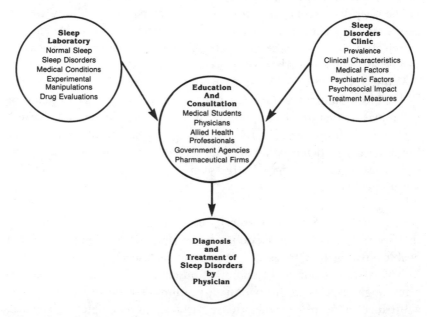

Fig. 1.2. Laboratory, clinical, and educational functions of the Sleep Research and Treatment Center. Practical data from the Sleep Laboratory and Sleep Disorders Clinic are conveyed through educational programs to the general medical community. The end result is improved diagnosis and treatment of sleep disorders in physicians' office settings. (Modified from Kales et al[39])

medical community through consultation and educational programs designed to improve physicians' ability to diagnose and treat sleep disorders, including insomnia, in the office setting.[39-41]

Another type of study conducted in the non-laboratory setting is the clinical trial of a hypnotic drug.[32] In these clinical trials, subjective data that complement the objective data from the sleep laboratory are gathered, providing an approximation of a drug's efficacy. Further, because they usually involve large numbers of subjects, they also give a comprehensive picture of the nature and prevalence of the drug's side effects. Such studies can be conducted in almost any clinical setting, therefore permitting investigation of hypnotic drugs in specific populations, such as in subjects who have insomnia and associated medical conditions.

Normal Patterns of Sleep

Identifying Sleep Stages

With the discovery of REMs, researchers divided sleep stages into REM sleep and NREM sleep (stages 1, 2, 3, and 4) based on each stage's characteristic EEG, EOG, and EMG patterns.[4] Just over ten years later, the definitions of these sleep stages were revised and expanded by an international committee of scientists who also standardized the recording techniques used in the sleep laboratory and the criteria for scoring sleep stages.[30] The definitions of sleep stages in Figure 1.3 conform to these standardized criteria.

During wakefulness, the EEG pattern is one of low amplitude and fast frequency, and there are rapid eye movements, eye blinking, and a relatively high-amplitude EMG.[30] When the eyes are closed, there are varying degrees of alpha activity (consisting of 8–13 cycles per second EEG activity). Stage 1 usually appears during the transition from wakefulness to sleep and after body movements during sleep. It is characterized by slow eye movements; low-amplitude, mixed-frequency EEG activity; and a level of muscle tonus (EMG) below that of relaxed wakefulness.

Stage 2 sleep generally consists of relatively low-amplitude, mixed-frequency EEG activity.[30] There are also intermittent sleep spindles (brief bursts of 12–14 cps EEG activity) and K complexes (EEG wave forms consisting of a high-amplitude, negative sharp wave immediately followed by a positive wave).

Stages 3 and 4 sleep are characterized by high-amplitude, slow-

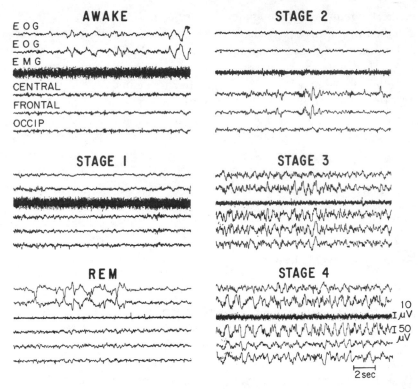

Fig. 1.3. Polygraphic characteristics of sleep stages. Sleep has its onset in stage 1, which is characterized by the absence of REMs and a low amplitude, fast-frequency EEG pattern. With the progression of sleep (stage 2), spindles of 12 to 16 cycles per second occur with low-amplitude, fast-frequency activity. In stages 3 and 4, deepening of sleep is characterized by high-amplitude slow waves covering 20% to 50% of the EEG record. REM sleep is characterized by a low-amplitude, fast-frequency EEG pattern, bursts of eye movements, and a markedly decreased level of muscle tonus. (From Kales, ed[7])

frequency EEG activity.[30] The values for these two sleep stages are often combined in sleep research studies and together are referred to as slow-wave sleep. During stages 2, 3, and 4, eye movements are absent and EMG activity remains at a level lower than that of wakefulness.

REM sleep is identified by a hypnopolygraphic pattern of relatively low-amplitude, mixed-frequency EEG activity resembling that of stage 1, episodic bursts of rapid eye movements, and a substantially reduced level of EMG activity.[30] During this sleep stage, muscle tonus, as re-flected by EMG amplitude, is at its lowest level of the sleep period (Fig. 1.3).[21-23]

Sleep Cycle of the Young Adult

A young adult's typical night of sleep begins with a brief period of stage 1 followed by stages 2, 3, and 4, respectively (Fig. 1.4).[4,36,37,42-46] The sleeper's patterns then return to stages 3 and 2. After about 70 to 100 minutes of NREM sleep, the first period of REM sleep begins. This periodic sequence of sleep stages, ending with a REM period, is defined as a sleep cycle. Averaging about 90 minutes in length, the sleep cycle is repeated four to six times each night, depending on the length of the sleep period.

As the night progresses, REM periods lengthen, and the amounts of stages 3 and 4 sleep diminish (particularly stage 4). Thus, slow-wave sleep is most prevalent early in the night and least prevalent late in the night, while the distribution of REM sleep follows the opposite pattern. REM sleep constitutes about 20 to 25 percent of a night's sleep; stage 2 makes up 50 to 60 percent of the sleep period; stages 3 and 4 account for 10 to 20 percent; and stage 1 constitutes 5 to 10 percent of total sleep time (Fig. 1.4).[4,36,37,42-46]

Age-Related Sleep Patterns

Age affects the length of sleep periods and the way they are distributed throughout a 24-hour day.[47-50] People sleep less as they grow older; the average time spent asleep becomes progressively shorter, from 16 hours at birth[51,52] to eight hours in young adults,[45,46,50] to even less in the elderly.[43,44,47,48,50,53-56] However, sleep latency (the time required to fall asleep) is fairly consistent across all adult age groups.[47] Thus, the increased wakefulness often experienced by the elderly is generally the result of more frequent and prolonged awakenings during the night.[43,47,48,50,53-56] In newborns and infants, sleep distribution throughout the 24-hour period is polyphasic.[52,57] Then, from their first year until age 5 or 6, children tend to take one afternoon nap. Older children and adults do not regularly nap. With advanced age,[49] however, napping once again becomes quite common.

Sleep stage patterns also change with age. Starting in childhood and continuing throughout life, REM sleep accounts for about 20 to 25 percent of total sleep time,[44,50] although both the absolute amount and percentage of REM sleep are inversely correlated with age.[44,54] Slow-wave sleep decreases even more dramatically with age.[43,44,50,53-56,58] Children spend about 20 to 25 percent of their total sleep in slow-wave sleep. This percentage begins to decrease in young adulthood and then diminishes progressively during middle-age and older years, so that in the elderly there is little or no slow-wave sleep.

Age-related changes in sleep patterns should be considered by the clinician who evaluates the sleep of an older person. It is particularly important to obtain a 24-hour sleep history because older people tend to take naps during the day and sleep less at night, yet report their curtailed nighttime sleep as their total sleep time.[38]

Physiologic Correlates of Sleep

General Physiology

The physiology of sleep has been studied extensively.[59-89] In general, most bodily processes slow down at sleep onset and either remain at low levels or are further reduced during NREM sleep. During REM sleep, physiologic activity rises above NREM levels and sometimes approaches the levels reached during wakefulness. The changes in body temperature regulation during sleep suggest the existence of two basic and opposite functional states: one homeostatic (during NREM sleep) and the other poikilostatic (during REM sleep).[82]

The EEG during NREM sleep becomes progressively slower in frequency and greater in amplitude; frequency is slowest and amplitude greatest during slow-wave sleep. In REM sleep, the EEG is activated, as indicated by an increase in frequency and a reduction in amplitude of the wave patterns.[4,30] Similar patterns occur in blood pressure,[59,67,68,79,87] heart rate,[59,67,87] cardiac output,[59,67] respiration rate,[59,62,65,83,84] whole body and brain temperature,[73,86] total body oxygen consumption,[64] and single neuronal brain activity.[60,70,74] These functions decrease at sleep onset and remain reduced without much variation during NREM sleep. In contrast, REM sleep is accompanied by faster firing rates for many neurons in the brain,[60,70,74] elevations in body and brain temperature,[73,78,86] greater cortical blood flow,[72,88] and increased oxygen consumption.[64] Penile erections also occur in conjunction with REM sleep.[71,76,77]

Within REM sleep there are two major physiologic phenomena: tonic events and phasic events. Tonic events are essentially maintained throughout the REM period. They include a continuous EEG pattern

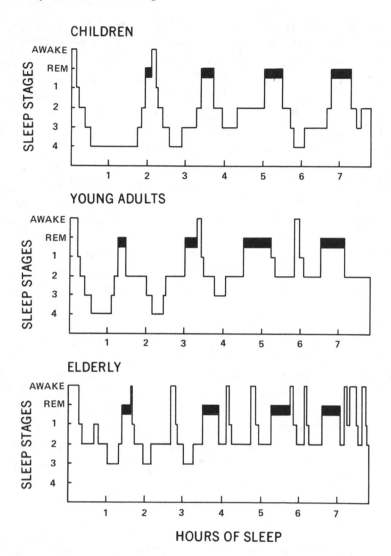

Fig. 1.4. Effects of age on normal sleep cycles. REM sleep (darkened area) occurs cyclically throughout the night at intervals of approximately 90 minutes in all age groups. REM sleep decreases slightly in the elderly, whereas stage 4 sleep decreases progressively with age, so that little, if any, is present in the elderly. In addition, the elderly have frequent awakenings and a notable increase in wake time after sleep onset. (Modified from Kales, ed[7])

of low-amplitude, fast-frequency waves;[4,30] lowered EMG activity in certain muscles;[21-23,30] and penile erections.[71,76,77] (The latter begin and end close to the onset and termination of REM periods.) Phasic events, on the other hand, are of brief duration, are discontinuous, and occur sporadically. They include conjugate REMs,[4,30] cardio-respiratory changes,[59,61,62,66,67,83,84] and occasional muscle twitching.[89]

During REM sleep, the previously mentioned tonic increases in physiologic activity are superimposed upon the preceding general NREM-related decreases. These tonic increases include those in respiration rate,[61,62,66,83,84] body and brain temperature,[73,74] and oxygen consumption.[64] Furthermore, cerebral blood flow is greater across all regions of the brain.[72] The phasic events of REM sleep are associated with further increases in physiologic activity. Blood pressure, heart rate,[59,67,68,79,87,88] cerebral blood flow,[72,88] and respiration rate,[59,61,62,66,83,84] either rise over their NREM-sleep levels in mean value as well as in variability, or exceed the values reached during the tonic phase of REM sleep.

Changes in muscle tonus are the one exception to the general pattern of reduced bodily activity during NREM sleep and increased activity during REM sleep.[21-23] The tonus of the trunk and limb muscles diminishes notably at sleep onset and remains low throughout NREM sleep. During REM sleep, however, muscle tonus diminishes even further. This relative atonia during REM sleep also involves the intercostal muscles, so that diaphragmatic breathing predominates during this sleep phase.[81] In addition, diaphragmatic activity is transiently inhibited during REM sleep, resulting in occasional brief periods of apnea or hypopnea.[69,85]

Circadian Influences on Sleep

Circadian (24-hour) rhythms in man regulate many bodily processes including sleep and wakefulness, body temperature, hunger, and most metabolic functions.[90-96] The sleep-wakefulness rhythm can be considerably influenced by external factors such as the light-dark cycle and ambient temperature. However, this rhythm as well as the ultradian, 90-minute periodicity of the REM/non-REM cycle are endogenous rhythms that persist in the absence of environmental variation. Under conditions of isolation where environmental influences are constant, the sleep-wakefulness rhythm is maintained but the length of this cycle increases to about 25 hours.[97] If such conditions are extended, the cycle length may increase to 30 to 50 hours. Circadian rhythms for body temperature,[97,98] sleep duration, and sleep structure appear to be closely related. Czeisler and Weitzman and their colleagues have shown that sleep duration depends more on the circadian phase of body temperature when a person goes to sleep than on how long the person has previously been awake. Further, these same investigators showed that the time selected for going to sleep occurred most often just after the low point of the temperature cycle had been attained. Similarly, the propensity for REM sleep increases following the trough in the temperature cycle.[98] Recently, Borbely[99] proposed that the mechanism underlying the sleep-wakefulness cycle involves an interaction of this circadian rhythm with the prior amount of wakefulness. In this theory, intensity of sleep is considered to be a function of the amount of time spent awake and is at its highest at the beginning of the sleep period. In support of this hypothesis, it has been shown that lower frequencies of the EEG (1 to 8 cycles per second) in all sleep stages decrease as the night progresses and increase with sleep deprivation.[100]

Neurotransmitters and Sleep

Early studies indicated a major role of serotonin (5-HT) as the active inducer and maintainer of slow-wave sleep (SWS) and the "primer" of REM sleep.[101-103] Those studies showed that: lesions of 5-HT-containing cell bodies in the raphe nuclei induce insomnia (primarily a decrease in SWS), which is not reversed following injection of the precursor of 5-HT, 5-hydroxytryptophan (5-HTP); inhibition of 5-HT synthesis with para-chlorophenylalanine (PCPA) leads to total insomnia, which can be immediately reversed following an injection of 5-HTP; and selective biochemical lesions of the 5-HT terminals induced by an intraventricular injection of 5,6-dihydroxytryptamine results in a marked decrease in both SWS and REM sleep.

Other studies point to a significant role of catecholamines in sleep.[104] Thus, inhibition of catecholamine synthesis by alpha-methylparatyrosine (AMPT) reverses the excitation and insomnia resulting from lesions in the raphe nuclei. Also, lesions of certain noradrenergic structures, such as the locus coeruleus, produce a decrease in cortical arousal that is related to the decrease of norepinephrine (NE) at thalamic and cortical terminals.

Further studies have demonstrated a variety of interactions between the serotonin and catecholamine systems in relation to both SWS and REM sleep, as well as an absence of an independent role of individual monoamines as mediators of specific sleep stages.[104] Actually, the firing rates of both the raphe nuclei (serotonergic) and the locus coeruleus (noradrenergic) follow the same pattern in wakefulness and sleep; highest in wakefulness, very low in SWS, and almost absent in REM sleep.[105,106]

More recent studies have indicated an interaction of at least three neurotransmitter systems in the regulation of sleep.[107] Thus, in addition to 5-HT and NE, acetylcholine (ACH) plays a major role in sleep, as evidenced by the activity of the cholinergic giant cells of the gigantocellular tegmental field (FTG) in the pontine reticular formation. These cells increase their firing rates during REM sleep as a result of the lowering of inhibition by both serotonergic and noradrenergic systems. Eventually, 5-HT and NE systems begin firing again, resulting in inhibition of the cholinergic giant cells and termination of the REM period. Thus, a reciprocal interaction between serotonergic and noradrenergic systems on the one hand, and cholinergic systems on the other, may underlie the basic oscillation of the sleep cycle.[107]

The interaction between the three neurotransmitter systems is believed to account for the different phenomenological aspects of REM sleep. Thus, during REM sleep, muscle atonia results from the lack of the inhibitory influence of the noradrenergic neurons of the locus coeruleus upon the FTG cholinergic neurons that activate the bulbospinal inhibitory system.[108] Similarly, cortical activation and phasic neuronal activity during REM sleep, such as the ponto-geniculo-occipital (PGO) spikes, originate from the abolition of the inhibitory control of serotonergic neurons of the raphe nuclei and catecholaminergic neurons of the locus coeruleus.[109] These neurons act upon executive neurons located in the dorsolateral ponto-mesencephalic reticular formation, which in turn mediate both EEG desynchronization and phasic events during REM sleep. Other, as yet unidentified, mechanisms also may be involved in the occurrence and regulation of the complex and subtle phenomena of sleep and wakefulness.[110] Recent experiments by Jouvet and his colleagues have suggested that serotonin may not be directly involved in REM sleep production.[111,112] Rather, it may act by controlling a factor in the cerebrospinal fluid that can induce REM sleep.

Hormonal Secretion and Sleep

The secretion of certain hypothalamic-pituitary hormones is closely related to the 24-hour sleep-wake cycle.[95,113-116] This relationship is made more significant by the fact that these hormones are regulated by the same biogenic amines that are active in the neuronal mechanisms underlying REM and NREM sleep.[101-104] Specifically, the biogenic-amine neurotransmitters serotonin, norepinephrine, and dopamine appear to have a significant role in regulating anterior pituitary hormone secretion through their effects on the hypothalamus and its releasing and inhibiting factors.[95,114,116]

Levels of urinary and plasma corticosteroids show an increase later in the night when REM sleep is predominant.[117,118] In contrast, growth hormone is secreted early in the night, when sleep stages 3 and 4 are most prevalent.[119,120] It is noteworthy that children, who have a rapid rate of growth, have high levels of stages 3 and 4 sleep early in the night.[44,50] Prolactin is secreted most heavily during the last few hours of sleep in both men and women.[121] The secretion of prolactin and growth hormone appears to depend greatly on sleep because partial or complete inversion of the sleep-wake cycle causes an immediate shift of prolactin and growth hormone secretion to the new sleep period.[122] However, this is not the case with cortisol, whose late-night peak persists for many days following sleep-wake inversion.[123]

The relationship between sleep and the secretion of gonadotropins, LH and FSH, depends upon the physiologic maturation of the subject.[113,116,124,125] For example, LH levels do not vary with sleep in prepubertal children but begin to fluctuate with the onset of puberty; at that time, LH is secreted periodically during sleep but not during wakefulness. The pattern of LH secretion changes again in adulthood. In adult males, both LH and FSH are secreted periodically, with many peaks within a 24-hour period; LH levels generally tend to rise slightly later in the night, when REM sleep is more prevalent. Testosterone levels are also higher later in the night. The simultaneous increases in both LH and testosterone during sleep of adult men suggest that LH "triggers" testosterone secretion, which has been reported to occur in conjunction with REM sleep. These latter hormonal changes may be related to the penile erection cycles that occur during REM sleep, but a precise association has not yet been defined.[113,114,126]

Role and Functions of Sleep

To understand the significance of the different sleep stages and of the amount of sleep obtained, investigators have studied subjects who habitually have "short" or "long" sleep times. Important contributions to the understanding of the functions of sleep have come from investigations of animals and humans who have been completely or partially deprived of sleep or selectively deprived of either REM or NREM sleep. These and other studies have provided the background for scientists to formulate various hypotheses on the role and functions of sleep.

Short and Long Sleep Duration

Several studies have evaluated the differences between individuals who habitually sleep for relatively long or short periods of time.[127-130] In one study of "long" and "short" sleepers, short sleepers appeared to be more efficient, energetic, ambitious individuals who were generally free of psychopathology.[127] The long sleepers, in contrast, seemed to be unsure of themselves and to be psychologically distressed. Other studies, however, failed to demonstrate significant psychologic differences between short and long sleepers.[129,130] For a more detailed discussion of this topic, see Chapter 3 (Sleep Laboratory Studies of Insomnia).

Extending or reducing subjects' sleep time or abruptly shifting their customary sleep period by three hours produces changes in attentiveness, mood, and performance.[131] It is assumed that these changes are caused by a disruption in the 24-hour, or circadian, sleep-wakefulness cycle. When the reduction of sleep time is gradual, it seems to be well tolerated as long as the reduction does not result in less than 4.5 to 5 hours of sleep per night.[132] However, it appears that subjects each have their own "sleep barriers"—minimum sleep requirements below which their performance or mood suffers. In this sense, it has been proposed that adaptation to sleep loss changes to an accumulation of sleep debt when the "sleep barrier" is crossed. On the other hand, as long as the minimum sleep requirement is met, getting additional sleep does not result in improved performance or mood.[133]

Total Sleep Deprivation

The effects of total sleep deprivation have been extensively researched because this topic has always stimulated a great deal of clinical interest.[134] Investigators have been intrigued by the fact that total deprivation of sleep for more than several days frequently results in disorders of thought and perception that resemble those seen in schizophrenic patients. Indeed, behavioral changes during total sleep deprivation are often dramatic and can be incapacitating. Fatigue, instability, and feelings of persecution, misperception, and disorientation are often reported or observed. These symptoms become more evident after about 100 hours of sleep deprivation[135,136] and intensify as sleep loss progresses.[137,138] However, there are distinct differences between symptoms of schizophrenia and effects of sleep deprivation. For example, the hallucinations of schizophrenic patients are most often auditory, whereas the illusions and hallucinations that may be associated with sleep deprivation are usually visual and tactile.

Decrements in performance are also common during prolonged wakefulness, especially for tasks that are lengthy and repetitive compared with those that are brief and have strong incentive qualities. Both behavioral changes and performance decrements during sleep deprivation follow a diurnal cycle; changes are usually more pronounced in the early morning hours, when the subject would normally be asleep. In spite of the dramatic changes often produced by total sleep deprivation, subjects quickly recover when allowed to sleep, and they suffer no permanent psychopathologic effects or impaired performance beyond the period of sleep deprivation.[137,138]

The recovery of different sleep stages following total sleep deprivation varies with how long the subject is deprived of sleep. When subjects are allowed to sleep after two to four nights of total sleep deprivation, the percentage of stage 4 sleep significantly exceeds baseline levels.[135,136] After longer periods of deprivation (200 hours), levels of both stage 4 and REM sleep increase considerably over baseline on the first recovery night.[137,138] In fact, some subjects demonstrate REM periods at sleep onset on the first recovery night.[138] Under normal circumstances this is rare, but it is often seen in patients who have narcolepsy/cataplexy[139] or in some cases of abrupt withdrawal of a REM-suppressant drug.

One study assessed the comparative importance of recovering either slow-wave sleep or REM sleep following total sleep deprivation by selectively allowing one or the other type of sleep on recovery nights.[140] The findings suggested that the effects of recovery from loss of either stages 3 and 4 or REM sleep were about the same in terms of motor and cognitive tasks and subjective mood. Thus, the total amount of sleep obtained upon recovery may be more important than the amount of a particular sleep stage.

Selective Deprivation of Sleep Stages

To determine the functions of specific stages of sleep, scientists have deprived subjects of certain sleep stages. Most of these experiments have involved deprivation of REM sleep and stage 4 sleep. Dement was the first to deprive human subjects of REM sleep by awakening them at the onset of REM periods.[141] The frequency of "attempts" to enter REM sleep increased progressively with each successive night of deprivation. When allowed to sleep undisturbed on recovery nights, the subjects had significantly more REM sleep than they did on baseline. Some behavioral and psychologic changes were reported during the deprivation period, including increases in appetite, anxiety, irritability, and difficulties in concentrating. Dement concluded that REM sleep deprivation could result in more permanent serious psychologic disturbances.[141]

Subsequent studies, however, failed to confirm this conclusion,[142,143] and additional studies showed that REM deprivation is not harmful even to schizophrenic[144] or depressed patients.[145] It has been suggested that REM deprivation may, in fact, have beneficial effects. Vogel and his colleagues, for example, have demonstrated that patients with endogenous depression may improve with REM-sleep deprivation.[145] Vogel points out that his finding is consistent with the REM-suppressing effect of antidepressant medications and the energizing effect on waking behavior that deprivation of REM sleep has in animals.

Stage 4 deprivation has been studied less extensively than REM deprivation, but the results generally show that on recovery nights, stage 4 sleep exceeds baseline levels. For example, when Agnew, Webb, and Williams deprived subjects of stage 4 sleep for two consecutive nights, the level of this sleep stage on recovery nights surpassed those of baseline.[146] Also, no psychologic disturbances were reported in this study.

In a subsequent study, the same researchers deprived one group of subjects of REM sleep and another group of stage 4 sleep, both for seven nights.[147] Different psychologic effects followed each type of deprivation. Stage 4 deprivation produced a depressive outlook, whereas REM deprivation caused increased irritability and emotional lability. Agnew and his associates concluded that REM deprivation results in a hyper-response state and that stage 4 deprivation causes a hypo-response state.

Functions of Sleep

Several theories have been proposed to answer the question of why sleep is necessary.[148-150] These ideas have evolved from studies of differences in sleep among species and from comparing the sleep of humans who are in different stages of development. The role of sleep also has been clarified by studies of neurophysiologic functioning and the effects of drugs on sleep.

In the phylogenetic theory, sleep is seen as a means of conserving energy; REM sleep serves a "sentinel" function, bringing about brief periodic awakenings to prepare the organism for immediate fight or flight without significantly disturbing the continuity of sleep.[151] Other findings consistent with this theory are that humans awaken more easily during REM sleep than during slow-wave sleep.[152] On the other hand, in animal studies, arousal from REM sleep is more difficult, and defenseless animals have much less REM sleep than do predators.[153] Also, in this sense, an ethological theory has been proposed by Webb,[154] who suggests that ecological pressures placed on a given species make non-responding important for survival and that sleep serves this purpose. In other words, sleep removes the individual from the environment during periods of time when waking activity is maladaptive.

The ontogenetic hypothesis is based on the fact that infants have a great deal of REM sleep.[44] In this hypothesis, the function of REM sleep is to assist in the development of the central nervous system, but it does not explain why REM sleep persists throughout life. A recent revision of this hypothesis suggests that REM sleep plays a dual role, depending upon the organism's stage of development.[155] During the neonatal period, it aids developmental processes, while in later stages of life, it helps to guard the integrity of the neural circuitry that is involved in memory consolidation.

It has also been suggested that REM sleep preserves cortical homeostasis.[156] During NREM sleep, there is a loss of cortical tonus, whereas during REM sleep neurophysiologic activation returns cortical tonus to a level approximating that of wakefulness. Another speculation is that REM sleep reorganizes neuronal firing patterns in the CNS that have somehow become disorganized during NREM sleep.[157]

REM sleep is widely thought to play a critical role in memory and learning.[158,159] One hypothesis suggests that information is reprogrammed during sleep, especially during REM sleep.[159] Similarly, REM sleep may help to integrate new experiences into the existing personality and may be involved in the transfer of recent memories onto long-term "storage tapes."[159]

Recently, Crick and his colleagues,[160] as well as Hopfield and his associates,[161] have postulated an active process of reverse learning that occurs during REM sleep. In other words, "We dream in order to forget."[160] In this theory, the mechanism of "unlearning" prevents the brain's memory storage from becoming overloaded. It is hypothesized that during REM sleep the brain stem stimulates the forebrain in a more or less random fashion, exciting inappropriate modes of brain activity (e.g., hallucinations), that can be triggered by random noise rather than by highly specific neuronal signals. In this way the cortex is modified by reducing the strength of individual synapses so that their activity is less likely in the future.

It has also been suggested that the function of sleep is to dissipate a "hypnotoxin" that accumulates during wakefulness. In the early 1900s, Legendre and Pieron reported that serum or CSF obtained from sleep-deprived dogs induced sleep in non-sleep-deprived dogs.[162] Monnier and his colleagues have since isolated a nonapeptide called delta sleep-inducing peptide, which in low doses has induced slow-wave sleep in rabbits.[163] More recently, Pappenheimer and his associates have isolated from human urine a glycopeptide (Factor S) that is also reported to induce slow-wave sleep in cats, rats, and rabbits.[164] All of these studies, however, have been difficult to replicate in other laboratories. Thus, the existence of a specific peptide that causes sleep has yet to be conclusively demonstrated.

REM sleep may facilitate protein synthesis and anabolism—another theory consistent with high amounts of REM sleep during infancy.[165,166] Oswald has proposed that the prolonged REM rebound following withdrawal from chronic use of certain drugs indicates accelerated protein synthesis in the brain.[166] The increased cerebral blood flow and brain temperature during REM sleep support this theory. Adam and Oswald have further postulated that NREM-REM sleep cycles reflect oscillations between rates of protein synthesis in the brain and in skeletal muscle.[165] Furthermore, the amount and percentage of REM sleep in mentally retarded people is considerably lower than that in individuals of normal intelligence.[167,168] However, Horne hypothesizes that increases in mitosis during the early part of the sleep period may only be a reflection of the sleep-independent low levels of corticosteroid output, since plasma levels of corticosteroids and adrenaline, which drop in the late evening, seem to be inversely related to rates of mitosis.[169]

In psychoanalytic terms, REM sleep is seen as restoring the ego cathexis that is partially lost during the regressive process of NREM sleep.[170] In this way, the ego can be easily reintegrated after sleep. REM sleep may also be necessary for the ego to sort and rearrange instinctual drives and related material or, as in Freud's view, to discharge instinctual drives.[171]

Finally, McGinty has argued that REM sleep is a more primitive state than NREM sleep.[172] Mature organization of sleep develops gradually and reflects the general maturation of the individual. Furthermore, certain aspects of sleep organization can be dissociated (as in narcoleptics[173,174] or persons with sleepwalking or night terrors[175-178]) or disturbed (as with insomnia or hypersomnia in certain psychiatric populations[10,179,180]), suggesting that optimum waking behavior is related to the organization of sleep.[172] Thus, the function of sleep may be to maintain waking behavior.

These theories, and others that have not been described here, are best interpreted not as singular answers to the puzzling question, "Why do we sleep?" but rather as attempts to understand such phenomena as differences among species or age-related, developmental differences in the neurophysiology of sleep that suggest a purposeful mechanism. Many questions have been raised and many hypotheses have been proposed regarding the functions of sleep, but the answers are yet unknown.

Summary

Relatively recent discoveries have led to the establishment of standardized criteria for recording and assessing sleep and to the extensive use of the sleep laboratory for studying normal sleep patterns. These studies have added considerably to our knowledge of normal sleep patterns, as well as of the physiology, neuroendocrinology, and underlying mechanisms of sleep.

Sleep is divided into REM sleep and four stages of NREM sleep. The patterns of these sleep stages are fairly consistent among age groups, with cycles of REM and NREM sleep occurring about every 90 minutes throughout the night. As people age, nightly awakenings are longer and more frequent, and a reduction in the amount of both REM sleep and stage 3 and 4 sleep occurs, particularly stages 3 and 4.

During NREM sleep, the various bodily systems generally become less active; however, bodily activity increases during REM sleep and may approach levels seen during the daytime. Within the REM sleep phase there are two major physiologic phenomena: tonic events, including the characteristic EEG pattern, markedly reduced muscle tonus activity, and penile erections; and phasic events, such as rapid-eye-movements, cardiorespiratory changes, and muscle twitching.

The circadian cycle of sleep and wakefulness is an endogenous rhythm; without environmental influences the cycle persists, although it gradually lengthens with continued isolation from external cues. The sleep-wakefulness cycle seems to be closely related to the circadian rhythm for body temperature; low body temperature at bedtime is associated with a longer duration of sleep, and after the nocturnal trough for body temperature is reached, there is an increased propensity for REM sleep.

The secretion of several hypothalamic-pituitary hormones is related to the sleep cycle; levels of corticosteroids increase late in the night when REM sleep predominates, while growth hormone secretion is at peak levels early in the night when stages 3 and 4 sleep are most prevalent. The biogenic amine neurotransmitters—serotonin, norepinephrine, and dopamine—are involved in the regulation of anterior pituitary hormone secretion as well as in the mechanisms for REM and NREM sleep.

Studies of long and short sleepers and of those who have been completely or partially deprived of sleep have contributed greatly to the understanding of the functions of sleep. Total sleep deprivation often results in dramatic and sometimes incapacitating behavioral changes and decrements in performance. However, there seem to be no permanent effects after subjects are allowed to recover their sleep. Studies have also suggested that the total amount of sleep obtained upon recovery may be more important than the amount recovered of a particular sleep stage.

To explain the functions of sleep, a number of hypotheses have been proposed regarding the role of sleep in: the survival of the organism; central nervous system development; cortical homeostasis; memory, learning, and unlearning; protein synthesis; ego cathexis and reintegration; and the organization of waking behavior. As yet, however, the puzzling questions remain unanswered.

References

1. Aserinsky E, Kleitman N: Regularly occurring periods of eye motility and concomitant phenomena during sleep. *Science 118*:273–274, 1953.
2. Aserinsky E, Kleitman N: Two types of ocular motility occurring in sleep. *J Appl Physiol 8*:1–10, 1955.
3. Dement WC, Kleitman N: Cyclic variations in EEG during sleep and their relation to eye movements, body motility and dreaming. *Electroencephalogr Clin Neurophysiol 9*:673–690, 1957.
4. Dement WC, Kleitman N: The relation of eye movements during sleep to dream activity: an objective method for the study of dreaming. *J Exp Psychol 53*:339–346, 1957.
5. Kleitman N: *Sleep and Wakefulness*. Chicago and London, The University of Chicago Press, 1963.
6. Gastaut H, Lugaresi E, Berti Ceroni G, Coccagna G (eds): *The Abnormalities of Sleep in Man*. Bologna, Aulo Gaggi Editore, 1968.
7. Kales A (ed): Sleep and dreams: recent research on clinical aspects, *Ann Intern Med 68*:1078–1104, 1968.
8. Kales A (ed): *Sleep Physiology and Pathology*. Philadelphia, Lippincott, 1969.
9. Kales A, Kales JD: Sleep disorders: recent findings in the diagnosis and treatment of disturbed sleep. *N Engl J Med 290*:487–499, 1974.
10. Kales A, Soldatos CR, Kales JD: Sleep disorders: Evaluation and management in the office setting, in Arieti S, Brodie HKH (ed): *American Handbook of Psychiatry*, ed 2. New York, Basic Books, 1981, vol VII, pp 423–454.
11. Mendelson WB, Gillin JC, Wyatt RJ: *Human Sleep and Its Disorders*. New York, Plenum Press, 1977.
12. Williams RL, Karacan I (eds): *Sleep Disorders: Diagnosis and Treatment*. New York, John Wiley & Sons, 1978.
13. Kales A, Caldwell A, Preston A, Healey S, Kales J: Personality patterns in insomnia: theoretical implications. *Arch Gen Psychiatry 33*:1128–1134, 1976.
14. Kales JD, Soldatos CR, Kales A: Diagnosis and treatment of sleep disorders, in Greist JN, Jefferson JW, Spitzer RL (eds): *Treatment of Mental Disorders*. New York, Oxford University Press, 1982, pp 473–500.
15. Soldatos CR, Kales A, Kales JD: Management of insomnia. *Annu Rev Med 30*:301–312, 1979.
16. Brazier MAB: *A History of the Electrical Activity of the Brain*. London, Pitman Medical Publishing Co., 1961.
17. Berger H: Uber das Elektroencephalogramm des Menschen. *Arch Psychiatr Nervenkr 87*:527–570, 1929.
18. Loomis AL, Harvey EN, Hobart GA: Cerebral states during sleep as studied by human brain potentials. *J Exp Psychol 21*:127–144, 1937.
19. Griesinger W: Berliner medicinisch-psychologische Gesellschaft. *Arch Psychiatr Nervenkr 1*:200–216, 1868.

20. Freud S: Project for a scientific psychology (1895), in Strachey, J (ed): *The Standard Edition of the Complete Psychological Works of Sigmund Freud, 1* (1886–1899). London, The Hogarth Press, 1966.
21. Berger RJ: Tonus of extrinsic laryngeal muscles during sleep and dreaming. *Science 134*:840, 1961.
22. Jacobson A, Kales A, Lehmann D, Zweizig JR: Somnambulism: all-night electroencephalographic studies. *Science 148*:975–977, 1965.
23. Jouvet M, Michel F, Mounier D: Analyse electroencephalographique comparee du sommeil physiologique chez le chat et chez l'homme. *Rev Neurol 103*:189–205, 1960.
24. Dement WC: Dream recall and eye movements during sleep in schizophrenics and normals. *J Nerv Ment Dis 122*:263–269, 1955.
25. Howell WH: A contribution to the physiology of sleep, based upon plethysmographic experiments. *J Exp Med 2*:313–345, 1897.
26. MacWilliam JA: Some applications of physiology to medicine III. Blood pressure and heart action in sleep and dreams. *Br Med J II*:1196–1200, 1923.
27. Regelsberger H: Uber vegetative Korrelationen im Schlafe des Menschen. *Z ges Neurol Psychiat 174*:727, 1942.
28. Ohlmeyer P, Brilmayer H, Huellstrung H: Periodische Vorgaenge im Schlaf. *Pfleuger Arch Ges Physiol 248*:559, 1944.
29. Kleitman N: Basic rest-activity cycle in relation to sleep and wakefulness, in Kales A (ed): *Sleep Physiology and Pathology.* Philadelphia, Lippincott, 1969.
30. Rechtschaffen A, Kales A (eds): *A Manual of Standardized Terminology, Techniques, and Scoring System for Sleep Stages of Human Subjects*, NIH no 204. National Institutes of Health, 1968.
31. Kales A, Kales JD, Bixler EO, Scharf MB: Methodology of sleep laboratory drug evaluations: further considerations, in Kagan F, Harwood T, Rickels K, Rudzik A, Sorer H (eds): *Hypnotics: Methods of Development and Evaluation.* New York, Spectrum Publishers, 1975, pp 109–126.
32. Kales A, Scharf MB, Soldatos CR, Bixler EO: Clinical evaluation of hypnotic drugs: contributions from sleep laboratory studies. *J Clin Pharmacol 19*:329–336, 1979.
33. Soldatos CR, Kales A: Role of the sleep laboratory in the evaluation of hypnotic drugs, in Priest RG, Ward J (eds): *Sleep Research* (Proceedings of the Northern European Symposium in Sleep Research). England, MTP Press Limited, 1979, pp 181–195.
34. Agnew HW, Webb WB, Williams RL: The first night effect: an EEG study of sleep. *Psychophysiology 2*:263–266, 1966.
35. Antrobus JS, Dement W, Fischer C: Patterns of dreaming and dream recall: an EEG study. *J Abnorm Soc Psychol 69*:341–344, 1964.
36. Kales A, Jacobson A, Kales JD, Kun T, Weissbuch R: All-night EEG sleep measurements in young adults. *Psychon Sci 7*:67–68, 1967.
37. Rechtschaffen A, Verdone P: Amount of dreaming: effect of incen-

tive, adaptation to laboratory, and individual differences. *Percept Mot Skills* 19:947–958, 1964.

38. Kales A, Soldatos CR, Kales JD: Taking a sleep history. *Am Fam Physician* 22:101–108, 1980.
39. Kales A, Bixler EO, Kales JD: Role of the sleep research and treatment facility: diagnosis, treatment and education, in Weitzman ED (ed): *Advances in Sleep Research, 1.* New York, Spectrum Publications, 1974.
40. Kales JD, Kales A, Bixler EO, Soldatos CR: Resource for managing sleep disorders. *JAMA* 241:2413–2416, 1979.
41. Kales JD, Kales A, Bixler EO, Soldatos CR: Sleep disorders: what the primary care physician needs to know. *Postgrad Med* 67:213–220, 1980.
42. Berger RJ: The sleep and dream cycle, in Kales A (ed): *Sleep Physiology and Pathology.* Philadelphia, Lippincott, 1969.
43. Feinberg I, Koresko RL, Heller N: EEG sleep patterns as a function of normal and pathological aging in man. *J Psychiatr Res* 5:107–144, 1967.
44. Roffwarg H, Muzio J, Dement W: Ontogenetic development of the human sleep-dream cycle. *Science* 152:604–619, 1966.
45. Williams RL, Agnew HW Jr, Webb WB: Sleep patterns in young adults: an EEG study. *Electroencephalogr Clin Neurophysiol* 17:376–381, 1964.
46. Williams RL, Agnew HW Jr, Webb WB: Sleep patterns in the young adult female: an EEG study. *Electroencephalogr Clin Neurophysiol* 20:264–266, 1966.
47. Bixler EO, Kales A, Jacoby JA, Soldatos CR, Vela-Bueno A: Nocturnal sleep and wakefulness: effects of age and sex in normal sleepers. *Int J Neurosci* (in press).
48. Webb WB: Sleep in older persons: sleep structures of 50-to-60-year-old men and women. *J Gerontology* 37:581–586, 1982.
49. Webb WB, Agnew HW Jr: Sleep cycling within twenty-four hour periods. *J Exp Psychol* 74:158–160, 1967.
50. Williams RL, Karacan I, Hursch CJ: *EEG of Human Sleep: Clinical Applications.* New York, John Wiley & Sons, 1974.
51. Kleitman N, Engelmann TG: Sleep characteristics of infants. *J Appl Physiol* 6:269–282, 1953.
52. Parmelee AH Jr, Wenner WH, Schulz HR: Infant sleep patterns: From birth to 16 weeks of age. *J Pediatr* 65:576–582, 1964.
53. Feinberg I: Changes in sleep cycle patterns with age. *J Psychiatric Res* 10:283–306, 1974.
54. Feinberg I, Carlson V: Sleep variables as a function of age in man. *Arch Gen Psychiatry* 18:239–250, 1968.
55. Hayashi Y, Endo S: All-night sleep polygraphic recordings of healthy aged persons: REM and slow-wave sleep. *Sleep* 5:277–283, 1982.
56. Spiegel R: *Sleep and Sleeplessness in Advanced Age* (Weitzman ED [series ed]: *Advances in Sleep Research,* vol 5). New York, SP Medical and Scientific Books, 1981.

57. Moore T, Ucko LE: Night waking in early infancy, part I. *Arch Dis Child* 32:333–342, 1957.
58. Kales A, Wilson T, Kales JD, Jacobson A, Paulson MJ, Kollar E, Walter RD: Measurements of all-night sleep in normal elderly persons: effects of aging. *J Am Geriatr Soc* 15:405–414, 1967.
59. Anch M, Orr WC, Karacan I: Stress, cardiac activity, and sleep. *J Human Stress* 2:15–24, 1976.
60. Arduini A, Berlucchi G, Strata P: Pyramidal activity during sleep and wakefulness. *Arch Ital Biol* 101:530–544, 1963.
61. Aserinsky E: Periodic respiratory pattern occurring in conjunction with eye movements during sleep. *Science* 150:763–766, 1965.
62. Bateman JRM, Pavia D, Clark SW: The retention of lung secretions during the night in normal subjects. *Clin Sci Mol Med* 55:523–527, 1978.
63. Berger RJ: Physiological characteristics of sleep, in Kales A (ed): *Sleep Physiology and Pathology*. Philadelphia, Lippincott, 1969, pp 66–79.
64. Brebbia RD, Altshuler KZ: Oxygen consumption rate and electroencephalographic stage of sleep. *Science* 150:1621–1623, 1965.
65. Broughton RS, Poire R, Tassinari CA: The electrodermogram (Tarchanoff effect) during sleep. *Percept Mot Skills* 20:181–182, 1965.
66. Bülow K: Respiration and wakefulness in man. *Acta Physiol Scand* 59(suppl 209):1–110, 1963.
67. Coccagna G, Lugaresi E, Farineti D, Didonato G: Changes in systemic and pulmonary arterial pressures during sleep in normal and some pathological disorders, in Mayer JS, Leshner H, Revich (eds): *Cerebral Vascular Disease*. Stuttgart, Thieme, 1976, pp 193–195.
68. Coccagna G, Mantovani M, Brignani F, Manzini A, Lugaresi E: Arterial pressure changes during spontaneous sleep in man. *Electroencephalogr Clin Neurophysiol* 31:277–281, 1971.
69. Duron: La fonction respiratoire pendant le sommeil physiologique. *Bull Physiopathol Respir* (Nancy) 8:1031–1057, 1972.
70. Evarts EV: Temporal patterns of discharge of pyramidal tract neurons during sleep and waking in the monkey. *J Neurophysiol* 27:152–171, 1964.
71. Fisher C, Gross J, Zuch J: A cycle of penile erection synchronous with dreaming (REM) sleep. *Arch Gen Psychiatry* 12:29–45, 1965.
72. Gücer G, Viernstein LJ: Intracranial pressure in the normal monkey while awake and asleep. *J Neurosurg* 51:206–210, 1979.
73. Henane R, Buguet A, Roussel B, Bittel J: Variations in evaporation and body temperatures during sleep in man. *J Appl Physiol: Respirat Environ Exercise Physiol* 42:50–55, 1977.
74. Huttenlocher PR: Evoked and spontaneous activity in single units of medial brain stem during natural sleep and waking. *J. Neurophysiol* 24:451–468, 1961.
75. Jouvet M: Telencephalic and rhombencephalic sleep in cat, in Wal-

stenholme GEW, O'Connor M (eds): *Nature of Sleep.* Boston, Little, Brown, 1961.

76. Karacan I, Goodenough DR, Shapiro A, Starker S: Erection cycle during sleep in relation to dream anxiety. *Arch Gen Psychiatry 15*:183–189, 1966.

77. Karacan I, Williams RL, Thornby JI, Salis PJ: Sleep-related penile tumescence as a function of age. *Am J Psychiatry 132*:932–937, 1975.

78. Kawamura H, Sawyer CH: Elevation in brain temperature during paradoxical sleep. *Science 150*:912–913, 1965.

79. Littler WA, Honour AJ, Carter RD, Sleight P: Sleep and blood pressure. *Br Med J 3*:346–348, 1975.

80. Orem J, Barnes CD: *Physiology in Sleep.* New York, Academic Press, 1980.

81. Parmeggiani PL: Regulation of the activity of respiratory muscles during sleep, in Fitzgerald RS, Gautren S, Lahiri S (eds): *The Regulation of Respiration During Sleep and Anesthesia.* New York: Plenum Press, 1978, pp 47–57.

82. Parmeggiani PL: Temperature regulation during sleep: a study in homeostasis, in Orem J, Barnes CD (eds): *Physiology in Sleep.* New York, Academic Press, 1980, pp 97–143.

83. Phillipson EA: Respiratory adaptations in sleep. *Ann Rev Physiol 40*: 133–156, 1978.

84. Phillipson EA: Control of breathing during sleep. *Am Rev Respir Dis 118*:909–939, 1978.

85. Pompeiano O: The neurophysiological mechanisms of the postural and motor events during desynchronized sleep, in Kety S, Evarts E, Williams H (eds): *Sleep and Altered States of Consciousness.* Baltimore, Williams and Wilkins, 1967, pp 351–423.

86. Rechtschaffen A, Cornwall P, Zimmerman W, Bassam M: Brain temperature variations with paradoxical sleep: implications for relationship among EEG, cerebral metabolism, sleep and consciousness. *Proceeding of Symposium on Sleep and Consciousness,* Lyon, France, 1965.

87. Snyder F, Hobson JA, Morrison DF, Goldfrank F: Changes in respiration, heart rate, and systolic blood pressure in human sleep. *J Appl Physiol 19*:417–422, 1964.

88. Townsend RE, Prinz PN, Obrist WD: Human cerebral blood flow during sleep and waking. *J Appl Physiol 35*:620–625, 1973.

89. Wolpert EA: Studies in psychophysiology of dreams: II, An electromyographic study of dreaming. *Arch Gen Psychiat (Chicago) 2*:231, 1960.

90. Aschoff J: Circadian rhythms in man. *Science 148*:1427–1432, 1965.

91. Halberg F: Chronobiology. *Ann Rev Physiol 31*:675–725, 1969.

92. Johnson LC, Colquhoun WP, Tepas DI, Colligan MJ: *Biological Rhythms, Sleep and Shift Work* (Weitzman ED [series ed]: *Advances in Sleep Research,* vol 7). New York, SP Medical and Scientific Books, 1981.

93. Kleitman N: Part 3: Periodicity (chps 15–19), in Kleitman N: *Sleep and Wakefulness*. University of Chicago Press, 1963, pp 131–192.
94. Moore-Ede MC, Sulzman FM, Fuller CA: *The Clocks that Time Us*. Cambridge, Harvard University Press, 1982.
95. Weitzman ED: Circadian rhythms and episodic hormone secretion in man. *Ann Rev Med* 27:225–243, 1976.
96. Wever RA: *The Circadian System of Man. Results of Experiments under Temporal Isolation*. New York, Springer-Verlag, 1979.
97. Czeisler CA, Weitzman ED, Moore-Ede MC, Zimmerman JC, Knauer RS: Human sleep: its duration and organization depend on its circadian phase. *Science* 210:1264–1267, 1980.
98. Czeisler CA, Zimmerman JC, Ronda J, Moore-Ede MC, Weitzman ED: Timing of REM sleep is coupled to the circadian rhythm of body temperature in man. *Sleep* 2:329–346, 1980.
99. Borbely AA, Tobler I, Groos G: Sleep homeostasis and the circadian sleep-wake rhythm, in Chase M, Weitzman ED (eds): *Sleep Disorders: Basic and Clinical Research* (Weitzman ED [series ed]: *Advances in Sleep Research*, vol 8). New York, SP Medical and Scientific Books, 1983, pp 227–243.
100. Borbely AA, Baumann F, Brandeis D, Strauch I, Lehmann D: Sleep-deprivation: effect on sleep stages and EEG power density in man. *Electroencephalogr Clin Neurophysiol* 51:483–493, 1981.
101. Jouvet M: Biogenic amines and the states of sleep. *Science* 163:32–41, 1969.
102. Jouvet M: The role of monoamines and acetylcholine-containing neurons in the regulation of sleep-waking cycle. *Ergebnisse der Physiologie* 64:166–308, 1972.
103. Rechtschaffen A, Lovell RA, Freedman D: The effect of parachlorophenylalanine on sleep in the rat: Some implications for the serotonin-sleep hypothesis, in Barchas J, Usdin E (eds): *Serotonin and Behavior*. New York, Academic Press, 1973, pp 401–418.
104. Morgane PJ: Serotonin: twenty-five years later. *Psychopharmacol Bull* 17:13–17, 1981.
105. Hobson JA, McCarley RW, Wyzinski PW: Sleep cycle oscillation: reciprocal discharge by two brainstem neuronal groups. *Science* 189:55–58, 1975.
106. McGinty DJ, Harper RM: Dorsal raphe neurons: depression of firing during sleep in cats. *Brain Res* 101:569–575, 1976.
107. McCarley RW: Mechanisms and models of behavioral state control: chairman's overview of part V, in Hobson JA, Brazier MAB (eds): *The Reticular Formation Revisited*. New York, Raven Press, 1980, pp 375–403.
108. Pompeiano O: Mechanisms responsible for spinal inhibition during desynchronized sleep: Experimental study, in Guilleminault C, Dement WC, Passouant P (eds): *Narcolepsy*. New York, Spectrum Publications, Inc, 1976, pp. 411–449.
109. Sakai K: Some anatomical and physiological properties of ponto-

mesencephalic tegmental neurons with special reference to the PGO waves and postural atonia during paradoxical sleep in the cat, in Hobson JA, Brazier MAB (eds): *The Reticular Formation Revisited.* New York, Raven Press, 1980, pp 427–447.

110. Koella WP: Neurotransmitters and sleep, in Wheatley D (ed): *Psychopharmacology of Sleep.* New York, Raven Press, 1981, pp 19–52.

111. Jouvet M, Sallanon M, Petitjean F, Bobillier P: Serotonergic and non-serotonergic mechanisms in sleep, in Chase M, Weitzman ED (eds): *Sleep Disorders: Basic and Clinical Research* (Weitzman ED [series ed]: *Advances in Sleep Research,* vol 8). New York, SP Medical and Scientific Books, 1983, pp 557–571.

112. Sallanon M, Buda C, Janin M, Jouvet M: L'insomnie provoquée par la p-chlorophénylalanine chez le chat. Sa réversibilité par l'injection intraventriculaire de liquide céphalorachidien prélevé chez des chats privés de sommeil paradoxal. *CR Acad Sci (Paris)* 292:113–117, 1981.

113. Rubin RT, Poland RE: Synchronies between sleep and endocrine rhythms in man and their statistical evaluation. *Psychoneuroendocrinology 1*:281–290, 1976.

114. Rubin RT, Poland RE, Rubin LE, Gouin PR: The neuroendocrinology of human sleep. *Life Sci 14*:1041–1052, 1974.

115. Weitzman ED: Biologic rhythms and hormone secretion patterns. *Hosp Pract 11*:79–86, 1976.

116. Weitzman ED, Boyer RM, Kapen S, Hellman L: The relationship of sleep and sleep stages to neuroendocrine secretion and biological rhythms in man. *Recent Prog Horm Res 31*:399–446, 1975.

117. Mandell AJ, Mandell MP: Biochemical aspects of rapid eye movement sleep. *Am J Psychiatry 122*:391–401, 1965.

118. Weitzman ED, Fukushima DK, Nogeire C, Roffwarg H, Gallagher TF, Hellman L: The twenty-four hour pattern of the episodic secretion of cortisol in normal subjects. *J Clin Endocrinol Metab 33*:14–22, 1971.

119. Parker DC, Sassin JF, Mace JW, Gotlin RW, Rossman LG: Human growth hormone release during sleep: electroencephalographic correlation. *J Clin Endocrinol Metab 29*:871–877, 1969.

120. Sassin JF, Parker DC, Mace JW, Gotlin RW, Johnson LC, Rossman LG: Human growth hormone release: relation to slow-wave sleep and sleep-waking cycles. *Science 165*:513–515, 1969.

121. Sassin JF, Frantz AG, Weitzman ED, Kapen S: Human prolactin: 24-hour pattern with increased release during sleep. *Science 177*:1205–1207, 1972.

122. Parker DC, Rossman LG: Sleep-wake cycle and human growth hormone, prolactin and luteinizing hormone, in Raiti S (ed): *Advances in Human Growth Hormone Research.* Washington DC, US Government Printing Office, 1974, pp 294–312.

123. Parker DC, Rossman LG, Kripke DF, Hershman JM, Gibson W, Davis C, Wilson K, Pekary E: Endocrine rhythms across sleep-wake cycles in normal young men under basal state conditions, in Orem J,

Barnes CD (eds): *Physiology in Sleep*. New York, Academic Press, 1980, pp 145–179.

124. Boyar RM, Rosenfeld RS, Kapen S, Finkelstein JW, Roffwarg HP, Weitzman ED, Hellman L: Human puberty: simultaneous augmented secretion of luteinizing hormone and testosterone during sleep. *J Clin Invest 54*:609–618, 1974.

125. Parker DC, Judd HL, Rossman LG, Yen SSC: Pubertal sleep-wake patterns of episodic LH, FSH, and testosterone release in twin boys. *J Clin Endocrinol Metab 40*:1099–1109, 1975.

126. Karacan I, Hartse K, Thornby J, Ware C, Cunningham G, Lantz G: Nocturnal penile tumescence, testosterone, and prolactin in impotent men. *Sleep Res 11*:76, 1982.

127. Hartmann E, Baekeland F, Zwilling G: Psychological differences between long and short sleepers. *Arch Gen Psychiatry 26*:463–468, 1972.

128. Stuss D, Broughton R: Extreme short sleep: personality profiles and a case study of sleep requirement. *Waking and Sleeping 2*:101–105, 1978.

129. Webb WB: Are short and long sleepers different? *Psychol Rep 44*: 259–264, 1979.

130. Webb WB, Friel J: Sleep stage and personality characteristics of natural long and short sleepers. *Science 171*:587–588, 1971.

131. Taub JM, Berger RJ: The effects of changing the phase and duration of sleep. *J Exp Psychol (Hum Percept) 2*:30–41, 1976.

132. Johnson LC, MacLeod WL: Sleep and awake behavior during gradual sleep reduction. *Percept Mot Skills 36*:87–97, 1973.

133. Naitoh P: Sleep deprivation in human subjects: a reappraisal. *Waking & Sleeping 1*:53–60, 1976.

134. Johnson LC: Psychological and physiological changes following total sleep deprivation, in Kales A (ed): *Sleep Physiology and Pathology*. Philadelphia, Lippincott, 1969, pp 206–220.

135. Berger RJ, Oswald I: Effects of sleep deprivation on behavior, subsequent sleep, and dreaming. *J Ment Sci 108*:457–465, 1962.

136. Williams HL, Hammack JT, Daly RL, Dement WC, Lubin A: Responses to auditory stimulation, sleep loss and the EEG stages of sleep. *Electroencephalogr Clin Neurophysiol 16*:269–279, 1964.

137. Johnson LC, Slye ES, Dement W: Electroencephalographic and autonomic activity during and after prolonged sleep deprivation. *Psychosom Med 27*:415–423, 1965.

138. Kales A, Tan TL, Kollar EJ, Naitoh P, Preston TA, Malmstrom EJ: Sleep patterns following 204 hours of sleep deprivation. *Psychosom Med 32*:189–200, 1970.

139. Kales A, Cadieux RJ, Soldatos CR, Bixler EO, Schweitzer PK, Prey WT, Vela-Bueno A: Narcolepsy-cataplexy I. Clinical and electrophysiologic characteristics. *Arch Neurol 39*:164–168, 1982.

140. Johnson LC: Are stages of sleep related to waking behavior? *Am Sci 61*:326–338, 1973.

141. Dement W: The effect of dream deprivation. *Science 131*:1705–1707, 1960.
142. Kales A, Hodemaker FS, Jacobson A, Lichtenstein EL: Dream deprivation: an experimental reappraisal. *Nature 204*:1337–1338, 1964.
143. Sampson H: Psychological effects of deprivation of dreaming sleep. *J Nerv Ment Dis 143*:305–317, 1966.
144. Vogel GW, Traub AC: REM deprivation, I. The effect on schizophrenic patients. *Arch Gen Psychiatry 18*:287–299, 1968.
145. Vogel GW, Traub AC, Ben-Horin P, Meyers GM: REM deprivation, II. The effects on depressed patients. *Arch Gen Psychiatry 18*:301–311, 1968.
146. Agnew HW, Webb WB, Williams RL: The effects of stage four sleep deprivation. *EEG Clin Neurophysiol 17*:68–70, 1964.
147. Agnew HW, Webb WB, Williams RL: Comparison of stage four and 1-REM sleep deprivation. *Percept Mot Skills 24*:851–858, 1967.
148. Drucker-Colin R, Shkurovich M, Sterman MB (eds): *The Functions of Sleep*. New York, Academic Press, 1979.
149. Hartmann EL: *The Functions of Sleep*. New Haven, Yale University Press, 1973.
150. Rechtschaffen A: The control of sleep, in Hunt W (ed): *Human Behavior and Its Control*. Cambridge, Schenkman, 1972, pp. 75–92.
151. Snyder F: Toward an evolutionary theory of dreaming. *Am J Psychiatry 123*:121–136, 1966.
152. Rechtschaffen A, Hauri P, Zeitlin M: Auditory awakening thresholds in REM and NREM sleep stages. *Percept Mot Skills 22*:927–942, 1966.
153. Allison T, Cicchetti DV: Sleep in mammals: ecological and constitutional correlates. *Science 194*:732–734, 1976.
154. Webb WB: Theories of sleep functions and some clinical implications, in Drucker-Colin R, Shkurovich M, Sterman MB (eds): *The Functions of Sleep*. New York, Academic Press, 1979, pp 19–35.
155. Drucker-Colin R: Protein molecules and the regulation of REM sleep: possible implications for function, in Drucker-Colin R, Shkurovich M, Sterman MB (eds): *The Functions of Sleep*. New York, Academic Press, 1979, pp 99–111.
156. Ephron HS, Carrington P: Rapid eye movement sleep and cortical homeostasis. *Psychol Rev 73*:500–526, 1966.
157. Weiss T: Discussion of "The D-state" by E. Hartmann. *Int J Psychiatry Med 2*:32–36, 1966.
158. Dewan EM: The Programming "P" hypothesis for REM sleep, in Hartmann E (ed): *Sleep and Dreaming*. Boston, Little, Brown, 1970, International Psychiatry Clinics Series, vol 7, pp 295–307.
159. Greenberg R, Leiderman P: Perceptions, the dream process and memory: an up-to-date version of notes on a mystic writing pad. *Compr Psychiatry 7*:517–522, 1966.
160. Crick F, Mitchison G: The function of dream sleep. *Nature 304*:111–114, 1983.

161. Hopfield JJ, Feinstein DI, Palmer RG: Unlearning has a stabilizing effect in collective memories. *Nature 304*:158–159, 1983.
162. Legendre R, Pieron H: Du developpement au cours de l'insomnie experimental, des proprietes hyponotoxiques des humeurs en relation avec le besoin croissant de sommeil. *C R Soc Biol (Paris) 70*:190–192, 1911.
163. Monnier M, Hatt AM, Cueni LB, Schoenenberger GA: Humoral transmission of sleep. VI. Purification and assessment of a hypnogenic fraction of "sleep dialysate" (factor delta). *Pfluegers Arch 331*:257–265, 1972.
164. Krueger JM, Pappenheimer JR, Karnofsky ML: The composition of sleep-promoting factor isolated from human urine. *J Biol Chem 257*: 1664–1669, 1982.
165. Adam K, Oswald I: Sleep is for tissue restoration. *J Roy Coll Physicians 11*:376–388, 1977.
166. Oswald I: Sleep, the great restorer. *New Scientist 46*:170–172, 1970.
167. Feinberg I, Braun M, Shulman E: EEG sleep patterns in mental retardation. *EEG Clin Neurophysiol 27*:128–141, 1969.
168. Petre-Quadens O, Jouvet M: Paradoxical sleep and dreaming in the mentally retarded. *J Neurol Sci 3*:608–612, 1966.
169. Horne JA: Restitution and human sleep: a critical review. *Physiological Psychology 7*:115–125, 1979.
170. Hawkins DR: A review of psychoanalytic dream theory in the light of recent psychophysiological studies of sleep and dreaming. *Br J Med Psychol 39*:85–104, 1966.
171. Fisher C: Psychoanalytic implications of recent research on sleep and dreaming. II. Implications of psychoanalytic theory. *J Am Psychoanal Assoc 13*:271–303, 1965.
172. McGinty DJ: Ontogenetic and clinical studies of sleep state organization and dissociation, in Drucker-Colin R, Shkurovich M, Sterman MB (eds): *The Functions of Sleep*. New York, Academic Press, 1979, pp 171–206.
173. Guilleminault C, Dement WC, Passouant P: *Narcolepsy* (Weitzman ED [series ed]: *Advances in Sleep Research*, vol 3). New York, Spectrum Publications Inc, 1976.
174. Roth B: *Narcolepsy and Hypersomnia*. Basel, S Karger, 1980.
175. Broughton RJ: Sleep disorders: disorders of arousal? *Science 159*:1070–1078, 1968.
176. Fisher C, Kahn E, Edwards A, Davis D: A psychophysiological study of nightmares and night terrors. *Psychoanal Contemp Sci 3*:317–398, 1974.
177. Kales A, Soldatos CR, Caldwell AB, Kales JD, Humphrey FJ II, Charney DS, Schweitzer PK: Somnambulism: clinical characteristics and personality patterns. *Arch Gen Psychiatry 37*:1406–1410, 1980.
178. Kales JD, Kales A, Soldatos CR, Caldwell AB, Charney DS, Martin ED: Night terrors: clinical characteristics and personality patterns. *Arch Gen Psychiatry 37*:1413–1417, 1980.

179. Kupfer D, Feinberg M, Gillin JC, Carroll BJ, Greden JF, Zis AP: Sleep and neuroendocrine abnormalities in affective disorders: new findings. *Psychopharmacol Bull* 17:20–22, 1981.

180. Snyder F: Electroencephalographic studies of sleep in psychiatric disorders, in Chase MH (ed): *The Sleeping Brain*. Los Angeles, Brain Information Service, 1972, pp 376–393.

2. Insomnia: Scope of the Problem

Insomnia, a term derived from Latin, literally denotes a total lack of sleep. In practical and clinical terms, however, it refers to a relative lack of sleep or an inadequate quality of sleep or both.[1] An extremely prevalent symptom, insomnia is associated with a variety of psychiatric and medical disorders as well as situational disturbances. Although it does not represent a specific disease entity, when insomnia becomes chronic and severe it greatly affects patients' lives. Consequently, they often perceive the symptom and associated condition as their primary disorder.

Physicians frequently hear the question, "How much sleep does a person need?," clearly reflecting people's concern over how their general health may be affected by lack of sleep. While it is difficult to demonstrate that chronic insomnia has distinct adverse effects on health, the disorder often has clear-cut and severe psychosocial effects. Indeed, when the disorder is longstanding, it impairs individuals' family relationships and work situations, as well as their general social functioning.

To evaluate and treat chronic insomnia successfully, physicians need to appreciate the full extent of its wide-ranging effects. This chapter explores the scope of the problem of insomnia in terms of its actual prevalence, people's subjective perceptions of their need for sleep, the relationship of sleep duration to health status, and the psychosocial consequences of insomnia. It also addresses the need to educate physicians regarding the overall management of chronic sleep difficulty.

Prevalence of Insomnia

Insomnia is the most common disorder of sleep.[2,3] A number of surveys have shown that it occurs more frequently with increasing age[3-10] and in women.[3,4,6-9] As women become older they complain more of difficulty falling asleep,[3,7,8] as well as reporting lighter sleep with more frequent awakenings.[7,11] An increased prevalence of insomnia has also been associated with psychologic disturbances[3,5,7,12,13,14] and lower socioeconomic status.[3,6,7,10,15] These two factors that increase the likelihood of insomniac complaints appear to be related, because mental health disorders are more prevalent among persons of lower socioeconomic status[16,17] and social class has been found to be inversely related to degree of life stress, as measured by life-change events.[18] Furthermore, the noise, crowding, and other conditions associated with disadvantaged social environments may also contribute to sleep disturbance.[19]

Two nationwide health surveys in the United States have shown that insomnia is experienced by a considerable proportion of the general population; one revealed a prevalence of 21 percent,[4] and the other, 32 percent.[9] Regional surveys have produced similar percentages. In the Los Angeles metropolitan area, the estimated prevalence of insomnia was 32 percent,[3] while a survey in Alachua County, Florida, showed a prevalence of 35 percent.[6] The slight variations in prevalence among these four large surveys were probably caused by differences in the questions asked. Specifically, the three surveys in closest agreement (32%, 32%, and 35%) asked about "difficulty sleeping at least sometimes,"[3,6,9] whereas the study reporting the lowest figure for sleep difficulty (21%) asked specifically about insomnia.[4]

In one of the U.S. nationwide surveys, insomnia was reported more frequently by older subjects and was more common among women (26%) than men (13%).[4] In the other U.S. health survey, which included more than 6,000 adults, difficulty falling asleep or staying asleep was a problem "at least sometimes" for 40 percent of the women and for 30 percent of the men. Sleep difficulties were more common among older subjects, especially women.[9]

In the Los Angeles metropolitan area survey, insomnia was more common among older individuals, particularly women, and among persons of lower educational and socioeconomic status.[3] It was also correlated with more frequent mental health difficulties and physical problems. The prevalence of current complaints of difficulty sleeping was 32 percent, while the prevalence of such complaints at any time during the respondents' lives was 42 percent.

Consistent with the other surveys, the Alachua County study showed that trouble sleeping was more prevalent among older people.[6] Also, hypnotic drugs were used more often by older subjects, particularly

Table 2.1. Prevalence of Insomnia

Area Represented in Survey	Sample Size	Prevalence of Difficulty Sleeping	Factors Affecting Prevalence*
United States[4]	1,064,004	21%	A, S
United States[9]	6,672	32%	A, S
Alachua County, Florida[6]	1,645	35%	A, S, SES
Los Angeles, California[3]	1,006	32%	A, S, SES

* A = Age; S = Sex; SES = Socioeconomic Status

by women and by divorced, widowed, or separated individuals. Among the 35 percent of respondents who had difficulty sleeping, the following categories of frequency were reported: 22 percent had difficulty sleeping "sometimes" and 13 percent, "often" or "all of the time."

Table 2.1 summarizes data on the prevalence of insomnia from the two nationwide surveys and two regional surveys conducted in the United States.

Two other surveys of note were conducted in the United Kingdom.[7,8] An assessment of over 2,000 adults in the cities of Dundee and Glasgow, Scotland, showed that sleep difficulty increased with age.[7] Reports of nervousness were also related to sleep difficulty; those who described themselves as being nervous reported more difficulty getting to sleep and staying asleep. This study also indicated that sleep difficulty was more prevalent among the less advantaged social classes. Finally, it showed that when compared with men, women reported that their sleep difficulty began at an earlier age and presented with more complaints of sleep disturbance, a higher incidence of nervousness, and more frequent use of hypnotic drugs. In a study conducted in Merseyside, England, the frequency of both nocturnal sleep disturbance and daytime naps increased with age.[8]

Because of its high prevalence in the general population, insomnia is understandably the sleep disturbance encountered most frequently by physicians. A nationwide survey of physicians indicated that 19 percent of all adult medical patients (aged 18 and older) complain of insomnia.[2] When medical specialties in this survey were compared, psychiatric patients had the highest percentage (35%) of complaints of insomnia. The frequency of complaints of insomnia for adult patients in other specialties was as follows: surgery, 22%; internal medicine, 18%; family–general practice, 16%; neurology, 16%; and obstetrics–gynecology,

12%. This survey also showed that insomnia, as well as other sleep disorders known to be associated with mental health problems (nightmares, night terrors, and hypersomnia), was more prevalent in highly populated areas. Further, in studies comparing psychiatric outpatients with non-patients, insomnia was found to be much more prevalent in the psychiatric population.[12,13] The frequency and chronicity of insomnia were strongly associated with the degree of psychiatric disturbance but not with specific diagnoses.

The Need for Sleep

While the need for sleep appears to vary greatly, little is known about the actual optimum amount of sleep. When allowed to sleep as they wish, most people desire about eight hours of sleep each night,[11,20] but some are reported to sleep no more than a few hours per night,[21-23] and others may insist that they need more than nine hours of sleep.[24]

Sleep-deprivation studies and the results of attempts at manipulating sleep length have contributed to an understanding of sleep needs,[25-33] and they have been fully discussed in Chapter 1 (The Study and Nature of Sleep). The best estimates of sleep need, however, are available from surveys indicating the amount of sleep that people consider ideal and the amount they actually obtain,[11] and correlations of these data with general health status.[4,34-40] Major surveys and studies concerned with sleep needs have reviewed in detail elsewhere.[41,42] Here we summarize the salient points from those studies.

Correlates of Sleep Quality and Quantity

Most people do not sleep as much as they would like. Among 1,550 adults surveyed by the Gallup Organization in 1979, nearly two-thirds (61%) reported sleeping less than eight hours nightly,[11] but only 38 percent regarded that amount as ideal (Table 2.2). Similarly, about half of those surveyed (48%) regarded 8.0 to 8.5 hours of sleep as optimal, although only 26 percent reported obtaining that amount. In another study, most of the subjects reported sleeping less than eight hours nightly,[8] even though eight hours of sleep is commonly considered ideal.

The Gallup survey also showed that among women, working full time appeared to affect the amount of sleep obtained because women working full time slept less than those working part-time.[11] Employment status was another factor affecting perception of sleep require-

Table 2.2. Sleep Length Estimates: Preferred Vs. Obtained

Number of Hours Sleep/Night	Percentage of Respondents (n = 1,550)	
	Perceived Sleep Need	Reported Sleep Duration
< 6.0 hrs.	3	10
6.0 to < 6.5 hrs.	9	16
6.5 to < 7.0 hrs.	2	5
7.0 to < 7.5 hrs.	18	24
7.5 to < 8.0 hrs.	6	6
8.0 to < 8.5 hrs.	48	26
8.5 to < 9.0 hrs.	2	2
9.0 to < 10.0 hrs.	6	6
> 10.0 hrs.	4	3
	98%	98%

(Adapted from *The Gallup Study of Sleeping Habits,* The Gallup Organization. Princeton, N.J., 1979.[11])

ments and the amount of sleep obtained. Blue-collar workers were more likely than white-collar employees to consider 8.0 to 8.5 hours of sleep ideal (47% vs. 33%), although neither group slept as much as they felt was optimal; most of the blue-collar workers (68%), and even more of the white-collar workers (78%), slept less than 8.0 to 8.5 hours each night.

Other variables affecting perception of ideal sleep time were age and geographic location.[11] Older respondents were less likely to feel a need for more than eight hours of sleep per night, and people living in the South tended to believe they needed more than eight hours per night.

Sleep Length and Health Status

A number of large-scale surveys have assessed the relationship of sleep duration to health status and to mortality rate.[4,34-40] Four of these studies were conducted in Alameda County (California) by the Human Population Laboratory between 1965 and 1974 in order to quantify the World Health Organization's concept of health.[34-37] The first of these studies examined the relationship between common health practices, including the amount of sleep obtained nightly and health status.[34] The subsequent three studies assessed the relationship between people's health practices and their mortality rate.[35-37] Another set of studies reported on data regarding sleep duration, use of sleeping pills, and mortality.[4,38,40] These data were obtained by the American Cancer Society during an epidemiologic study of more than 1 million Americans in which subjects were followed up annually in terms of mortality rate, and every two years for additional questionnaire information.[38] In addition to the Alameda County and American Cancer Society studies, two other studies,[43,44] one including sleep duration as a health practice,[44] showed that "good" health practices were related to the level of health. These studies, however, were conducted in highly selected populations and used small samples.

The first of the Alameda County studies was conducted by Belloc and Breslow as part of their general study of the relationship of physical health status and health practices.[34] By examining nearly 7,000 people, they found that the amount of sleep most frequently related to good health is seven to eight hours. Most of the respondents reported that amount, with similar results for men and women. Those who estimated that they usually slept nine or more hours were less healthy than average, and those who slept less than six hours were least healthy. Belloc and Breslow identified five other health practices that were associated with a general index of good physical health: regular meals, near-average weight, physical activity, avoidance of smoking, and moderate consumption of alcoholic beverages. Although each of these health practices was positively related to health, the differences among mortality rates associated with specific health practices were generally small. However, the health practices were shown to be cumulative; those who reported observing all or most of the good practices were in better physical health, even if they were older, than those who followed only a few. In fact, those over age 75 who followed all of the good practices had about the same level of physical health as those aged 35 to 44 who followed fewer than three.[34]

Sleep length appears to be correlated with mortality rate, although causality is not clear because illness may cause insomnia or a need for more sleep, rather than the reverse. Five and a half years after the 1965 survey, Belloc found that men who reported sleeping eight hours had lower mortality rates than those who slept more or less than that amount.[35] The optimum amount for women was seven hours of sleep, but those who reported sleeping six hours or less were not at a disadvantage with regard to mortality. Each of the health practices, including hours of sleep obtained, was related to mortality rate in the expected direction, but the differences were slight. Again, however, when the health practices were considered together, the number of health practices showed a striking inverse relationship with mortality rates, especially for men. For example, the average life expectancy of men aged 45 who reported six or seven good practices was more than 11 years longer than that of men reporting fewer than four.[35]

In 1974, Wiley and Comacho re-interviewed a subsample of respondents to Belloc and Breslow's 1965 survey.[36] They found that most of the health practices that were correlated with concurrent health status and risk of mortality in the 1965 study were also predictive of health status in those interviewed nine years later. There was a marked correlation between subjects' sleep length in 1965 and their subsequent health scores. Seven or eight hours of sleep per night was associated with the most favorable health scores; both sexes scored the highest health ratings at the socially accepted norm of eight hours. Sleeping less than seven hours per night appeared to be a significant health risk for both men and women.[36] Further analysis of these data showed that mortality rates from ischemic heart disease, cancer, stroke, and all causes combined were lowest for individuals sleeping seven or eight hours per night.[37]

In the first of the reports on sleep duration and mortality from the American Cancer Society data, Hammond found that men in certain age groups who reported sleeping less than four hours per night were up to ten times more likely to have died within two years as those who reported sleeping 7.0 to 7.9 hours.[4] There were no controls, however, for the potential effects of various medical illnesses. In a subsequent study, Hammond and Garfinkel found that deaths caused by coronary artery disease, stroke, and aortic aneurysm were more prevalent in both men and women older than age 40 who reported sleeping more than 7.0 to 7.9 hours, and especially among those who reported sleeping more than 10.0 hours.[39]

In a follow-up of the original American Cancer Society study, Kripke and his associates found that reports of insomnia were not consistently associated with mortality when the data were controlled for various factors, including a history of any of four major illnesses, including diabetes, heart disease, stroke, or high blood pressure.[40] However, men who reported sleeping less than four hours per night were 2.8 times as likely to have died within the six-year follow-up period as were men who reported 7.0 to 7.9 hours of sleep per night. Women who slept less than four hours per night were 1.5 times more likely to have died within the follow-up period than were those who slept 7.0 to 7.9 hours per night. Similar findings were associated with excessive sleep: men and women who reported sleeping ten hours or more had about 1.8 times the mortality rate of those who reported 7.0 to 7.9 hours of sleep. In the same study, those who often used sleeping pills had 1.5 times the mortality rate of those who never had used sleep medication. Overall, the data supported the common notion that the asymptomatic or healthy person sleeps about eight hours a night. The authors point out, however, that their data need to be interpreted conservatively because they were not able to control for all major illnesses.[40]

Although this information on optimum sleep length may be useful in understanding the role of sleep in general health status, the clinician needs to keep in mind that the need for sleep varies widely from person to person. An additional problem in quantitatively assessing sleep needs arises with insomniacs, who frequently overestimate their sleep difficulty[45-51] (see also Chapter 3, Sleep Laboratory Studies of Insomnia).

Psychosocial Correlates of Insomnia

Insomnia as a Chronic Psychobehavioral Disorder

More than 30 million people in the United States are disabled by chronic conditions, and half of them are considered to have major disabilities.[52] Among these disabling conditions are psychobehavioral disorders (such as chronic pain syndromes and obesity), which, although functional in nature, are characterized by excessive somatic symptomatology.[53] We believe that chronic insomnia should be included in this category. Unlike chronic medical illnesses that have distinct organic pathology, such as arthritis, diabetes, and emphysema, chronic psychobehavioral disorders usually lack any demonstrable pathology, or, if pathology is present, the symptoms are grossly disproportionate to it.

The treatment of chronic psychobehavioral disorders such as insomnia is a major challenge to modern medicine. These conditions are usually refractory to conventional medical treatment and have a major economic impact. Conservatively estimated, the cost of chronic disabling conditions in the United States, in general, is well over $100 billion annually.[52] The cost of one psychobehavioral disorder alone, chronic pain, was estimated to be between $35 and $50 billion in 1976.[54] Similarly, one of the most costly consequences of chronic insomnia may be its economic impact on the public.

Insomnia, as is the case with many chronic psychobehavioral disorders, is potentially reversible. Therefore, those factors that lead to chronicity in insomniacs, as outlined below, need to be identified so that treatment strategies can be developed by physicians who care for these patients.

Reaction of the Patient, Family, Physician,
and Social Environment to Insomnia

Patients with insomnia usually are highly invested in and preoccupied with their symptoms, and they derive a great deal of secondary gain from them.[55-57] Either consciously or unconsciously, these patients allow their symptoms to exempt them from normal daily functioning. They may become less and less involved in family activities, and they often detach themselves from parental responsibilities and marital and sexual interactions. At work they typically function on a level much lower than normal; they are usually not fully alert and their concentration is often impaired because of a lack of sleep or a hangover from sleep medications. This leads to tardiness, abuse of sick leave, and loss of productivity.

Chronic illness is affected not only by personal factors; it is interwoven with the attitudes of the family, society, and the health care team.[58] In our evaluation and treatment of cases of chronic insomnia, we have found that the development and persistence of the disorder results from an interaction of behavioral, social, medical, and psychologic factors.[55,57,59,60] Changes in patients' social and cultural framework, as well as disruptions in their interpersonal relationships, can lead to chronic illness, particularly if they are predisposed to illness and perceive the changes as important to them.[61,62] Once insomnia is established, patients' lifestyles, particularly interactions with those close to them, change significantly. In turn, others' reactions to the insomniacs' sleep difficulty can influence its course. For example, those in the patients' immediate environment may expect or even unwittingly oblige them to remain sick.[63]

As Fordyce has suggested for treating any chronic condition, it is inadvisable to rely solely on the concept of the "disease model" by attributing all of the manifest symptomatology to the physical or emotional factors that precipitated the onset of the illness.[64] Simply looking for underlying pathology, whether organic or psychologic, may minimize the importance of the patient's environment. Thus, the biopsychosocial model of illness provides the best approach to under-standing chronic insomnia.[60,65-68]

As with other chronic psychobehavioral disorders, an elaborate network is involved when an individual develops chronic insomnia: the network includes the illness itself, the patient, the family, the physi-cian, and society. Each component affects and is affected by the other components.

Role of the Illness When sleep disturbance becomes more longstand-ing, the potential arises for maladaptive learning or conditioning, which, in turn, may contribute to the development and the persis-tence of chronic insomnia (see also Chapter 5, Psychiatric Factors in Insomnia). In chronic insomnia, psychologic conflicts are inter-nalized, leading to chronic emotional arousal. This, in turn, produces physiologic activation, which causes insomnia. The patient may then develop a fear of sleeplessness, as well as become conditioned to expect poor sleep, both contributing to further emotional and psychologic arousal and continued insomnia.[55] In fact, studies have shown that chronic emotional arousal can contribute to the development of a wide variety of illnesses.[61,69,70] Additionally, the symptoms of a chronic illness such as insomnia can easily generate ample sympathy and atten-tion and thus, considerable secondary gain. In this way, the insomnia itself may have a reinforcing effect because it provides patients with an effective way to manipulate their environment and avoid many aspects of daily life.[64]

Role of the Patient "Being sick" often incorporates far more than mere organic pathology.[71] Many people with serious organic pathol-ogy do not assume the sick role, whereas others with little or no dis-cernible change in their physical condition readily assume this role.[72] Thus, development of chronicity is not necessarily dependent only upon the etiology or pathogenesis of the condition.[73]

Many insomniacs use their disorder and the entire concept of "being ill" in such a way that the impact of the insomnia extends far beyond its physiologic consequences. For many insomniac patients, chronicity may continue after the initial and precipitating causes have long dis-appeared.[74,75] Insomnia, like other chronic psychobehavioral disorders and medical illnesses, is profoundly influenced by the background, lifestyle, and temperament of the person who is experiencing it.[76]

Studies have shown that personality factors play a major role in the development and persistence of chronic insomnia.[50,55-57,59,68,77-81] When compared with control subjects, insomniacs perceive themselves as having been more emotionally upset as children and less content with their parents and their family lives.[79] As children, they tended to express this discontent through an internalizing pattern of somatization, focused on problems of eating and sleeping, rather than by overt behavioral difficulties. Thus, at risk for developing chronic insomnia are people who were emotionally deprived in childhood, which has led them to feel inadequate, insecure, and dependent as adults. It is therefore understandable that the insomniac may develop feelings of entitlement and expect to be nurtured and cared for by others.

As a group, chronic insomniacs have been characterized as having experienced depression, self-doubt, and inferiority.[50,55,68,79] They also have difficulty in interpersonal relations; they need and demand sympathy and support, but are often too self-preoccupied to be attentive to the feelings of others. More importantly, insomniac patients tend to internalize their emotions rather than expressing them outwardly.[50,55,68,77-79,81] Some deny or reject feelings of depression, anxiety, and inadequacy and develop chronic somatic complaints and medical impairment as an "acceptable" solution to their longstanding conflicts in living. The role of personality factors in the onset and persistence of insomnia is discussed more extensively in Chapter 5 (Psychiatric Factors in Insomnia).

Role of the Family   A "sick" person invariably affects other members of the family.[63,71] Well-intended efforts by family members to help the patient with chronic insomnia inadvertently may provide considerable secondary gain. For example, family members may accept the insomniac's excuses and rationalizations for avoiding responsibilities. Also, family members may not expect the patient to get well or genuinely desire improvement since they may unconsciously prefer the patient to be less involved in family and other activities. When this situation develops, the patient and the family are in a stable equilibrium around the patient's sick role, and both gratify their needs through the "sickness."[63]

Family members may experience inner conflict over conscious desires for the patient to become well and unconscious motives for keeping the patient ill. A compromise-formation is likely, with the family expressing concern for improvement but at the same time conveying a tacit message that sickness is expected. The patient then experiences a "double bind" situation, and, as a consequence, may respond ambivalently in terms of the desire to get well.[63]

Role of the Social Environment A major social consequence of chronic insomnia is its frequent impact on the patient's employment—overall performance, relationship to supervisors, and interaction with co-workers. Because of sleep loss and fear of its consequences, insomniacs may be tardy or absent repeatedly and perform poorly while on the job. Furthermore, they usually rationalize their unsatisfactory work performance to their co-workers and supervisors, which eventually provokes considerable resentment and may ultimately cost them their jobs. Additionally, the welfare and compensation structure in our society often tends to foster disability and downward functioning rather than rehabilitation. In particular, disability benefits which depend upon continued illness may reinforce persistence of the sick role and failure to return to work.[82] Another disincentive to rehabilitation and return to functioning is the generally high level of reimbursement by third-party payers for technical diagnostic and therapeutic procedures. In contrast, the compensation is much less adequate for physicians' counseling and supportive care designed to improve patients' emotional status and coping abilities.[83]

In a larger social context, Rogers has pointed out the need to educate the public regarding maintenance of health and the best use of preventive, supportive, and treatment services.[76] In this regard, Cohen notes that in our present-day society individuals are less willing to endure tension and anxiety, whereas in earlier times it was more customary to "tough out" periods of stress.[84] Today's social environment, as represented by television commercials, suggests that when individuals experience distress it should be promptly alleviated by a pill or potion to relieve pain, calm anxiety, or bring on sleep. Thus, our social environment provides powerful reinforcers for the individual who experiences transient insomnia to resort to alcohol, over-the-counter sleep aids, or prescribed medication. Through portrayals in cartoons and articles on sleep in the popular press, the general culture promotes the self-labeling concept "I am an insomniac and helpless" rather than the image of individuals actively trying to solve problems of living or interpersonal conflicts. Cohen disputes the notion that all human societies must inevitably resort to chemical pacifiers, citing the prohibitions of Moslems, Mormons, and Seventh-Day Adventists against tranquilizing chemical substances.[85]

Role of the Physician   Physicians who are generally confident in dealing with the medical aspects of patients' acute disease processes appear to be less comfortable managing patients with chronic insomnia. Because of their preoccupation with their symptoms and investment in the secondary gain they receive, these patients are difficult to treat. Thus, physicians at times may feel anxious, frustrated, manipulated, and angry, and they may not spend enough time with these patients to obtain a thorough history. This is a critical omission because taking a comprehensive sleep history is essential for determining the onset and clinical course of insomnia, its clinical characteristics, and its impact on the individual and his or her family.[86]

This lack of a thorough evaluation combined with physicians' frustration with these patients may create a sense of obligation to do something for chronic insomniacs. Thus, they may simply prescribe hypnotic medication—not as an adjunctive treatment, but as the only treatment—knowing that it is not a solution but feeling that it is the best "treatment" available. Or, they may provide patients with secondary gain by prescribing more "rest" and fewer activities—a recommendation that is usually counterproductive.[87] Or, finally, because they feel pressured by insomniac patients or do not believe that they can understand the condition adequately, they may refer such patients to sleep laboratories for expensive diagnostic procedures that may contribute little to the management of insomnia.[57,59,88-91]

Because of their preoccupation with their symptoms and the secondary gain they derive from them, insomniac patients are often resistant to treatment.[56,57,59] The resulting frustration, experienced by doctor and patient alike, often leads to mutual avoidance; the patient may then begin "doctor shopping," and the physician may distance himself from the patient. Such patients often have significant emotional difficulties, but the physician may be reluctant to recommend psychiatric evaluations because of patients' negative attitudes and reactions toward psychiatric referral. These attitudes are particularly likely when the patient insists that, aside from the insomnia, there are no other problems.

It is clear, then, that the primary care physician can play a crucial role in the evaluation and treatment of chronic insomnia by taking a longitudinal view of the development and continuation of the disorder.[56,57,59] But our experience has also shown that in order to manage chronic insomnia effectively, the physician must be aware that the disorder is multidimensional; any approach that is directed to only one

Table 2.3. Psychosocial Factors Contributing to Chronic Insomnia

---

Patient
  Childhood vulnerability
  Inadequate coping patterns for life stress
  Internalization of emotions
  Role of "being sick"
  Concurrent physical or psychiatric disorder

Illness
  Fear of sleeplessness and its consequences
  Conditioning to expect poor sleep
  Reinforcement by secondary gain

Family
  Provide secondary gain
  Unconscious motives for keeping the patient ill
  Lowered expectations of patient

Physician
  Inadequate evaluation
  Overreliance on diagnostic services
  Overdependence on hypnotic medication
  Labeling of patient

Social Environment
  Patients' lowered self-image through poor work performance
  Disincentives for rehabilitation
  Inadequate public/physician education

---

of the factors involved in insomnia, such as relying only on prescribing a hypnotic drug, is likely to be inadequate or unsuccessful (see also Chapters 8–11, which discuss the treatment of insomnia).

Table 2.3 lists a number of the psychosocial and behavioral factors involved in the development and persistence of insomnia. The case of a 38-year-old woman illustrates many of these factors:

Case 1. This patient had a history of chronic insomnia of 12 years' duration. The onset of the disorder appeared to coincide with her decision not to marry her boyfriend of a number of years after he had given her an ultimatum to do so. She recalled much unhappiness during childhood and indicated that she frequently experienced sleep difficulty both as a child and as an adolescent.

Her parents maintained an overprotective attitude toward her, and she was unable to express her feelings and concerns to them and develop a meaningful close relationship. This pattern of difficulty with close interpersonal relationships was repeated with her boyfriends, and she had never married. She related to her parents and friends primarily through her complaints of sleep difficulty and associated fatigue. She was particularly preoccupied with thoughts that the sleeplessness adversely affected her physical appearance, and she used this concern to avoid many of her social relationships and obligations.

She gave a history of moving from one job to another within relatively short intervals of time. When seen for evaluation and treatment, she was working for the state government in a responsible and desirable position. She was continually preoccupied with her sleeplessness and its potential consequences. She was habitually tardy for work because she felt unprepared to leave the house after a terrible night of sleeplessness. She thought she "looked bad," in addition to feeling tired and needing more sleep.

She continued to be late for work and eventually even convinced her supervisor to make a regular exception so she could begin work later each day. However, even this arrangement was not sufficient; she abused the special privilege and also developed a chronic pattern of taking advantage of sick leave. Her abuse of the special arrangements and sick leave eventually led to a confrontation with her supervisor, and she lost her position.

She had previously seen many physicians, who treated her almost exclusively with hypnotic medication on an irregular, long-term basis. Our approach was multidimensional and involved consideration of intrapsychic, interpersonal, familial, social, and vocational factors, in addition to the adjunctive use of hypnotic medication for about two weeks at the beginning of her treatment. After several months, her sleep difficulty had improved considerably, and she continued to be involved in individual therapy and, later, group therapy.

Physician Education on Insomnia

The need for physician education on insomnia is exemplified by the high prevalence of this condition among medical patients. In fact, many medical illnesses themselves and/or their treatments may cause insomnia (see Chapter 6, Medical and Other Pathophysiologic Factors). Therefore, it is important for physicians to be able to distinguish between chronic insomnia, which is a self-perpetuating condition, and transient insomnia, which is frequently secondary to medical conditions. Also, physicians need to be thoroughly prepared to manage patients with transient or chronic insomnia because iatrogenic factors themselves (eg, certain prescribed medications) may lead to sleep difficulty. Also, by simply prescribing hypnotic medication and thereby neglecting a thorough assessment of the underlying factors in insomnia, the physician may contribute to the development of chronic insomnia or the persistence of an already existing condition (see Chapter 7, Evaluation of Insomnia).

The National Institute of Drug Abuse (NIDA) report, "Sedative-Hypnotic Drugs: Risks and Benefits"[92] and the Institute of Medicine (IOM) report, "Sleeping Pills, Insomnia and Medical Practice,"[93] provided a valuable service in alerting physicians and the public to potential dangers in hypnotic drug use. In their conclusions, the IOM recommended that major educational programs should be developed for physicians and other health care professionals in the diagnosis and treatment of insomnia. Project Sleep was subsequently initiated by the Public Health Service as a program to educate physicians and patients about insomnia and other sleep disorders. Unfortunately, from the practicing physician's standpoint, the project addressed the complex multidimensional aspects involved in diagnosing and treating insomnia in an incomplete and unsystematic manner rather than presenting detailed scientific information on the biopsychobehavioral and social correlates of insomnia. For example, limited attention was paid to the important role of stress and psychologic conflicts in insomnia and the multi-modal treatment of this disorder, which includes stress management, office counseling, behavior therapy, and psychotherapy as well as judicious, adjunctive use of pharmacotherapy where indicated. Also missing from the project were validated testing instruments to evaluate the effectiveness of their educational efforts.

The need for physician education on insomnia should be viewed in relation to the difficulty of physicians' role in dealing with this condition because it is different from their accustomed role in evaluating and treating medical illnesses in their clinical practices. Insomnia is not a specific disease entity, but rather a symptom whose development and persistence may relate to a variety of biopsychobehavioral factors. Thus, the evaluation and treatment of this condition is complex and multidimensional.

There are a number of common shortcomings in the evaluation and treatment of insomnia.[57,59,94] An incomplete evaluation may result from neglecting to take a comprehensive history,[94] which should include not only a sleep history[86] but also drug and psychiatric histories. The drug history may identify pharmacologic factors as contributing to the insomnia, and the psychiatric history can often illuminate an association between the development of certain psychologic conflicts and the onset of sleep difficulty. Treatment of insomnia is often unsuccessful because the physician approaches the disorder from a unidimensional, "either-or" perspective. Rather than treating the patient from a multidimensional standpoint, as will be discussed in this book

(Chapters 8 through 11), the physician too often focuses on only one treatment approach, such as hypnotic drugs or psychotherapy alone.

To enhance physicians' knowledge of sleep disorders, our Sleep Research and Treatment Center developed two audiovisual programs for physician education on a nationwide basis. The first teaching program was based on a 60-minute film, "Evaluation and Treatment of Sleep Disorders"[95]; the second program, "The National Sleep Disorders Update: A Television Workshop," which was co-produced with the Network for Continuing Medical Education (NCME), was a learning and self-assessment experience based on a 50-minute videotape.[91] Together, the two programs have been viewed by over 50,000 physicians and health professionals. Each program included a pre-test and post-test, the results of which showed that the participants' knowledge about sleep disorders improved significantly.

By analyzing physicians' responses to the tests from both teaching programs, we were able to delineate specific strengths and weaknesses in their knowledge of insomnia.[91,95] Physicians were highly aware of the importance of psychologic factors in the etiology of insomnia. Most recognized that hypnotic drugs are not the pharmacologic treatment of choice for insomnia associated with endogenous or major depression and that such patients should be treated by administering most or all of the daily dose of a sedative tricyclic antidepressant at bedtime. However, they were not as well informed about the sedative tricyclic antidepressants themselves. Some thought that the therapeutic dose is determined by the level of daytime sedation produced by the drugs; however, the antidepressant action is the proper gauge for establishing dosage. Others thought that the basic antidepressant activity of these drugs begins within two or three days even though the antidepressant effect usually does not begin until after about two weeks.

The physicians were fairly well aware that most hypnotic drugs lose their effectiveness within two weeks of consecutive nightly use.[91,95] However, some mistakenly thought that most hypnotic drugs are effective when used continuously for one month or longer. Many failed to recognize that the abrupt withdrawal of hypnotic drugs can intensify insomnia, and that certain hypnotic drugs may affect the plasma levels of anticoagulants. They were also unaware that, as in the case of barbiturates, high doses of other non-benzodiazepine hypnotics can seriously suppress respiration.

The results of these educational programs and our clinical practice

and consultation suggest a need for physicians to expand their knowledge of sleep disorders, especially regarding the evaluation and treatment of insomnia. Whereas physicians appear to be fairly well aware
that psychologic factors are causative in insomnia, they need to be
better informed concerning the various treatment strategies for this
prevalent disorder. For example, for the majority of chronic insomniac patients who are anxious, ruminative, apprehensive, neurotically
depressed, or somatically preoccupied, neither hypnotic drugs nor
psychotherapy alone is usually sufficient as the sole treatment modality. Rather, psychotherapy is initiated to provide support and assist in
developing insight regarding the conflicts that underlie the insomnia,
while the initial and short-term prescription of a hypnotic drug is
beneficial to break the vicious circle of fear of sleeplessness and insomnia.

Finally, because of a lack of systematic pre- and postgraduate medical education on sleep disorders, physicians are often confused by
information that may overemphasize the role of physiologic factors in
the pathogenesis of insomnia. This has led to a mystique regarding the
importance of and necessity for sleep laboratory studies in the evaluation of sleep disorders in general and of insomnia in particular. In
reality, sleep laboratory diagnostic studies are not indicated for the
evaluation of many patients with sleep disorders, including the vast
majority of those with insomnia.[57,88,91,96,97] Suspicion of sleep apnea is
the major indication for referral to the sleep laboratory.[89,90] Insomniac
patients, however, have been found to be at no greater risk for this
disorder than control subjects[67] (see also Chapter 3, Sleep Laboratory
Studies of Insomnia).

Summary

Insomnia is a term referring to a relative deficiency in the amount or
quality of sleep. Although a symptom of psychiatric and medical disorders and situational disturbances, insomnia is often perceived as a
primary disorder because it has great impact on patients' lives.

The most common disorder of sleep, it occurs more frequently in
the elderly, in women, in those with psychologic disturbances, and in
persons of lower socioeconomic status. Regional and nationwide surveys show that about one-third of the adult U.S. population reports
current difficulties in sleeping.

Most people do not sleep as much as they would like. In a recent survey, most respondents reported that they slept less than eight hours, even though most believed that eight hours of sleep is preferable. Factors affecting the amount of sleep obtained included age, geographic location, employment status, and for women, working full time as opposed to part-time.

A number of studies have shown that obtaining seven or eight hours of sleep and other "good" health practices are positively correlated with improved health status and lower mortality rate. Sleeping less than seven hours per night appeared to be a significant health risk for both men and women. However, these studies could not completely control for the effects of medical illness, so it is not clear if abnormally shortened or lengthened sleep duration is a cause or an effect of medical illness.

As a psychobehavioral disorder, chronic insomnia is best understood using the biopsychosocial model of illness. It is a condition that affects and is affected by several aspects of the patient's life: personality factors, the illness itself, family and marital relationships, physician-patient interaction, and social environment. Patient factors contributing to the illness are a tendency to internalize emotions and to have certain vulnerabilities rooted in childhood that are expressed as inadequacy, insecurity, and dependency as an adult. The illness itself, in addition to being a source of chronic emotional arousal, can cause the patient to develop a fear of sleeplessness, and to become conditioned to expect poor sleep—both factors contributing to the persistence of the disorder. Family members may also affect a patient's insomnia, often providing secondary gain through sympathy and support or by tacitly encouraging the persistence of sleep difficulty because their own needs are being met in some way. The social environment may also contribute to the persistence of insomnia by providing health benefits that may be disincentives to rehabilitation and by reimbursing technical medical procedures at higher rates than rehabilitative counseling. Also, the television promotion of over-the-counter sleep aids may encourage patients to be more passive than active in attempting to master the stressful events in their lives that lead to sleep disturbances.

Physicians need to be better informed about the management of insomnia. The results from pre- and post-tests of two nationwide educational programs on sleep disorders show that a significant degree of knowledge was obtained by the physicians and allied health professionals who participated in the programs. There is a need, however, for physicians to better understand the important role of stress and psychologic conflicts in insomnia and to expand their skills in the multimodal treatment of insomnia, which includes stress management, office counseling, behavior therapy, and psychotherapy as well as judicious adjunctive use of pharmacotherapy where indicated. Finally, there is an overall need for physicians to better understand that the development and persistence of insomnia may relate to a number of biopsychobehavioral and social factors and that the disorder's evaluation and treatment are therefore multidimensional.

References

1. Kleitman N: Insomnia or hyposomnia, in Kleitman N: *Sleep and Wakefulness*. Chicago, University of Chicago Press, 1963, pp. 274–279.
2. Bixler EO, Kales A, Soldatos CR: Sleep disorders encountered in medical practice: a national survey of physicians. *Behav Med* 6:1–6, 1979.
3. Bixler EO, Kales A, Soldatos CR, Kales JD, Healey S: Prevalence of sleep disorders in the Los Angeles metropolitan area. *Am J Psychiatry* 136:1257–1262, 1979.
4. Hammond EC: Some preliminary findings on physical complaints from a prospective study of 1,064,004 men and women. *Am J Public Health* 54:11–23, 1964.
5. Johns MW, Egan P, Gay TJA, Masterton JP: Sleep habits and symptoms in male medical and surgical patients. *Br Med J* 2:509–512, 1970.
6. Karacan I, Thornby JI, Anch M, Holzer CE, Warheit GJ, Schwab JJ, Williams RL: Prevalence of sleep disturbance in a primarily urban Florida county. *Soc Sci and Med* 10:239–244, 1976.
7. McGhie A, Russell SM: The subjective assessment of normal sleep patterns. *J Ment Sci* 108:642–654, 1962.
8. Tune GS: Sleep and wakefulness in normal human adults. *Br Med J* 2:269–271, 1968.
9. *Selected Symptoms of Psychological Distress*. Rockville MD, US Department of HEW, 1970.
10. Weiss HR, Kasinoff BH, Bailey MA: An exploration of reported sleep disturbance. *J Nerv Ment Dis* 134:528–534, 1962.
11. The Gallup Organization: *The Gallup Study of Sleeping Habits*, Princeton, NJ, 1979.
12. Sweetwood H, Grant I, Kripke DF, Gerst MS, Yager J: Sleep disorder over time: psychiatric correlates among males. *Br J Psychiatry* 136:456–462, 1980.
13. Sweetwood HL, Kripke DF, Grant I, Yager J, Gerst MS: Sleep disorder and psychobiological symptomatology in male psychiatric outpatients and male nonpatients. *Psychosom Med* 38:373–378, 1976.
14. Price VA, Coates TJ, Thoresen CE, Grinstead OA: Prevalence and

correlates of poor sleep among adolescents. *Am J Dis Child 132*:583–586, 1978.

15. Simonds JF, Parraga H: Prevalence of sleep disorders and sleep behaviors in children and adolescents. *J Am Acad Child Psychiatry 21*: 383–388, 1982.

16. Hollingshead A, Redlich RC: *Social Class and Mental Illness.* New York, John Wiley & Sons, 1958.

17. Srole L, Langner TS, Michael ST, Opler MK, Rennie TAC: *Mental Health in the Metropolis: The Midtown Manhattan Study.* New York, McGraw-Hill, 1962.

18. Dohrenwend BS: Social class and stressful events, in Hare EH, Wing JK (eds): *Psychiatric Epidemiology.* New York, Oxford University Press, 1970.

19. Pierce CM: The ghetto: An extreme environment. *J Natl Med Assoc 67*:162–166, 1975.

20. Lewis HE: Sleep patterns on polar expeditions, in Wolstenholme GEW, O'Connor M (eds): *Ciba Foundation Symposium on the Nature of Sleep.* London, Churchill, 1961, pp 322–328.

21. Jones HS, Oswald I: Two cases of healthy insomnia. *Electroencephalogr Clin Neurophysiol 24*:378–380, 1968.

22. Meddis R, Pearson AJD, Langford G: An extreme case of healthy insomnia. *Electroencephalogr Clin Neurophysiol 35*:213–214, 1973.

23. Stuss D, Broughton R: Extreme short sleep: personality profiles and a case study of sleep requirement. *Waking and Sleeping 2*:101–105, 1978.

24. Hartmann E: Sleep requirements: long sleepers, short sleepers, variable sleepers, and insomniacs. *Psychosomatics 14*:95–103, 1973.

25. Agnew HW, Webb WB, Williams RL: Comparison of stage four and 1-REM sleep deprivation. *Percept Mot Skills 24*:851–858, 1967.

26. Berger RJ, Oswald I: Effects of sleep deprivation on behavior, subsequent sleep, and dreaming. *J Ment Sci 108*:457–465, 1962.

27. Dement W: The effect of dream deprivation. *Science 131*:1705–1707, 1960.

28. Johnson LC, Slye ES, Dement W: Electroencephalographic and autonomic activity during and after prolonged sleep deprivation. *Psychosom Med 27*:415–423, 1965.

29. Kales A, Hodemaker FS, Jacobson A, Lichtenstein EL: Dream deprivation: an experimental reappraisal. *Nature 204*:1337–1338, 1964.

30. Kales A, Tan TL, Kollar EJ, Naitoh P, Preston TA, Malmstrom EJ: Sleep patterns following 204 hours of sleep deprivation. *Psychosom Med 32*:189–200, 1970.

31. Naitoh R: Sleep deprivation in human subjects: a reappraisal. *Waking and Sleeping 1*:53–60, 1976.

32. Vogel GW, Traub AC: REM deprivation, I. The effect on schizophrenic patients. *Arch Gen Psychiatry 18*:287–300, 1968.

33. Williams HL, Hammack JT, Daly RL, Dement WC, Lubin A: Responses to auditory stimulation, sleep loss, and the EEG stages of sleep. *Electroencephalogr Clin Neurophysiol 16*:269–279, 1964.

34. Belloc NB, Breslow L: Relationship of physical health status and health practices. *Prev Med 1*:409–421, 1972.
35. Belloc NB: Relationship of health practices and mortality. *Prev Med 2*:67–81, 1973.
36. Wiley JA, Camacho TC: Life-style and future health: Evidence from the Alameda County study. *Prev Med 9*:1–21, 1980.
37. Wingard DL, Berkman LF: Mortality risk associated with sleeping patterns among adults. *Sleep 6*:102–107, 1983.
38. Hammond EC: Smoking in relation to the death rates of 1 million men and women. *Natl Cancer Inst Monogr 19*:127–204, 1966.
39. Hammond EC, Garfinkel L: Coronary heart disease, stroke, aortic aneurysm: factors in the etiology. *Arch Environ Health 19*:167–182, 1969.
40. Kripke DF, Simons RN, Garfinkel L, Hammond EC: Short and long sleep and sleeping pills. *Arch Gen Psychiatry 36*:103–116, 1979.
41. Hauri P: *The Sleep Disorders*. Kalamazoo, Mich., The Upjohn Company, 1977.
42. Kales JD, Kales A: Rest and sleep, in Taylor RB, Ureda JR, Denham JW (eds): *Health Promotion: Principles and Clinical Applications*. Norwalk, Conn., Appleton-Century-Crofts, 1982, pp 307–337.
43. Palmore E: Health practices and illness among the aged. *The Gerontologist 4*(10):313–316, 1970.
44. Pratt L: The relationship of socioeconomic status to health. *Am J Publ Health 61*:281–291, 1971.
45. Bixler EO, Kales A, Leo LA, Slye T: A comparison of subjective estimates and objective sleep laboratory findings in insomniac patients. *Sleep Res 2*:143, 1973.
46. Carskadon MA, Dement WC, Mitler MM, Guilleminault C, Zarcone V, Spiegel R: Self-reports versus sleep laboratory findings in 122 drug-free subjects with complaints of chronic insomnia. *Am J Psychiatry 133*: 1382–1388, 1976.
47. Kales A, Bixler EO: Sleep profiles of insomnia and hypnotic drug effectiveness, in Burch N, Altshuler HL (eds): *Behavior and Brain Electrical Activity*. New York, Plenum, 1975, pp 81–91.
48. Frankel BL, Coursey RD, Buchbinder R, Snyder F: Recorded and reported sleep in chronic primary insomnia. *Arch Gen Psychiatry 33*:615–623, 1976.
49. Hoddes E, Carskadon M, Phillips R, Zarcone V, Dement W: Total sleep time in insomniacs (abstract). *Sleep Res 1*:152, 1972.
50. Monroe LJ: Psychological and physiological differences between good and poor sleepers. *J Abnorm Psychol 72*:255–264, 1967.
51. Schwartz BA, Guilbaud G, Fischgold H. Etudes electroencephalographiques. Le sommeil de nuit: I. L' "insomnie" chronique. *Presse Med 71*: 1474, 1963.
52. Rice DP, Hodgson TA: *Scope and impact of chronic disease in the United States*. Nat Arthritis Adv Bd Forum on Public Policy and Chr Disease, 1978.
53. American Psychiatric Association: *Diagnostic and Statistical Manual of*

Mental Disorders (DSM-III), ed 3. Washington, D.C.: American Psychiatric Association, 1980.

54. Bonica JJ: Introduction to symposium on pain: part 1. *Arch Surg 112*: 749–761, 1977.

55. Kales A, Caldwell AB, Preston TA, Healey S, Kales JD: Personality patterns in insomnia. *Arch Gen Psychiatry 33*:1128–1134, 1976.

56. Kales A, Kales JD, Bixler EO: Insomnia: An approach to management and treatment. *Psychiatr Ann 4*:28–44, 1974.

57. Soldatos CR, Kales A, Kales JD: Management of insomnia. *Ann Rev Med 30*:301–312, 1979.

58. Callahan EM, Carroll S, Revier P, Gilhooly E, Dunn D: The 'sick role' in chronic illness: some reactions. *J Chron Dis 19*:883–897, 1966.

59. Kales A, Soldatos CR, Kales JD: Sleep Disorders: Evaluation and management in the office setting, in Arieti S, Brodie HKH (eds): *American Handbook of Psychiatry*, ed 2. New York, Basic Books, 1981, vol 7, pp 423–454.

60. Tan T-L, Kales JD, Kales A, Soldatos CR, Bixler EO: Biopsychobehavioral correlates of insomnia, IV: Diagnosis based on the DSM-III. *Am J Psychiatry* (in press).

61. Hinkle LE Jr: The effect of exposure to culture change, social change, and changes in interpersonal relationship on health, in Dohrenwend BS, Dohrenwend BP (eds): *Stressful Life Events: Their Nature and Effects*. New York, Wiley, 1974, pp 9–44.

62. Hinkle LE Jr, Wolff HG: Ecologic investigations of the relationship between illness, life experiences and the social environment. *Ann Intern Med 49*:1373–1388, 1958.

63. Bursten B, D'Esopo R: The obligation to remain sick. *Arch Gen Psychiatry 12*:402–407, 1965.

64. Fordyce WE: *Behavioral Methods for Chronic Pain and Illness*. St. Louis, Mosby, 1976.

65. Kales JD, Kales A, Bixler EO, Soldatos CR, Cadieux RJ, Kashurba GJ, Vela-Bueno A: Biopsychobehavioral correlates of insomnia, V: clinical characteristics and behavioral consequences. *Am J Psychiatry* (in press).

66. Kales A, Bixler EO, Vela-Bueno A, Cadieux RJ, Soldatos CR, Kales JD: Biopsychobehavioral correlates of insomnia, III: polygraphic findings of sleep difficulty and their relationship to psychopathology. *Int J Neurosci* (in press).

67. Kales A, Bixler EO, Soldatos CR, Vela-Bueno A, Caldwell AB, Cadieux RJ: Biopsychobehavioral correlates of insomnia, I: Role of sleep apnea and nocturnal myoclonus. *Psychosomatics 23*:589–600, 1982.

68. Kales A, Caldwell AB, Soldatos CR, Bixler EO, Kales JD: Biopsychobehavioral correlates of insomnia, II: MMPI pattern specificity and consistency. *Psychosom Med 45*:341–356, 1983.

69. Levi L: Psychosocial stress and disease: A conceptual model, in Gunderson EKE, Rahe RH (eds): *Life Stress and Illness*. Springfield, Ill., Charles C Thomas & Sons, 1974.

70. Suwa N, Yamashita I: *Psychophysiological Studies of Emotional and Mental Disorders.* Tokyo, Ihaku Shoin, 1974.

71. Parson T: *Social System.* Glencoe, Ill., Free Press (Division of Mac-Millan Company), 1951.

72. Mechanic D, Volkart E: Stress, illness behavior and sick role. *Am Soc Rev 26*:51–58, 1961.

73. Daitz BD: The challenge of disability. *Am J Public Health 55*:528–534, 1965.

74. Haber LD: Disabling effects of chronic disease and impairment. *J Chron Dis 24*:469–487, 1971.

75. Haber LD: Disabling effects of chronic disease and impairment–II: functional capacity limitations. *J Chron Dis 26*:127–151, 1973.

76. Rogers DE: The doctor himself must become the treatment. *Pharos 37*: 124–129, 1974.

77. Coursey RD, Buchsbaum M, Frankel BL: Personality measures and evoked responses in chronic insomniacs. *J Abnorm Psychol 84*:239–249, 1975.

78. Haynes SN, Follingstad DR, McGowan WT: Insomnia: sleep patterns and anxiety level. *J Psychosom Res 18*:69–74, 1974.

79. Healey ES, Kales A, Monroe LJ, Bixler EO, Chamberlin K, Soldatos CR: Onset of insomnia: Role of life-stress events. *Psychosom Med 43*: 439–451, 1981.

80. Marks PA, Monroe LJ: Correlates of adolescent poor sleepers. *J Abnorm Psychol 85*:243–246, 1976.

81. Monroe LJ, Marks PA: MMPI differences between adolescent poor and good sleepers. *J Consult Clin Psychology 45*:151–152, 1977.

82. Better SR, Fine PR, Simison D, Doss GH, Walls RT, McLaughlin DE: Disability benefits as disincentives to rehabilitation. *Milbank Memorial Fund Quarterly/Health and Society 57*:412–427, 1979.

83. Cluff LE: Chronic disease, function and the quality of care. *J Chron Dis 34*:299–304, 1981.

84. Cohen S: Methaqualone: a new twist. *Drug Abuse and Alcoholism Newsletter 11(1)*:1–4, 1982.

85. Cohen S: Pleasure and pain. *Drug Abuse and Alcoholism Newsletter 11 (5)*:1–4, 1982.

86. Kales A, Soldatos CR, Kales JD: Taking a sleep history. *Am Fam Physician 22*:101–108, 1979.

87. Goldman R: Rest: its use and abuse in the aged. *J Am Geriatr Soc 25*: 433–438, 1977.

88. Kales A, Kales JD: Sleep disorders: recent findings in the diagnosis and treatment of disturbed sleep. *N Engl J Med 290*:487–499, 1974.

89. Kales A, Kales JD, Soldatos CR: Insomnia and other sleep disorders. *Med Clinics N Am 66*:971–991, 1982.

90. Kales A, Soldatos CR, Kales JD: Sleep disorders. *Med North Am 1*: 3299–3314, 1983.

91. Kales JD, Kales A, Bixler EO, Soldatos CR: Resource for managing sleep disorders. *JAMA 241*:2413–2416, 1979.

92. Cooper J (ed): *Sedative-Hypnotic Drugs: Risks and Benefits.* Washington DC, Dept. of HEW, National Institute on Drug Abuse, 1977.
93. National Academy of Sciences: *Sleeping Pills, Insomnia, and Medical Practice.* Washington DC, Institute of Medicine, Division of Mental Health & Behavioral Medicine, 1979.
94. Kales A, Kales JD, Bixler EO, Martin E: Common shortcomings in the evaluation and treatment of insomnia, in Kagan F, Harwood T, Rickels K, Rudzik A, Sorer H (eds): *Hypnotics: Methods of Development and Evaluation.* New York, Spectrum Publications, 1975, pp 29–40.
95. Kales JD, Kales A, Bixler EO, Soldatos CR: Sleep disorders: What the primary care physician needs to know. *Postgrad Med 67*:213–220, 1980.
96. Oswald I: Assessment of insomnia. *Br Med J 283*:874–875, 1981.
97. Regestein QR, Reich P: A sleep clinic within a general hospital psychiatry service. *Gen Hosp Psychiatry 2*:112–117, 1980.

3. Sleep Laboratory Studies of Insomnia

Sleep laboratory studies utilizing all-night polygraphic recordings can be valuable for researching certain aspects of both normal and disturbed sleep. By using the laboratory to assess the sleep of normal subjects, investigators have defined sleep patterns and delineated the effects of age and sex on sleep.[1-13] Insomnia, however, has been less thoroughly studied in the sleep laboratory; there have been fewer studies of insomnia than of normal sleep, and most studies of insomnia have used relatively small subject samples. In addition, for methodologic reasons, most studies of insomniacs have been limited to subjects not using medication. Because these subjects tend to have less severe insomnia than those who do use sleep medication, most studies of insomnia are not representative of the degree of sleep difficulty experienced by chronic insomniacs in everyday life. In spite of these limitations, sleep laboratory studies have demonstrated differences in sleep between insomniacs and normal subjects and have helped to clarify the relationship between insomniacs' subjective estimates of their sleep difficulty and objective measurements of their insomnia.

The first section of this chapter briefly delineates methodologic problems that are encountered in sleep laboratory studies. In the next section, patterns of nocturnal sleep and wakefulness in normal subjects are described. Then, assessment of insomnia in the sleep laboratory is discussed in terms of sleep efficiency, sleep stage patterns, and physiologic correlates. The final section addresses a pertinent topic that has been thoroughly evaluated through the use of sleep laboratory studies—the etiologic role of sleep apnea and nocturnal myoclonus in chronic insomnia.

Methodologic Considerations

Two major methodologic considerations that may markedly affect the results of a sleep laboratory study are the length of the recording period and adaptation to the laboratory environment. In relation to the length of the recording time, two basic designs are used for sleep laboratory studies.[2] One design uses an "ad-lib" protocol in which subjects are allowed to stay in bed as long as they wish. In the other design, the length of the recording period is fixed and constant for each night in the laboratory. The schedule of the ad-lib design is more typical of subjects' nightly schedules in everyday life, and the data from such a study may be more representative of subjects' usual sleep-wakefulness patterns. On the other hand, since the length of the recording period may vary from night to night in the ad-lib design, investigators cannot control for the amount of time subjects spend in bed. This makes comparisons difficult between groups of subjects, across various conditions, or within groups of subjects with regard to wake time after sleep onset, total wake time, and the amount of time spent in each sleep stage because the value of each variable depends on the total time spent in bed.

Sleep must be recorded for several consecutive nights if it is to be evaluated accurately because subjects must adapt or readapt to the sleep laboratory environment. On the first night in the sleep laboratory, subjects take longer to fall asleep, awaken more often, and have more total wake time than on subsequent nights, when they have adjusted to their new environment.[14-16] Thus, data from the first night in the sleep laboratory do not represent subjects' customary sleep patterns and are generally not included in the average values that represent baseline sleep patterns in a study protocol. By the second or third night in the sleep laboratory, data are quite characteristic of subjects' customary, or baseline, sleep patterns. Similar but less pronounced adaptation effects have been noted when subjects return to the laboratory after varying periods at home.[17] Thus, a readaptation night is generally included whenever subjects return to the laboratory even though they were initially adapted to it.

Nocturnal Sleep and Wakefulness in Normal Subjects

Since the sleep patterns of normal subjects are influenced considerably by age, and to a lesser extent by sex, knowledge of sleep and its variations in normal subjects is essential for physicians who evaluate the sleep of insomniac patients. Several sleep laboratory studies with large sample sizes have defined sleep patterns of normal subjects.[2,3,] [12,13] Three of these studies used an ad-lib design,[3,12,13] and the other study employed a constant eight-hour recording period.[2] Each of these, four studies assessed the effects of age on sleep, and three of the studies also evaluated the differences in sleep patterns between men and women. In each study, the subjects were allowed to adapt to the laboratory environment on the first night, and nocturnal sleep was recorded for several consecutive nights thereafter.

Sleep Efficiency

Measurements of sleep efficiency, or how well or poorly a person sleeps, vary among different age groups and between the sexes. In studies in which the length of the recording period is held constant, sleep efficiency is composed of three major measurements—sleep latency (the time it takes to fall asleep), wake time after sleep onset, and total wake time (the combined values for sleep latency and wake time after sleep onset).

Sleep Latency Sleep latency changes very little with age. In one study,[13] the mean values for sleep latency across 11 age groups comprised of individuals aged 3–69 years ranged from eight to 18 minutes. The oldest group (70–79 years old) took an average of 24 minutes to fall asleep. In a study where we divided the subjects into three age groups,[2] the mean values for sleep latency among the three groups were remarkably similar: ages 19–29, 20.7 minutes; ages 30–49, 21.7 minutes; and ages 50–80, 23.1 minutes (Table 3.1).

Wake Time After Sleep Onset Wake time after sleep onset increases considerably with age.[2,12,13] In the previously mentioned study of 11 age groups, this increase began at around age 40.[13] For the seven age groups younger than age 40, mean wake time after sleep onset ranged from 6 to 11 minutes. This value nearly doubled to 19 minutes for subjects aged 40–50, and continued to rise, reaching 40 minutes for ages 60–70 and 83 minutes for ages 70–80. A similar trend was seen in our study of three age groups (Table 3.1).[2] While the two younger age groups averaged 19 and 26 minutes of wakefulness after sleep onset, respectively, those in the 50–80-year age group were awake for 50 minutes, nearly twice as long.

Older persons are more wakeful after sleep onset because they have more and longer awakenings. In the study of 11 age groups, the groups between the ages of 13 and 40 averaged between 2.0 and 2.6 nightly awakenings.[13] In the next four age groups (40 to 80 years), however, the number of awakenings increased, with mean values of 3.8, 5.2, 5.9, and 7.7 awakenings, respectively. The awakenings also became longer in these four decades, with respective mean values of 4.9, 4.4, 6.8, and 10.8 minutes. Our findings in the study of three age groups[2] demonstrated a similar relationship between age and wakefulness following sleep onset. As seen in Table 3.1, the awakenings of the two youngest age groups were similar both in mean number (6.0 and 7.7, respectively) and duration (3.2 and 3.4 minutes, respectively). The oldest age group, however, had more awakenings (11.0) and a longer duration (4.6 minutes). These findings confirm results previously reported by Webb and Campbell.[18]

Men awaken more often during the night than women.[2,12,13] This difference appears to begin after puberty. In one study, boys and girls through age 12 averaged fewer than two nightly awakenings.[13] Then, in men through age 39, this number rose to three, while women continued to awaken fewer than two times a night during the same time period. Men had more awakenings than women until both groups reached the decade of 70 to 79 years. Between ages 40 and 69, the number of awakenings in women increased from 3.1 to 4.4, and in men, from 4.6 to 7.6. Similarly, in our study, men had an average of 10.2 awakenings per night while women had 7.8 awakenings; this relationship was consistent within all three age groups.[2]

Older men also have been reported to have more wakefulness after sleep onset. In a comparison of 40 men and 40 women who were 50 to 60 years old, the men were awake 8.1 percent of the time after sleep onset and the women were awake only 5.1 percent of the time.[12] In our study, however, men had an average time awake after sleep onset that was only slightly longer than that of women.[2]

Total Wake Time　　Total wake time also increases with age, primarily because older people have more wakefulness following sleep onset. In the 11-age-group study, those groups under age 50 were awake on average from 16 to 28 minutes.[13] However, the amount of total wake time was progressively greater across the last three age groups; from 34 minutes in subjects aged 50–60, to 53 minutes in those aged 60–70, and 108 minutes in subjects aged 70–80. Similarly, total wake time in our three-age-group study increased from a mean of 40 minutes in the youngest group to 73 minutes in the oldest (Table 3.1).[2]

Distribution of wakefulness throughout the night differs among age

Table 3.1. Sleep Patterns and Age[a]

	19–30 years old		30–49 years old		50–80 years old		Total	
	Insomniacs	Normal Controls	Insomniacs	Normal Controls	Insomniacs	Normal Controls	Insomniacs	Normal Controls
Sleep latency (min)	42.2†	20.7	47.1†	21.7	45.2†	23.1	44.9†	22.1
Wake time after sleep onset (min)	21.2	18.9	37.2†	25.9	58.4*	50.3	34.6	34.7
Total wake time (min)	63.4†	39.6	84.3†	47.6	103.6†	73.4	79.5†	56.8
Number of awakenings	4.2*	6.0	6.5	7.7	9.3	11.0	6.0†	8.7
Duration of awakenings (min)	5.0*	3.2	5.7†	3.4	6.3*	4.6	5.8*	4.0

a Values presented are the means of nights 2–4
† p<0.01, for comparisons between insomniacs and controls
* p<0.05, for comparisons between insomniacs and controls
(From Kales et al[38])

groups as well. The oldest of our three age groups spent more time awake during each of the final seven hours of the night than did either of the two younger groups. This finding is similar to what has previously been reported for elderly women.[18] However, within each of the three age groups the distribution of wakefulness for hours two through eight was quite similar; all three age groups had more sleep disruption during the final hours of the night. This trend was most pronounced in the oldest age group.

Unusual Sleep Requirements of Normal Subjects

The sleep of persons who do not have a sleep complaint but have unusual sleep requirements has been evaluated in the sleep laboratory.[19-26] For example, the sleep of "short" sleepers, who obtained an average of 5.5 hours of sleep per night, was compared with that of "long" sleepers, who slept an average of 8.5 hours each night.[19] The two groups had the same amounts of slow-wave sleep (stages 3 and 4), but the "long" sleepers spent significantly more time in REM sleep. Since "short" sleepers and "long" sleepers were found to differ also in terms of their personality patterns, the implication was that the amount of REM sleep was related to subjects' personality patterns.[27] However, we believe a more likely explanation is that "long" sleepers have more REM sleep simply because REM sleep normally increases when sleep is prolonged.

Other studies have assessed the relationship between sleep duration, sleep stages, and personality patterns in short and long sleepers as well as in variable-length sleepers.[28-30] Hartmann and Brewer found that sleep duration of variable-length sleepers fluctuated as a function of their life stress; subjects reported that more sleep was obtained during periods of increased stressfulness.[28] An inverse relationship was found between sleep duration and level of Type A behavior; habitual short sleepers scored highest in Type A behavior.[29] In a subsequent study, variable sleepers were found to have the lowest level of Type A behavior.[30] Findings from both studies of variable sleepers led the investigators to suggest that varying sleep duration is a useful mechanism for coping with stress.[28,30]

Studies of "short" sleepers have demonstrated that these subjects appear to have relatively efficient sleep patterns because they have the same amount of stage 4 and REM sleep (at the expense of stage 2 sleep) as controls sleeping for seven to eight hours.[25,26] More extreme cases of short sleep in people who regularly sleep for only an hour or two each night, yet do not complain of insomnia or the effects of sleep loss, have also been evaluated in the sleep laboratory.[20-24] For example, two men who reported that they obtained only three hours of sleep each night slept just under that amount in the laboratory.[20] Much of their sleep was spent in stages 3 and 4. Another study of an extreme short sleeper also showed a relatively high amount of stages 3 and 4 sleep but a low level of REM sleep.[23] When the sleep of a 70-year-old woman who slept an average of only 67 minutes was assessed, the distribution of sleep stages and the proportion of time spent in each of them were found to be fairly normal.[21]

Nocturnal Sleep and Wakefulness in Insomniac Subjects

A number of sleep laboratory studies have evaluated the sleep patterns of subjects who complained of insomnia. In 1967, Monroe studied the sleep characteristics of 16 "poor sleepers" and 16 "good sleepers."[31] Karacan and his associates initially compared ten insomniacs with ten control subjects[32] and subsequently completed another study with an additional 11 insomniac subjects and their matched controls.[33] In other studies, Frankel and his associates compared 18 insomniacs with age- and sex-matched controls,[34] Gillin and his associates compared the sleep of 18 insomniacs with that of 41 normal control subjects and 56 depressed patients,[35] and Gaillard compared the sleep of 16 insomniacs with 16 age- and sex-matched controls.[36] Another group of investigators assessed the sleep of 12 insomniacs and 12 good sleepers in their home environment.[37]

All of these studies were somewhat limited by relatively small samples of insomniacs, the absence of a control group, or both. To derive data from a larger sample, we evaluated the sleep of 150 insomniacs ranging in age from 19 to 80 years and compared their sleep characteristics with those of 100 normal control subjects.[38] Both insomniacs and controls were divided into three age groups (ages 19–29, 30–49, and 50–80) for age-related comparisons. In order for the insomniac and control samples to differ primarily in terms of the presence of a sleep complaint, the insomniacs selected were in good general health and not taking any medication. This latter restriction, while necessary to avoid affecting the sleep laboratory recordings by medication, most likely led to fewer differences between the insomniacs and their controls because it has been shown that insomniacs who take medication are generally more severely disturbed than those who do not.[39,40]

Sleep Efficiency

Sleep Latency Our insomniac sample had a significantly longer mean sleep latency than did the normal controls[38] (Table 3.1). This finding confirms previous reports by other investigators.[31-33,35,36] In each age group, the insomniacs took longer to fall asleep than did the respective group of normal controls. Within the insomniac sample, however, sleep latency was unrelated to age or to sex.[38] This finding is similar to that reported by Carskadon and her associates.[41]

Wake Time After Sleep Onset The total insomniac and control groups in our study had similar amounts of wakefulness after sleep onset (Table 3.1).[38] This confirms the findings of a previous study.[32] Wake time after sleep onset increased with age in both the insomniac sample and control subjects.[2,38] However, insomniacs over age 30 were awake after sleep onset for longer periods of time than were the controls.

There appears to be some disagreement among researchers as to whether insomniacs awaken more often than normal sleepers during the night. Monroe[31] and Gaillard[36] reported that insomniacs awakened more often than controls, while Beutler[42] and Coates[37] found no differences. We found an age-related increase in the number of nightly awakenings in insomniacs, as well as in their controls.[2,38] This confirms the findings of Carskadon in insomniac patients.[41] In our study, the controls in the youngest age group actually had more nightly awakenings than the insomniacs.[38] When the duration of nightly awakenings was considered, the sleep of insomniacs was more disturbed than that of controls, with the insomniacs in all three age groups having longer nightly awakenings than the controls. As a result, the insomniacs and controls in the youngest age group did not differ in terms of wake time after sleep onset, whereas insomniacs in the two older age groups had greater values than their respective controls. These data, together with our finding of a consistently longer sleep latency for insomniac subjects than for controls, indicate that insomniacs' primary difficulty is initiating sleep, whether at the beginning of the sleep period or following awakenings during the night.

The insomniacs in our study did not show any sex-related differences in wakefulness following sleep onset. This contrasts with our finding that among normal controls, men awakened more often than women.[2,38]

Total Wake Time   The insomniac group in our study had more total wake time as a whole than the control group because all of the insomniac age groups had longer sleep latencies than their respective controls, and the middle and older age groups had more wakefulness following sleep onset. These data also confirm previous findings.[31,36,37] Other investigators have reported that, when compared with normal controls, insomniac subjects spend less time in bed asleep.[32,33,36]

In our insomniac sample as well as in our controls, total wake time was strongly influenced by age, increasing in each successive age category[2,38] (Table 3.1). In addition, each age group of insomniacs had more total wake time than its respective control group. Other studies have shown that total wake time increases with age in normals,[43,44] but the relationship between age and total wake time in insomniac subjects has not been previously assessed.

The distribution of wakefulness throughout the night differed among our three insomniac groups (Fig. 3.1).[38] The oldest insomniacs had significantly more wakefulness than did the youngest insomniacs for hours 3, 4, 6, 7, and 8. During hours 7 and 8 the middle-aged group also had significantly more wakefulness than the youngest insomniacs. The distribution of wakefulness for each group of insomniacs differed from their controls, principally during the first several hours of the recording period. The youngest insomniacs had significantly more wakefulness during hours 1 and 2, the middle-aged insomniacs during hours 1 through 5, and the older insomniacs during the first three hours.

Variability in Sleep Efficiency   Several investigators have reported that insomniacs have a more variable night-to-night sleep efficiency than normal subjects.[33,36,37] A similar night-to-night variability was seen when we compared insomniacs' and control subjects' sleep efficiency over three consecutive nights.[38] Although sleep latency was consistent from night to night for both groups, insomniacs were considerably less stable than controls from night to night in terms of wake time after sleep onset.

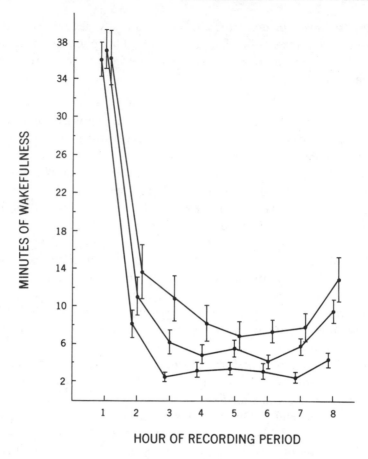

Fig. 3.1. Distribution of wakefulness by hour of night. The minutes of wakefulness for each hour of the recording period for insomniac subjects are represented in terms of mean values. Each bar indicates ± one standard error of the mean. The values for the youngest to oldest age groups are offset from left to right, respectively, for each hour. (From Kales et al[38])

*Subjective Estimates and Objective Measurements
of Sleep Efficiency*

In the sleep laboratory the accuracy of an insomniac's perception of sleep difficulty can be objectively evaluated. To measure this accuracy, normal and insomniac subjects estimate the quality and efficiency of the previous night's sleep in the sleep laboratory each morning. These estimates are then compared with objective measurements of the subjects' sleep. Both normal sleepers and insomniacs significantly overestimate the time it takes them to fall asleep and underestimate their total sleep time.[31,41,45-48] In one study of 122 insomniac subjects, 60 subjects consistently overestimated their sleep latency by more than 15 minutes, 15 of whom overestimated it by more than an hour.[41] Forty-two subjects underestimated their total sleep time by more than 60 minutes. In the same study, 57 patients said they slept less than five hours, but only ten (17.5%) actually did. Subjects did not, however, overestimate the number of times they awakened during the night. In fact, these values are often underestimated. One explanation for insomniacs overestimating their degree of sleep difficulty may be that they are much less likely than controls to perceive having been asleep; when awakened by investigators after the first five minutes of sleep, poor sleepers reported having been asleep only 12 percent of the time compared to 30 percent for controls.[49]

We found that both insomniacs and normal subjects tended to overestimate their sleep latency, while only insomniacs underestimated their total sleep time.[46] For insomniac subjects the correlation between subjective estimates and objective measurements was moderately strong, indicating general agreement between the estimates and actual measurements. This suggests that a physician should consider a patient's complaint of disturbed sleep to be reliable, although somewhat exaggerated.

Insomniacs appear to sleep better in the sleep laboratory than at home according to comparisons of sleep recordings made in the home environment and the sleep laboratory.[46] Even subjective estimates support this finding, with insomniacs reporting that they slept as well or better in the sleep laboratory environment than they typically did at home. The laboratory conditions themselves may help to distract insomniacs from their typical, disturbing rumination and also allow them to sleep longer because they feel more protected and secure in the laboratory environment. Normal controls, on the other hand, may find these same conditions distracting and disturbing.[34] In this regard, Haynes and his associates found that experimentally induced presleep stress actually resulted in a reduction in sleep latency values for insomniac subjects and increases in sleep latency for controls.[50] Their findings as well as ours suggest that values obtained in the sleep laboratory may bias the data toward less sleep difficulty in insomniacs and more sleep difficulty in control subjects.

Sleep Stage Patterns

In Normal Sleepers

The amount of both stages 3 and 4 sleep (slow-wave sleep)[1,4,5,7,9,10,13] and REM sleep[4,5,7,10,13] in normal sleepers appears to diminish with increasing age. The actual amount of slow-wave sleep identified depends at least in part upon the amplitude criterion used. The lower the amplitude requirement, the more sleep time will be designated as slow-wave sleep. For example, using a 50 microvolt minimum amplitude requirement, we found normal young adults to have 22 percent of their time asleep in slow-wave sleep, while elderly normal sleepers had 12 percent.[7] In another study that used a lower amplitude criterion (40 μv), subjects aged 3–29 years spent between 19 and 23 percent of the recording period in slow-wave sleep. This amount decreased for those in the next five age groups (30 to 79 years) to about 13, 10, 8, 5, and 6 percent, respectively.[13] Webb,[12] who eliminated amplitude from his scoring criteria, reported a mean of 21 percent slow-wave sleep in a sample of normal young adults, while his 50- to 60-year-olds had 20 percent slow-wave sleep. Therefore, as proposed by several researchers, it is likely that age-related changes in slow-wave sleep at least partially reflect a reduction in wave amplitude.[1,6,12]

The percentage of REM sleep also changes with age. Children aged 3 to 5 years were found to spend about 30 percent of a night's sleep in REM sleep.[13] This percentage decreases to 28 percent between ages 6 and 9, and to 26 percent between ages 10 and 29. During the next 20 years, REM sleep remains at around 25 percent, and then it drops to 22 percent between ages 50 to 69. People in their 70s spend only about 18 percent of their sleep time in REM sleep. Thus, REM sleep decreases with age, primarily during the first three decades of life. Decreases in REM sleep have been considered by some investigators to reflect both these normal age-related changes as well as pathological changes in the functional integrity of the brain that are independent of age.[4,6,8] REM sleep has been found to be a physiologic index of degree of intellectual impairment. Significant correlations between REM sleep and cognitive functioning test scores have been reported for patients with organic brain syndrome or mental retardation, as well as for normal elderly subjects.[44]

The amount of stage 1 or "drowsy" sleep appears to increase progressively as people age. Young children (ages 3–5 years) spend about 2 percent of their night's sleep in this stage, an amount that increases to more than 6 percent in older people (ages 50–59 years) and to more than 8 percent in the elderly (ages 60–80).[13]

In Insomniac Subjects

There is little agreement among studies comparing the percentages of sleep stages in insomniac and control subjects. In two studies, poor sleepers had a lower percentage of REM sleep than controls, even though they had the same number of REM periods.[31,51] In another study, insomniacs had a higher percentage of stage 4 sleep than did controls,[33] while in three other studies they had lower percentages.[34,36,37] Finally, we have reported that insomniacs and controls have similar percentages of sleep stages.[46] Although the percentage of REM sleep did not differ significantly between the two groups, insomniacs showed a greater night-to-night variability for this sleep stage.

Two studies assessed the relationship between insomniacs and controls using the multivariate technique of discriminant analysis,[35,37] which evaluates multiple variables simultaneously. Both studies were able to correctly classify insomniacs and controls by including measures of both sleep efficiency and sleep stages. In terms of sleep stages, both studies found only REM-related variables useful in discriminating between the two groups. In one study, insomniacs differed from controls by having fewer absolute minutes but a greater percentage of REM sleep.[35] In the other study, the sleep of insomniacs was characterized by REM sleep being more fragmented and a greater proportion occurring early in the night.[37]

Physiologic Correlates of Insomnia

Insomniacs and good sleepers appear to differ in terms of physiologic activity prior to and during sleep.[31,50-54] When Monroe compared "good" and "poor" sleepers, he found that the poor sleepers' heart rate, peripheral vasoconstriction, and rectal temperature were elevated during a 30-minute presleep period in bed.[31] Also, during sleep, poor sleepers had more body movements (7.8) than good sleepers (5.8). They also showed increased peripheral vasoconstriction, greater skin resistance, higher rectal temperature, and less total sleep time. Their heart rate was also slightly faster, but not significantly so. These findings suggest that poor sleepers have greater physiologic arousal both before and during sleep.[31,51] Similarly, when comparing "deep" and "light" sleepers, Zimmerman found that light sleepers were more physiologically active during sleep, but the differences were not as great as those between Monroe's poor and good sleepers.[54] In another study, insomniacs were found to have greater levels of arousal prior to sleep as evidenced by higher levels of muscle tension and heart rate and lower levels of finger temperature compared to controls.[52] These differences, however, were not present during sleep.

Rechtschaffen and Monroe have speculated that poor sleepers' physiologic activation during sleep is a continuation of their heightened autonomic levels prior to sleep.[51] They also theorized that a physiologic disturbance might prevent poor sleepers from lowering the level of their presleep arousal to the extent that normal sleepers do. In a related study, insomniacs were found to have higher levels of muscle tension than control subjects, as measured by frontalis EMG activity before sleep.[53] While there was a positive correlation between degree of EMG activity and number of awakenings during the night, this was not the case with sleep latency.

Hauri evaluated good sleepers' first 3.5 hours of sleep after they had spent 6 hours in one of three conditions: relaxation, intensive mental exercise, or physical exercise.[55] Physical exercise raised heart rate and rectal temperature prior to sleep, but, compared with Monroe's data, these values declined at a much faster rate after the subjects were asleep. Thus, physical arousal before sleep does not necessarily lead to greater physiologic activity during sleep; rather, poor sleepers' high autonomic levels during sleep may stem from an inability to subdue their heightened levels of arousal before they go to bed. Our findings that insomniac and control subjects primarily differ in their degree of difficulty in falling asleep and not in staying asleep strongly support the concept that the major factor accounting for disturbed sleep in insomnia is increased autonomic activity prior to sleep.[2,38]

Insomniacs also differ from controls in terms of certain physiologic events associated with sleep stages.[56] Insomniacs are more restless during the night than are controls because they have more body movements. They also have more variable sleep-spindle density, which suggests that insomniacs may have a somewhat unstable sleep-spindle production mechanism.

While insomnia is more frequent in older persons, there are conflicting findings relating to the presence of greater physiologic arousal during sleep in the elderly.[57] Zepelin has found that auditory arousal thresholds during sleep decrease with age. In addition, older subjects were noted to have higher heart rates during sleep than younger subjects. However, no significant correlations were found between heart rate and the degree of sleep disturbance on a given night. Further, body temperature, number of vasoconstrictions, and galvanic skin responses were reduced in the elderly subjects.

Sleep Apnea and Nocturnal Myoclonus

Because the sleep laboratory is useful for measuring physiologic data, it has been used to determine whether sleep apnea (abnormal degree of respiratory irregularity during sleep) and nocturnal myoclonus (periodic jerking of the legs during sleep) are associated with insomnia. Several investigators have reported that sleep apnea and nocturnal myoclonus frequently cause insomnia.[58-63] Specifically, it has been suggested that sleep apnea causes between 10 and 20 percent of all cases of insomnia,[58,59,61] and that nocturnal myoclonus is causative in 10 to 25 percent.[58,62] These studies did not include normal control groups, however. We therefore compared 200 subjects who had a primary complaint of insomnia with 100 normal control subjects, utilizing sleep laboratory recordings and data from the Minnesota Multiphasic Personality Inventory (MMPI).[64] The insomniacs included 82 men and 118 women with a mean age of 42.3 years.

Studies of Normal Subjects

Sleep apnea and nocturnal myoclonus were evaluated in 100 normal subjects (41 men and 59 women) who had a mean age of 40 years.[65,66] None of the subjects had the clinical condition of sleep apnea (SA); ie, they did not meet the criteria of at least 30 apneic periods per night (minimum duration per episode, 10 seconds) or at least five events per hour of sleep. However, 12 of the subjects (six men and six women) had some sleep apneic activity (SAA) in the form of at least three apneic periods per night (Table 3.2). SAA was more common, but not significantly so, in men (14.6%) than in women (10.2%), and in older subjects (mean age of 47.9 years for those with SAA vs. 39.0 years for those without). Further, SAA and age were positively correlated, and the mean body weight of subjects with SAA was significantly greater than of those without SAA when height was controlled. In relation to sleep stages, SAA occurred significantly more often in REM sleep.[65]

Six subjects (three men and three women) had the clinical condition of nocturnal myoclonus, characterized by three or more epochs of 30 or more leg-muscle discharges, each lasting more than 0.5 seconds and less than 5.0 seconds, with a period of 5 to 120 seconds between discharges. Five additional subjects (three men and two women) had at least one but not more than two epochs of 30 or more discharges. Thus, a total of 11 subjects (six men and five women) had some nocturnal myoclonic activity (NMA) in a night's recording (Table 3.2). The six subjects with the clinical condition of nocturnal myoclonus were significantly older (61.0 yrs.) than those with only NMA (51.0 yrs.), and the 11 subjects with NMA were significantly older than those without NMA (38.1 yrs.). Both those subjects with and those without NMA were almost identical in weight when height was controlled.[66]

Our studies[64,65] confirmed and extended a number of previous findings. First, our data confirmed that SAA occurs more often in men,[67] and that it becomes more prevalent with age.[67-69] Nevertheless, SAA has been reported to occur even in children aged 9 to 13.[70] Several studies have reported a high prevalence for the condition of SA in elderly subjects,[68,71-73] but when we evaluated 60 elderly subjects (ages 50–81 yrs.), the prevalence for sleep apnea was considerably lower.[74] In other studies, the investigators did not exclude those elderly subjects who may have had sleep complaints or physical illnesses,[68,71,72] or they utilized a more liberal criterion for defining the length of sleep apneic periods (8 vs. 10 seconds).[73] These differences in methodology probably account for the relatively low prevalence of sleep apnea that we found in healthy elderly subjects[74] as compared to the extremely high prevalence reported for the elderly by others.

As with SAA, NMA tends to be slightly more common in men than in women, and men tend to have more events.[66] The correlation of NMA with age is stronger, however, and it appears to begin at a later age. In contrast to subjects who had SAA, only those over age 30 had NMA, and older subjects tended to have more events. Also, unlike SAA, NMA appears to be more strongly related to non-REM (NREM) sleep than to REM sleep and is independent of body weight. Thus, NMA and the clinical condition of nocturnal myoclonus appear to be primarily a function of age.

Sleep Apneic Activity in Insomniacs

In our study investigating the prevalence of sleep apnea, none of the subjects in either the insomniac or the control group had the clinical

Table 3.2. Sleep Apnea and Nocturnal Myoclonus in Insomnia

	Sleep Apneic Activity		Nocturnal Myoclonic Activity	
	Insomniacs	Normal Controls	Insomniacs	Normal Controls
Percentage of Total Sample	10.5%	12.0%	11.0%	11.0%
Percentage of Men[a]	13.4%	14.6%	12.2%	14.6%
Percentage of Women[a]	8.5%	10.2%	10.2%	8.5%
Mean Age (yrs)[b]	46.1 ± 3.2	47.9 ± 4.0	48.1 ± 3.6	56.4 ± 3.6
Mean Number of Episodes[b]	9.1 ± 1.3	9.5 ± 2.2	106.5 ± 16.9	171.3 ± 41.2
Mean Duration of Episodes[b] (secs)	16.2 ± 1.0	13.8 ± 0.7	2.2 ± 0.2	2.0 ± 0.2

[a] Percentage calculated from the number of the same sex within the total sample
[b] Mean values are presented with ± the standard error
(From Kales et al[64])

condition of sleep apnea.[64,65] SAA had a similar prevalence among the insomniacs (10.5%) and the control subjects (12.0%), and it occurred with a similar frequency in the two groups (9.1 episodes per insomniac subject with SAA and 9.5 episodes per control subject with SAA) (Table 3.2).

SAA did not affect the degree of sleep difficulty in the insomniacs.[64] Specifically, insomniacs with SAA did not differ significantly from insomniacs without SAA in terms of sleep latency, wake time after sleep onset, or total wake time. These two insomniac subgroups also had very similar clinical scores on the MMPI. Similar results were found when control subjects with SAA were compared with those without SAA. The MMPI data further showed that the insomniacs with SAA also had more psychopathology than the normal controls with SAA, both in terms of the mean values of all eight clinical scales as well as the mean number of elevated MMPI scales per individual.[64] Thus, the insomniac and control groups did not differ in terms of the presence of SAA, but rather in terms of the degree of psychopathology.

Nocturnal Myoclonic Activity in Insomniacs

In our study, the clinical condition of nocturnal myoclonus was present in essentially the same percentage of insomniacs (5%) and control subjects (6%), and NMA was detected in 11 percent of each group.[64,66] Also, the number of NMA episodes per night was not significantly different (insomniacs, 106 episodes; controls, 171 episodes) (Table 3.2). When insomniacs who had NMA were compared with those who did not have NMA, the two groups' sleep-efficiency measurements were essentially the same, as were their values for the various MMPI parameters.[64] Comparisons between normal subjects with NMA and those without NMA yielded generally similar results.

Similar to the MMPI results for the subgroups with SAA, the analysis of the MMPI data demonstrated that the insomniacs with either nocturnal myoclonus or nocturnal myoclonic activity had more psychopathology than did the normals with either nocturnal myoclonus or nocturnal myoclonic activity.[64] This was measured both in terms of the mean values of the eight clinical scales as well as in terms of the number of abnormally elevated MMPI scales per subject. Thus, as with the subjects who had SAA, the major difference between the insomniacs and their controls was the presence of psychologic disturbances, not the presence of nocturnal myoclonus or nocturnal myoclonic activity.

The results of our studies[39,64,75,76] and of others[31,42,53,77-79] show that psychologic difficulties are most often critical in the development and persistence of chronic insomnia (see also Chapter 5, Psychiatric Factors in Insomnia). These factors should, therefore, be the object of investigations into the diagnosis and treatment of this disorder. Our results are not at variance, as they may seem to be, with the findings of others;[58-63] rather, our methodologic approach differs from that of other studies. Little evidence of psychopathology will result when studies rely primarily on anecdotal data, do not include comprehensive psychiatric interviews, or fail to administer psychologic tests to all subjects. Similarly, if control groups are not used when patients are assessed for possible physiologic causes of insomnia (ie, sleep apnea and nocturnal myoclonus), investigators will tend to assume a high incidence of these physiologic causes. In fact, these same phenomena are equally prevalent in controls without resulting in symptomatic sleep disturbances.[64-66]

In stressing the importance of physiologic factors in insomnia, some investigators may be confusing causality with correlation. For example, findings from several studies suggest that nocturnal myoclonic activity is no more frequent in insomniacs than controls[64,66] or may be a result of poor sleep rather than a cause of it,[80,81] or part of the response to arousal from sleep rather than a cause of it.[82] Further, some patients with chronic insomnia may just meet the arbitrary criteria for the minimum number of sleep apneic events to qualify for this diagnosis (30 apneic episodes per seven hours of sleep).[83] As some investigators have suggested, however, this threshold may be too low and lack clinical relevance, as evidenced by the fact that such patients are usually asymptomatic.[67,84,85] Finally, in a study in which various sleep centers used the Association of Sleep Disorders Centers' (ASDC) classification system[86] to establish diagnoses for patients with sleep disorders, prevalence of sleep apnea and nocturnal myoclonus varied markedly among the centers, from 0 to 18.5 percent and from 2.8 to 26.3 percent, respectively.[58] The variations in patient populations from one setting to another may account, in part, for this high level of inconsistency. These disparate results, however, may also reflect the limitations of the ASDC diagnostic system[87,88] (see also Chapter 5, Psychiatric Factors in Insomnia), as well as the possibility that some investigators may have overfocused on physiologic factors without using adequate controls.

In conclusion, on the basis of our studies of the prevalence of sleep apnea and nocturnal myoclonus in both normal sleepers[65,66] and insomniac subjects[64] and our review of the work of others,[58-63,67-73,80-85] we have demonstrated that sleep apnea and nocturnal myoclonus are rarely causative factors in insomnia. Nevertheless, doctors should question the bed partners of patients complaining of insomnia, or of any medical condition for that matter, if sleep apnea or nocturnal myoclonus are suspected.

Summary

Sleep laboratory studies can provide valuable research data on sleep difficulty. If certain methodologic considerations are taken into account, investigators can use the sleep laboratory to clarify and compare sleep efficiency variables, sleep stage patterns, and physiologic correlates in both normal sleepers and subjects presenting with disturbed sleep.

Age and sex affect the amount of time normal sleepers spend awake. In normal subjects, total wake time increases with age. Although the time it takes to fall asleep does not vary with age, the time spent awake during the night is significantly greater among older normal sleepers. Also, men awaken more often and for longer periods during the night than women, but these differences are relatively small.

In insomniac subjects, age also exerts a strong influence on nocturnal wakefulness, but sex does not seem to be a factor. Sleep latency does not change with age, but, as with normal controls, time awake after sleep onset increases with age. The most striking difference between insomniacs and control subjects is the insomniacs' difficulty in initiating sleep, whether at the beginning of the sleep period or when returning to sleep following awakenings during the night. Insomniacs also have more night-to-night variability in sleep efficiency, particularly in terms of wakefulness after sleep onset.

When sleepers' subjective estimates of their sleep are compared with objective measurements, both normal sleepers and insomniacs significantly overestimate their sleep latency and underestimate their total sleep time. However, sleep laboratory recordings demonstrate that insomniac subjects usually have a significantly greater degree of sleep difficulty than controls. Further, there is a strong correlation between perceived and actual sleep difficulty, so a patient's complaint of disturbed sleep can be considered valid, although often exaggerated.

Insomniacs and controls appear to differ considerably in terms of various physiologic measures, with insomniacs showing much more physiologic activation before sleep in the form of increased heart rate, muscle tension, rectal temperature, and peripheral vasoconstriction. Increased body movements during the night suggest that higher autonomic levels continue throughout the sleep period in some insomniacs. However, other studies have found no differences between insomniacs and controls in terms of the degree of physiologic arousal during the night, a finding which may relate to the relatively low prevalence of the specific complaint of difficulty staying asleep among insomniacs.

Physiologic factors are seldom the primary cause of insomnia. In carefully controlled studies comparing insomniac and normal subjects, no significant differences were found in sleep apneic and nocturnal myoclonic activity. No subjects in either group had the clinical condition of sleep apnea, while about 5 percent of both our insomniacs and controls had nocturnal myoclonus, which in all cases was asymptomatic. Other studies have shown that nocturnal myoclonic activity may be a result of poor sleep rather than a cause of it. In the case of sleep apnea, a few patients with chronic insomnia may just meet the arbitrary minimum criterion for diagnosis of this condition, but this threshold may be too low and lack clinical relevance because such patients are usually asymptomatic. Finally, there is a marked difference in the MMPI findings between insomniac and control groups, underscoring the causative role of psychopathology in the development and persistence of chronic insomnia.

References

1. Agnew HW Jr, Webb WW, Williams RL: Sleep patterns in late middle age males: an EEG study. *Electroencephalogr Clin Neurophysiol* 23:168–171, 1967.
2. Bixler EO, Kales A, Jacoby JA, Soldatos CR, Vela-Bueno A: Nocturnal sleep and wakefulness: effects of age and sex in normal sleepers. *Int J Neurosci* (in press).
3. Feinberg I: Changes in sleep cycle patterns with age. *J Psychiatric Res* 10:283–306, 1974.
4. Feinberg I, Carlson VR: Sleep variables as a function of age in man. *Arch Gen Psychiatry* 18:239–250, 1968.
5. Hayashi Y, Endo S: All-night sleep polygraphic recordings of healthy aged persons: REM and slow-wave sleep. *Sleep* 5:277–283, 1982.
6. Kahn E, Fisher C: The sleep characteristics of the normal aged male. *J Nerv Ment Dis* 148:477–494, 1969.
7. Kales A, Wilson T, Kales JD, Jacobson A, Paulson MJ, Kollar E, Walter RD: Measurements of all-night sleep in normal elderly persons: effects of aging. *J Am Geriatr Soc* 15:405–414, 1967.
8. Prinz PN: Sleep patterns in the healthy aged: relationship with intellectual function. *J Gerontol* 32:179–186, 1977.
9. Prinz PN, Preskind ER, Vitaliano PP, Raskind MA, Eisdorfer C, Zemcuznikov N, Gerber CJ: Changes in sleep and waking EEGs of nondemented and demented elderly subjects. *J Am Geriatr Soc* 30:86–93, 1982.
10. Roffwarg H, Muzio J, Dement W: Ontogenetic development of the human sleep–dream cycle. *Science* 152:604–619, 1966.
11. Spiegel R: *Sleep and Sleeplessness in Advanced Age* (Weitzman ED [series ed]: *Advances in Sleep Research*, vol 5). New York, SP Medical and Scientific Books, 1981.
12. Webb WB: Sleep in older persons: sleep structure of 50- to 60-year-old men and women. *J Gerontol* 37:581–586, 1982.
13. Williams RL, Karacan I, Hursch C: *EEG of Human Sleep: Clinical Applications,* New York, Wiley, 1974.
14. Agnew HW, Webb WB, Williams RL: The first night effect: an EEG study of sleep. *Psychophysiology* 2:263–266, 1966.
15. Dement WC, Kahn E, Roffwarg HP: The influence of the laboratory situation on the dreams of the experimental subject. *J Nerv and Ment Dis* 140:119–131, 1965.

16. Rechtschaffen A, Verdone, P: Amount of dreaming: effects of incentive, adaptation to laboratory and individual differences. *Percept and Mot Skills 19*:947–958, 1964.
17. Scharf MB, Kales A, Bixler EO: Readaptation to the sleep laboratory in insomniac subjects. *Psychophysiology 12*:412–415, 1975.
18. Webb WB, Campbell SS: Awakenings and the return to sleep in an older population. *Sleep 3*:41–46, 1980.
19. Hartmann E: Sleep requirement: long sleepers, short sleepers, variable sleepers, and insomniacs. *Psychosomatics 14*:95–103, 1973.
20. Jones HS, Oswald I: Two cases of healthy insomnia. *Electroencephalgr Clin Neurophysiol 24*:378–380, 1968.
21. Meddis R, Pearson AJD, Langford GL: An extreme case of healthy insomnia. *Electroencephalgr Clin Neurophysiol 35*:213–214, 1973.
22. Schneider D, Gnirss F: Three cases of extreme idiopathic hyposomnia, in Levin P, Koella WP (eds): *Sleep 1974. Instinct, Neurophysiology, Endocrinology, Episodes, Dreams and Intracranial Pathology*. Basel, S Karger, 1975, pp 460–483.
23. Stuss D, Broughton R: Extreme short sleep: Personality profiles and a case study of sleep requirement. *Waking and Sleeping 2*:101–105, 1978.
24. Velok G, Passouant P, Cadilhac P, Baldy-Mouliner M: Données polygraphiques sur les insomnics. *Rev Neurol 119*:269–278, 1968.
25. Webb WB, Agnew HW Jr: Sleep stage characteristics of long and short sleepers. *Science 168*:146–147, 1970.
26. Webb WB, Friel J: Sleep stage and personality characteristics of "natural" long and short sleepers. *Science 171*:587–588, 1971.
27. Hartmann EL: *The Functions of Sleep*. New Haven and London, Yale University Press, 1973, pp 53–70.
28. Hartmann E, Brewer J: When is more or less sleep required: A study of variable sleepers. *Comprehens Psychiatry 17*:275–284, 1976.
29. Hicks RA, Pellegrini RJ, Martin S, Garbesi L, Elliott D, Hawkins J: Type A behavior and normal habitual sleep duration. *Bull Psychon Soc 14*:185–186, 1979.
30. Hicks RA, Lingen S, Eastman PC: Habitual variable sleep and Type A behavior. *Bull Psychon Soc 14*:469–470, 1979.
31. Monroe LJ: Psychological and physiological differences between good and poor sleepers. *J Abnorm Psychol 72*:255–264, 1967.
32. Karacan I, Williams RL, Salis PJ, Hursch CJ: New approaches to the evaluation and treatment of insomnia (preliminary results). *Psychosomatics 12*:81–88, 1971.
33. Karacan I, Williams RL, Littell RC, Salis PJ: Insomniacs: unpredictable and idiosyncratic sleepers, in Koella WP, Levin P (eds): *Sleep: Physiology, Biochemistry, Psychology, Pharmacology, Clinical Implications* (Proceedings of the First European Congress on Sleep Research, Basel, 1972). Basel, S Karger, 1973, pp 120–132.
34. Frankel BL, Coursey RD, Buchbinder R, Snyder F: Recorded and reported sleep in chronic primary insomnia. *Arch Gen Psychiatry 33*:615–623, 1976.

35. Gillin JC, Duncan W, Pettigrew KD, Frankel BL, Snyder F: Successful separation of depressed normal and insomniac subjects by EEG sleep data. *Arch Gen Psychiatry 36*:85–90, 1976.
36. Gaillard JM: Chronic primary insomnia: Possible physiopathological involvement of slow wave sleep deficiency. *Sleep 1*:133–147, 1978.
37. Coates TJ, Killen JD, George J, Marchini E, Silverman S, Hamilton S, Thorensen C: Discriminating good sleepers from insomniacs using all-night polysomograms conducted at home. *J Nerv Ment Disease 170*:224–230, 1982.
38. Kales A, Bixler EO, Vela-Bueno A, Cadieux RJ, Soldatos CR, Kales JD: Biopsychobehavioral correlates of insomnia, III: polygraphic findings of sleep difficulty and their relationship to psychopathology. *Int J Neurosci* (in press).
39. Kales A, Caldwell AB, Soldatos CR, Bixler EO, Kales JD: Biopsychobehavioral correlates of insomnia, II: MMPI pattern specificity and consistency. *Psychosom Med 45*:341–356, 1983.
40. Soldatos CR, Kales A: Sleep disorders: research in psychopathology and its practical implications. *Acta Psychiatr Scand 65*:381–387, 1982.
41. Carskadon MA, Dement WC, Mitler MM, Guilleminault C, Zarcone VP, Spiegel R: Self-reports versus sleep laboratory findings in 122 drug-free subjects with complaints of chronic insomnia. *Am J Psychiatry 133*:1382–1388, 1976.
42. Beutler LE, Thornby JI, Karacan I: Psychological variables in the diagnosis of insomnia, in Williams RL and Karacan I (eds): *Sleep Disorders: Diagnosis and Treatment*. New York, John Wiley & Sons, 1978, pp 61–100.
43. Brezinova V: The number and duration of the episodes of various EEG stages of sleep in young and older people. *Electroencephalogr Clin Neurophysiol 39*:273–278, 1975.
44. Feinberg I, Koresko RL, Heller N: EEG sleep patterns as a function of normal and pathological aging in man. *J Psychiatr Res 5*:107–144, 1967.
45. Hoddes E, Carskadon M, Phillips R, Zarcone V, Dement W: Total sleep time in insomniacs. *Sleep Res 1*:152, 1972.
46. Kales A, Bixler EO: Sleep profiles of insomnia and hypnotic drug effectiveness, in Burch N, Altshuler HL (eds): *Behavior and Brain Electrical Activity*. New York, Plenum Publishing Corporation, 1975, pp 81–91.
47. Lewis SA: Subjective estimates of sleep: an EEG evaluation. *Br J Psychol 60*:203–208, 1969.
48. Schwartz BA, Guilbaud G, Fischgold H: Etudes electroencephalographiques le sommeil de nuit: I. L' "insomnie" chronique. *Presse Med 71*:1474, 1963.
49. Borkovec TD, Lane TW, VanOot PH: Phenomenology of sleep among insomniacs and good sleepers: wakefulness experience when cortically asleep. *J Abnorm Psychol 90*:607–609, 1981.
50. Haynes SN, Adams A, Franzen M: The effects of presleep stress on sleep-onset insomnia. *J Abnorm Psychol 90*:601–606, 1981.
51. Rechtschaffen A, Monroe LJ: Laboratory studies of insomnia, in Kales

A (ed): *Sleep: Physiology and Pathology.* Philadelphia, Lippincott, 1969, pp 158–169.

52. Freedman RR, Sattler HL: Physiological and psychological factors in sleep-onset insomnia. *J Abnorm Psychol 91*:380–389, 1982.

53. Haynes SN, Follingstad DR, McGowan WT: Insomnia: sleep patterns and anxiety level. *J Psychosom Res 18*:69–74, 1974.

54. Zimmerman WB: *Psychological and Physiological Differences between "Light" and "Deep" Sleepers,* unpublished doctoral dissertation. University of Chicago, 1967.

55. Hauri P: Effects of evening activity on early night sleep. *Psychophysiology 4*:267–277, 1968.

56. Soldatos CR, Scarone S, Bixler EO, Scharf M, Kales A: Sleep characteristics and phasic physiological events in insomnia patients. *Sleep Res 7*:248, 1978.

57. Zepelin H: Normal age-related change in sleep, in Chase MH, Weitzman ED (eds): *Sleep Disorders: Basic and Clinical Research.* New York, Spectrum Publications, Inc, 1983, pp 431–444.

58. Coleman RM, Roffwarg HP, Kennedy SJ, Guilleminault C, Cinque J, Cohn MA, Karacan I, Kupfer DJ, Lemmi H, Miles LE, Orr WC, Phillips ER, Roth T, Sassin JF, Schmidt HS, Weitzman ED, Dement WC: Sleep-wake disorders based on a polysomnographic diagnosis. *JAMA 247*:997–1003, 1982.

59. Dement WC, Guilleminaut C: Sleep disorders: the state of the art. *Hosp Pract 8(11)*:57–71, 1973.

60. Dement WC, Zarcone VP: Pharmacological treatment of sleep disorders, in Barchas JD, Berger PA, Ciaranello RD, Elliott GR (eds): *Psychopharmacology: From Theory to Practice.* New York, Oxford University Press, 1977, pp 243–259.

61. Guilleminault C, Eldridge FL, Dement WC: Insomniacs with sleep apnea: a new syndrome. *Science 181*:856–858, 1973.

62. Guilleminault C, Raynal D, Weitzman ED, Dement W: Sleep-related periodic myoclonus in patients complaining of insomnia. *Trans Am Neurol Assoc 100*:19–22, 1975.

63. Zorick FJ, Roth T, Hartze KM, Piccione PM, Stepanski EJ: Evaluation and diagnosis of persistent insomnia. *Am J Psychiatry 138*:769–773, 1981.

64. Kales A, Bixler EO, Soldatos CR, Vela-Bueno A, Caldwell AB, Cadieux RJ: Biopsychobehavioral correlates of insomnia, I: role of sleep apnea and myoclonus nocturnus. *Psychosomatics 23*:589–600, 1982.

65. Bixler EO, Kales A, Soldatos CR, Vela-Bueno A, Jacoby JA, Scarone S: Sleep apneic activity in a normal population. *Res Commun Chem Pathol Pharmacol 36*:141–152, 1982.

66. Bixler EO, Kales A, Vela-Bueno A, Jacoby JA, Scarone S, Soldatos CR: Nocturnal myoclonus and nocturnal myoclonic activity in a normal population. *Res Commun Chem Pathol Pharmacol 36*:129–140, 1982.

67. Block AJ, Boysen PG, Wynne JW, Hunt LA: Sleep apnea, hypopnea and oxygen desaturation in normal subjects. *N Engl J Med 300*:513–517, 1979.

68. Carskadon MA, Dement WC: Respiration during sleep in the aged man. *J Gerontol 36*:420–423, 1981.
69. Webb P: Periodic breathing during sleep. *J Appl Physiol 37*:899–903, 1974.
70. Carskadon MA, Harvey K, Dement WC: Respiration and sleep in children. *Sleep Res 6*:47, 1977.
71. Ancoli-Israel S, Kripke DF, Mason W, Messin S: Sleep apnea and nocturnal myclonus in a senior population. *Sleep 4*:349–358, 1981.
72. Coleman RM, Miles LE, Guilleminault CC, Zarcone VP, van den Hoed J, Dement WC: Sleep-wake disorders in the elderly: a polysomnographic analysis. *J Am Geriatr Soc 29*:289–296, 1981.
73. Krieger J, Turlot JC, Mangin P, Kurtz D: Breathing during sleep in normal young and elderly subjects: hypopneas, apneas, and correlated factors. *Sleep 6*:108–120, 1983.
74. Bixler EO, Kales A, Cadieux RJ, Vela-Bueno A, Soldatos CR, Jacoby JA, Locke T: Sleep apneic activity in older normal subjects (in preparation).
75. Healey ES, Kales A, Monroe LJ, Bixler EO, Chamberlin K, Soldatos CR: Onset of insomnia: Role of life-stress events. *Psychosom Med 43*:439–451, 1981.
76. Kales A, Caldwell AB, Preston TA, Healey S, Kales JD: Personality patterns in insomnia: Theoretical implications. *Arch Gen Psychiatry 33*:1128–1134, 1976.
77. Coursey RD, Buchsbaum M, Frankel BL: Personality measures and evoked responses in chronic insomniacs. *J Abnorm Psychol 84*:239–249, 1975.
78. Monroe LJ, Marks PA: MMPI differences between adolescent poor and good sleepers. *J Consult Clin Psychol 45*:151–152, 1977.
79. Monroe LJ, Marks PA: Psychotherapists' descriptions of emotionally disturbed adolescent poor and good sleepers. *J Clin Psychol 33*:263–269, 1977.
80. Coleman RM: Periodic movements in sleep (nocturnal myoclonus) and restless legs syndrome, in Guilleminault C (ed): *Sleeping and Waking Disorders: Indications and Techniques.* Menlo Park, Calif, Addison–Wesley, 1982, pp 265–295.
81. Coleman RM, Pollak CP, Weitzman ED: Periodic movements in sleep (nocturnal myoclonus): relation to sleep disorders. *Ann Neurol 8*:416–421, 1980.
82. Lugaresi E, Cirignotta F, Montagna P, Coccagna G: Myoclonus and related phenomena during sleep, in Chase MH, Weitzman ED (eds): *Sleep Disorders: Basic and Clinical Research* (Weitzman ED [series ed]: *Advances in Sleep Research,* vol 8). New York, Spectrum Publications, 1983, pp 123–127.
83. Guilleminault C, Tilkian A, Dement WC: The sleep apnea syndromes. *Annu Rev Med 27*:465–484, 1976.
84. Block AJ: Letter to the editor. *Sleep 6*:164–166, 1983.

85. Orr WC, Imes NK, Martin RJ, Rogers RM: Sleep apnea in sympto-
    matic and asymtomatic groups. *Clinical Research* 26:38A, 1978.
86. Association of Sleep Disorders Centers: Diagnostic classification of sleep
    and arousal disorders. *Sleep* 2(1):1–137, 1979.
87. Kales JD, Soldatos CR, Kales A: Diagnosis and treatment of sleep
    disorders, in Greist JH, Jefferson JW, Spitzer RL (eds): *Treatment of
    Mental Disorders.* New York: Oxford University Press, 1982, pp 473–
    500.
88. Reynolds CF III, Coble PA, Black RS, Holzer B, Carroll R, Kupfer DJ:
    Sleep disturbances in a series of elderly patients: polysomnographic find-
    ings. *J Am Geriatr Soc* 28:164–170, 1980.

4. Onset, Clinical Characteristics, and Behavioral Correlates

When evaluating any medical disorder, physicians need to know about the condition's onset, clinical course, and characteristics. It is also important to identify any factors that are causing, contributing to, or correlated with the disorder. These considerations are essential for the thorough assessment of a chronic condition because multiple factors are often involved in the initiation and persistence of a long-standing disorder.[1-3] Proper understanding and management of these factors are necessary for a positive treatment outcome.[4,5]

The literature on sleep disorders is sparse regarding the onset and clinical course of chronic insomnia. Few studies have mentioned the clinical characteristics of insomnia and even fewer have comprehensively evaluated them, underscoring the extent to which this disorder has been neglected in terms of clinical research. A number of factors may account for the lack of data pertaining to the clinical correlates of insomnia. First, chronic insomnia is not a specific disorder itself but, rather, a symptom of a wide range of psychiatric and medical disorders, making it more difficult to define and select study samples. Another problem is that transient or intermittent difficulty in sleeping is a ubiquitous problem, and objective criteria are inadequate for determining who should be classified as an insomniac; clinicians as well as researchers have to rely primarily on a person's subjective complaints. Finally, recent research has focused on attempts to develop objective criteria for diagnosing insomnia and to determine physiologic causes for the disorder, while little attention has been directed to describing the clinical characteristics of these patient populations.

This chapter begins with a discussion of the demographic characteristics of various samples of insomniac patients. Then, the onset of insomnia is discussed, particularly in relation to stressful life events. Also described are the type and duration of specific sleep complaints and subjective estimates of sleep disturbance reported by patients with chronic insomnia. Next is a discussion of the physical and mental health, behavioral, and psychosocial correlates of this condition. Finally, the relationship of insomnia to drug and alcohol use, cigarette smoking, and the use of caffeinated beverages is examined.

Most of the material in this chapter has been derived from four of our recent studies. One of these studies was part of a large survey of more than 1,000 households in the Los Angeles metropolitan area (LAMAS study), in which data from a general population were collected on the prevalence, onset, duration, and physical and mental health correlates of sleep disorders, including insomnia.[6] In the second study (clinical characteristics study) data on the clinical characteristics of insomnia were gathered through interviews and comprehensive sleep histories conducted with 100 patients who had a primary complaint of insomnia. Whenever possible, these data were compared with data from 100 control subjects.[7] The third study (MMPI individual response study)[7] contrasts responses to specific items on the Minnesota Multiphasic Personality Inventory (MMPI) related to sleep, health, and psychosocial factors between all insomniacs (214) and control subjects for whom these data were available from previous studies.[8,9] Finally, in a sample of 31 poor and 31 good sleepers (life-stress events study)[10] the role of life-stress events[11-15] in the onset of insomnia was evaluated using the Schedule of Recent Experience (SRE), which identifies and standardizes a broad spectrum of events normally experienced in American life.

Demographics

Complaints of difficulty in sleeping appear to be more prevalent among persons of lower socioeconomic status. In the LAMAS study, current complaints of insomnia were more frequent among individuals who had less advanced education and lower incomes, or whose occupations required operation of machinery (those classified as operative).[6] Similarly, in studying the prevalence of sleep disorders in 309 children, Simonds and Parraga found that of the children who had nighttime awakenings, 76 percent were in lower socioeconomic groups, as were 69 percent of those categorized as "restless" sleepers.[16] Further, a Gallup survey reported that subjects who sought treatment for their sleep difficulty were most likely to be in lower income groups, to live in a central part of a large city, and to have blue-collar employment status.[17] These findings that insomnia is more prevalent among individuals of low educational and socioeconomic status confirm previous observations.[18,19] Because insomnia is also often associated with higher levels of psychopathology, these findings might be explained by data from earlier studies showing a higher incidence of mental health disturbances in groups with limited education and lower income.[20,21] This in turn may reflect the inverse relationship between the degree of life stress as measured by life-change events and the level of social class, as measured by education.[22]

Since our clinical characteristics study was conducted in a university medical center setting, with a largely middle-class population, it is not surprising that there were no significant differences in socioeconomic status or educational level between insomniac patients and control subjects.[7] Also, few differences were found between insomniacs and controls in terms of marital status and general living arrangement; about one-fifth of each group reported currently living alone, while slightly fewer insomniacs than controls were married. Of the insomniacs who had been married, more, but not significantly so, had been divorced at least once, compared to controls.

Onset, Type, and Duration of Insomnia

Chronic insomnia can begin at any age, but in the majority of patients, persistent difficulty sleeping usually starts before the age of 40. It appears to begin earlier in patients who complain of difficulty falling asleep, as well as in those with a more severe current complaint. Life stresses appear to play a major role in the onset of the problem because in most patients there is an increase in stressful life events around the time the disorder begins. Difficulty falling asleep is the most common complaint reported among patients with chronic insomnia. Further, the problem is generally of many years' duration.

Age at Onset

The insomniacs in the LAMAS study reported that their sleep problem began at a mean age of 36.8 years, with the following distribution in ten-year periods: younger than 10, 22 subjects (7%); 11–20 years old, 37 (11%); 21–30 years old, 72 (22%); 31–40 years old, 58 (18%); 41–50 years old, 52 (16%); 51–60 years old, 44 (14%); 61–70 years old, 25 (8%); and older than 70 years, 14 (4%).[6] Both men and women had similar ages at onset, 36.5 years and 37.1 years, respectively. Those with difficulty falling asleep had the earliest mean age at onset, followed in order by those having difficulty staying asleep, and those experiencing early final awakening (37, 39, and 40 years, respectively).

In the clinical characteristics study,[7] the mean age for the onset of insomnia was 35.1 years, suggesting that chronic insomnia often begins by early adulthood. By 10-year epochs, the distribution of the ages at onset was as follows: age 1–10, 4 patients; age 11–20, 15 patients; age 21–30, 25 patients; age 31–40, 20 patients; age 41–50, 17 patients; age 51–60, 13 patients, and age 61–70, 6 patients. Thus, about two-thirds of the insomniacs in this study started having sleep difficulty before age 40, and about one-fifth, before age 20. An even earlier onset for insomnia has also been noted in another study where 27 percent of an adult chronic insomniac sample reported that sleep difficulty began by the age of 10 years.[23]

In our clinical characteristics study, women seeking treatment tended to develop insomnia at an earlier age (30.7 years) than did men (39.3 years). Also, insomnia began earlier in insomniacs who had difficulty falling asleep (32.2 years) than in those whose major difficulty was staying asleep or awakening too early (38.8 years).

It is quite likely that the severity of insomnia in the LAMAS group was less than that in our clinical characteristics sample because the subjects in this survey were selected based on demographic criteria, while those in the clinical study were chosen from a group who had requested treatment for a sleep problem. The earlier mean age at onset for those insomniacs seen in our clinic seems to suggest that insomnia begins earlier in those who develop more severe symptomatology.

Stressful Life Events at Onset

In the life-stress events study,[10] both the subjective and objective measures of the Schedule of Recent Experience (SRE) indicated that the poor sleepers (PS) experienced more stressful life events during the year their insomnia began than in previous or subsequent years, and more than a control group of good sleepers (GS) (Fig. 4.1). Specifically, 74 percent of 31 poor sleepers reported that stressful life experiences were connected with the onset of their insomnia. Moreover, the eight subjects who did not make this connection on the SRE revealed, in a different context, that at least one major life event occurred when

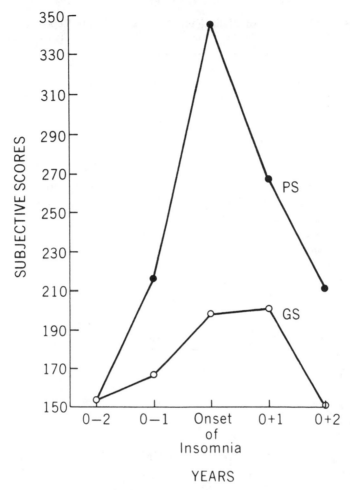

Fig. 4.1. Stressful life events and the onset of insomnia. Mean subjective ratings of the life events for poor sleep subjects (PS) and good sleep subjects (GS) over a five-year period. (From Healey et al[10])

their insomnia began. Although stressful life events do coincide with the onset of other sleep disorders, the percentage of insomniacs reporting such events is higher than among patients with other sleep disorders with organic etiologies, such as narcolepsy[24] or sleep apnea,[25] as well as those considered to be psychogenic, such as adult sleepwalking,[26] night terrors,[27] and nightmares.[28]

When PS and GS were compared with regard to the specific kinds of events they experienced when their insomnia began (ie, work-

Table 4.1. Comparison of Mean Number of Life Events Reported by Poor Sleepers (PS) and Good Sleepers (GS) During Year of Insomnia Onset

Category	Items in Category	Mean	
		PS	GS
Area of Activity			
Work	7	0.8	0.6
Financial	4	0.2	0.2
Legal	2	0.1	0.1
Family	13	1.6	1.1
Personal	13	2.7	1.6*
Health	4	0.6	0.2††
Total (less health)	39	5.4	3.6†
Type of Event			
Desirable	4	1.1	0.7
Ambiguous	23	1.7	1.9
Undesirable	16	2.7	1.0††
Entrances and exits (losses) from the social field			
Entrances	2	0.3	0.2
Exits	6	1.2	0.5†
Death only	3	0.4	0.2

†† $p < 0.001$
† $p < 0.01$
* $p < 0.05$
(Modified from Healey et al[10])

related, financial, legal, family, personal, and health), the PS had a greater number of personal events[10] (Table 4.1). The PS also had more events that were undesirable than the GS when these events were categorized as desirable, undesirable, and ambiguous. Furthermore, significantly more PS (87%) than GS (48%) reported the occurrence of these undesirable events. By contrast, there were no significant differences between the two groups in reporting either desirable or ambiguous events. Although the groups did not differ statistically with regard to the number reporting the entrance of a new person into their lives, PS reported nearly twice as many departures or losses from within their social fields as did GS. In addition, more than three times as many PS reported at least one such loss. No differences between PS and GS were found, however, in terms of losses attributed to death.

In support of the contribution of life stresses to the onset of sleep difficulty, we found that most of the sample (75%) in our clinical characteristics study had experienced some stressful event at about the time insomnia began.[7]

Type and Duration of Complaint

Difficulty falling asleep was the most severe symptom in 73 percent of the subjects in our clinical characteristic study.[7] The remaining 27 percent had severe difficulty staying asleep either throughout the night or in the form of early final awakenings. More women (72%) than men (51%) had difficulty falling asleep as their primary complaint.

Roth and his associates, in studying 54 insomniacs seeking treatment for their sleep problem, also found difficulty falling asleep to be the most common complaint (83%), either alone or in combination with other symptoms.[29] Further, those with difficulty falling asleep were reported to be younger. Early final awakening was the symptom least likely to be primary (11%) in their sample. No relationship between sex and type of complaint was found in Roth's study.

Monroe and Marks, in studying the prevalence of difficulty falling asleep in 831 emotionally disturbed adolescents, found 32 percent of them to have "some" difficulty and 20 percent with "characteristic" difficulty falling asleep,[30] an incidence of sleep difficulty that is higher than that reported for general adult populations[6,18,31,32] but comparable to prevalence figures for psychiatric outpatients.[33,34] Of those emotionally disturbed adolescents who were referred to physicians specifically for sleep difficulties, 51 percent were found to have considerable difficulty falling asleep, and 25 percent, some difficulty falling asleep, suggesting that this complaint is the one most frequently reported.[30]

The mean duration of insomnia in our clinical characteristics study was 14.0 years, indicating that the condition was, in general, quite chronic.[7] The long-term nature of insomnia may reflect both serious underlying psychopathology and lack of adequate evaluation and treatment.[35-37] In this regard, the vast majority of insomniacs manifest significant psychopathology, as measured by the MMPI[8,9,38-41] (see also Chapter 5, Psychiatric Factors in Insomnia) and as demonstrated by the psychosocial consequences experienced by insomniacs, which are described later in this chapter.

Behavioral Correlates

Studies assessing the behavior of insomniacs have produced a fairly consistent picture of how insomniacs think and act during the day, prior to bedtime, during the night when unable to sleep, upon awakening, during the morning, and during the day following a night of poor sleep.[7,17] Insomniacs are typically characterized as being tense and anxious persons who ruminate about daytime problems while attempting to get to sleep. They report that their sleep is easily disturbed by such external factors as noise, temperature, and light, as well as by the continuing internal distress generated by their ruminative thoughts. Upon awakening from a night of poor sleep, they feel tense, irritable, depressed, and physically and mentally tired. During the day they are socially withdrawn and depressed, with a considerable degree of somatization, decreased productivity, and self-preoccupation.

Presleep Behavior

Significantly fewer insomniacs than controls in our clinical characteristics study reported being sleepy at bedtime. Instead, they were much more likely to be tense, anxious, and worried, and often felt like their "minds were racing"[7] (Table 4.2). Further, more insomniacs than controls said they were mentally tired and depressed. When questioned about bedtime thoughts, insomniacs were more likely to relate the following concerns: getting enough sleep, health, death, work, and personal problems. Other studies have shown that insomniacs have high levels of tension and ruminative apprehension at bedtime.[17,38-40,42] For example, in our study, fewer insomniacs than controls responded positively to the MMPI question, "Most nights I go to sleep without thoughts or ideas bothering me."[7] Also, the Gallup survey showed that more than one-third (35%) of the subjects who reported sleep difficulty attributed it to "thinking over" problems, 25 percent said they had insomnia due to an inability to relax, and 11 percent could not sleep because of being "overstimulated."[17] Finally, in their study of adolescents, Price and her associates noted that most chronic poor sleepers attributed their sleep difficulty to worry, tension, and personal, family, and school problems. In contrast, most of those who slept poorly on an occasional basis could not identify a cause.[42]

In an attempt to induce sleep, significantly more insomniacs than normals in our clinical characteristics study said they did the following: "tried hard," read, turned on the light, got out of bed, went to the bathroom, ate some food, took medication, drank water or milk, or drank alcoholic beverages.[7]

Table 4.2. Presleep Behavior

	Insomniacs	Controls
Feelings		
"Mind racing"	48%	15% †
Tense–anxious	44%	2% †
Worried	35%	6% †
Depressed	24%	2% †
Desperate	10%	0% †
Mentally tired	56%	39% †
Sleepy	31%	71% †
Thoughts		
Getting enough sleep	77%	12% †
Personal problems	49%	30% *
Work	47%	29% *
Health	36%	16% †
Death	14%	3% *
Activities		
Reading	53%	37% *
Eating	31%	7% †
Drinking water, milk, etc.	31%	13% †
Drinking alcoholic beverages	15%	3% *
Taking sleep medication	51%	0% †
Trying hard to sleep	48%	17% †
Turning on light	21%	5% †
Getting out of bed	43%	21% †
Going to bathroom	61%	28% †

† p<0.01
* p<0.05
(From Kales et al[7])

Nighttime Behavior

Studies have identified three general groups of factors as contributing to insomniacs' disrupted nighttime sleep: psychologic issues including dreams and nightmares, as well as the continuation of ruminative concerns from the daytime; physiologic distress associated with pain or the need to urinate; and environmental conditions, such as noise, temperature, and light.[7,17] In the clinical characteristics study, the following factors were considered disruptive, in order of frequency: need to urinate, noise, temperature, dreams or nightmares, changes in humidity, light, physical pain, and the disruption felt to be produced by the presence of a bed partner.[7] Similar findings were reported in the Gallup survey.[17] About one in every four subjects attributed sleep problems to one of the following: a need to use the bathroom, muscle or joint aches, light, or noise. Women were more likely than men to report their partner's snoring as a problem (18% vs 7%), as well as an inability to relax, thinking over problems, and needing to use the bathroom.

Postsleep Behavior

Insomniacs in our clinical characteristics study felt considerably worse than controls in the morning.[7] Significantly more insomniacs than controls were sleepy, groggy, physically and mentally tired, depressed, worried, tense, anxious, and irritable. Fewer insomniacs than controls were rested, alert, "ready to get going," and sociable, and more felt as if their minds were "racing." Furthermore, insomniacs characteristically felt tired in the morning, whereas controls were more likely to report feeling tired in the afternoon.

Daytime Behavior

The insomniacs in our clinical characteristics study reported that their sleep difficulty had adversely affected their social lives, personal relationships, and work situations.[7] After their insomnia began, 26 percent had less satisfactory intimate relationships, 21 percent had less frequent social contacts, and 15 percent had fewer friends. At work, 39 percent became less productive after their insomnia began, 17 percent were less compatible with their co-workers, 11 percent were absent more often, and 10 percent were less compatible with their supervisors. Also, almost one-third of the insomniacs (30%) lost some ability to achieve their goals after their insomnia began, and 17 percent were more likely to lose their tempers. Almost one-third (32%) thought less of themselves because of their sleep disorder, but most (81%) reported receiving more care or sympathy from significant others. Simonds and Parraga's study of sleep behaviors in children indicated that almost half (45%) were reported by their parents to act differently during the day following a poor night's sleep.[16]

In our MMPI study, responses to individual MMPI questions also indicated a higher prevalence of psychosocial difficulties in insomniacs, although the items were not phrased to specifically determine whether the difficulties were consequences of their sleep loss.[7] On 16 of these 25 items (64%), more insomniacs than controls demonstrated impaired social skills or negative social attitudes. Insomniacs significantly more often responded negatively to such statements as, "I believe that my home life is as pleasant as that of most people I know"; "I seem to make friends about as quickly as others do"; "I like children"; "I like parties and socials"; and "My sex life is satisfactory."

Marchini and her associates compared the daytime activities and thought content of insomniacs who had difficulty staying asleep with those of control subjects.[43] Their findings are similar to those reported above. Specifically, the insomniacs in their study were more passive, unconcerned, and mentally and physically inactive, thus suggesting a general pattern of social withdrawal and depression. While they did not acknowledge thinking about problems more often than controls, they did report being more preoccupied with themselves. At night, insomniacs had a greater degree of mental activity than good sleepers, leading the authors to conclude that insomniacs are hypoactive during the day but hyperactive at night.[43]

It is difficult to estimate to what degree the negative behavioral correlates of insomniac patients are a consequence of their psychologic difficulties or of their chronic sleep loss. The number and magnitude of these negative behaviors suggest that both factors contribute. We have observed, however, in sleep laboratory studies that chronic insomniacs' behavior does not change notably when their sleep is improved by drugs for intermediate or even long-term periods. Also, other studies have demonstrated that shortening of sleep duration is not a stressor per se.[44-46] Thus, while daytime difficulties may be somewhat related to sleeplessness and fatigue, it is more likely that the psychologic disturbances associated with insomnia are primarily responsible for both the patients' diurnal and nocturnal problems.

General Health Correlates

Insomniacs consistently display characteristics of poor physical and mental health when compared with controls (Table 4.3). They report poorer childhood health; more current medical illnesses, particularly of the psychosomatic type; more hospitalizations; more suicide ideation; stronger family histories for emotional problems; and greater degrees of tension, anxiety, depression, and loneliness.

Physical Health

Insomniacs tend to have more health complaints than normal controls, both as children and as adults, and they do appear to have poorer

Table 4.3. Health Correlates in Insomnia

	Insomniacs	Controls
Physical Health		
Poor in childhood	19%	11%
Poor currently	43%	3% †
Under doctor's care	55%	11% †
"Psychosomatic" illnesses	59%	31% †
Work limited by illness	49%	17% †
Number of hospitalizations	2.7	1.4†
Mental Health		
More nervous than others	51%	11% †
Ready to go to pieces	51%	12% †
Feeling life is a strain	46%	7% †
Less happy than others	52%	20% †
Lacking self-confidence	44%	20% †
Loneliness	43%	7% †
Feeling blue	35%	2% †
Future hopeless	17%	0% †
Suicidal ideation	25%	10% *

† p<0.01
* p<0.05
(From Kales et al[7])

health in a number of respects. In our clinical characteristics study, insomniacs were less healthy as children than were normal controls.[7] Specifically, more insomniacs (19%) than controls (11%) reported their health as having been only fair, poor, or very poor in childhood. Within the insomniac sample, two times more women (26%) than men (11%) reported poor health during childhood.

Insomniacs' current health was much less satisfactory than controls' on several measures.[7] First, 43 percent reported their current health as fair, poor, or very poor, compared with only 3 percent of the controls, and more insomniacs than controls reported having had some illness in their lifetime (86% vs 53%). Furthermore, hospitalizations were about twice as common among the insomniacs. Also, slightly more than two-fifths of the insomniacs were currently being treated for a medical illness other than insomnia, compared with only about 10 percent of the controls. Psychosomatic-type illnesses, such as allergies, asthma, colitis, elevated blood pressure, migraine headaches and ulcers, were reported by about two times more insomniacs than controls (59% vs 31%). About one-half of the insomniacs said that health problems had limited their work capacity at some time in their lives, compared with only about one-sixth of the control subjects. Problems such as tiredness, depression, nervousness, anxiety, insomnia, or dependence on drugs or alcohol addiction caused these work limitations in one-fourth of the insomniacs but in only 2 percent of the controls.

Compared with the total sample of subjects from the LAMAS study, individuals with a current complaint of insomnia more frequently reported a persistent or recurring health problem, experienced more multiple health problems, and had been hospitalized more often and for longer periods of time during the previous year.[6]

Looking at health-related items in the MMPI individual response study, we found that more insomniacs than controls appeared to have problems regarded as possibly being emotionally based.[7] In fact, on 53 of 58 questions related to such health problems, insomniacs' responses indicated more somatization than those of the controls. Differences were significant on 30 items, including headache, diarrhea, constipation, stomach discomfort, palpitations and shortness of breath, nonspecific pain, tiredness, and weakness.

The poor sleepers in the life-stress events study were sick more often and hospitalized more often than controls.[10] Similarly, Roth, et al, in their study of chronic insomniacs seeking treatment for their sleep problem, found a high level of symptomatology using the Cornell Medical Index.[29] Monroe also administered the Cornell Medical Index to his 16 good sleepers and 16 poor sleepers.[40] The poor sleepers had a mean of 15 somatic symptoms, while the good sleepers reported only five.

The results of the studies discussed above become more meaningful in light of data from another study,[47] in which patients in a large insomniac sample were diagnosed using the multiaxial criteria of the *Diagnostic and Statistical Manual of Mental Disorders* (DSM-III).[48] This study showed that insomniacs' perceptions of having physical illnesses are exaggerated compared with the actual medical diagnoses based on thorough evaluations. Only 5 percent of the chronic insomniacs had a diagnosis of a physical illness, which was considered to be the major focus of treatment.[47] On the other hand, another 18 percent of the chronic insomniacs were given a psychiatric diagnosis of somatoform disorder, indicating the presence of somatic complaints in the absence of a physical disorder.

In looking at typical health habits in our clinical characteristics study, we found that fewer insomniacs than controls currently smoked cigarettes.[7] However, because cigarette smoking is known to cause sleep disturbance, particularly difficulty falling asleep,[49] it is interesting to note that all of the insomniacs who reported smoking had difficulty falling asleep. Similar percentages of insomniacs and controls reported high daily consumption of caffeinated beverages, as did men and women insomniacs.[7] Insomniacs with difficulty falling asleep drank about as much coffee as those who had difficulty staying asleep. It has been shown that sleep may be disturbed when three or more cups of coffee are taken close to bedtime,[50] but it is unlikely that many people have such a habit. Thus, insomniacs did not have a high prevalence of cigarette smoking or caffeine use, but there was a positive correlation between smoking and the degree of difficulty falling asleep. This was not the case for caffeine use.

Mental Health

Our clinical characteristics study[7] showed that insomniacs also had more mental health problems than controls. Suicidal ideation was reported by about one-fourth of the insomniacs but by only about 10 percent of the controls, and attempts at suicide were reported four times more often by insomniacs. Among the insomniacs, twice as many women as men had suicide ideation. Also, a family member's hospitalization for emotional problems was reported more than twice as often by the insomniacs as by the control group. When the type of complaint was considered, insomniacs with difficulty falling asleep more often reported a family history of hospitalization resulting from emotional problems (49%) than did those with difficulty staying asleep (23%). In the life-stress events study, suicidal thoughts were reported more often among insomniacs than good sleepers, and more insomniacs had histories of emotional disturbance.[10]

Further evidence that insomniacs have poor mental health was obtained from both the LAMAS[6] and the life-stress events studies.[10] In the LAMAS study, individuals with insomnia more often felt that they needed help with emotional or family problems,[6] specifically, with tension, depression, and loneliness. Tension was a more frequent complaint among those who had difficulty falling asleep or difficulty staying asleep, and depression was more common for those who had difficulty staying asleep and those who woke too early. Loneliness was a common complaint for all three groups. However, insomniacs did not use mental health services more often than non-insomniac respondents.

Finally, more insomniacs than normal subjects from the life-stress events study complained of a lack of energy, trouble concentrating, and nervousness.[10]

Further evidence of poor mental health among insomniacs was found in our analysis of related items on the MMPI (Table 4.3).[7] Insomniacs, more often than controls, responded positively to the following items: "I am certainly lacking in self-confidence," "I brood a great deal," "I wish I could be as happy as others seem to be," "Even when I am with people I feel lonely much of the time," and "Most of the time I feel blue." They also reported more frequently than controls that they tended to "take things hard," considered life a "strain," saw the future as "hopeless," had not lived the "right kind of life," sometimes felt about to "go to pieces," and thought that something was wrong with their mind. Additional MMPI items indicated that insomniacs were more likely to feel worried, anxious, "high strung," more nervous than most others, and not usually calm.

Similarly, in Monroe's study of good and poor adult sleepers, the poor sleepers had a higher level of emotional symptomatology on the Cornell Medical Index (9.2 vs 1.3).[40] When the same author studied good and poor sleep in a large sample of emotionally disturbed adolescents,[30] he found that sleep quality is "extremely vulnerable to underlying neurotic conflicts and relatively unaffected by psychopathic personality dynamics." Specifically, anxiety, fear, depression, somatic concerns, and multiple neurotic manifestations were the most significant characteristics associated with sleep problems in his adolescent group. The most common descriptors were shy, sensitive, quiet, silent, slow, and reserved, as opposed to the "acting-out" descriptors more often associated with emotionally disturbed youths.

Coursey and associates have reported the results of a multivariate study employing only psychologic test data to determine the factors discriminating insomniacs from controls.[38] Two factors were identified: the first, described the insomniacs as anxious, depressed, and worried, and the second, characterized them as overly preoccupied with bodily functioning and seeking less external stimulation (ie, they internalized their concerns).

Using a different method of analysis to discriminate between insomniacs and controls, Beutler divided a sample of 22 insomniacs into four subgroups, based upon objective parameters obtained in the sleep laboratory.[51] The insomniacs were split into groups in terms of either high or low values on two different dimensions (sleep latency and number of awakenings). When each of the four groups was compared to controls, the group with low values for both sleep latency and number of awakenings did not differ from its controls. The insomniacs who had only sleep maintenance difficulty were reported to be more schizoid, naive, active, and attention-seeking, while those with high sleep latency values were more neurotic. The insomniacs with both types of problems were found to be similar to those with pure sleep latency problems.

When we divided a sample of 150 insomniacs and 100 controls into four subgroups as Beutler did, we found that as the degree of sleep difficulty increased, the degree of psychopathology also increased.[52] Finally, a stepwise discriminant function was able to discriminate at least three-fourths of each subgroup of insomniacs and their controls by using only MMPI variables. The variables that most effectively discriminated between insomniacs and controls included measures of anxiety and overall psychopathology.

Drug or Alcohol Treatment as a Factor

The vast majority of the insomniacs (88%) in the clinical characteristics study had used drugs or alcohol to help themselves sleep at some time in their lives.[7] Of that group, 70 percent currently used drugs or alcohol frequently to help them sleep (CFT), 18 percent reported past or infrequent use (PIT), and 12 percent had never taken either drugs or alcohol to help them sleep (NT). Insomniacs with difficulty falling asleep tended to use drugs more often than those who had difficulty staying asleep. Specifically, only 16 percent of those who had difficulty falling asleep had never used drugs or alcohol to help them sleep, while this was true for 26 percent of the patients with difficulty staying asleep.

Because the CFT group made up the major proportion of our sample of insomniacs who sought treatment, comparisons made with the other two treatment groups were considerably weakened. Therefore, we selected another control sample of 70 insomniac subjects who had not sought treatment and were not currently using drugs or alcohol for their insomnia symptoms (CFT controls).

Insomniacs' estimates of their typical sleep latency and their total sleep time reflect a significant degree of sleep disturbance compared to controls' estimates. Further, they report desiring about the same amount of sleep as normal controls do, indicating that their problem is not one of unrealistic expectations, but rather one of obtaining less sleep, or at least a perception that they obtain less sleep. All of the treatment groups and the CFT controls reported similar subjective estimates of sleep difficulty; however, the CFT group reported a significantly greater degree of insomnia when not treating their symptoms. It was also found that those who had never treated their symptom of insomnia with drugs or alcohol had developed sleep difficulty at a later age. Those who treated their symptoms either currently or in the past were most likely to report life stresses at the time of onset.

Onset and Clinical Characteristics

Insomnia began at about the same age for those in the CFT group, the CFT insomniac control group, and the PIT group (34, 31, and 32 years, respectively) (Table 4.4). However, the NT group had a much later age at onset, 41 years. All four groups had similar mean durations of insomnia (CFT group, 14 years; control group, 14 years; PIT group, 12 years; and NT group, 15 years). Thus, these data support our hypothesis that when insomnia develops earlier in life, it is more severe, or perceived as such, and the use of sleep medication, including alcohol, is more likely.

A stressful event was experienced at the onset of insomnia by most of the subjects in both the CFT and PIT groups (77% and 87%, respectively); while considerably fewer subjects in both the NT and CFT control groups identified life stresses at the onset of their sleep difficulty (43% and 51%, respectively).

Table 4.4. Clinical Characteristics of Insomnia

	CFT	CFT Controls	PIT	NT	Total Sample
Men (%)	47.1	45.7	40.9	42.9	47.0
Women (%)	52.9	54.3	59.1	57.1	53.0
Event at Onset (%)	76.7	50.9	86.7	42.9	75.0
Age at Onset (yrs)	34.1 ± 2.1	30.9 ± 2.1	32.2 ± 3.2	40.9 ± 7.5	35.1
Current Age (yrs)	47.9 ± 1.6	45.0 ± 1.4	45.4 ± 3.7	55.0 ± 5.1	47.9
Duration (yrs)	14.2 ± 1.5	13.8 ± 1.5	12.5 ± 3.1	14.6 ± 4.2	14.4

CFT = Current, frequent treatment group
CFT Controls = Current, frequent treatment control group
PIT = Past or infrequent treatment group
NT = No treatment group

Subjective Estimates of Sleep Disturbance

Sleep Latency Our insomniac group's estimated sleep latency was about four times that of the normal control group (insomniacs, 63 min; controls, 17 min).[7] When specific sleep complaint was considered, insomniacs who had difficulty falling asleep reported a sleep latency more than twice that of insomniacs who had difficulty staying asleep (83 min vs 34 min). Women insomniacs in our clinical characteristics study reported taking longer to fall asleep than did men (72 vs 57 min), which is consistent because approximately three-fourths of the insomniac women had difficulty falling asleep as their primary complaint. In studying insomniacs who sought treatment for their sleep problem, Roth and his colleagues reported an estimated sleep latency of about 97 minutes.[29]

The CFT group estimated sleep latency to be 59 minutes, which was close to the 73 minutes estimated by the CFT control group.[7] Both of these estimates exceed that of the normal control group (17 min) by at least 3.5 times. Furthermore, the CFT group's estimate of what sleep latency would be if they were not taking any drugs or alcohol (205 min) was about three times that of the CFT control group and about 12 times that of the normal control group. The other two subgroups' estimated sleep latencies were about the same as the CFT control group (PIT and NT, 79 mins).

These data support our hypothesis that insomniacs who take drugs or alcohol to help themselves sleep have more severe sleep difficulty than those who do not. Recently we reported the findings from the analysis of the MMPI on a large sample of insomniac subjects.[9] This study demonstrated that those insomniacs who used drugs or alcohol to help them sleep generally showed more psychopathology than those who did not and that the MMPI profile patterns of the two groups were almost identical. Furthermore, the MacAndrew Alcoholism Scale[53] was unelevated in both groups.[9] Thus, the use of drugs or alcohol by chronic insomniacs appears to be a function of the patients' general level of distress and not a function of a specific pattern of psychopathology.

Total Sleep Time As a group, the insomniacs reported considerably less total sleep time than the normal control subjects (325 vs 431 min).[7] Estimates of total sleep time were not affected by the type of sleep complaint; patients with either difficulty falling asleep or difficulty staying asleep reported obtaining similar amounts of sleep. The men and women insomniac patients in our study reported about the same amounts of total sleep time.[7] Similarly, the insomniacs studied by Roth's group reported a total sleep time of 5.4 hours (324 minutes).[29]

When treatment groups were considered, both the CFT group and the CFT control group reported similar amounts of total sleep time (321 and 313 minutes, respectively), which amounted to only about three-fourths of the normal control group's estimate (431 minutes). The CFT group estimated that they would have an even shorter sleep time (211 min) if they were not to take any medication. In comparison, both PIT and NT subjects reported a total sleep time of 264 minutes.

When asked how much sleep they would like to get each night, the insomniac sample as a whole, each of the insomniac subgroups, and the normal control group responded with similar desired sleep times.[7] This ranged from about 7.3 hours to 7.6 hours within the various insomniac groups, compared to the control subjects' desired estimate of 7.4 hours.

Health Correlates

The frequent use of drugs or alcohol to aid sleep was correlated with poor health or the perception of poor health.[7] The CFT group rated their current health as fair, poor, or very poor about four times more often than the insomniac control group and about 15 times more often than the normal control group. Furthermore, about three times as many of the CFT group (61%) as the CFT control group (20%) were being treated for a current illness, while only 11 percent of the normal control group reported current treatment. Similarly, the CFT group reported more hospitalizations than either of the two control groups. Not surprisingly, more of the CFT group and CFT controls reported work limitations because of poor health than normal controls.

The CFT group felt they had less satisfactory childhood health than the normal control subjects.[7] Health during childhood was described as fair, poor, or very poor by similar percentages of the CFT group and their insomniac controls. However, a much lower percentage of the normal control group reported poor childhood health.

Finally, the mental health of the CFT group appeared to be more disturbed than that of the insomniac controls.[7] The normal control group, however, was much less disturbed than either of these two groups. Both the CFT and insomniac control samples reported suicidal ideation about twice as often as the normal controls. Further, more than two-fifths of the CFT group reported a family history of hospitalizations for emotional problems, which was a significantly higher percentage than for the two control groups.

Summary

Among the general population, the complaint of insomnia is more common in individuals of lower socioeconomic status, education, and occupational level—in whom higher levels of stress, mental disturbance, and psychopathology have previously been found. Among insomniacs, the most frequent type of sleep complaint is difficulty falling asleep. Chronic insomnia usually begins in mid-adulthood, in most instances before age 40, and generally persists for many years. Women tend to develop the disorder at a younger age than men, and it appears earlier in insomniacs who have a primary complaint of difficulty falling asleep than in insomniacs who complain of having trouble staying asleep. Stressful life events, especially personal events and those related to loss, are commonly associated with the onset of sleep difficulty.

Insomniac patients manifest typical behaviors prior to sleep, during the night when their sleep is disturbed, and during the day. At bedtime they have difficulty relaxing; they describe themselves as feeling tense, anxious, worried, or depressed, and as though their "minds were racing." There are frequent concerns about getting enough sleep, health, personal problems, and even death. They report that they attempt to cope with their tension and rumination by reading, eating, drinking, taking medications or alcohol, or getting out of bed. During the night, insomniacs often experience disrupted sleep and arousals, which they perceive as being caused most frequently by dreams, nightmares, continuing ruminative concerns, and environmental factors such as noise, light, or temperature. In the morning, they more frequently report feeling physically and mentally tired, and during the day, they characteristically feel depressed, worried, tense, irritable, and preoccupied with themselves. Thus, it is not surprising that these patients often report adverse effects on social lives, personal relationships, and employment.

Poor health, either actual or perceived, is more prevalent among insomniacs than good sleepers both during childhood and adulthood. Adult insomniacs report they are hospitalized more often than controls, are more often treated for medical illness (particularly psychosomatic disorders), and are more frequently limited in their work performance because of health complaints. Insomniacs' use of cigarettes and caffeine, health habits known to cause sleep difficulty because of their stimulant effects, appears to be similar to that of normal controls. However, when smoking was present it was associated with a greater degree of difficulty falling asleep.

Poor mental health is characteristic of chronic insomniacs. When compared with good sleepers, more insomniacs feel a need for help with family problems and emotional symptomatology, such as nervousness, tension, depression, and loneliness. Also, mental health problems are more likely to be seen in insomniacs' families, and insomniacs themselves are more likely to attempt suicide than good sleepers.

Insomniacs' estimates of their typical sleep latency and their total sleep time reflect a significant degree of sleep disturbance compared with controls' estimates. Further, they desire about the same amount of sleep as normal controls, indicating that their problem is not one of unrealistic expectations, but rather one of obtaining less sleep, or at least a perception that they obtain less sleep.

Insomniacs who take drugs or alcohol to help them sleep report that without treatment they have a much greater degree of sleep difficulty than those who do not treat their symptoms. Further, they have more health complaints and a greater degree of psychopathology than either other insomniacs or normal controls. Their most common complaint is difficulty falling asleep. Also, insomniacs who use or have used drugs or alcohol for their sleep difficulty, compared with those who do not, report their insomnia as beginning earlier in their lives and indicate that more life-stress events were associated with the onset of their sleep problem.

References

1. Callahan EM, Carroll S, Revier P, Gilhooly E, Dunn D: The 'sick role' in chronic illness: some reactions. *J Chron Dis* 19:883–897, 1966.
2. Elliott GR, Eisdorfer C: *Stress and Human Health.* New York, Springer Publishing Company, 1982.
3. Hinkle LE Jr: The effect of exposure to culture change, social change, and changes in interpersonal relationship on health, in Dohrenwend BS, Dohrenwend BP (eds): *Stressful Life Events: Their Nature and Effects.* New York, John Wiley & Sons, 1974, pp 9–44.
4. Fordyce WE, Brockway JA: Chronic pain and its management, in Usdin G, Lewis JM (eds): *Psychiatry in General Medical Practice.* New York, McGraw-Hill, 1979, pp 352–368.

5. Rogers DE: The doctor himself must become the treatment. *Pharos* 37:124–129, 1974.
6. Bixler EO, Kales A, Soldatos CR, Kales JD, Healey S: Prevalence of sleep disorders in the Los Angeles metropolitan area. *Am J Psychiatry* 136:1257–1262, 1979.
7. Kales JD, Kales A, Bixler EO, Soldatos CR, Cadieux RJ, Kashurba GJ, Vela-Bueno A: Biopsychobehavioral correlates of insomnia, V: clinical characteristics and behavioral correlates. *Am J Psychiatry* (in press).
8. Kales A, Caldwell AB, Preston TA, Healey S, Kales JD: Personality patterns in insomnia. *Arch Gen Psychiatry* 33:1128–1134, 1976.
9. Kales A, Caldwell AB, Soldatos CR, Bixler EO, Kales JD: Biopsychobehavioral correlates of insomnia. II. Pattern specificity and consistency with the Minnesota Multiphasic Personality Inventory. *Psychosom Med* 45:341–356, 1983.
10. Healey ES, Kales A, Monroe LJ, Bixler EO, Chamberlin K, Soldatos CR: Onset of insomnia: role of life-stress events. *Psychosom Med 43*: 439–451, 1981.
11. Holmes TH, Rahe RH: The social readjustment rating scale. *J Psychosom Res 11*:213–218, 1967.
12. Lundberg U, Theorell T, Lind E: Life changes and myocardial infarction: individual differences in life change scaling. *J Psychosom Res 19*: 27–32, 1974.
13. Rabkin JG, Struening EL: Life events, stress, and illness. *Science 194*: 1013–1020, 1976.
14. Rahe RH: Life change measurement as a predictor of illness. *Proc R Soc Med 61*:1124–1126, 1968.
15. Rahe RH, Arthur RJ: Life change and illness studies: past history and future directions. *J Human Stress 4(1)*:3–15, 1978.
16. Simonds JF, Parraga H: Prevalence of sleep disorders and sleep behaviors in children and adolescents. *J Am Acad Child Psychiatry 21*:383–388, 1982.
17. The Gallup Organization: *The Gallup Study of Sleeping Habits.* Princeton, NJ, 1979.
18. Karacan I, Thornby JI, Anch M, Holzer CE, Warheit GJ, Schwab JJ, Williams RL: Prevalence of sleep disturbance in a primarily urban Florida county. *Soc Sci and Med 10*:239–244, 1976.
19. McGhie A, Russell SM: The subjective assessment of normal sleep patterns. *J Ment Sci 108*:642–654, 1962.
20. Hollingshead A, Redlich RC: *Social Class and Mental Illness.* New York, John Wiley & Sons, 1958.
21. Srole L, Langner RS, Michael ST, Opler MK, Rennie TAC: *Mental Health in the Metropolis: The Midtown Manhattan Study.* New York, McGraw-Hill Book Co, 1962.
22. Dohrenwend BS: Social class and stressful events, in Hare EH, Wing JK (eds): *Psychiatric Epidemiology.* New York, Oxford University Press, 1970.
23. Hauri P, Olmstead E: Childhood-onset insomnia. *Sleep 3*:59–65, 1980.

24. Kales A, Cadieux RJ, Soldatos CR, Bixler EO, Schweitzer PK, Prey WT, Vela-Bueno A: Narcolepsy-cataplexy. I. Clinical and electrophysiologic characteristics. *Arch Neurol 39*:164–168, 1982.
25. Kales A, Cadieux RJ, Bixler EO, Soldatos CR, Vela-Bueno A, Misoul C, Locke TW: Obstructive sleep apnea, I: Onset, clinical course, and characteristics, (in preparation).
26. Kales A, Soldatos CR, Caldwell AB, Kales JD, Humphrey FJ II, Charney DS, Schweitzer PK: Somnambulism: clinical characteristics and personality patterns. *Arch Gen Psychiatry 37*:1406–1410, 1980.
27. Kales JD, Kales A, Soldatos CR, Caldwell AB, Charney DS, Martin ED: Night terrors: clinical characteristics and personality patterns. *Arch Gen Psychiatry 37*:1413–1417, 1980.
28. Kales A, Soldatos CR, Caldwell AB, Charney DS, Kales JD, Markel D, Cadieux R: Nightmares: clinical characteristics and personality patterns. *Am J Psychiatry 137*:1197–1201, 1980.
29. Roth T, Kramer M, Lutz T: The nature of insomnia: a descriptive summary of a sleep clinic population. *Compr Psychiatry 17*:217–220, 1976.
30. Monroe LJ, Marks PA: Psychotherapists' descriptions of emotionally disturbed adolescent poor and good sleepers. *J Clin Psychol 33*:263–269, 1977.
31. Hammond EC: Some preliminary findings on physical complaints from a prospective study of 1,064,004 men and women. *Am J Public Health 54*:11–23, 1964.
32. U.S. Department of HEW: *Selected Symptoms of Psychological Distress.* Rockville MD, 1970.
33. Bixler EO, Kales A, Soldatos CR: Sleep disorders encountered in medical practice: a national survey of physicians. *Behav Med 6*:1–6, 1979.
34. Sweetwood H, Grant I, Kripke DF, Gerst MS, Yager J: Sleep disorders over time: psychiatric correlates among males. *Br J Psychiatry 136*:456–462, 1980.
35. Kales A, Soldatos CR, Kales JD: Sleep disorders: evaluation and management in the office setting, in Arieti S, Brodie HKH (eds): *American Handbook of Psychiatry.* New York, Basic Books Inc, 1981, vol 7, pp 423–454.
36. Kales JD, Soldatos CR, Kales A: Diagnosis and treatment of sleep disorders, in Greist JH, Jefferson JW, Spitzer RL (eds): *Treatment of Mental Disorders.* New York, Oxford University Press, 1982, pp 473–500.
37. Soldatos CR, Kales A, Kales JD: Management of insomnia. *Ann Rev Med 30*:301–312, 1979.
38. Coursey RD, Buchsbaum M, Frankel BL: Personality measures and evoked responses in chronic insomniacs. *J Abnorm Psychol 84*:239–249, 1975.
39. Haynes SN, Follingstad DR, McGowan WT: Insomnia: sleep patterns and anxiety level. *J Psychosom Res 18*:69–74, 1974.
40. Monroe LJ: Psychological and physiological differences between good and poor sleepers. *J Abnorm Psychol 72*:255–264, 1967.

41. Monroe LJ, Marks PA: MMPI differences between adolescent poor and good sleepers. *J Consult Clin Psychology 45*:151–152, 1977.
42. Price VA, Coates TJ, Thoresen CE, Grinstead OA: Prevalence and correlates of poor sleep among adolescents. *Am J Dis Child 132*:583–586, 1978.
43. Marchini EJ, Coates TJ, Magistrad JG, Waldum SJ: What do insomniacs do, think, and feel during the day? A preliminary study. *Sleep 6*:147–155, 1983.
44. Akerstedt T, Gillberg M: Sleep, stress and recuperation, in Koella WP (ed): *Sleep 1980: Circadian Rhythms, Dreams, Noise and Sleep, Neurophysiology, Therapy.* Basel, S Karger, 1981, pp 98–101.
45. Horne JA: A review of the biological effects of total sleep deprivation in man. *Biol Psychol 7*:55–102, 1978.
46. Horne JA: Sleep deprivation, stress and sleep function, in Koella WP (ed): *Sleep 1980: Circadian Rhythms, Dreams, Noise and Sleep, Neurophysiology, Therapy.* Basel, S Karger, 1981, pp 95–97.
47. Tan T-L, Kales JD, Kales A, Soldatos CR, Bixler EO: Biopsychobehavioral correlates of insomnia, IV: diagnosis based on the DSM-III. *Am J Psychiatry* (in press).
48. American Psychiatric Association: *Diagnostic and Statistical Manual of Mental Disorders, ed 3.* Washington DC, American Psychiatric Association, 1980.
49. Soldatos CR, Kales JD, Scharf MB, Bixler EO, Kales A: Cigarette smoking associated with sleep difficulty. *Science 207*:551–553, 1980.
50. Karacan I, Thornby JI, Anch AM, Booth GH, Williams RL, Salis PJ: Dose-related sleep disturbances induced by coffee and caffeine. *Clin Pharmacol Ther 20*:682–689, 1976.
51. Beutler LE, Thornby JI, Karacan I: Psychological variables in the diagnosis of insomnia, in Williams RL, Karacan I (eds): *Sleep Disorders: Diagnosis and Treatment.* New York, John Wiley & Sons, 1978, pp 61–100.
52. Kales A, Bixler EO, Vela-Bueno A, Cadieux RJ, Soldatos CR, Kales JD: Biopsychobehavioral correlates of insomnia, III: Polygraphic findings of sleep difficulty and their relationship to psychopathology. *Int J Neurosci* (in press).
53. MacAndrew C: The differentiation of male alcoholic outpatients from nonalcoholic psychiatric patients by means of the MMPI. *Q J Studies Alcohol 26*:238–246, 1965.

5. Psychiatric Factors in Insomnia

This chapter describes the critical role of psychiatric factors in the development and persistence of insomnia. Only by understanding this relationship will the physician be adequately prepared to evaluate and treat insomniac patients, who are typically reluctant to acknowledge their underlying psychologic difficulties.[1-3] Although physicians have often assumed that psychologic factors are central in the etiology of most cases of chronic insomnia, this relationship has been challenged by some sleep researchers.[4-7] Other investigators have confirmed the importance of psychiatric factors; however, their data have been based on relatively small samples,[8-13] and thus, may not be fully representative of this complex disorder. Many of the conclusions presented in this chapter are derived from several large-scale studies we conducted to determine the precise role of psychologic factors in the clinical course of insomnia.[14-20] These studies involve the role of predisposing emotional factors and of stressful life events in the etiology of insomnia,[14,20] assessment of personality patterns with the Minnesota Multiphasic Personality Inventory (MMPI),[15,17] and psychiatric evaluation and diagnosis of patients with chronic insomnia[19] using the criteria of the *Diagnostic and Statistical Manual of Mental Disorders*, third edition (DSM-III), of the American Psychiatric Association.[21]

Role of Predisposing Emotional Factors and Stressful Life Events

When we examined the role of stressful life events in the development of chronic insomnia, we found that such events, when mediated by certain predisposing emotional factors and inadequate coping mechanisms, are indeed closely related to the onset of long-term sleep difficulty.[14,20] Our findings regarding the type and frequency of life-stress events that are associated with the onset of insomnia are discussed in detail in Chapter 4 (Onset, Clinical Characteristics, and Behavioral Correlates). Here, we report on the role of predisposing emotional factors and maladaptive coping mechanisms that mediate the effects of life-stress events in the development of insomnia.

When insomniacs are compared with control subjects regarding their perceptions of childhood emotional experiences, they less frequently report that they "felt good" as children or had positive experiences with their families.[14] They also had more nightmares, problems sleeping, and eating difficulties as children. This childhood pattern of discontent with family life and numerous somatic complaints continued into adulthood. When recalling the time before their insomnia began, the patients viewed themselves as having had less satisfying relationships with their parents than did controls. They also had problems in other interpersonal relations and had comparatively poor self-concepts: they were less likely to seek sustaining personal friendships and more likely to express feelings of inferiority. In terms of somatic concerns, they were less satisfied with their general health status before their insomnia began. These findings of lifelong emotional difficulties preceding chronic insomnia may explain why episodes of stress-induced sleeplessness are transient for most people, while for others they become an ingrained pattern.[14]

The following case vignettes illustrate how underlying psychologic difficulties can lead to personal vulnerability and inadequate coping mechanisms. The resulting inability to properly manage stressful life events in adaptive ways places the person at risk for developing chronic insomnia:

Case 1. A 48-year-old married woman presented with a primary complaint of insomnia that had persisted over the last 12 years. During her early childhood, she had experienced considerable anxiety and general fearfulness in response to her sister having developed a brain tumor. The patient vividly recalled her distress when the sister completely lost her hair for a period of time. Thirty years later, when the sister's brain tumor recurred, she became progressively debilitated and died a year later. The patient recalled that her sister "was like a vegetable" for about one year prior to her death. This situation was so anxiety-provoking for the patient that she rarely visited her sister.

The last time she saw her sister, she tried to encourage her to sleep. However, the sister stated, "I don't want to close my eyes. I'm afraid I won't wake up." The patient clearly dated the onset of her insomnia to that time and indicated that when she attempted to go to sleep, she often thought of her deceased sister and would then experience general anxiety. Furthermore, her history revealed a lifetime pattern of excessive concern over the possibility of physical illness in her family. She had trouble managing stressful situations, and instead attempted to deny or avoid them.

Case 2. An 18-year-old unmarried mother of a 2-year-old son had developed insomnia at age 12. At that time, her mother and stepfather had serious marital distress, with the stepfather having threatened the mother with physical abuse. These events produced a recrudescence of earlier experiences in childhood. She recalled that when she was four years old and lying in bed, she heard screams while her father was chasing and beating her mother. Following this incident and her parents' subsequent divorce, she had intermittent periods of insomnia and nightmares as well as behavioral problems. At the time of her evaluation, she was consciously aware of fears of going to sleep. She said, "Maybe I'm afraid to sleep because I'm scared something will happen to me or my little boy."

In addition to reporting more emotional difficulties during childhood and before their insomnia began, insomniac subjects continue to experience greater psychologic distress than controls during the course of their sleep difficulty.[14,20] Specifically, at the time of assessment, chronic insomniacs feel more dissatisfied with their lives than control subjects, have less positive self-concepts, and have greater difficulty in interpersonal relationships.[14] Also, they are less satisfied with themselves, their social lives, leisure time, living arrangements, and health status. Underlying feelings of inadequacy are reflected in their responses on the Adjective Check List[22] and in their one-word descriptions of themselves; they primarily use adjectives that fall into the categories of "bad," "weak," or "passive." They also have more health complaints than control subjects and are hospitalized more often. Thus, the insomniacs' poor self-concepts, difficulties in socialization, and frequent health complaints at the time of assessment indicate that the personal vulnerability they experienced in childhood and before their insomnia began continues after the onset of their insomnia.[14]

Psychologic Testing

We have extensively studied the personality patterns of patients with sleep disorders,[15,17,23-27] including those of insomniac patients.[15,17] The MMPI was used in these studies because, of all the available objective measures of personality, it has been the most widely used standardized inventory in clinical practice.[28-35]

We first used the MMPI to evaluate the personality patterns of 128 insomniac subjects studied at the University of California at Los Angeles (UCLA) Neuropsychiatric Institute.[15] Subsequently, another 300 insomniac subjects, as well as 100 normal controls, were given the MMPI at The Pennsylvania State University (PSU) College of Medicine in Hershey, Pennsylvania.[17]

Although these samples of subjects with insomnia were drawn from populations in completely different geographic regions, the two groups were remarkably similar in three respects: their MMPI code patterns, the percentage of insomniac subjects with at least one clinical scale that was abnormally elevated (ie, with a T-score at or above 70), and the mean number of abnormally elevated scales per subject. The predominant characteristic of both groups' personality patterns was a strong tendency to internalize psychologic conflicts rather than to express them outwardly.[15,17]

The two insomniac samples differed from the control group in similar ways—they had the same age-related shifts in MMPI patterns, similar sex differences, and moderately more psychologic disturbance among subjects who used drugs or alcohol. In fact, each group of insomniacs differed significantly from the control group on almost every comparison. When the two groups of insomniacs were compared, however, there were no significant differences.[17]

MMPI Scale Elevations

When compared with controls, subjects with insomnia had higher mean values on all eight clinical scales of the MMPI (Table 5.1).[17] For individual scales, insomniacs had mean T-scores that were significantly higher on seven of the eight scales: 1-Hs (Hypochondriasis), 2-D (Depression), 3-Hy (Conversion Hysteria), 4-Pd (Psychopathic Deviate), 6-Pa (Paranoia), 7-Pt (Psychasthenia), and 8-Sc (Schizophrenia). The exception was 9-Ma (Hypomania), which is often low when 2-D is high.[29] In addition, insomniacs had at least one abnormally elevated scale almost three times more often than did controls, and the mean number of elevated scales per person for the insomniacs was five times greater.[17]

In both insomniac samples, the three highest mean scores, in decreasing rank order, were 2-D, 7-Pt, and 3-Hy.[15,17] Scale 2-D was preponderant among the elevated scales: 53 percent of the PSU sample and 61 percent of the UCLA sample had abnormal elevations on scale 2-D. In general, this scale indicates a depressed mood, poor morale,

Table 5.1. MMPI Scale Scores in Insomniacs and Controls[a]

	PSU Insomniacs (n = 279)		Controls (n = 97)		UCLA Insomniacs (n = 122)	
	Mean	S.E.	Mean	S.E.	Mean	S.E.
L	50.1	± 0.4	49.1	± 0.7	47.9	± 0.6
F	7.4	± 0.2†	4.2	± 0.3	8.4	± 0.4†
K	13.9	± 0.3†	15.8	± 0.5	14.0	± 0.4†
Hypochondriasis (Hs)	63.2	± 0.8†	50.2	± 0.8	63.4	± 1.1†
Depression (D)	71.6	± 1.0†	52.8	± 1.1	73.9	± 1.4†
Conversion Hysteria (Hy)	66.8	± 0.7†	54.8	± 0.8	67.6	± 1.0†
Psychopathic Deviate (Pd)	65.0	± 0.7†	56.2	± 1.1	66.7	± 1.2†
Masculine–Feminine						
(M)	65.5	± 0.9	62.3	± 1.7	70.8	± 1.3†
(F)	45.2	± 0.7	45.5	± 1.3	43.0	± 1.2
Paranoia (Pa)	60.7	± 0.6†	55.4	± 0.9	61.0	± 0.9†
Psychasthenia (Pt)	67.7	± 0.8†	53.7	± 0.9	68.1	± 1.2†
Schizophrenia (Sc)	66.4	± 0.9†	54.5	± 1.0	67.7	± 1.3†
Hypomania (Ma)	57.2	± 0.7	55.0	·± 1.0	59.9	± 1.0†

a = Values reported only for those subjects with valid MMPIs
PSU = Pennsylvania State University; UCLA = University of California at Los Angeles
† = p<0.01, when compared to controls
(From Kales et al[17])

and unhappiness, and it reflects internalized reactions to stress that are handled by pessimistic thinking, inhibition of anger, self-depreciation, and persistent worrying.

One-third to one-half of the subjects in both groups of insomniacs had pathologic elevations on each of several additional MMPI scales, which, in order of the greatest number of elevations, were scales 7, 3, 8, 1, and 4.[15,17] Scale 7-Pt reflects chronic anxiety, multiple fears, and obsessive apprehensions. Scale 3-Hy is usually associated with a style of repression, denial, and inhibition and may indicate conversion symptoms, which would tend to be manifested as various types of pain lacking an organic basis. A negative self-image, difficulties in expressing anger, a tendency to withdraw from interpersonal contact, disturbed thought processes, and at the extreme, a breakdown of reality testing, are associated with scale 8-Sc. Scale 1-Hs indicates preoccupation about one's health and overreaction to minor physical symptoms, while Scale 4-Pd suggests deficits of conscience, social alienation, and failures of judgment.

The two scales on which the fewest number of subjects had elevated scores were scales 6-Pa (Paranoia) and 9-Ma (Hypomania).[15,17] Scale 6 is usually associated with projection of anger and ideas of being victimized or mistreated by others. Scale 9 connotes pressured and outwardly directed activity, excitability, irritability, and unrealistically expansive ideas. The insomniac subjects' low scores on these scales are consistent with their tendency to internalize emotions; the anger of the insomniac is turned into self-blame or is repressed, rather than being expressed outwardly as irritability, hostility, or assertive action.[15,17]

MMPI Code Patterns

MMPI personality profiles for individual subjects are usually examined in terms of a profile pattern or code type, which is formulated by combining the subject's three highest scores, in any order. The results of our studies were striking in that seven code patterns (largely representing neurotic-depressive profiles) were found in 50 percent of the UCLA sample and in 43 percent of the PSU sample.[15,17] Table 5.2 shows the frequency with which these seven code types appeared in the insomniac samples as well as in the control sample.

Table 5.2. Frequency of MMPI Code Types in Insomniacs and Controls[a]

MMPI Code Type	PSU Insomniacs (n = 279)		Controls (n = 97)		UCLA Insomniacs (n = 122)	
	Number	%	Number	%	Number	%
278	34.0	12.2	2.0	2.0	15.5	12.7
231/312	26.5	9.5	1.0	1.0	15.5	12.7
237/273	21.3	7.6	1.0	1.0	3.5	2.9
127/271	13.7	4.9	0.0	0.0	6.0	4.9
234	12.0	4.3	1.0	1.0	6.5	5.3
247	6.3	2.3	1.0	1.0	8.0	6.6
248	5.5	2.0	0.0	0.0	6.0	4.9
Totals	119.3	42.8	6.0	6.0	61.0	50.0

a = Code types reported only for those subjects with valid MMPIs
(From Kales et al[17])

The most prevalent code patterns in both insomniac groups were the 2-7-8 and 2-3-1 code types.[15,17] The 2-7-8 code type, which was found in 12.2 percent of the PSU insomniacs and in 12.7 percent of the UCLA group, was preponderant among subjects under age 30. It reflects a chronic, ruminative depression and a schizoid, identity-confusion pattern. The next most common code type, 2-3-1, which indicates a somatized depression, was found mainly in subjects 30 years and older.

The other five code types and the personality patterns that they characterize were as follows: 2-3-7, a diffusely apprehensive and anxious depression; 1-2-7, an apprehensive, "worrying" depression with a particular focus on health concerns; 2-3-4, a "smiling depression" with passive-aggressive elements; 2-4-7, a moody depression with a passive-dependent life style; and 2-4-8, an alienated, distrustful type of depression.[15,17] The proportion of these neurotic-depressive profiles increased progressively from the youngest to the oldest age group. In contrast, scale 7-Pt became less prevalent within the code patterns as the subjects' ages increased.

The following excerpts from two of our patients' MMPI reports describe the personality patterns associated with two code types commonly found in patients who have chronic insomnia:

Case 3. Code-pattern 2-1-3. The MMPI report of a 72-year-old man with a 5-year history of insomnia included the following description of his personality patterns. "This patient seems to be a depressed, irritable, somewhat tense individual who is overconcerned with his bodily functions. He may complain of specific medical problems that have no physical basis."

"In times of prolonged emotional stress he may develop psychophysiological symptoms, such as headaches and gastrointestinal disorders. He appears to be a person who represses and denies emotional distress. While he may respond readily to advice and reassurance, he may be unwilling to accept a psychologic interpretation of his difficulties."

"He finds it difficult to assert himself, and he avoids situations where his performance might be inferior to that of others. He has some difficulty in dealing with hostile feelings. To the extent that he controls the direct expression of these feelings, he may be a bitter, resentful, and perhaps somewhat irresponsible person. Also, he is likely to have problems in establishing close personal relationships."

Case 4. Code-pattern 2-3-7. The report of a 39-year-old man with a 3-year history of insomnia provided the following information. "This patient is a tense, anxious, depressed individual who is over-controlled, has difficulty expressing his feelings, and is filled with self-doubt. Although he may seem industrious and conscientious in his work, he is torn between a need to be competitive and a fear of failure. He may suffer from fatigue, weakness, and low energy level."

"He is a rigid person who may react to anxiety with phobias, compulsions, or obsessive rumination. Chronic tension and excessive worry are common, and resistance to treatment may be extreme, despite obvious distress. He has problems centering around the control and expression of hostile feelings. Depending upon social factors, as well as other personality features, he may deal with his hostility overtly, in direct antisocial behavior, or covertly, in resentfulness, bitterness, and irresponsibility. This person feels unable to deal with the environmental pressures facing him or to utilize his skills or abilities to full advantage. At present, he feels unable to cope with life as he sees it. He may respond to these feelings of inadequacy with increased rigidity or withdrawal, depending upon individual factors."

Drug and Alcohol Use As Correlates of Psychopathology

Use of drugs and alcohol to induce sleep did not seem to be related to a specific pattern of psychopathology in the insomniac subjects; both users and non-users showed much higher levels of psychopathology than the control subjects.[17] Although those insomniacs who used drugs or alcohol to help themselves sleep generally showed a greater degree of psychopathology than non-users, the MMPI profile patterns of these two groups were almost identical. Furthermore, the MacAndrew Alcoholism Scale,[36] which may indicate a potential for alcohol dependence, was unelevated in both groups. Thus, the use of drugs or alcohol by chronic insomniacs appears to be a function of the patients' general level of distress and not a function of a specific pattern of psychopathology.[17] For the same reasons, the insomniacs' use of drugs or alcohol did not indicate a potential for dependence on these substances.

The Internalization Hypothesis

The MMPI studies show that subjects with chronic insomnia consistently have high levels of psychopathology and exhibit certain personality patterns. In the two populations studied, 76 and 85 percent of the insomniac subjects had one or more abnormally elevated clinical scales on the MMPI.[15,17] This high rate of psychopathology is similar to that found in various psychiatric patient populations, in which the percentage of patients who have at least one elevated clinical scale on the MMPI ranges from 70 to 80 percent.[33] The insomniacs in our studies also had higher levels of psychopathology than those reported for other sleep disorders that are also considered psychogenic in origin (nightmares,[25] sleepwalking in adults,[26] and night terrors[27]), as well as for sleep disorders that are considered to have organic etiologies (narcolepsy/cataplexy[23] and sleep apnea[24]).

In both of our samples, insomnia was associated with MMPI profiles indicating neurosis, depression, anxiety, obsessiveness, and hysterical repression.[15,17] With age, changes in personality reflected in the MMPI profiles progressed from ruminative depression and schizoid, identity-confusion patterns in younger subjects to somatized depression and distress over fears of declining health, pain, and suffering for the older age groups. Such differences are consistent with age-related shifts in MMPI patterns seen in any type of normal or pathologic noninsomniac populations.[28,35,37] However, given these expected changes in personality as a function of age, it is striking that the specificity of MMPI patterns of internalization persisted across the different age groups. Thus, the personality patterns of insomniacs of all ages were characterized by neurotic depression, apprehension, inhibition, rumination, and an inability to outwardly discharge anger.

The high incidence of specific types of psychopathology among insomniacs in these studies has led us to hypothesize that the mechanism underlying insomnia is based on the internalization of psychologic disturbance.[3,15,17] Thus, we have proposed that unresolved and internalized psychologic conflicts lead to emotional arousal, and, in turn, to physiologic activation before and during sleep. Insomnia then follows from this persistent emotional arousal and the resulting physiologic activation. Our hypothesis is consistent with previous research showing that emotional arousal causes physiologic changes that in turn can induce general psychophysiologic dysfunction.[38-42]

Persons who turn their anxieties inward or who are depressed and fearful of pain and suffering appear to be "pre-sensitized" to physical distress. In addition, this predisposition coupled with a process of conditioning may contribute to the development of chronic insomnia as follows: When individuals experience sleeplessness, they are easily frightened of further sleep loss and its possible consequences and are thus acutely apprehensive of insomnia. They become overly focused on their sleeplessness and on the self-fulfilling prophecy, "I am an insomniac, and I may never get another good night's sleep!" This internalized fear itself becomes emotionally and physiologically activating and may displace or compound the original psychologic conflicts. This additional physiologic arousal may then further aggravate the sleep problem in a circular and escalating progression that eventually establishes a conditioned pattern of chronic insomnia.[3,15,17]

While we believe that conditioning of poor sleep is an important contributing factor in the development and perpetuation of chronic insomnia, other investigators consider disturbed sleep that is conditioned as a separate diagnostic entity, psychophysiologic insomnia.[43,44] In a multi-center study, the percentage of patients with chronic insomnia who were diagnosed as having psychophysiologic insomnia ranged from 1 to 33 percent among the different sleep disorders centers.[4] We consider this extreme inconsistency between centers as indicating a lack of specificity and reliability for this diagnosis.

The striking within-group homogeneity of neurotic depressive patterns in our insomniacs also has been seen in patients with headache or psychogenic pain,[45,46] other chronic psychologic disorders. Thus, our results support the generalization that although there are a variety of "neurotic depressive roads" and internalizing patterns to insomnia, the general psychologic manifestations are remarkably similar. The homogeneity of the MMPI profiles in our chronic insomniacs is strong evidence that these patients' psychopathology is primary rather than secondary to their sleep disorder.[15,17] In contrast, patients suffering from narcolepsy/cataplexy, a chronic sleep disorder clearly of organic origin with secondary psychiatric manifestations, have heterogeneous MMPI profiles.[23]

Other Psychologic-Test Studies

Findings from other studies of personality patterns of adult insomniacs are in general agreement with ours.[8-13,47-49] Further evidence of a strong emotional component to insomnia has been provided by Monroe and Marks, who found a high level of psychopathology in adolescent insomniacs.[50-52] These authors showed that among emotionally disturbed adolescents, those who slept poorly could be differentiated from those who slept well, based on higher levels of anxiety, tension, obsession, depression, sensitivity, and somatic concerns.[50] Using norms appropriate for adolescents, they also showed that the poor sleepers had MMPI scores that were significantly higher on scales 2-D, 3-Hy, and 1-Hs, and lower on 9-Ma.[51] Moreover, psychotherapists described the emotionally disturbed poor sleepers as nervous, anxious, fearful, phobic, depressed, obsessed, shy, and as having excessive fatigue and somatic complaints.[52] In contrast, the emotionally disturbed adolescents who were good sleepers were described as impulsive, aggressive, provocative, demanding, resentful, critical, and argumentative. These findings, establishing a clear-cut dichotomy between the inhibited pattern of neuroticism in the adolescent poor sleepers and the acting-out pattern of psychopathy in the adolescent good sleepers, are consistent with our findings for adult insomniacs.[15,17]

Several studies have provided additional findings supporting the hypothesis that insomniac patients internalize their emotions, thereby becoming more physiologically aroused.[9,47-49,53] Most notable is Monroe's study of physiologic activation during sleep in "good" and "poor" sleepers.[49] Poor sleepers in his study had significantly more vasoconstriction and body movements and significantly higher rectal temperatures than good sleepers. These results indicate that poor sleepers have a higher level of physiologic activation during sleep and led Monroe to describe his poor sleepers as "more awake-like" throughout the night. The apparent higher levels of physiologic activation in the poor sleepers could well have been secondary to emotional arousal because their MMPI profiles were consistently more disturbed than those of his good sleepers. Thus, the physiologic and psychologic data in Monroe's study can be interpreted as an extension into the night of heightened daytime and presleep emotional arousal.

Similarly, Haynes and his associates in two separate studies showed that insomniacs, compared to controls, had higher levels of autonomic activity prior to sleep.[47,53] In one study insomniac college students had more manifest anxiety and higher levels of muscle tension,[47] and in the other study insomniac subjects had a higher mean heart rate.[53] Following experimentally induced presleep stress, insomniac subjects were found to have reductions in their sleep latency, whereas increases were noted for controls. These findings were interpreted as indicating that the presleep stress had disrupted the characteristic ruminative cognition of the insomniacs, leading to an improvement in sleep induction,[47] whereas, in the controls, presleep stress lengthened sleep latency.[53]

Coursey and his associates[9] found that a small group of adult insomniacs were more anxious than normals, as shown by higher scores on the Taylor Manifest Anxiety Scale.[54] Their patients were also significantly more depressed than were normal controls, as measured by the MMPI and Zung's Self-Rating Depression Scale.[55] They were also more prone to worry, especially with regard to the past and the future. The authors concluded that the insomniacs were, in general, depressed, anxious, hypochondriacal, and excessively worried. Consistent with the hypothesis of internalization, they postulated that the insomniacs' chronic, obsessive worrying is an active and self-stimulating state that may well be responsible for sleep difficulty.[9]

In a survey of nearly 300 insomniacs, Lichstein and Rosenthal similarly found that 90 percent of the subjects attributed their delayed sleep onset to "intrusive cognitions" rather than to somatic distress.[48] Cognitive factors delaying sleep included: "mind very active," thinking, worrying, planning, analyzing, and difficulty controlling disturbing thoughts at bedtime. This presleep cognition is very similar to that reported by our patients with chronic insomnia (see also Chapter 4, Onset, Clinical Characteristics, and Behavioral Correlates).

Psychiatric Diagnoses

DSM-III Diagnoses of Insomniac Patients

The *Diagnostic and Statistical Manual of Mental Disorders* (DSM-III)[21] is well suited for diagnosing the psychiatric conditions associated with insomnia. DSM-III provides specific criteria for making each diagnosis and for enhancing reliability between diagnosticians.[56-58] In addition, the multi-axial system of evaluation permits consideration of disorders that may otherwise be overlooked. Axis I includes psychiatric clinical syndromes, such as anxiety and depression. Axis II consists of personality disorders and specific personality traits, and Axis III includes physical disorders or conditions. DSM-III encourages multiple diagnoses on both Axes I and II so that conditions are fully described. It is also possible to have more than one diagnosis within a single class of disorders.[21]

To determine the prevalence and types of psychopathology in patients with chronic insomnia, we conducted general medical examinations and psychiatric interviews of 100 patients with a complaint of chronic insomnia.[19] An extensive case narrative for each subject, based on complete medical, psychiatric, and physical examinations, was reviewed by two psychiatrist-raters, who then independently assigned diagnoses to each of the cases using the DSM-III multi-axial classification. The raters did not participate in the evaluations and were blind to the conclusions of the sleep disorders team. Multiple diagnoses were established on any of the three axes as well as within an axis. Each patient was assigned a principal diagnosis based on the major focus of treatment designated by the psychiatrist-rater.

All 100 patients had at least one Axis I or Axis II diagnosis.[19] Additionally, most patients had multiple diagnoses within and between axes. Using a special measure of inter-rater agreement,[59-61] a high degree of agreement between the two raters for the principal diagnoses was found on Axis I and Axis II, 79 and 71 percent, respectively.[19] This degree of inter-rater agreement was similar to that previously reported for the original reliability studies of the DSM-III, again confirming the general reliability of this diagnostic system.[21,58] Axis I diagnoses (psychiatric disorders) were the principal diagnoses in 69 patients and additional diagnoses in 45, while Axis II diagnoses (personality disorders and traits) were principal in 26 patients and additional in 68.[19] Axis III diagnoses (physical illnesses) were principal in five cases and additional in 23; however, even the five cases with a principal diagnosis of physical illness had additional diagnoses on Axis I and/or Axis II.

Affective disorder was identified in more than two-thirds of the sample (n = 71) and was the principal diagnosis in 52 cases (Table 5.3).[19] Dysthymic disorder (depressive neurosis) was the most common of the affective disorders (n = 45), and atypical depression was the next most common (n = 14). The diagnosis of dysthymic disorder includes the previously used diagnostic categories of "neurotic" or "characterologic" depression.[21,62] Thus, patients with dysthymic dis-

Table 5.3. Diagnoses of Psychiatric Disorders in Patients with Chronic Insomnia: DSM-III (Axis I) (n = 100)

Diagnostic Class	Principal Diagnosis	Additional Diagnosis[a]	Total Number of Patients
Affective Disorders	52	22	71
Anxiety Disorders	5	10	15
Adjustment Disorders	4	1	5
Somatoform Disorders	3	15	18
Organic Mental Disorders	3	3	6
Substance Use Disorders	1	25	17
V-Codes	1	0	1
Psychosexual Disorders	0	7	7
No Axis I Diagnoses	0	0	8

a Except for 19 patients who had 22 additional diagnoses of affective disorder and 16 patients who had 25 additional diagnoses of substance use disorder, no other diagnostic categories had any patients with more than one additional diagnosis.
(From Tan et al[19])

order, in addition to manifesting symptoms of depressed mood, often are characterized by high levels of either free-floating or somatized anxiety. In our patients diagnosed as having atypical depression we find that they often claim that they do not feel depressed, but instead are preoccupied with their sleeplessness. Denial is common in insomniacs, but most of these patients eventually acknowledge their depression if the psychiatric interview is thorough enough.

We reserved the diagnosis of somatoform disorder for only those patients who believed that the physical effects of their insomnia were extremely severe. Also, many patients had a principal diagnosis of affective disorder, thus precluding the diagnosis of hypochondriasis. Despite these exclusions, the diagnosis of somatoform disorder was quite prevalent (n = 18).[19]

Only 15 patients met the diagnostic requirements for anxiety disorder, and in only five cases was this a principal diagnosis.[19] However, it must be kept in mind that in the presence of a depressive disorder diagnosis, DSM-III discourages the diagnosis of anxiety disorder.[21] Anxiety is actually extremely common among patients with chronic insomnia, but an anxiety disorder diagnosis was infrequent because 71 patients had a depressive disorder. Others have suggested that DSM-III tends to overdiagnose affective disorders.[63] This appeared to be the case in our study, primarily because dysthymic disorder was overdiagnosed at the expense of anxiety disorder.

We found a high prevalence of substance use disorder (17%); abuse of hypnotics and mixed-substance abuse were the most common types, followed by hypnotic dependence.[19] In only one case was this the principal diagnosis. Thus, it is an error to assume that substance use is a primary cause of insomnia; rather, substance abuse is usually a reliable indicator of underlying psychopathology.

Nearly all of the patients (94%) had Axis II diagnoses of either prominent personality trait or personality disorder (Table 5.4), indicating that insomniacs may have enduring maladaptive patterns of perceiving, thinking, and relating to others, which makes their condition difficult to treat. Furthermore, in close agreement with our MMPI studies,[15,17] these patients exhibited personality characteristics and traits consistent with patterns of internalization (compulsive, avoidant, dependent, schizoid, and passive-aggressive) far more often than they showed characteristics and traits of "acting-out" patterns (histrionic, narcissistic, borderline, and antisocial).[19] These findings, combined with the high prevalence of depressive diagnoses on Axis I and compulsive

Table 5.4. Diagnoses of Personality Disorders and Traits in Chronic Insomnia: DSM-III (Axis II) (n = 100)

Axis II Diagnoses	Principal Diagnosis	Additional Diagnosis	Total Number of Patients[a]
Personality Disorders			
Compulsive	7	11	18
Borderline	6	5	11
Histrionic	5	0	5
Schizoid/Schizotypal	4	3	7
Other	2	5	7
Mixed	1	6	7
Personality Traits			
Compulsive	1	27	28
Dependent	0	6	6
Avoidant	0	4	4
Other	0	12	12
No Axis II Diagnoses	0	0	6

a Each patient with an Axis II diagnosis had one personality disorder or personality trait diagnosis, except for nine patients, each of whom had one personality disorder and one personality trait diagnosis, and two other patients, each of whom had two personality trait diagnoses.
(From Tan et al[19])

personality disorders or traits on Axis II, strongly support our hypothesis that a psychophysiologic mechanism underlies insomnia. In this mechanism, internalization produces a state of constant emotional arousal, resultant physiologic activation, insomnia, fear of sleeplessness and its consequences, and more emotional arousal.

The following case history illustrates the Axis I (dysthymic disorder) and Axis II (compulsive personality disorder) diagnoses most frequently noted in our sample of patients with chronic insomnia:

Case 5. A 49-year-old, married accountant referred himself to our Sleep Disorders Clinic. He had had insomnia for nine years. He related that he had always been overly sensitive to noise and to other disruptions while he was trying to fall asleep, and that this problem became acute when his insomnia began. At that time, he was additionally beset with excessive worry and concerns relative to financial difficulties in his business.

His history revealed a troubled childhood. His father was an alcoholic and physically abusive towards him. He also recalled lying awake as a teenager and fearing that his father might call him in the middle of the night to assist in the family bakery if one of the employees had not shown up for work. More recently, in addition to persistent difficulties in getting along with his parents, he began to have marital problems. His characteristic pattern of handling conflict in close relationships was to become excessively worried and ruminative about his concerns. He could not express feelings openly and was generally pessimistic.

The mental status examination revealed an anxious and depressed person who acknowledged becoming bogged down in minutiae. During the interview, he was generally circumstantial but in an overly detailed manner. Psychological testing suggested that the patient was excessively rigid, with perfectionistic standards that often caused him performance anxiety. He was described as extremely anxious and unhappy over a lack of satisfaction with his life. Also, his concern over being able to control his impulses was manifested through compulsive behavior and a general pattern of being overcontrolled.

Other Diagnostic Studies

Some investigators who have studied patients with chronic insomnia have provided anecdotal reports or used the diagnostic classification proposed by the Association of Sleep Disorders Centers (ASDC).[43] The latter classification, which we feel is generally limited in its clinical usefulness, includes about 70 diagnoses, many of which are not well substantiated or are based on electrophysiologic criteria that have relatively little clinical significance.[64] Unlike the DSM-III, the ASDC classification does not follow a multi-axial system. Most important, this classification provides only three diagnoses to describe psychiatric conditions associated with insomnia, whereas the DSM-III has 17 major diagnostic classes and 345 individual diagnoses to describe psychiatric conditions on Axis I and II.[21]

Our finding of a high prevalence of psychiatric disorders in insomnia is seemingly at variance with studies in which the ASDC classification was used. The most striking characteristic of the largest of these studies, which involved a number of sleep clinics, was the extreme variability of the range within individual diagnoses across the various clinics.[4] For example, the prevalence of sleep apnea in insomniacs varied from 0 to 18.4 percent, and the prevalence of psychiatric disorders varied from 3.9 to 66.8 percent—a 16-fold difference between the two extremes. The extreme variation between different centers for diagnosing psychiatric disturbances in insomnia is probably due to the fact that patients who have high levels of psychologic distress are being assigned to mutually exclusive non-psychiatric diagnoses within the ASDC classification system. For example, other investigators have pointed out, and we agree, that a diagnosis of "pseudo-insomnia," a subjective complaint without objective findings, is of little benefit to the patient's evaluation and treatment.[65,66] Further, our data show that patients who would have been diagnosed as "drug and alcohol dependency" or "psychophysiological disorder" have a high prevalence of psychiatric disturbances. Accordingly, if the categories of "drug and alcohol dependency," "subjective complaint without objective findings," and "psychophysiological disorder" were included in a broader category of psychiatric diagnosis in several studies,[4,7,67,68] the total prevalence of a diagnosis of psychiatric disorder would approximate that found in our study.

Other factors help to explain the differences between our diagnostic findings and those of other investigators. In one study that showed only a 14 percent prevalence of psychiatric disorders, the investigators failed to include an adequate control group; further, psychologic tests were administered to only 56 percent of their patients.[7] It is, therefore, not surprising that they found a low prevalence of psychiatric disorders in their sample and an extremely high prevalence for sleep apnea and nocturnal myoclonus (18%). In two of the four studies employing the ASDC classification,[67,68] the prevalence of psychiatric disorders was found to be higher than in the other two studies using the same classification.[4,7] Furthermore, the investigators have questioned the validity, reliability, and clinical usefulness of the ASDC nosology.[68] Specifically, they reported being limited in detecting the full extent of existing psychopathology because this nosology includes only three diagnostic categories for all psychiatric conditions.[67]

The physician should critically analyze studies that fail to comprehensively assess possible causative or contributory psychiatric factors in chronic insomnia. Such reports may lead the physician to conclude that physiologic factors are often etiologic for this disorder (see also Chapter 3, Sleep Laboratory Studies in Insomnia), and therefore, that diagnostic sleep laboratory studies are essential to the evaluation of most patients with chronic insomnia. Our findings,[16,64,69,70] as well as those of others,[71-73] indicate that such procedures are seldom necessary for the evaluation of patients with chronic insomnia. Instead, as we discuss in Chapter 7 (Evaluation of Insomnia), we believe that the physician is best able to evaluate and treat the insomniac patient in the office setting[2,3,64,74] by taking a medical history and complete sleep history,[75] conducting a physical examination, and carefully assessing the patient's emotional status. Then, also as described in Chapter 7 (Evaluation of Insomnia), diagnosis of insomniac patients is best accomplished by using the International Classification of Diseases (ICD–9–CM)[76] combined with the DSM-III.[21]

Summary

The psychiatric factors involved in the development and persistence of insomnia have been assessed in a number of large-scale studies of stressful life events, personality patterns, and psychiatric diagnoses. Stressful life events are closely associated with the onset of chronic insomnia and are mediated by certain predisposing personality factors. When compared with controls, insomniacs tend to be more discontented, both as children and as adults; their interpersonal relations are less satisfying; and their self-concepts are comparatively poor. These patterns of personal vulnerability often lead to inadequate coping mechanisms for dealing with stress and to the development and persistence of chronic insomnia.

MMPI profiles of insomniacs' personalities demonstrate a high degree of specificity and consistency across patients. Patients with chronic insomnia exhibit high levels of psychopathology with specific personality patterns characterized by neurotic depression, rumination, chronic anxiety, inhibition of emotions, and inability to express anger. They typically handle stresses and conflicts by internalizing their emotions, which leads to emotional arousal, physiologic activation, and sleeplessness, thereby creating a vicious circle. This process is the major force underlying both the development and persistence of chronic sleep difficulty.

The high levels of psychopathology among insomniacs have been further demonstrated through diagnostic studies of these patients. In chronic insomniac patients, psychiatric diagnoses are extremely prevalent, whereas physical disorders are much less common. The most common diagnoses are dysthymic disorder (previously called neurotic or characterologic depression) and compulsive personality disorder or trait. Another indication of a high level of psychologic disturbance in chronic insomniacs is the preponderance of multiple psychiatric diagnoses. Although our findings of the high incidence of psychopathology associated with chronic insomnia seem to be at variance with other studies in which the ASDC classification of sleep disorders is used, we feel that this is a reflection of the clinical limitations of the ASDC classification, which we believe is not compatible with the multiaxial DSM-III classification system.

In summary, several types of studies conducted with chronic insomniacs have demonstrated a strong etiologic link between psychiatric factors and insomnia. Not only do these patients manage stress ineffectively; they have high levels of psychopathology, as well as homogeneous personality patterns, and, most often, one or more psychiatric diagnoses. In both psychiatric diagnostic studies and psychological testing, these patients characteristically manifest high levels of anxiety, obsessive-compulsiveness, rumination, depression, and hypochondriasis.

References

1. Kales A, Kales JD, Bixler EO: Insomnia: an approach to management and treatment. *Psychiatr Ann 4*:28–44, 1974.
2. Kales A, Soldatos CR, Kales JD: Sleep disorders: evaluation and management in the office setting, in Arieti S, Brodie HKH (eds): *American Handbook of Psychiatry*, ed 2. New York, Basic Books, 1981, vol 7, pp 423–454.
3. Soldatos CR, Kales A, Kales JD: Management of insomnia. *Ann Rev Med 30*:301–312, 1979.
4. Coleman RM, Roffwarg HP, Kennedy SJ, Guilleminault C, Cinque J, Cohn MA, Karacan I, Kupfer DJ, Lemmi H, Miles LE, Orr WC, Phillips ER, Roth T, Sassin JF, Schmidt HS, Weitzman ED, Dement WC: Sleep-wake disorders based on a polysomnographic diagnosis: a national cooperative study. *JAMA 247*:997–1003, 1982.
5. Dement WC, Guilleminault C: Sleep disorders: the state of the art. *Hosp Pract 8(11)*:57–71, 1973.
6. Dement WC, Zarcone VP: Pharmacological treatment of sleep disorders, in Barchas JD, Berger PA, Ciaranello RD, Elliott, GR (eds), *Psychopharmacology: From Theory to Practice*. New York, Oxford University Press, 1977, pp 243–259.
7. Zorick FJ, Roth T, Hartze KM, Piccione PM, Stepanski EJ: Evaluation and diagnosis of persistent insomnia. *Am J Psychiatry 138*:769–773, 1981.
8. Beutler LE, Thornby JI, Karacan I: Psychological variables in the diagnosis of insomnia, in Williams RL, Karacan I (eds): *Sleep Disorders: Diagnosis and Treatment*. New York, Wiley, 1978, pp 61–100.
9. Coursey RD, Buchsbaum M, Frankel BL: Personality measures and evoked responses in chronic insomniacs. *J Abnorm Psychol 84*:239–249, 1975.
10. Elenewski JJ: *A Study of Insomnia: The Relationship of Psychopathology to Sleep Disturbance*. University of Miami, 1971.
11. Freedman RR, Sattler HL: Physiological and psychological factors in sleep-onset insomnia. *J Abnorm Psychol 91*:380–389, 1982.

12. Piccione P, Tallarigo R, Zorick F, Wittig R, Roth T: Personality differences between insomniac and non-insomiac psychiatry outpatients. *J Clin Psychiatry* 42:261–263, 1981.
13. Roth T, Kramer M, Lutz T: The nature of insomnia: a descriptive summary of a sleep clinic population. *Compr Psychiatry* 17:217–220, 1976.
14. Healey ES, Kales A, Monroe LJ, Bixler EO, Chamberlin K, Soldatos CR: Onset of insomnia: role of life-stress events. *Psychosom Med* 43: 439–451, 1981.
15. Kales A, Caldwell AB, Preston TA, Healey S, Kales JD: Personality patterns in insomnia. *Arch Gen Psychiatry* 33:1128–1134, 1976.
16. Kales A, Bixler EO, Soldatos CR, Vela-Bueno A, Caldwell AB, Cadieux RJ: Biopsychobehavioral correlates of insomnia, I: role of sleep apnea and nocturnal myoclonus. *Psychosomatics* 23:589–600, 1982.
17. Kales A, Caldwell AB, Soldatos CR, Bixler EO, Kales JD: Biopsychobehavioral correlates of insomnia, II: pattern specificity and consistency with the Minnesota Multiphasic Personality Inventory. *Psychosom Med* 45:341–356, 1983.
18. Kales A, Bixler EO, Vela-Bueno A, Cadieux RJ, Soldatos CR, Kales JD: Biopsychobehavioral correlates of insomnia, III: polygraphic findings of sleep difficulty and their relationship to psychopathology. *Int J Neurosci* (in press).
19. Tan TL, Kales JD, Kales A, Soldatos CR, Bixler EO: Biopsychobehavioral correlates of insomnia, IV: diagnosis based on the DSM-III. *Am J Psychiatry* (in press).
20. Kales JD, Kales A, Bixler EO, Soldatos CR, Cadieux RJ, Kashurba GJ, Vela-Bueno A: Biospsychobehavioral correlates of insomnia, V: clinical characteristics and behavioral correlates. *Am J Psychiatry* (in press).
21. American Psychiatric Association: *Diagnostic and Statistical Manual of Mental Disorders (DSM-III)*, ed 3. Washington DC, American Psychiatric Association, 1980.
22. Gough H, Heibrun A: *The Adjective Check List Manual*. Palo Alto, California, Consulting Psychologists Press, 1965.
23. Kales A, Soldatos CR, Bixler EO, Caldwell A, Cadieux RJ, Verrechio JM, Kales JD: Narcolepsy-cataplexy II. Psychosocial consequences and associated psychopathology. *Arch Neurol* 39:169–171, 1982.
24. Kales A, Caldwell AB, Cadieux RJ, Vela-Bueno A, Ruch L, Mayes S: Obstructive sleep apnea, II: associated psychopathology and psychosocial consequences (in preparation).
25. Kales A, Soldatos CR, Caldwell AB, Charney DS, Kales JD, Markel D, Cadieux R: Nightmares: clinical characteristics and personality patterns. *Am J Psychiatry* 137:1197–1201, 1980.
26. Kales A, Soldatos CR, Caldwell AB, Charney DS, Kales JD, Humphrey FJ II, Schweitzer PK: Somnambulism: clinical characteristics and personality patterns. *Arch Gen Psychiatry* 37:1406–1410, 1980.
27. Kales JD, Kales A, Soldatos CR, Caldwell AB, Charney DS, and Martin ED: Night terrors: clinical characteristics and personality patterns. *Arch Gen Psychiatry* 37:1413–1417, 1980.

28. Dahlstrom WG, Welsh GS, Dahlstrom LE: *An MMPI Handbook* (vol 1). Minneapolis, University of Minnesota Press, 1972.
29. Dahlstrom WG, Welsh GS, Dahlstrom LE: *An MMPI Handbook* (vol 2). Minneapolis, University of Minnesota Press, 1975.
30. Drake LE, Oetting ER: *An MMPI Code Book for Counselors.* Minneapolis, University of Minnesota Press, 1959.
31. Gilberstadt H, Duker J: *A Handbook for Clinical and Actuarial MMPI Interpretation.* Philadelphia, Saunders, 1965.
32. Hathaway SR, McKinley JC: *The Minnesota Multiphasic Personality Inventory Manual.* New York, Psychological Corporation, 1967.
33. Hathaway SR, Meehl PE: *An Atlas for the Clinical Use of the MMPI.* Minneapolis, University of Minnesota Press, 1951.
34. Marks PA, Seeman W: *The Actuarial Description of Abnormal Personality.* Baltimore, Williams & Wilkins, 1973.
35. Swenson WM, Pearson JS, Osborne D: *An MMPI Source Book.* Minneapolis, University of Minnesota Press, 1973.
36. MacAndrew, C: The differentiation of male alcoholic outpatients from nonalcoholic psychiatric outpatients by means of the MMPI. *Q J Studies Alcohol 26*:238–246, 1965.
37. Gynther MD: Aging and personality, in Butcher, JN (ed): *New Developments in the Use of the MMPI.* Minneapolis, University of Minnesota Press, 1979, pp 39–68.
38. Hinkle LE Jr: The effect of exposure to culture change, social change, and changes in interpersonal relationships on health, in Dohrenwend, BS, Dohrenwend, BP (eds): *Stressful Life Events: Their Nature and Effects.* New York, Wiley, 1974, pp. 9–44.
39. Levi L: General discussion, in Levi L (ed): *Stress and Distress in Response to Psychosocial Stimuli.* Stockholm, Almqvist and Wiksell, 1972.
40. Levi L: Psychosocial stress and disease: a conceptual model, in Gunderson EKE, Rahe RH (eds): *Life Stress and Illness.* Springfield, Ill., Charles C Thomas, 1974.
41. Levi L: Parameters of emotion: an evolutionary and ecological approach, in Levi L (ed): *Emotions—Their Parameters and Measurement.* New York, Raven Press, 1974.
42. Suwa N, Yamashita I: *Psychophysiological Studies of Emotional and Mental Disorders.* Tokyo, Ihaku Shoin, 1974.
43. Association of Sleep Disorders Centers: Diagnostic classification of sleep and arousal disorders. *Sleep 2* (1):1–137, 1979.
44. Hauri P: Treating psychophysiologic insomnia with biofeedback. *Arch Gen Psychiatry 38*:752–758, 1981.
45. Kudrow L, Sutkus BJ: MMPI pattern specificity in primary headache disorders. *Headache 19*:18–24, 1979.
46. Strassberg DS, Reimherr F, Ward M, Russell S, Cole A: The MMPI and chronic pain. *J Consult Clin Psychol 49*:220–226, 1981.
47. Haynes SN, Follingstad DR, McGowan WT: Insomnia: sleep patterns and anxiety level. *J Psychosom Res 18*:69–74, 1974.
48. Lichstein KL, Rosenthal TL: Insomniacs' perceptions of cognitive versus

somatic determinants of sleep disturbance. *J Abnorm Psychol 89*:105–107, 1980.

49. Monroe LJ: Psychological and physiological differences between good and poor sleepers. *J Abnorm Psychol 72*:255–264, 1967.

50. Marks PA and Monroe LJ: Correlates of adolescent poor sleepers. *J Abnorm Psychol 85*:243–246, 1976.

51. Monroe LJ, Marks PA: MMPI differences between adolescent poor and good sleepers. *J Consult Clin Psychol 45*:151–152, 1977.

52. Monroe LJ, Marks PA: Psychotherapists' descriptions of emotionally disturbed adolescent poor and good sleepers. *J Clin Psychol 33*:263–269, 1977.

53. Haynes SN, Adams A, Franzen M: The effects of presleep stress on sleep-onset insomnia. *J Abnorm Psychol 90*:601–606, 1981.

54. Byrne D: Manifest anxiety, in *Introduction to Personality*. Englewood Cliffs, NJ, Prentice-Hall, 1966.

55. Zung WW: A self-rating depression scale. *Arch Gen Psychiatry 12*:63–70, 1965.

56. Spitzer RL, Endicott J, Robins E: Clinical criteria for psychiatric diagnosis and DSM-III. *Am J Psychiatry 132*:1187–1192, 1975.

57. Spitzer RL, Endicott J, Robins E: Research diagnostic criteria: rationale and reliability. *Arch Gen Psychiatry 35*:773–782, 1978.

58. Spitzer RL, Forman JBW, Nee J: DSM-III field trials: I. Initial interrater diagnostic reliability. *Am J Psychiatry 136*:815–817, 1979.

59. Cohen J: A coefficient of agreement for nominal scales. *Educational and Psychological Measurement 20*:37–46, 1960.

60. Fleiss JL: Measuring nominal scale agreement among many raters. *Psychol Bull 76*:378–382, 1971.

61. Fleiss JL: *Statistical Methods for Rates and Proportions*. New York, Wiley, 1973.

62. Akiskal HS: Dysthymic disorder: psychopathology of proposed chronic depressive subtypes. *Am J Psychiatry 140*:11–20, 1983.

63. Frances A, Cooper AM: Descriptive and dynamic psychiatry: a perspective on DSM-III. *Am J Psychiatry 138*:1198–1202, 1981.

64. Kales JD, Soldatos CR, Kales A: Diagnosis and treatment of sleep disorders, in Greist JH, Jefferson JW, Spitzer RL, (eds): *Treatment of Mental Disorders*. New York, Oxford University Press, 1982, pp 473–500.

65. Regestein QR, Reich P: Current problems in the diagnosis and treatment of chronic insomnia. *Perspect Biol Med 21*:232–239, 1978.

66. Bootzin RR, Nicassio PM: *Behavioral Treatments for Insomnia (Progress in Behavior Modification*, vol 6). New York, Academic Press, 1978, pp 1–45.

67. Reynolds CF III, Coble PA, Black RS, Holzer B, Carroll R, Kupfer DJ: Sleep disturbances in a series of elderly patients: polysomnographic findings. *J Am Geriatr Soc 28*:164–170, 1980.

68. Reynolds CF III, Shubin RS, Coble PA, Kupfer DJ: Diagnostic classifi-

cation of sleep disorders: implications for psychiatric practice. *J Clin Psychiatry 42*:296–299, 1981.

69. Bixler EO, Kales A, Soldatos CR, Vela-Bueno A, Jacoby JA, Scarone S: Sleep apneic activity in a normal population. *Res Commun Chem Pathol Pharmacol 36*:141–152, 1982.
70. Bixler EO, Kales A, Vela-Bueno A, Jacoby JA, Scarone S, Soldatos CR: Nocturnal myoclonus and nocturnal myoclonic activity in a normal population. *Res Commun Chem Pathol Pharmacol 36*:129–140, 1982.
71. Oswald I: Assessment of insomnia. *Br Med J 283*:874–875, 1981.
72. Regestein QR, Reich P: A sleep clinic within a general hospital psychiatry service. *Gen Hosp Psychiatry 2*:112–117, 1980.
73. Regestein QR, Reich P: *Sleep Bulletin*, no. 186. Los Angeles, Brain Information Service, May 1980, p 27.
74. Kales A, Kales JD, Soldatos CR: Insomnia and other sleep disorders. *Medical Clinics of North America 66*:971–991, 1982.
75. Kales A, Soldatos CR, Kales JD: Taking a sleep history. *Am Fam Physician 22*:101–108, 1980.
76. WHO Center for Classification of Diseases for North America, National Center for Health Statistics: *International Classification of Diseases, 9th Revision, Clinical Modification (ICD-9-CM)*. Ann Arbor, Mich.: Edwards Brothers, 1978.

6. Medical and Other Pathophysiologic Factors in Insomnia

Although psychologic difficulties frequently underlie chronic insomnia, many other factors cause and contribute to sleep disturbance. The aging process, situational factors, medical conditions, hospital environment, and drugs themselves may adversely affect sleep. In most cases of chronic insomnia several factors are involved, which may act simultaneously or in succession.

The causative and contributing factors of insomnia discussed in this chapter can induce transient sleeplessness or act as initiators of chronic insomnia. For example, people may abruptly alter their sleep-wake schedules in response to academic pressures or a change in employment and, as a result, sleep poorly for a short time. But if someone were particularly vulnerable to stressful life events and reacted with inadequate coping mechanisms, these same circumstances might induce long-term sleep difficulty.

The first two sources of sleep difficulty examined in this chapter, the aging process and situational disturbances, are a part of human experience and therefore eventually experienced by everyone. Three other causes of insomnia, while not ubiquitous, are common: medical conditions, effects of the hospital environment, and drugs. The latter two areas, in particular, represent potential sources for iatrogenic sleep disturbances.

Aging

Older people are predisposed to insomnia because the aging process has distinct effects on the sleep–wakefulness cycle. A full description of how age affects sleep is given in Chapter 3 (Sleep Laboratory Studies of Insomnia), so the process is explained only briefly here.

Normal Sleep and Aging

As people age, they experience changes in both their total sleep time and sleep patterns. The elderly not only sleep less and have more nocturnal awakenings than younger people, they also have virtually no stage 4 sleep.[1-12] Because this is the deepest stage of sleep, as measured by auditory awakening threshold,[13,14] its absence may help to explain why elderly people often complain that their sleep is light. Sleep laboratory evidence that the elderly sleep less at night also validates their frequent complaints of insufficient sleep. When different age groups are compared, the time spent awake each night is relatively low until age 50, then it increases rapidly and progressively; the number of nightly awakenings at age 60 is nearly three times that at age 20.[12]

Curtailed nighttime sleep, however, is offset by a tendency to take daytime naps. In one survey, subjective data showed that total sleep time decreased between ages 20 and 59, but increased after that point.[15] In spite of poor nighttime sleep, older subjects slept more in a 24-hour period than middle-aged individuals because of their midday naps. Thus, advancing age may produce a disruption of sleep-wakefulness patterns, rather than a worsening of sleep per se.

Insomnia in the Elderly

When older people have insomnia, they differ distinctly from their younger counterparts. Older insomniacs sleep less than younger insomniacs.[16] This difference is almost entirely the result of their greater wakefulness after sleep onset because sleep latency does not change substantially with age. In comparing elderly insomniacs and controls, the primary difference was the insomniacs' greater difficulty in initially falling asleep, as well as returning to sleep once having awakened during the night.

Younger and older insomniac patients also differ psychologically; personality patterns, as measured by the Minnesota Multiphasic Personality Inventory (MMPI), vary among different insomniac age groups.[17,18] Older insomniac patients tend to deny and repress their conflicts, whereas younger patients are more likely to acknowledge their anxiety and depression and recognize the connection between their insomnia and their emotional problems. Thus, older patients are more apt to overly focus on their sleeplessness and related somatic concerns and, as a result, avoid recognizing their underlying problems.

Of course, insomnia in old age can be caused by difficulties other than psychologic conflicts or age-related changes in sleep patterns. Indeed, older people's sleep is often disrupted by the pain and discomfort of medical illnesses, which are much more common among the elderly.[19-21] Sleeplessness can also be brought on by the fear, anxiety, and depression older people experience when they realize their health is declining.

Situational Disturbances

Almost everyone has experienced insomnia at one time or another, usually because of stress, environmental factors, or a change in schedule. Transient sleep difficulties may develop in reaction to such stresses as the loss of a loved one, job or academic pressures, or major life changes, such as marriage or divorce.[19,21] Environmental factors, such as overcrowding, excessive noise, or extremes in weather, also can be a source of sleep disruption (see also Chapter 8, General Measures for Treating Insomnia). Finally, wakefulness can result from a lack of physical activity or from a desynchronization of biologic rhythms, as in night-shift work or "jet lag."[22-31] Sleep difficulty arising from situational disturbances needs to be differentiated from sleep disturbances that are part of a chronic asynchrony between individuals' circadian rhythms and environmental cues, for example, the delayed sleep phase syndrome.[32]

Shift Work

Changes in sleep schedules interfere with circadian fluctuations in body temperature and mental efficiency.[22-31] These two functions normally follow a similar 24-hour curve; they decline in the early hours of sleep, begin to rise sharply before awakening and reach their peak at about 10:00 AM.[22,24,29] When the sleep schedule is abruptly changed, a significant period must pass before body temperature adjusts, efficiency is regained in tasks requiring sustained attention and judgment,[22,24,29] and sleep patterns return to normal.[24,29-31] The adjustment usually takes several days, but individuals adapt at different rates,[24,28,29] and behavioral phenomena return to normal more quickly than physiologic measures.[24,27,29]

When subjects accustomed to sleeping at night suddenly begin to sleep during the day, they sleep for a shorter time, awaken more often, and experience more changes in sleep stages.[25,26,30,31] Two weeks after this reversal of the sleep period, they continue to sleep less than when they slept at night. The type of sleep they obtain and its temporal distribution also changes; they have less REM sleep, and their propensity for REM sleep, along with that for stage 2, shifts toward the early portion of the sleep period. Time spent awake, on the other hand, moves toward the latter part of sleep.[26] Another important change induced by reversal of the sleep-wakefulness cycle is a dissociation between sleep-stage patterns and corticosteroid levels.[30,31] This dissociation can cause fatigue, daytime sleepiness, psychomotor impairment, anxiety, depression, and various somatic complaints.

Jet Travel and Other Factors

Flights from west to east are theoretically more fatigue-producing because the time shifts ahead as one travels eastward and inner circadian rhythms lag behind.[24,29] However, other factors enter into the effects of long-distance flights across time zones in either direction—these are the amount of fatigue caused by preflight rest-activity schedules, the stress of long-distance travel, the amount of sleep loss incurred, and the type of activity required on arrival.[25]

Social factors often impinge on people's sleep schedules.[22,24,26,29,33] Staying up late on weekends or napping on holidays, for example, sometimes leads to disrupted sleep patterns. A more serious problem arises when there is a strong emotional component superimposed upon the basic physiologic disturbance, as in "cramming" for exams, working through the night during a natural disaster, or serving on a war front. In such cases as these, to focus only on the physiologic aspects without considering the accompanying stress and its psychologic consequences is mechanical, superficial, and against the individual's best interests.

Medical Causes of Insomnia

Insomnia often develops when medical disorders cause pain, physical discomfort, anxiety, or depression.[19-21,34,35] In these cases, both physical and emotional factors must be considered because all disease processes evoke an emotional response. In cardiovascular disorders, for example, insomnia may be caused by anxiety and depression combined with such physical factors as anoxia-induced brain impairment. Similarly, cancer patients often have sleep difficulty because of pain, metabolic and systemic derangements, effects of irradiation, and apprehension regarding the illness and its treatment.

Cardiovascular Disorders

Patients with cardiovascular disease often have disturbed sleep. Sleep disruption may be due to episodes of nocturnal angina, the occurrence of cardiac arrhythmias, or the presence of left ventricular failure.[34,35] Nocturnal dyspnea is a major symptom of left ventricular failure; patients often obtain relief by sitting on the edge of the bed or walking about so that blood accumulates in their veins, reducing venous return to the heart.[36,37]

Patients with nocturnal angina pectoris often complain of sleep difficulty. Compared with normal sleepers, they take longer to fall asleep, have longer periods of wakefulness, and have less stages 3 and 4 sleep.[38] Similarly, patients recovering from acute myocardial infarction experience more nighttime wakefulness, more shifts in sleep stages, and less REM sleep.[39] One patient who was monitored continuously slept only slightly more than four hours during a 24-hour period[40] and spent about 90 percent of his sleep time in stage 2. A crucial point, however, is that such dramatic sleep disturbances following myocardial infarction can be caused not only by the disease itself, but also by cardiovascular and CNS drugs or the coronary-care-unit environment.

Pulmonary Disorders

Chronic Obstructive Pulmonary Disease (COPD)   Sleep disturbance is common among patients with COPD.[41-45] In one study, 20 COPD patients slept an average of less than six hours, had high levels of stage 1 sleep, and awakened frequently (about 30 times each night).[44] Because their sleep was fragmented, the subjects had little REM sleep and practically none of stages 3 and 4 sleep. Sleep apnea did not appear to be a major problem because only one patient had frequent apneic episodes (30 per night, with a mean duration of 14 seconds). Nevertheless, respiratory dysfunction worsens considerably in these patients when they sleep.[46] In one study, subjects slept poorly because of many awakenings, with a mean total sleep time of only 218 minutes.[45] Disordered breathing was found to lead to arousal or changes in sleep stages.

In COPD patients, the degree of alveolar hypoventilation increases progressively from wakefulness through the successive stages of NREM sleep with breathing dysfunction reaching its nadir during REM sleep;[41] a mean nocturnal oxygen desaturation of 26 percent has been reported.[45] As alveolar hypoventilation increases, pulmonary arterial pressure rises as well,[41] and cardiac arrhythmias may appear.

Asthma   Asthma can cause both children and adults to have difficulty sleeping.[47-49] Adult patients with asthma frequently have attacks of nocturnal dyspnea and complain of being unable to sleep properly. In fact, they do sleep less than normal subjects because they awaken often during the night and early in the morning. They also obtain less stage 4 sleep.[47] Asthmatic episodes in adults, however, do not appear to be related to particular sleep stages or time of night. In a study where 91 asthmatic episodes were observed, 73 occurred during NREM sleep and 18 during REM sleep.[47]

When asthmatic children were studied in the sleep laboratory and compared with control subjects, the children with asthma slept less, had more awakenings, and had less stage 4 sleep.[48] Of the 20 asthmatic episodes recorded, five occurred during REM sleep, a number proportionate with the amount of time spent in this sleep stage. No episodes occurred in the first third of the night, when slow-wave sleep predominated. This suggests two possibilities: respiratory difficulty diminishes during slow-wave sleep, or respiratory impairment remains constant, but there is less tendency to respond to a disturbing stimulus during the deeper stages of sleep.

Sleep Apnea   Sleep apnea is characterized by many periods of breath cessation (30 or more) during a night's sleep, each 10 seconds or longer.[50-52] There are three types of sleep apnea: central, obstructive, and mixed. In central sleep apnea there is a cessation of air flow through the nares and mouth and a simultaneous interruption of thoracic and abdominal respiratory efforts. In obstructive or "upper airway" sleep apnea, thoracic and abdominal movements continue, but air flow through the nares and mouth is interrupted. Features of both central and obstructive sleep apnea are present in mixed sleep apnea.

Some investigators have reported that patients with nocturnal breath cessations, particularly those with central sleep apnea, may complain of insomnia.[53-55] In our experience, however, these patients rarely pre-

sent with insomnia as the chief complaint even though many brief
EEG arousals are associated with sleep apneic events. In one study of
200 insomniac patients and 100 normal controls, none of the 300 subjects had sleep apnea.[56,57] Thus, insomniacs do not appear to be at high
risk for sleep apnea. Instead, middle-aged men with excessive daytime
sleepiness and obesity are particularly at high risk.[50-52]

Patients with obstructive sleep apnea, by far the most common type,
usually present with a history of excessive daytime sleepiness, sleep attacks, and nocturnal breath cessations punctuated by loud snoring and
gasping sounds.[51,52] Less common symptoms include excessive body
movements during sleep, secondary enuresis, and morning headaches.
Patients may be aware of difficulty breathing and choking, but if this
is not the case, evidence of these symptoms usually can be provided by
a bedpartner who has observed the patient's respiration.

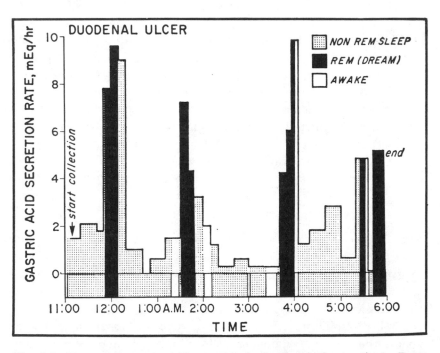

Fig. 6.1. Nocturnal gastric acid secretion in duodenal ulcer patients. Rates
are presented in terms of both time of night and sleep stage, and are representative of four of five patients. Gastric acid secretion is at relatively high
levels throughout the night with peak levels reached during periods of REM
sleep. (From Armstrong et al[59])

Gastrointestinal Disorders

Duodenal ulcer is frequently associated with sleep disturbance.[58] Patients with duodenal ulcer secrete more gastric acid than control subjects during sleep,[58-61] particularly REM sleep,[59] and this is probably responsible for their nocturnal pain and discomfort (see Figures 6.1 and 6.2). In a group of patients with active ulcer disease, 22 of 24 secretion peaks occurred during REM sleep.[59] In healthy controls, findings of a consistently low level of gastric acid secretion throughout the night were demonstrated in two studies.[59,62] In another study of patients with duodenal ulcers, gastric acid secretion was found to be episodic throughout the night but unrelated to REM periods.[63] The finding of a lack of correlation between REM sleep and gastric acid secretion may be accounted for by the use of patients with inactive ulcers (more than two months without symptoms). Also, further analyses of the data in this study demonstrate that gastric acid secretion

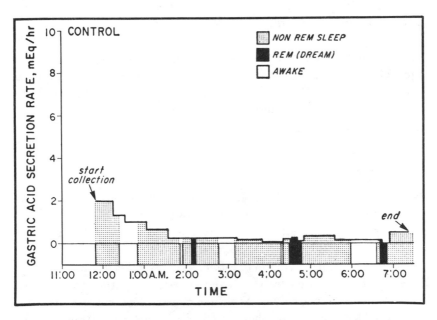

Fig. 6.2. Nocturnal gastric acid secretion in healthy controls. Rates are presented in terms of both time of night and sleep stage, and are representative of all three control subjects. Note the low levels of gastric acid secretion throughout the night. (From Armstrong et al[59])

peaks occur throughout the night in about 60–90 minute intervals. Hiatal hernia can also result in nocturnal pain and discomfort because it can induce esophageal reflux when patients are in a horizontal position.[37]

Chronic Renal Insufficiency

Patients with chronic renal insufficiency, as well as those with kidney transplants often have disturbed sleep.[64-66] In one study comparing the subjective estimates of sleep for dialysis patients and their spouses, the patients reported significantly worse sleep on non-dialysis nights.[64]

In the sleep laboratory, patients with chronic renal insufficiency and chronic uremia awaken for long periods of time from all stages of sleep and at all times of the night.[65,66] Furthermore, they get less than normal amounts of stages 3 and 4 sleep. The degree of sleep disturbance in these patients is correlated with the levels of urea in their blood.[65] Extrarenal purification by hemodialysis or peritoneal dialysis improves their sleep considerably; their sleep cycles become regular, they have fewer awakenings, and they have more slow-wave sleep. Sleep disturbance and blood urea level are positively correlated.

Patients with kidney transplants also appear to have problems sleeping.[66] When compared with control subjects, they spend more time awake, have more REM sleep periods, and obtain less stage 4 sleep. The time between sleep onset and the first REM period (REM latency) is also increased in these patients.

Eating Disorders

Anorexia Nervosa Troubled sleep is among the many problems encountered by patients with anorexia nervosa. They have difficulty falling asleep and staying asleep, and they are particularly prone to early final awakenings.[67-69] Although anorexia is associated with disturbances in mood and general emotional state, the insomnia experienced by these patients is more closely related to poor nutrition than to the psychologic dysfunction.[67,70] After treatment, anorectic patients obtain more sleep and do not have early final awakenings. Fasting also affects the type of sleep obtained; amounts of REM and stages 3 and 4 sleep are below normal prior to treatment, then increase with weight gain.[67,71,72] Stages 3 and 4 sleep reach normal levels early in the weight-gain period, but REM sleep does not change until the later stages of improvement.[68]

Obesity   Obesity seems to be related to insomnia in two ways: rapid weight loss produces sleep problems, and the "night-eating syndrome" includes insomnia as one of its symptoms.[73-75] The troubled sleep experienced by obese patients when they lose a great deal of weight subsides toward the end of treatment, when they start to eat more and gain weight.[73] In one study, 40 to 120 mg/day of fenfluramine, a nonamphetamine appetite suppressant, was associated with weight reduction and increased sleep difficulty in four slightly overweight and one extremely obese subjects.[74] It is unclear, however, whether these changes in sleep were caused by the drug or by weight reduction.

Nighttime eating behavior appears to be common among overweight patients. The "night-eating syndrome," which consists of nocturnal hyperphagia, insomnia, and morning anorexia, was identified in 18 of 25 obese patients being treated at a clinic.[75] Those with the syndrome found it extremely difficult to lose weight and had many complications and reactions during weight reduction; only six of the 25 patients reduced successfully. Most of the patients ate at night when they were gaining weight and during periods of stress. This suggests that, in people who are overweight and have sleep difficulty, both conditions may be related to an inability to cope properly with stress.

Endocrine Conditions

Thyroid Dysfunction   Sleepiness has often been noted in patients with hypothyroidism.[76,77] When monitored in the sleep laboratory, however, their sleep latency and wake time after sleep onset were similar to those of normal controls.[78] The most striking finding was their reduced amount of stages 3 and 4 sleep (slow-wave sleep). After treatment, when they had become euthyroid, the patients' levels of slow-wave sleep were no longer significantly lower than those of the controls. They also had more frequent alpha waves and improved intellectual performance on psychologic testing. It is also of note that in hypothyroid infants, sleep-spindle formation is impaired.[79]

Hyperthyroidism has an opposite effect on slow-wave sleep.[80,81] Dramatic increases in these sleep stages were found in one study, where slow-wave sleep accounted for up to 70 percent of hyperthyroid patients' total sleep time.[80] In normal subjects, it is rare for the combined values for stages 3 and 4 sleep to exceed 25 percent. After treatment resulted in a euthyroid condition, the abnormally high percentages of these sleep stages began to approach normal levels.

Pregnancy   Sleep laboratory studies of pregnant women show that the amounts and types of sleep they obtain vary during the different stages of pregnancy.[82-84] During early pregnancy, women tend to sleep longer, take more naps, and complain of being sleepy.[82,83] In the second trimester, their sleep essentially returns to normal. However, the later stages of pregnancy are characterized by difficulty falling asleep and numerous nocturnal awakenings. Stage 4 sleep is also suppressed at this time, and may be nearly absent in the last trimester of pregnancy.[82-84] Subjective accounts confirm sleep difficulty in late pregnancy; in 100 women who were more than 38 weeks pregnant, 68 reported changes in their sleep, most of them during the last trimester.[85] In most cases, these sleep difficulties were caused by physiologic discomfort rather than by psychologic factors.

After parturition, sleep worsens and then gradually returns to normal. On the first postpartum night, women spend much more time awake and have considerably less REM sleep.[82,83] Sleep disturbance diminishes considerably by the third postpartum night, and about two to three weeks after parturition, sleep patterns return to normal. In a few cases, however, total sleep time and stage 4 levels do not return to normal until four to six weeks postpartum. Emotional disturbances during pregnancy and the postpartum period are very common, and the possible correlation of sleep disturbance with postpartum psychosis is of special clinical importance.

Neurologic Conditions

Headaches   Migraine headaches appear to occur in relation to sleep; patients with migraine frequently awaken at night or in the morning with a headache.[86] Sleep-laboratory studies have shown that nocturnal migraines and cluster headaches are associated with REM sleep.[87] Of 19 nighttime migraine headaches that occurred in one study, 17 began either during a REM period or shortly before or after one. It may be that the pain-arousal threshold is lowered during REM sleep because the auditory awakening threshold is lower during REM sleep than during stages 2, 3, or 4.[88]

Methysergide, used by some patients to prevent migraine headaches of a vascular type, can cause sleeplessness. Even though it often prevents headaches, about 20 percent of patients discontinue the drug because of its side effects, including insomnia. This effect of the drug might be related to its action as a serotonin antagonist.[89]

Parkinson's Disease   Sleep disturbances are common among Parkinsonian patients; these patients frequently have difficulty in both falling and staying asleep,[90-92] while, in a few cases, there may be excessive daytime sleepiness.[90] In one study, treatment with levodopa resulted in general clinical improvement of a group of Parkinsonian patients but did not improve their sleep difficulty.[92] As patients with Parkinson's disease improve with levodopa administration, they may become aware of sleep difficulties that actually pre-existed, thereby incorrectly implicating the drug treatment as a cause of their insomnia. A non-intention tremor is characteristic of Parkinson's disease. Although Parkinson's tremor usually disappears following sleep onset, it may return during incomplete arousals from sleep.[93]

Neuropathologic States   A number of experimental studies in animals have identified some of the mechanisms underlying sleep and wakefulness. The role of the ascending reticular activating system in maintaining an activated cortical EEG and alert behavior is well established.[94,95] Moruzzi and his co-workers further showed the importance of the bulbar reticular formation for the normal occurrence of EEG slow-wave sleep.[94] However, Clemente and Sterman[96] have also stressed the involvement of a basal forebrain cortical inhibitory system in the regulation of this sleep phase. Additionally, Jouvet has demonstrated the necessary integrity of the rostral pons for the appearance of REM sleep.[97]

The structures of the human brain involved in waking and sleeping have been, within limits, specified by findings from neurosurgical exploration and neuropathologic studies.[98-109] However, it must be kept in mind that the importance of a particular brain region in regard to a given function does not in any way imply that this is the only part of the brain involved in determining sleep and wakefulness, because their regulation is the result of the mutual interaction of many brain structures.[109]

Arousing and activating systems in the brain are largely concentrated in the junction between the rostral midbrain and the posterior diencephalon.[90] Destruction of this area is always followed by deep coma, and the patient is unarousable, both clinically and electroencephalographically;[99,100,103] this behavior is similar to that observed in cats with a midbrain transection ("cerveau isole").[90] Lesions of the posterior hypothalamus sparing the midbrain reticular formation produce the most typical cases of hypersomnia.[98,104,106] Further, lesions involving extensive cortical areas cause loss of both consciousness and arousal reaction.[101]

Sleep-inducing areas of the brain are located close to those involved in wakefulness. Insomnia has been observed after lesions to the thalamus, which suggests that these structures have a sleep-inducing influence.[108] Further, thalamotomized patients show a significant reduction of spindle activity following surgery,[108] suggesting a prominent role for the thalamus in sleep mechanisms. A lesion of the ventral pons interrupting the descending motor pathways but sparing the brain stem reticular-activating system causes the "locked-in" syndrome;[105,107] these patients are tetraplegic but are fully awake and alert with hyposomnia or insomnia.

Broughton[93] has summarized von Economo's description of two groups of patients in his classical reports on encephalitis lethargica.[102] One group of patients was hypersomnic or comatose and had pathology mainly of mesencephalic or diencephalic origin. The other group of patients, who displayed excessive movements, unresponsiveness, and an inability to sleep, had lesions predominantly in the area of the preoptic nucleus.[93]

Table 6.1 lists medical conditions that frequently result in disturbed sleep.

Sleep Disruption in the Hospital Environment

Patients who are about to undergo surgery or who have recently experienced surgery often have seriously disrupted sleep.[110-115] Their insomnia can be caused by the physical and psychologic effects of the procedure itself, the effects of anesthetic agents and other medications, frequent interruptions by medical and nursing personnel, and the general noise and activity level of the hospital environment.

In one study, patients were evaluated both before and after elective surgery; eight had a hernia repair and four had either a gastrectomy or highly selective vagotomy.[110] Preoperatively, the mean duration of sleep in this group was just under six hours; those patients anticipating

Table 6.1. Medical Conditions Associated with Sleep Disturbance

Cardiovascular Disorders
   Coronary insufficiency
   Left ventricle failure
   Cardiac arrhythmias
Pulmonary Disorders
   Chronic obstructive pulmonary disease
   Asthma
   Sleep apnea
Gastrointestinal Disorders
Chronic Renal Insufficiency
Eating Disorders
   Anorexia nervosa
   Obesity
Endocrine Conditions
   Thyroid dysfunction
   Pregnancy
Neurologic Conditions
   Headaches
   Parkinson's disease
   Thalamic lesions

major surgical procedures slept less well than those scheduled for hernia repair. After surgery, the patients slept on average about 40 minutes less than they did on the preoperative baseline nights. All of the patients who had hernia repairs had markedly suppressed REM sleep on the first postoperative night, while none of the gastrectomy patients had any REM sleep. Patients who have undergone cardiac surgery also have a loss of REM sleep.[111] This suppression of REM sleep in patients who have had major surgery may be caused by the higher doses and more prolonged administration of anesthetic agents, analgesics, and other medications.[110]

The many interruptions imposed upon surgical patients during the night are extremely disruptive to their sleep.[114,115] In one study that assessed the sleep of patients following heart surgery, the mean number of potential interruptions of sleep varied from 59.5 on the first night after surgery to 5.5 on the eighth postoperative night.[115] The most common disruptions were monitoring of vital signs and measures related to promoting respiration. In another study, interactions between hospital staff and patient numbered highest on the first day after surgery, with up to 56 interactions in eight hours.[114] During the first three days after surgery, each patient was interrupted at least once every hour.

These findings have motivated investigators to suggest ways of reducing the number of interruptions while still providing adequate, intensive-care nursing.[111-116] Ideas for minimizing interruptions include: distinguishing between essential and non-essential tasks; reorganizing nursing procedures, such as routine monitoring of vital signs, to allow a maximum amount of uninterrupted sleep; informing other personnel about why they should not interrupt a patient's sleep unnecessarily; and minimizing stimuli by dimming lights, muting telephones, and providing privacy.

Drug-Induced Insomnia

Drugs can cause insomnia either while they are being taken or after their withdrawal (Table 6.2). A patient's current drug regimen and previous responses to drugs and their withdrawal are therefore crucial aspects of a thorough evaluation and important guides to treatment.

Certain drugs' direct effects on the CNS may cause insomnia. For example, amphetamines and other CNS stimulants that are taken to suppress appetite, to control narcolepsy, and for other conditions are more likely to cause insomnia if they are taken close to bedtime.[19,117,118] Steroid preparations can also cause acute and severe insomnia,[119] as illustrated in the following case report.

> *Case 1.* A 59-year-old woman requested evaluation of chronic insomnia that had begun 11 years earlier. At age 48 she developed thyroiditis, was placed on corticosteroid therapy, and shortly thereafter began to experience severe insomnia. After four months, the steroids were discontinued, but the insomnia persisted.
>
> Our evaluation led us to propose that the use of steroid medication had precipitated the patient's insomnia, but that sleeplessness continued because of significant psychologic conflicts in her life. This hypothesis was supported by the fact that the patient's response to stress contrasted with those of her two sisters, both of whom had intermittently received corticosteroid therapy for a collagen disease. Both women developed insomnia while on steroid therapy, but their sleep improved notably whenever the medication was discontinued.

Other drugs can cause insomnia through their side effects (Table 6.2). Drugs used in the treatment of hypertension, such as propranolol,[120,121] methyldopa,[122,123] and rauwolfia,[124] frequently produce insomnia. Methysergide, a serotonin-blocking drug that is used to prevent severe migraine, also causes side effects of overstimulation and

Table 6.2. Drug-Induced Insomnia

Drug Administration
    CNS stimulants
    Steroids
    Bronchodilators
    Beta-blockers
    Methyldopa
    Rauwolfia
    Energizing antidepressants
    Methysergide
    Short half-life benzodiazepines

Drug Withdrawal
    Non-benzodiazepine hypnotics
    Short and intermediate half-life benzodiazepines

---

insomnia.[89] Because of their stimulant effects on the CNS, the broncho-dilating drugs, which contain ephedrine, theophylline, and norepinephrine, can lead to sleep difficulties.[125] Other drugs that may cause insomnia are monoamine-oxidase inhibitors used in the treatment of depression,[126] as well as energizing tricyclic antidepressants, such as imipramine and protriptyline,[127] and second generation antidepressants, such as nomifensine[128] (see also chapter 11, Use of Antidepressants in Treating Insomnia).

It is important not to overlook the stimulant properties of caffeine in coffee and colas. The use of caffeine may prolong the time needed to fall asleep and increase wakefulness during the night.[129,130] Cigarette smoking also affects sleep,[131] probably because it increases the secretion of epinephrine.[132,133] We found that people who smoke on a regular basis sleep poorly, and when they abruptly stop smoking, their sleep improves moderately.[131]

Hypnotic Drugs

We have described three types of insomnia that are related to the withdrawal of hypnotic drugs: drug withdrawal insomnia,[134] early morning insomnia,[135] and rebound insomnia.[136-138]

Drug Withdrawal Insomnia This sleep disturbance is part of the general abstinence syndrome that follows the abrupt withdrawal of non-benzodiazepine hypnotics that have been taken in large nightly doses for a long time. People with this syndrome have severe difficulty falling asleep, their sleep is fragmented and disrupted, and they have an increase in REM sleep (REM rebound).[134]

Drug withdrawal insomnia is the result of both a psychologic process and physiologic changes that are induced by drug withdrawal.[134] When patients abruptly stop using a non-benzodiazepine hypnotic drug that has been taken in large nightly doses for a prolonged period, they frequently feel apprehensive about being able to sleep without the drug. They also are affected physically by an abstinence syndrome that includes jitteriness and nervousness. The insomnia that evolves from this combination can be severe, especially in terms of difficulty in falling asleep.

Patients' sleeplessness is often further aggravated by sleep and dream alterations induced by hypnotic-drug withdrawal; "rebound" increases in REM sleep are often associated with intensified and more frequent dreaming, and sometimes nightmares. Patients may experience altered sleep and dream patterns and drug withdrawal insomnia even on nights when they have taken the drug but have slept past its duration of action.[134]

Early Morning Insomnia and Daytime Anxiety   Early morning insomnia is a significant increase in wakefulness during the final hours of the night on which a rapidly eliminated hypnotic has been taken.[135] This condition occurs even if the drug has been taken in single, nightly doses for relatively short-term periods. Early morning insomnia typically appears after the drug has been taken nightly for one or two weeks, when tolerance begins to develop and the drug begins to lose its effectiveness. As tolerance develops to the rapidly eliminated drug, sleep generally continues to be improved during the first two-thirds of the night, but it worsens significantly during the last third of the night. Early morning insomnia may not be specific to benzodiazepines because it is known that other rapidly eliminated drugs, such as alcohol, can disrupt sleep.[139,140] Daytime anxiety is a corollary of early morning insomnia; it consists of an increase in levels of tension and anxiety on days following nights of drug administration.[135,141,142]

The following case history illustrates the clinical difficulties that may occur when a patient experiences early morning insomnia and daytime anxiety while taking a hypnotic drug:

Case 2. A 33-year-old woman called the Sleep Disorders Clinic for information regarding the possible side effects of the sleep medication she had been taking. She indicated that several weeks previously her physician had prescribed triazolam (Halcion), 0.5 mg, for a transient sleep disturbance. During the first week, she took the drug nightly and her sleep was improved. However, she did experience an episode of amnesia that lasted for several hours during one of the days following drug use. Although this was upsetting to her, she continued to take the medication, but after about one week of nightly use, she began to experience difficulty staying asleep during the last several hours of her usual sleep period. She was particularly distressed by the fact that she began to be extremely "jumpy and irritable" during the day. Consequently, she stopped taking the medication and noted an improvement in her daytime mood. Two days before calling the clinic, she again took the drug on one occasion. When she awoke the next day, she found that she was extremely anxious, stating, "I couldn't stand myself." She indicated that when she first began to experience worsened sleep and daytime mood during drug use, she attributed it to her emotional status and not to the drug because the side effects were the opposite of the drug's expected effects. But after discussing her sleep difficulties and daytime anxieties with her husband, she began to question whether it was actually the drug itself that had caused the changes.

Rebound Insomnia and Rebound Anxiety   Rebound insomnia is a specific type of insomnia that follows withdrawal of benzodiazepine drugs that have short or intermediate half-lives.[136-138] When these drugs are withdrawn, wakefulness can increase above baseline levels, even if the drug has been taken in single, nightly doses for short-term periods. The frequency and intensity of rebound insomnia are strongly related to the half-life of the drug. If the benzodiazepine withdrawn has a short half-life (eg, midazolam[143] and triazolam[144-148]), rebound insomnia usually occurs and is severe. With benzodiazepines of intermediate half-life, rebound insomnia often occurs following withdrawal and is of moderate intensity. Withdrawal of benzodiazepines with a long half-life seldom produces withdrawal sleep disturbance, and then only of a mild degree.[138,149,150] Because benzodiazepine hypnotics with relatively short half-lives produce frequent and severe rebound phenomena both during administration and especially following withdrawal, we believe that these drugs may have a greater potential than intermediate or long half-life benzodiazepine hypnotics for reinforcing drug-taking behavior and producing hypnotic drug dependence.

Summary

The aging process, situational factors, medical conditions, hospital environment, and the administration and withdrawal of certain drugs may adversely affect sleep. Older people are predisposed to sleep disruption because the aging process has distinct effects on the quantity as well as the quality of sleep; the elderly have many nocturnal awakenings with a reduction in total sleep time at night and virtually no stage 4 sleep.

Situational disturbances that result in sleep disruption are ubiquitous and may include marital-, family-, and job-related stresses, environmental factors, and changes in sleep-wakefulness schedules. In nightshift work or the jet-lag syndrome, wakefulness can result from a desynchronization of biologic rhythms secondary to abrupt changes in sleep–wakefulness schedules; sleep is shorter in duration and interrupted by frequent awakenings, and the circadian rhythms for body temperature and mental efficiency are altered with resultant impairments in vigilance, attention, and general performance.

In all medical conditions, both physical and emotional factors need to be considered. Insomnia is most likely to be associated with those medical disorders with a greater degree of pain, anxiety, depression or general discomfort. Cardiovascular disorders, such as coronary insufficiency, left ventricular failure and cardiac arrhythmias, are frequently associated with disrupted sleep. In certain pulmonary disorders, breathing dysfunction may occur during sleep (sleep apnea) or be accentuated by sleep (chronic obstructive pulmonary disease). In both sleep apnea and chronic obstructive pulmonary disease, as well as in other pulmonary disorders such as childhood or adult asthma, sleep is severely disrupted by frequent awakenings and shifts in sleep stages. The nocturnal pain of patients with duodenal ulcers may be related to peaks in gastric acid secretion noted to occur during sleep. Eating disorders can also affect sleep; weight loss is associated with disrupted sleep and weight gain with improved sleep. In pregnancy, particularly the later stages, sleep is often seriously disrupted. Other conditions that may result in sleep disruption and sleep loss include chronic renal insufficiency, hyperthyroidism, Parkinson's disease, and pain states, such as headaches.

The hospital environment itself may contribute to sleep difficulty. Anxiety and pain related to various surgical and diagnostic procedures, the effects of anesthetic agents and other medications, frequent interruptions by medical personnel, and the general noise and activity level of the hospital environment are all contributing factors.

Finally, certain drugs, when administered or withdrawn, may result in sleep disturbances. Stimulants, steroids, bronchodilators, energizing antidepressants, monoamine oxidase inhibitors, beta-adrenergic receptor blockers, and other drugs used in hypertension may often cause insomnia. Also, it has been well established that abrupt withdrawal of non-benzodiazepines and benzodiazepine agents, after the use of high doses or prolonged use or both, results in an abstinence withdrawal syndrome that includes drug withdrawal insomnia. More recently, two withdrawal syndromes have been identified as occurring with benzodiazepine drugs, even with the use of only single nightly doses for relatively short periods of time. One of these syndromes, early morning insomnia and daytime anxiety, occurs during the administration of rapidly eliminated sedative-hypnotic drugs and consists, respectively, of a significant worsening of sleep late in the sleep period, and associated increases in tension and anxiety during the next day. Rebound insomnia and rebound anxiety, the second of these withdrawal syndromes, is more specific to benzodiazepine drugs; it frequently occurs and is of an intense degree following the abrupt withdrawal of benzodiazepines with short half-lives.

References

1. Agnew HW Jr, Webb WW, Williams RR: Sleep patterns in late middle aged males: an EEG study. *Electroencephalogr Clin Neurophysiol* 23:168–171, 1967.
2. Bixler EO, Kales A, Jacoby JA, Soldatos CR, Vela-Bueno A: Nocturnal sleep and wakefulness: effects of age and sex in normal sleepers. *Int J Neurosci* (in press).
3. Feinberg I: Changes in sleep cycle patterns with age. *J Psychiatric Res* 10:283–306, 1974.
4. Feinberg I, Carlson V: Sleep variables as a function of age in man. *Arch Gen Psychiatry* 18:239–250, 1968.
5. Hayashi Y, Endo S: All-night sleep polygraphic recordings of healthy aged persons: REM and slow-wave sleep. *Sleep* 5:277–283, 1982.
6. Kahn E, Fisher C: The sleep characteristics of the normal aged male. *J Nerv Ment Dis* 148:477–494, 1969.
7. Kales A, Wilson T, Kales JD, Jacobson A, Paulson MJ, Kollar E, Walter RD: Measurements of all-night sleep in normal elderly persons: effects of aging. *J Am Geriatr Soc* 15:405–414, 1967.
8. Prinz PN: Sleep patterns in the healthy aged: relationship with intellectual function. *J Gerontol* 32:179–186, 1977.
9. Roffwarg H, Muzio J, Dement W: Ontogenetic development of the human sleep-dream cycle. *Science* 152:604–619, 1966.
10. Webb WB: Sleep in older persons: sleep structures of 50- to 60-year-old men and women. *J Gerontol* 37:581–586, 1982.

11. Williams RL, Agnew HW Jr, Webb WB: Sleep patterns in young adults: an EEG study. *Electroencephalogr Clin Neurophysiol* 17:376–381, 1964.
12. Williams RL, Karacan I, Hursch CJ: *EEG of Human Sleep: Clinical Applications.* New York, Wiley, 1974.
13. Rechtschaffen A, Hauri P, Zeitlin M: Auditory awakening thresholds in REM and NREM sleep stages. *Percept Mot Skills* 22:927–942, 1966.
14. Zepelin H: Normal age-related change in sleep, in Chase MH, Weitzman, ED (eds): *Sleep Disorders: Basic and Clinical Research.* New York, Spectrum Publications, Inc, 1983, pp 431–444.
15. Tune GS: Sleep and wakefulness in normal human adults. *Br Med J* 2:269–271, 1968.
16. Kales A, Bixler EO, Vela-Bueno A, Cadieux RJ, Soldatos CR, Kales JD: Biopsychobehavioral correlates of insomnia, III: polygraphic findings of sleep difficulty and relation to psychopathology. *Int J Neurosci* (in press).
17. Kales A, Caldwell AB, Preston TA, Healey S, Kales JD: Personality patterns in insomnia: theoretical implications. *Arch Gen Psychiatry* 33:1128–1134, 1976.
18. Kales A, Caldwell AB, Soldatos CR, Bixler EO, Kales JD: Biopsychobehavioral correlates of insomnia, II: MMPI pattern specificity and consistency. *Psychosom Med* 45:341–356, 1983.
19. Kales A, Soldatos CR, Kales JD: Sleep disorders: evaluation and management in the office setting, in Arieti S, Brodie HKH (eds): *American Handbook of Psychiatry*, ed 2. New York, Basic Books, 1981, vol VII, pp 423–454.
20. Reynolds CF III, Coble PA, Black RS, Holzer B, Carroll R, Kupfer DJ: Sleep disturbances in a series of elderly patients: polysomnographic findings. *J Am Geriatr Soc* 28:164–170, 1980.
21. Soldatos CR, Kales A, Kales JD: Management of insomnia. *Ann Rev Med* 30:301–312, 1979.
22. Colquhoun WP, Blake MJF, Edwards RS: Experimental studies of shift work I: a comparison of rotating and stabilized 4-hour shift systems. *Ergonomics* 11:437–453, 1968.
23. Hauty GT, Adams T: Phase shifts of the human circadian system and performance deficit during the periods of transition: II. West-East flight. *Aerospace Med* 37:1027–1033, 1966.
24. Johnson LC, Tepas DI, Colquhoun, WP, Colligan MJ: *Biological Rhythms, Sleep and Shift Work* (Weitzman ED [series ed]: *Advances in Sleep Research*. Vol 7). New York, SP Medical and Scientific Books, 1981.
25. Klein KE, Bruner H, Holtmann H, Rehme H, Stolze J, Steinhoff WD, Wegmann HM: Circadian rhythm of pilots' efficiency and effects of multiple time zone travel. *Aerospace Med* 41:125–132, 1970.
26. Kripke DF, Cook B, Lewis OF: Sleep of night workers: EEG recordings. *Psychophysiology* 7:377–384, 1971.
27. McFarland RA: Air travel across time zones. *Am Sci* 63:23–30, 1975.

28. Mills JN: Air travel and circadian rhythm. *J R Coll Physicians Lond* 7:122–131, 1973.

29. Moore-Ede MC, Sulzman FM, Fuller CA: *The Clocks That Time Us.* Cambridge, Harvard University Press, 1982.

30. Weitzman ED, Kripke DF: Experimental 12-hour shift of the sleep-wake cycle in man: effects on sleep and physiologic rhythms, in Johnson LC, Tepas DI, Colquhoun WP, Colligan MJ (eds): *Biological Rhythms, Sleep and Shift Work* (Weitzman ED [series ed]: *Advances in Sleep Research,* vol 7). New York, SP Medical and Scientific Books, 1981, pp 93–110.

31. Weitzman ED, Kripke DF, Goldmacher D, McGregor P, Nogeire C: Acute reversal of the sleep-waking cycle in man. *Arch Neurol* 22:483–489, 1970.

32. Weitzman ED, Czeisler CA, Coleman RM, Spielman AJ, Zimmerman JC, Dement WC, Richardson GS, Pollak CP: Delayed sleep phase syndrome: a chronobiologic disorder with sleep onset insomnia. *Arch Gen Psychiatry* 38:737–746, 1981.

33. Webb WB, Agnew HW: Are we chronically sleep deprived? *Psychonomic Science* 6:47–48, 1975.

34. Kales JD, Kales A: Nocturnal psychophysiological correlates of somatic conditions and sleep disorders. *Int J Psychiatry Med* 6:43–62, 1975.

35. Williams RL: Sleep disturbances in various medical and surgical conditions, in Williams RL, Karacan I, Frazier SH (eds): *Sleep Disorders: Diagnosis and Treatment.* New York: Wiley, 1978, pp 285–302.

36. Robin ED: Some interrelations between sleep and disease. *Arch Int Med* 102:669–675, 1958.

37. Simpson RG: Nocturnal disorders of medical interest. *The Practitioner* 202:259–268, 1969.

38. Karacan I, Williams RL, Taylor WJ: Sleep characteristics of patients with angina pectoris. *Psychosomatics* 10:280–284, 1969.

39. Broughton R, Baron R: Sleep patterns in the intensive care unit and on the ward after acute myocardial infarction. *Electroencephalogr Clin Neurophysiology* 45:348–360, 1978.

40. Deamer RM, Scharf M, Kales A: Sleep patterns in the coronary care unit. *U.S. Navy Med* 59:19–23, 1972.

41. Coccagna G, Lugaresi E: Arterial blood gases and pulmonary and systemic arterial pressure during sleep in chronic obstructive pulmonary disease. *Sleep* 1:117–124, 1978.

42. Fleetham J, West P, Mezon B, Conway W, Roth T, Kryger M: Sleep, arousals, and oxygen desaturation in chronic obstructive pulmonary disease. *Am Rev Respir Dis* 126:429–433, 1982.

43. Flick MR, Block AJ: Continuous in vivo monitoring of arterial oxygenation in chronic obstructive lung disease. *Ann Intern Med* 86:725, 1977.

44. Giblin E, Garmon A, Anderson S, Kline N, DeLancey D: Characteris-

tics of sleep and incidence of apnea in patients with chronic obstructive pulmonary disease. *Sleep Res 9*:198, 1980.

45. Wynne JW, Block AJ, Boysen PG Jr: Oxygen desaturation in sleep: sleep apnea and COPD. *Hospital Practice 15*:77–85, 1980.

46. Pierce AK, Jarrett CE, Werkle G, Miller WF: Respiratory function during sleep in patients with chronic obstructive lung disease. *J Clin Invest 45*:631–636, 1966.

47. Kales A, Beall GN, Bajor GF, Jacobson A, Kales JD: Sleep studies in asthmatic adults: relationship of attacks to sleep stage and time of night. *J Allergy 41*:164–173, 1968.

48. Kales A, Kales JD, Sly RM, Scharf MB, Tan TL, Preston TA: Sleep patterns of asthmatic children: all-night electroencephalographic studies. *J Allergy 46*:300–308, 1970.

49. Montplaisir J, Walsh J, Malo JL: Nocturnal asthma: features of attacks, sleep and breathing patterns. *Am Rev Respir Dis 125*:18–22, 1982.

50. Gastaut H, Tassinari CA, Duron B: Polygraphic study of the episodic diurnal and nocturnal (hypnic and respiratory) manifestations of the Pickwick syndrome. *Brain Res 2*:167–186, 1966.

51. Guilleminault C, Dement WC (eds): *Sleep Apnea Syndromes*. New York, Alan R. Liss, Inc., 1978.

52. Lugaresi E, Coccagna G, Mantovani M: *Hypersomnia with Periodic Apneas* (Weitzman ED [series ed]: *Advances in Sleep Research*, vol 4). New York, SP Medical and Scientific Books, 1978.

53. Dement WC, Zarcone VP: Pharmacological treatment of sleep disorders, in Barchas JD, Berger PA, Ciaranello RD, Elliott GR (eds): *Psychopharmacology: From Theory to Practice*. New York, Oxford University Press, 1977, pp 243–259.

54. Guilleminault C, Eldridge FL, Dement WC: Insomnia with sleep apnea: a new syndrome. *Science 181*:856–858, 1973.

55. Zorick FJ, Roth T, Hartze KM, Piccione PM, Stepanski EJ: Evaluation and diagnosis of persistent insomnia. *Am J Psychiatry 138*:769–773, 1981.

56. Bixler EO, Kales A, Soldatos CR, Vela-Bueno A, Jacoby JA, Scarone S: Sleep apneic activity in a normal population. *Res Commun Chem Pathol Pharmacol 36*:141–152, 1982.

57. Kales A, Bixler EO, Soldatos CR, Vela-Bueno A, Caldwell AB, Cadieux RJ: Biopsychobehavioral correlates of insomnia, I: role of sleep apnea and nocturnal myoclonus. *Psychosomatics 23*:589–600, 1982.

58. Dragstedt LR: Cause of peptic ulcer. *JAMA 169*:203–209, 1959.

59. Armstrong RH, Burnap DB, Jacobson A, Kales A, Ward S, Golden J: Dreams and gastric secretions in duodenal ulcer patients. *The New Physician 14*:241–243, 1965.

60. Levin E, Kirsner JB, Palmer WL, Butler C: The variability and periodicity of the nocturnal gastric secretion in normal individuals. *Gastroenterology 10*:939–951, 1948.

61. Wolff P, Levine J: Nocturnal gastric secretions of ulcer and nonulcer patients under stress. *Psychosom Med 17*:218–226, 1955.

62. Stacher G, Presslich B, Starker H: Gastric acid secretion and sleep stages during natural night sleep. *Gastroenterology 68*:1449–1455, 1955.

63. Orr WC, Hall WH, Stahl ML, Durkin MG, Whitsett TL: Sleep patterns and gastric acid secretion in duodenal ulcer disease. *Arch Intern Med 136*:655–660, 1976.

64. Daly RJ, Hassall C: Reported sleep on maintenance haemodialysis. *Br Med J 2*:508–509, 1970.

65. Passouant P, Cadhilhac J, Baldy-Moulinier M, Mion CH: Etude du sommeil nocturne chez des uremiques chroniques soumis a une epuration extrarenale. *Electroencephalogr Clin Neurophysiol 29*:441–449, 1970.

66. Karacan I, Williams RL, Bose J, Hursch CJ, Warson SR: Insomnia in hemodialytic and kidney transplant patients. *Psychophysiology 9*:137, 1972.

67. Crisp AH, Stonehill E, Fenton GW: The relationship between sleep, nutrition and mood: a study of patients with anorexia nervosa. *Postgrad Med J 47*:207–213, 1971.

68. Lacey JH, Crisp AH, Kalucy RS, Hartmann MK, Chen CN: Weight gain and the sleeping electroencephalogram: study of 10 patients with anorexia nervosa. *Br Med J 4*:556–558, 1975.

69. Neil JF, Merikangas JR, Foster FG, Merikangas KR, Spiker DG, Kupfer DJ: Waking and all-night sleep EEG's in anorexia nervosa. *Clin Electroenceph 11*:9–15, 1980.

70. Crisp AH: Sleep, activity, nutrition and mood. *Br J Psychiatry 137*: 1–7, 1980.

71. Karacan I, Rosenbloom AC, Londono JH, Salis PJ, Thornby JI, Williams RL: The effect of acute fasting on sleep and the sleep-growth hormone response. *Psychosomatics 14*:33, 1973.

72. Parker CC, Rossman LG, Vanderlaan EF: Persistence of rhythmic human growth hormone release during sleep in fasted and nonisocalorically fed normal subjects. *Metabolism 21*:241–252, 1972.

73. Crisp AH, Stonehill E: Sleep patterns, daytime activity, weight changes and psychiatric status: a study of three obese patients. *J Psychosom Res 14*:353–358, 1970.

74. Lewis SA, Oswald I, Dunleavy DLF: Chronic fenfluramine administration: some cerebral effects. *Br Med J 3*:67–70, 1971.

75. Stunkard AJ, Grace WJ, Wolff HG: The night-eating syndrome: a pattern of food intake among certain obese patients. *Am J Med 19*:78–86, 1955.

76. Ord WM: On myxoedema, a term proposed to be applied to an esential condition in the "cretinoid" affection occasionally observed in middle-aged women. *Trans Roy Med Chir Soc 61*:57–78, 1878.

77. Ord WM: A case of hyperpyrexia in acute rheumatism treated by icepack. *Trans of Committee of Clin Soc of London.* (Suppl to vol 21), 182–186, 1888.

78. Kales A, Heuser G, Jacobson A, Kales JD, Hanley J, Zweizig JR,

Paulson MJ: All-night sleep studies in hypothyroid patients, before and after treatment. *J Clin Endocrinol Metabol* 27:1593–1599, 1967.

79. Schultz MA, Schulte FJ, Akiyama Y, Parmelee AH Jr: Development of electroencephalographic sleep phenomena in hypothyroid infants. *Electroenceph Clin Neurophysiol* 25:351–358, 1968.

80. Dunleavy DLF, Oswald I, Brown P, Strong JA: Hyperthyroidism, sleep and growth hormone. *Electroencephalogr Clin Neurophysiol 36*: 259–263, 1974.

81. Ross JJ, Agnew HW, Williams RL, Webb WB: Sleep pattern in preadolescent children: an EEG-EOG study. *Pediatrics 42*:324–335, 1968.

82. Karacan I, Heine W, Agnew HW Jr, Williams RL, Webb WB, Ross JJ: Characteristics of sleep patterns during late pregnancy and the postpartum periods. *Am J Obstet Gynecol 101*:579–586, 1968.

83. Karacan I, Williams RL: Current advances in theory and practice relating to postpartum syndromes. *Psychiatry Med 1*:307–328, 1970.

84. Petre-Quadens O, DeBarsy AM, Devos J, Sfaello Z: Sleep in pregnancy: evidence of foetal-sleep characteristics. *J Neurol Sci 4*:600–605, 1967.

85. Schweiger MS: Sleep disturbance in pregnancy: a subjective survey. *Am J Obstet Gynecol 114*:879–882, 1972.

86. Bing R: *Lehrbuch der Nervenkrankheiten*. Basel, B. Schwabe, 1945.

87. Dexter JD, Weitzman ED: The relationship of nocturnal headaches to sleep stage patterns. *Neurology 20*:513–518, 1970.

88. Dexter JD, Riley TL: Studies in nocturnal migraine. *Headache 15*:51–62, 1975.

89. Graham JR: Methysergide for prevention of headache. *N Engl J Med 270*:67–72, 1964.

90. Bricolo A: Neurosurgical exploration and neurological pathology as a means for investigating human sleep semiology and mechanisms, in Lairy GC, Salzarulo P (eds): *The Experimental Study of Human Sleep: Methodological Problems*. Amsterdam, Elsevier Scientific Publishing Co, 1975.

91. Freemon FR: Sleep in patients with organic diseases of the nervous system, in Williams RL, Karacan I (eds): *Sleep Disorders: Diagnosis and Treatment*. New York, Wiley, 1978, pp 261–284.

92. Kales A, Ansel RD, Markham CH, Scharf MB, Tan TL: Sleep in patients with Parkinson's disease and normal subjects prior to and following levodopa administration. *Clin Pharmacol Ther 12*:397–406, 1971.

93. Broughton R: Neurology and sleep research. *Can Psych Assn J 16*: 283–292, 1971.

94. Moruzzi G, Magoun HW: Brainstem reticular formation and activation of the EEG. *Electroencephalog Clin Neurophysiol 1*:455–473, 1949.

95. Batini CF, Moruzzi G, Palestini M, Rossi GF, Zanchetti A: Effects of complete pontine transection on the sleep-wakefulness rhythm: the midpontine pretrigeminal prepaartion. *Arch Ital Biol 97*:1–12, 1959.

96. Clemente CD, Sterman MB: Limbic and other forebrain mechanisms in sleep induction and behavioral inhibition. *Progress in Brain Research 27*:34–47, 1967.

97. Jouvet M: Recherches sur les structures nerveuses et las mecanismes responsables des differentes phases du sommeil physiologique. *Arch Ital Biol 100*:125–206, 1962.

98. Bergamasco B, Bergamini L, Doriguzzi T, Sacerdote I: Il ciclo nictemerale nel coma. Possibilita prognostiche. *Riv Pat Nerv Ment 87*:312–318, 1966.

99. Bricolo A, Turella G, Dalle Ore G, Terzian H: A proposal for electroencephalographic evaluation of acute traumatic coma in neurosurgical practice. *Electroenceph Clin Neurophysiol 34*:789, 1973.

100. Bricolo A, Turella G, Signorini GC, Mazza C, Dalle Ore G: Su di un particolare quadro EEG del coma acuto traumatico caratterizzato dalla presenza di spindles. *Rev Neurol 40*:269–280, 1970.

101. Brierley J, Adams J, Graham D, Simpson J: Neocortical death after cardiac arrest. A clinical, neurophysiological and neuropathological report of two cases. *Lancet 2*:560–565, 1971.

102. Economo von C: Sleep as a problem of localization. *J Nerv Ment Dis 71*:249–259, 1930.

103. Jefferson G: The reticular formation and clinical neurology, in *Henry Ford Hospital, Int. Symp.* Boston-Toronto, Little Brown Co, 1958, pp 729–738.

104. Jouvet M, Pellin B, Mounier D: Etude polygraphique des differentes phases du sommeil au cours des troubles de conscience chronique (comas prolonges). *Rev Neurol 105*:181–186, 1961.

105. Markand ON, Dyken ML: Sleep abnormalities in patients with brain stem lesions. *Neurology 26*:769–776, 1976.

106. Passouant P, Cadilhac J, Delange M, Baldy-Moulinier M, Kassabgui N: Differentes stades électriques et organization en cycle des comas post-traumatiques. Enregistrement polygraphique de longue durée. *Rev Neurol 111*:391, 1964.

107. Plum F, Posner J: *The Diagnosis of Stupor and Coma*. Philadelphia, Davis Co, 1966.

108. Puca F, Bricolo A, Turella G: Effect of L-Dopa or Amantadine therapy on sleep spindles in Parkinsonism. *Electroenceph Clin Neurophysiol 35*:327–330, 1973.

109. Rossi GF: Brain-stem facilitating influences on EEG synchronization. Experimental findings and observations in man. *Acta Neurochir 13*:256–288, 1965.

110. Ellis BW, Dudley HAF: Some aspects of sleep research in surgical stress. *J Psychosomatic Res 20*:303–308, 1976.

111. Johns MW, Large AA, Masterton JP, Dudley HAF: Sleep and delirium after open heart surgery. *Br J Surg 61*:377–381, 1974.

112. Murphy F, Bentley S, Ellis BW, Dudley H: Sleep deprivation in patients undergoing operation: a factor in the stress of surgery. *Br Med J 2*:1521–1522, 1977.

113. Orr WC, Stahl ML, Greenfield LJ: Physiological sleep patterns after open-heart surgery. *J Psychophys 12*:232, 1975.

114. Walker BB: The postsurgery heart patient: amount of uninterrupted

time for sleep and rest during the first, second, and third postoperative days in a teaching hospital. *Nurs Res 21*:164–169, 1972.

115. Woods NF: Patterns of sleep in postcardiotomy patients. *Nurs Res 21*:347–352, 1972.

116. Dlin BM, Rosen H, Dickstein K, Lyons JW, Fischer HK: The problems of sleep and rest in the intensive care unit. *Psychosomatics 12*: 155–163, 1971.

117. Nicholson AN, Stone BM: Effect of some stimulants on sleep in man. *Br J Pharm 66*:476P, 1979.

118. Smith DE, Wesson DR, Buxton ME, Seymour RB, Ungerleider JT, Morgan JP, Mandell AJ, Jara G: Amphetamine use, misuse, and abuse, in *Proceedings of the National Amphetamine Conference, 1978.* Boston, GK Hall and Co., 1979.

119. Williams GH, Dluhy RG: Diseases of the adrenal cortex, in Petersdorf RG, Adams RD, Braunwald E, Isselbacher KJ, Martin JB, Wilson JD (eds): *Harrison's Principles of Internal Medicine.* New York, McGraw-Hill Book Company, 1983, ed 10, pp 634–657.

120. Petrie WM, Maffucci RJ, Woosley RL: Propranolol and depression. *Am J Psych 139*:92–93, 1982.

121. Stephen S: Unwanted effects of propranolol. *Am J Card 18*:463–468, 1966.

122. Hamilton M, Kopelman H: Treatment of severe hypertension with methyldopa. *Br Med J 1*:151–155, 1963.

123. Smirk H: Hypotensive action of methyldopa. *Br Med J 1*:146–151, 1963.

124. Muller JC, Pryor WW, Gibbons JE, Orgain ES: Depression and anxiety occurring during rauwolfia therapy. *JAMA 159*:836–839, 1955.

125. Andersson KE, Persson CGA: Extrapulmonary effects of theophylline. *Eur J Resp Dis Sup 61*:17–28, 1980.

126. Schoonover SC: Depression, in Bassuk EL, Schoonover SC, Gelenberg AJ (eds): *The Practitioner's Guide to Psychoactive Drugs.* New York, Plenum Medical Book Co., 1983, ed 2, pp 19–77.

127. Kales A, Kales JD, Jacobson A, Humphrey FJ II, Soldatos CR: Effects of imipramine on enuretic frequency and sleep stages. *Pediatrics 60*: 431–436, 1977.

128. Pohl R, Gershon S: Nomifensine: a new antidepressant. *Psychiatric Annals 11*:391–395, 1981.

129. Karacan I, Thornby JI, Anch AM, Booth GH, Williams RL, Salis PJ: Dose-related sleep disturbances induced by coffee and caffeine. *Clin Pharmacol Ther 20*:682–689, 1976.

130. Levy M, Zylber-Katz E: Caffeine metabolism and coffee-attributed sleep disturbances. *Clin Pharmacol Ther 33*:770–775, 1983.

131. Soldatos CR, Kales JD, Scharf MB, Bixler EO, Kales A: Cigarette smoking associated with sleep difficulty. *Science 207*:551–553, 1980.

132. Ague C: Urinary catecholamines, flow rate and tobacco smoking. *Biol Psychol 1*:229–236, 1974.

133. Cryer PE, Haymond MW, Santiago JV, Shah SD: Norepinephrine

and epinephrine release and adrenergic mediation of smoking-associated hemodynamic and metabolic events. *N Engl J Med 295*:573, 1976.

134. Kales A, Bixler EO, Tan TL, Scharf MB, Kales JD: Chronic hypnotic-drug use: ineffectiveness, drug-withdrawal insomnia, and dependence. *JAMA 227*:513–517, 1974.

135. Kales A, Soldatos CR, Bixler EO, Kales JD: Early morning insomnia with short-acting benzodiazepines. *Science 220*:95–97, 1983.

136. Kales A, Scharf MB, Kales JD: Rebound insomnia: a new clinical syndrome. *Science 201*:1039–1041, 1978.

137. Kales A, Scharf MB, Kales JD, Soldatos CR: Rebound insomnia: a potential hazard following withdrawal of certain benzodiazepines. *JAMA 241*:1692–1695, 1979.

138. Kales A, Soldatos CR, Bixler EO, Kales JD: Rebound insomnia and rebound anxiety: a review. *Pharmacology 26*:121–137, 1983.

139. Rundell OH, Lester BK, Griffiths WJ, Williams HL: Alcohol and sleep in young adults. *Psychopharmacologia 26*:201–218, 1972.

140. Yules RB, Lippman ME, Freedman DX: Alcohol administration prior to sleep. *Arch Gen Psych 16*:94–97, 1967.

141. Carskadon MA, Seidel WF, Greenblatt DJ, Dement WC: Daytime carryover of triazolam and flurazepam in elderly insomniacs. *Sleep 5*:361–371, 1982.

142. Morgan K, Oswald I: Anxiety caused by a short-life hypnotic. *Br Med J 284*:942, 1982.

143. Kales A, Soldatos CR, Bixler EO, Goff PJ, Vela-Bueno A: Midazolam: dose-response studies of effectiveness and rebound insomnia. *Pharmacology 26*:138–149, 1983.

144. Kales A, Kales JD, Bixler EO, Scharf MB, Russek E: Hypnotic efficacy of triazolam: sleep laboratory evaluation of intermediate-term effectiveness. *J Clin Pharmacol 16*:399–406, 1976.

145. Mamelak M, Csima A, Price V: A comparative 25 night sleep laboratory study on the effects of quazepam and triazolam on the sleep of chronic insomniacs. *J Clin Pharmacol* (in press).

146. Roth T, Kramer M, Lutz T: Intermediate use of triazolam: a sleep laboratory study. *J Int Med Res 4*:59–62, 1976.

147. Vogel GW, Barker K, Gibbons P, Thurmond A: A comparison of the effects of flurazepam 30 mg and triazolam 0.5 mg on the sleep of insomniacs. *Psychopharmacology 47*:81–86, 1976.

148. Vogel G, Thurmond A, Gibbons P, Edwards K, Sloan KB, Sexton K: The effect of triazolam on the sleep of insomniacs. *Psychopharmacologia 41*:65–69, 1975.

149. Kales A, Kales JD: Sleep laboratory studies of hypnotic drugs: efficacy and withdrawal effects. *J Clin Psychopharmacol 3*:140–150, 1983.

150. Kales A: Benzodiazepines in the treatment of insomnia, in Usdin E, Skolnick P, Tallman JF Jr, Greenblatt D, Paul SM (eds): *Pharmacology of Benzodiazepines*. London, Macmillan Press Ltd, 1982, pp 199–217.

7. Evaluation of Insomnia

Proper evaluation of the insomniac patient is a prerequisite for developing an appropriate management plan. Not infrequently, physicians have dealt with the complaint of insomnia by simply prescribing hypnotic medication without completing the necessary evaluation. This practice may lead to overreliance on medication and inattention to the initial stresses underlying insomnia, thus increasing the potential for the condition to become chronic. In order to assist physicians in managing insomnia properly, we offer in this chapter a detailed approach to evaluating sleep difficulty. In the case of transient insomnia, the evaluation is relatively straightforward. Chronic insomnia, however, is a more complex matter and, consequently, the topic to which most of this chapter is devoted.

Evaluation of patients with chronic insomnia should include a sleep history, drug history, and psychiatric history, as well as a complete medical history and physical examination.[1-3] Patients with transient or situational insomnia do not usually require such an extensive evaluation because the cause of their symptom is often easily identified.[4] While assessing these patients, the clinician should concentrate on determining the initial cause of sleep difficulty, which is usually a temporary situational factor. Current precipitating stressors are emphasized rather than the more global aspects of the patient's personality or interpersonal functioning that would be the focus when patients complain of chronic sleep difficulty. In most cases of transient insomnia, the sleep difficulty subsides when the stress-inducing factors are effectively addressed.[2,4]

The techniques for evaluating transient insomnia associated with a current stress are similar to those used in crisis intervention work.[5-7] For example, the patient should first be asked to describe his presenting problem as spontaneously and fully as possible. In this stage of the interview, an attitude conveying interest and persistence is more productive than a barrage of questions. The next step is to elicit a chronologic account of the onset and course of the problem.[1] When and in what setting did the sleep difficulty first appear, and what life events occurred just prior to or concurrent with the appearance of the insomnia? Were there major changes in the patient's life, such as a new job or loss of a job, a new baby in the home, or a death in the family? How has the insomnia affected the patient's life and that of his or her family?[8]

As a final aspect of evaluating transient insomnia, the clinician determines whether there are precursors for the development of chronic insomnia. This involves looking for coping patterns of internalization,[9,10] predisposing factors of vulnerability during childhood,[11] and poor sleep habits that have recently formed and may contribute, through conditioning, to the development of chronic insomnia.[12]

The evaluation of patients with chronic insomnia is frequently incomplete because an adequate history is not taken in terms of sleep, psychologic factors, or drug use.[1,13] This is often the case because patients with chronic insomnia tend to focus on their sleep difficulty, essentially considering sleeplessness to be the entire problem.[3,14] Their preoccupation with the symptom hinders the physician's efforts to conduct a thorough evaluation, specifically in terms of taking an adequate history and eliciting underlying difficulties. Thus, skill and persistence in taking the required histories is invaluable to the physician in conducting an evaluation.[1]

Sleep History

Obtaining a sleep history is most useful in the evaluation of insomnia if the physician is knowledgeable about sleep disorders and is a skilled interviewer.[1] When conducting the interview, the physician should discourage patients from focusing excessively on their symptoms of sleeplessness. This tendency is quite typical of obsessive-compulsive or hypochondriacal patients, who ruminate about their sleep difficulties and tend to give detailed accounts of every minor event that occurs during the night.

The physician's own sleep habits should not bias the evaluation of the patient's disorder.[1] Not only do individual sleep needs vary considerably,[15] but, as we have stated earlier, the subjective complaint of insomnia is often disproportionate to the amount of sleep actually ob-

Table 7.1. Guidelines for Taking a Sleep History

Define specific sleep problem
Assess disorder's clinical course
Differentiate between sleep disorders
Evaluate sleep-wakefulness patterns
Question bed partner
Evaluate impact of the disorder

tained.[16,17] Physicians should not assume that certain sleep habits and routines that are helpful to them are of equal value to their patients. It is also wise to avoid preconceived ideas about the causes of insomnia because they vary widely among patients.

In addition to obtaining a sleep history when insomnia is the patient's primary complaint, the physician should ask general questions about sleep problems during the standard evaluation of any medical patient.[1] If a patient has sleep difficulty, the physician should obtain information about its characteristics and clinical course, its duration, the circumstances under which it developed, any precipitating or accentuating factors, any previous treatment and its results, and the impact of the sleep problem on the patient's life (Table 7.1).[1,8]

Define the Specific Sleep Problem

Because the treatment for insomnia often varies according to the type of sleep difficulty and its causes, the nature of the complaint must be determined.[1] If the patient has trouble falling asleep, the clinician should ask more questions about the patient's bedtime routine and determine the nature of his or her mental activity while trying to fall asleep. The histories of insomniacs who have difficulty falling asleep usually indicate that when they attempt to go to sleep, they have excessive, ruminative mentation and "racing thoughts," and they appear to be aroused in that they report feeling "keyed up and unable to slow down."[8] If the patient has a complaint of difficulty staying asleep, the possibility of medical problems or interference from the environment should be more thoroughly investigated. Among insomniac patients, there is a high prevalence of nightmares, which, in turn, can also seriously disrupt sleep.[18] Early final awakenings, on the other hand, may be symptomatic of major (endogenous) depression, and warrant inquiry about other symptoms of depression, including thoughts of suicide.[19]

When patients report that they sleep only a few hours at night, their perceptions of the quality of sleep should be clarified. Many "short sleepers"[20-22] who do not complain of insomnia frequently sleep less than most "insomniacs"; short sleepers, however, report that they feel rested and alert in the morning, whereas most insomniacs complain of feeling tired and sluggish. Thus, the physician's emphasis should be on the patient's complaint of insomnia, rather than on the amount of time actually asleep.[2,17,23]

Assess the Disorder's Clinical Course

By assessing the clinical course of chronic insomnia, the physician can determine not only the events precipitating the disorder's onset but also those factors responsible for its persistence. This is important because the treatment approach for insomnia usually will be guided by identifying the relationships that exist between the course of the disorder, developmental problems, stressful life events, and psychopathology.[1] In regard to these issues, insomnia can develop at any age,[8,24-26] and its onset is usually related to life-stress events and emotional difficulties.[8-11] Insomnia also tends to be a chronic condition; most patients with the disorder have the complaint for many years.[8,24,27]

Differentiate Between Sleep Disorders

Patients' complaints about their sleep are often general and vague and may even represent symptoms of more than one sleep disorder.[1] For the physician to differentiate between sleep disorders, the description of the patient's symptomatology must be carefully considered. For example, when a patient complains of "tiredness," the physician must determine whether this represents fatigue, weakness, exhaustion, or, as is sometimes the case, excessive daytime sleepiness. With a thorough sleep history, this usually can easily be done. Chronic tiredness is frequently a complaint of insomnia and may be related to an underlying medical condition or an emotional disturbance (see "Medical Assessment" and "Psychiatric Assessment" sections in this chapter). Actual sleepiness during the day frequently signals the presence of a disorder of excessive sleepiness (narcolepsy, hypersomnia, or sleep apnea). To rule out a disorder of excessive sleepiness, the physician should ask whether the patient has irresistible sleep attacks, associated with any auxiliary symptoms of narcolepsy,[28-32] or daytime sleepiness or sleep

attacks, associated with nocturnal breath cessations and the characteristic snorting or gasping sounds of sleep apnea.[33-38]

Evaluate 24-hour Sleep–Wakefulness Patterns

To determine whether daytime activities or naps are affecting the patient's sleep, it is important to consider the entire 24-hour day, not
just the eight-hour sleep period.[1-3] Elderly patients, for example, often
complain of trouble sleeping at night but, in fact, may take several
naps during the day. A 24-hour history will also point out any poor
habits of living, such as irregular bedtime schedules, which often contribute to sleep difficulty. Low or inconsistent levels of physical activity during the day are also frequently reported by insomniac patients.
On the other hand, vigorous physical exercise or stimulating mental activity close to bedtime can contribute to difficulty in falling asleep.[12,39]

Having the patient keep a sleep diary for one or two weeks can be
useful in assessing 24-hour sleep–wakefulness patterns,[1] particularly in
terms of detecting disordered schedules and routines. To keep a sleep
diary, the patient notes the time of retiring, including naps, and re-
cords the time and length of the day's general activities. Keeping a diary is not advisable for insomniac patients who are highly obsessive-
compulsive or hypochondriacal, however, because it could reinforce
their preoccupation with sleep difficulty.[12]

Question the Bed Partner

Questioning the bed partner is not meant to verify the patient's complaints of insomnia because the patient's account is most often reliable.
The main reason for interviewing the bed partner is to obtain evidence
of possible sleep apnea,[33-38] nocturnal myoclonus,[40-44] or any other ob-
servable nocturnal phenomenon, such as sleepwalking,[45] night terrors,[46]
or nocturnal wandering.[47] Although infrequent, the condition of sleep
apnea or nocturnal myoclonus may disturb patients' sleep without
their being aware of them. These conditions should, therefore, be pre-
liminarily ruled out in the office setting by questioning the bed partner. If sleep apnea is clinically suspected, a sleep laboratory recording
is required to determine the type and severity of apneic episodes.

There are two types of sleep apnea: obstructive and central.[33-38] Obstructive sleep apnea is almost invariably associated with a major com-

plaint of excessive daytime sleepiness, but seldom with a primary complaint of insomnia. Central sleep apnea may occasionally be associated with some disruption of nocturnal sleep, but again, excessive daytime sleepiness is the most predominant and prevalent symptom.

The bed partner can best indicate if the patient exhibits any signs of sleep apnea. If the patient snores heavily, snorts and gasps periodically, and there are periods of breath cessation lasting longer than 10 seconds, obstructive sleep apnea should be suspected.[34,35,38] At times, the snorting and gasping sounds are so loud that the bed partner moves to another room. A tape recording of the patient's snoring sounds can help the physician make a preliminary diagnosis[1,48,49] of obstructive sleep apnea, which can be confirmed through diagnostic recordings in the sleep laboratory.

Patients with central sleep apnea may not make snorting and gasping sounds.[34,35] However, they usually report other symptoms associated with sleep apnea, such as nocturnal choking sensations, general nocturnal distress, and frequent morning headaches, along with excessive daytime sleepiness, which is generally less severe than when it accompanies obstructive sleep apnea. Of course, the bed partner can also help to describe the interruptions in breathing that occur with central sleep apnea.

Another sleep disorder that, when present, is frequently observed and noted by the bed partner is nocturnal myoclonus.[40-44] Patients who have this periodic leg jerking may be oblivious to their symptoms until they are informed by their bed partner. Seldom does the degree of muscle activity characteristic of nocturnal myoclonus result in arousal that is sufficient to be considered a causative factor in insomnia.[40,42]

Evaluate the Impact of Insomnia

Because the condition of chronic insomnia generally has serious psychosocial consequences,[8] the physician should thoroughly explore the disorder's impact on the patient's life. For example, the patient may use the symptom to obtain considerable secondary gain. It is not unusual for insomniacs to avoid family and social interactions routinely by insisting they are too tired or by protesting that a certain activity will disturb their sleep. The insomniac patient may also avoid sexual relations, claiming to be too tired or that his or her presleep routine would be disturbed, and may even demand that the spouse sleep in a separate bed or a separate room. By determining how insomnia affects the patient's life and interpersonal relationships, the physician is better prepared to initiate an appropriate treatment plan.

Medical Assessment

A thorough medical history should be taken from patients presenting with a complaint of insomnia, and they should be given a complete physical examination.[50,51] Also, routine clinical laboratory tests, such as urinalysis, blood count, and sedimentation rate, as well as an EKG, should be obtained.[52] A standard medical history includes identification of demographic data, a search for other presenting complaints besides sleep difficulty, a symptom-oriented account of any present illness, a detailed past history, and a general family history.

During the physical examination, the physician should attend to every system. Even though the findings are usually minimal, a thorough examination not only rules out certain physical conditions, but also reassures the patient that his or her health has not suffered because of sleep loss. This information tends to relieve the patient's preoccupation with sleeplessness and its possible consequences.

Insomnia may be related directly to physical factors, so symptoms and signs of medical illness should be thoroughly assessed (see also Chapter 6, Medical and Other Pathophysiologic Factors in Insomnia). The discomfort and pain of arthritis, chronic pain states, and various types of headache often contribute to insomnia.[53,54] In these conditions, pain experienced during the day may be perceived as worsening at bedtime when environmental stimuli diminish and attention turns inward. Other examples of nocturnal pain and discomfort related to medical illness are epigastric distress in patients with ulcers, the anginal pain of myocardial ischemia, and joint and muscle aches in various rheumatic diseases. Patients with malignancies, in addition to dealing with pain, often stay awake because of fear of impending death or permanent disability. Similarly, patients with angina pectoris or cardiac arrhythmias often fear going to sleep because of possible attacks during the night, when they feel most vulnerable and helpless. As shown by these examples, insomnia related to medical illness is usually caused by both physical and emotional factors because an emotional response always accompanies a disease process.[2,3,14]

As part of the medical assessment, attention should be given to past surgery and hospitalizations for medical illness. Hospitalizations and periods before and after surgery are fraught with anxiety, and the environment of the hospital itself may promote transient sleep disruption.[55,56] Furthermore, the sedative, analgesic, and pre-anesthetic medications that are often used for surgery may interfere with sleep and dream patterns. Sleep may be interrupted by hospital procedures, such as injections and the routine measurement of vital signs, or simply by the noise and strangeness of the environment.[57] Finally, in addition to causing transient insomnia, these factors can act as precursors to the development of chronic sleeplessness (see also Chapter 6, Medical and Other Pathophysiologic Factors in Insomnia).

Drug History

As also discussed in detail in Chapter 6, insomnia can be aggravated or caused by stimulant drugs, steroids, energizing antidepressants, or beta-adrenergic blockers.[58-76] These drugs, even in therapeutic doses, are more likely to delay sleep onset when taken close to bedtime. Stimulant substances included in the average diet can cause problems as well. Difficulty falling asleep can result from drinking coffee[61] or cola before retiring for the night, as well as from cigarette smoking.[62] Alcohol can lead to changes in REM sleep[63] and sleep disruption, mainly in the form of early morning awakenings.[64] Benzodiazepines with short half-lives have also been found to produce early morning insomnia,[65] as well as increases in daytime levels of anxiety and tension.[65-67] Abrupt withdrawal of high doses of non-benzodiazepine hynotics may cause both insomnia and nightmares,[68] while withdrawal of relatively low doses of short- and intermediate-acting benzodiazepine agents may produce rebound insomnia.[69-71]

A drug history includes information about the current use of any medication, both prescribed and non-prescribed (Table 7.2). Insomniacs often take a baffling assortment of drugs, and if this is the case, it is helpful to record the following information: how long the patient has been taking each drug and its current dosage, any past change in dosage, side effects, and the drug's effectiveness. Similar information should be obtained for drugs used in the past, with an emphasis on the period following drug withdrawal. Withdrawal phenomena, including insomnia, may be related to a hypnotic drug's elimination half-life, dosage, and the length of its administration.[68-76] With both current and past drug use, the clinician should look for associations between drug-use patterns and the onset and/or exacerbation of sleep disturbance.

Table 7.2. Steps in Taking a Drug History for Insomnia

Consider caffeine consumption and cigarette smoking as contributing factors

Investigate drinking habits and dependence on alcohol

Rule out drug use as a causative factor, for example, stimulants, bronchodilators, or beta blockers

Assess for the presence of sleep difficulties related to drug withdrawal, including early morning insomnia and rebound insomnia

The drug history should not be limited to determining the patient's use of medication; it should also include current or past use of other substances that affect sleep, such as alcohol, caffeine, nicotine or illicit drugs. The physician should ask specifically about consumption of alcoholic beverages. If the patient drinks habitually, it should be noted how long he or she has been drinking, what the drinking habits are on a daily and weekly basis, and whether or not he or she becomes intoxicated. An important issue is whether the patient is dependent on alcohol. If so, past and current alcohol-withdrawal symptoms should be noted, and the patient's social and occupational functioning should be assessed. Impaired functioning caused by alcohol dependence may lead to more irregular patterns of sleep and wakefulness, compounding the patient's sleep difficulty.

Psychiatric Assessment

Because psychologic factors play a major role in the development of insomnia[2-4] (see also Chapter 5, Psychiatric Factors in Insomnia), the psychiatric history (Table 7.3) is integral to a complete evaluation of the insomniac patient. Chronic insomniacs generally show high levels of psychopathology[9,10,77-81] and tend to internalize emotional conflicts,[9,10] which leads to psychophysiologic activation[77-79,81,82] and a state of hyperarousal. When 100 patients with chronic insomnia were assigned diagnoses according to the American Psychiatric Association's *Diagnostic and Statistical Manual of Mental Disorders* (DSM-III),[83] each patient had at least one psychiatric diagnosis; in fact, 95 patients had a principal diagnosis of a psychiatric condition.[84] Even the five patients who had a medical condition as a principal diagnosis had additional psychiatric diagnoses. Thus, even when physical factors are primary, emotional components can contribute considerably to patients' sleep difficulties.[84]

As the psychiatric history unfolds, a clear association often emerges between the development of certain psychologic conflicts and the onset of sleep difficulty.[2,4,11] Establishing a connection between life-stress events and the onset of insomnia helps the physician and patient to better understand the development and clinical course of the patient's sleep disturbance. This not only makes the evaluation more comprehensive but also ultimately enhances the physician's ability to establish a diagnosis that accurately reflects both the patient's sleep disturbance and the patient's overall emotional status. The following case illustrates the connection between life-stress events and specific fears and anxieties occurring at the onset of insomnia:

Case 1. A 43-year-old homemaker was evaluated in our Sleep Disorders Clinic because of a long history of chronic insomnia. When the patient was first interviewed, she was vague as to when her insomnia started and was unsure about any precipitating circumstances. The next day, however, the patient called the clinic and indicated that while riding the train home after her interview, she experienced an acute anxiety reaction as she recalled when her sleep difficulties began and the circumstances surrounding their onset.

She related that when she was about seven years old, she began to have difficulty falling asleep because she would overhear her parents arguing and fighting as she tried to sleep. When she told her mother about her distress and difficulty sleeping, the mother insisted that she recite a particular prayer each night before going to sleep. Saying this prayer, however, created additional anxieties and fears that contributed to her difficulty in falling asleep. Specifically, she was afraid of the prayer's implied message that she might die before morning.

> "Now I lay me down to sleep,
> I pray the Lord my soul to keep,
> If I should die before I wake,
> I pray the Lord my soul to take."

For a time she was able to fall asleep only by disobeying her mother and not reciting the prayer she feared so much. She then frequently awakened because of terrifying nightmares that often depicted her own death or that of her parents. The nightmare content most likely arose from a combination of her fear of the prayer, her guilt at disobeying her mother's command, and her anxiety and anger over her parents' frequent disagreements.

Just as the psychiatric history is one of the most valuable components of an evaluation, it is also especially challenging. Many patients deny their psychologic difficulties and insist that sleeplessness is their only problem.[2,3,14] Moreover, insomniac patients tend to be obsessional.

These factors, coupled with the constraints on physicians' time, often result in a failure to take an adequate psychiatric history, which is one of the most common shortcomings in the evaluation of insomnia.

During the psychiatric evaluation, the physician should follow certain principles of interviewing.[85,86] The basic requirement for a sound psychiatric interview is the establishment of a meaningful doctor–patient relationship; the interviewer needs to be not only attentive, but genuinely interested and concerned. Only when satisfactory rapport develops can the physician elicit clinically important information related to the patient's emotional status. Rapport is most needed with insomniac patients who tend to deny their psychologic problems and instead focus unduly on the sleep difficulty itself. Warmth and caring on the part of the physician should not, of course, be confused with lack of professional attitude. A skilled clinician can combine empathy and objectivity, drawing upon one or the other as needed.

Directive interviewing in an authoritarian style is less successful than an approach that encourages the patient's active participation and spontaneous conversation. In this context, effective interviewers are good listeners, and ask open-ended rather than closed questions that are answered with yes or no. Of course, the physician should not leave the patient completely undirected, but should encourage the flow of relevant thoughts and feelings from the patient through both verbal and nonverbal communications. When the physician actively encourages expression, patients realize that they have alternatives in dealing with others and with their feelings, rather than simply internalizing their emotions. Such an interviewing strategy is absolutely necessary with insomniac patients; because they internalize their emotions, they discourage people from interacting with them.

The physician should proceed from exploring the dimensions of the sleep difficulty itself to sifting through the various areas of current and past functioning of the patient.[4] Such areas include family, vocational, and social spheres. Particular attention should be given to significant life events that may have precipitated or aggravated the patient's insomnia.[8,11]

Assessment of the patient's emotional functioning should cover his or her entire life, particularly the developmental years. It is important to determine whether psychologic difficulties during childhood, especially those resulting from major family disruptions, caused the patient to acquire inadequate mechanisms for coping with stress. Family events such as death, divorce, and separation can create a psychologic vulnerability, predisposing a person to insomnia.[8,11]

An assessment of the patient's mental status is particularly important in detecting patterns of depression, anxiety, rumination, obsessive-compulsiveness, hypochondriasis, and, in the elderly, organicity.[84] Most of the information needed to evaluate mental status is obtained during the process of taking a psychiatric history. While interviewing the patient, the physician will have had an opportunity to note the patient's appearance, overall behavior, level of activity, speech and communication, and organization of thought. The interview also yields most of the information needed to assess the patient's mood, content of thought, perception, level of awareness, orientation, concentration, memory, recall, fund of knowledge, abstract thinking and judgment, and understanding of his or her condition.

At times the physician needs to ask specific questions to determine the status of the patient's mental functions.[4] This is particularly true for assessing mood. Although many insomniac patients are depressed, they may not display depression or admit to being depressed.[84] If the interviewer senses underlying depression, patients should be asked whether they have feelings of apprehension, worry, dissatisfaction, disappointment, helplessness, hopelessness, loss of self-esteem, anger, or irritability. Such patients should also be asked whether they have any vegetative symptoms of depression, such as loss of appetite or decreased libido. If depression is not immediately apparent, it may surface later as the interview progresses or during a subsequent interview. Suicidal ideation may also be revealed and requires specific questioning.

Another area that sometimes needs further exploration is the sensorium. This is particularly useful for elderly patients or those who show signs of brain damage or dysfunction. The physician should not

Table 7.3. Principles for the Psychiatric History

Determine the role of life-stress events and coping patterns

Obtain a developmental history

Assess the premorbid personality and adjustment

Consider associated psychiatric symptomatology: anxiety, obsessive-compulsiveness, depression, and hypochondriasis

Rule out the presence of organicity or suicidal ideation

---

feel inhibited about asking questions concerning the patient's memory or judgment. If questions are matter-of-fact and brief explanations are given whenever necessary, the patient generally will respond with a positive attitude.

Diagnosis of Insomnia

For diagnosing insomnia and other sleep disorders, we recommend[2,4] the use of both the International Classification of Diseases, 9th edition, clinical modification (ICD-9-CM) of the World Health Organization[87] and the DSM-III of the American Psychiatric Association.[83] Both official classifications are employed because a multiaxial system is necessary for diagnosing the actual sleep disorder, as well as the organic and nonorganic psychiatric disorders, personality traits or disorders, and any medical conditions that may be present. Thus, the ICD-9-CM is used for diagnosing the sleep disorder and any concurrent medical conditions, and the DSM-III is used to diagnose the psychiatric disorders frequently associated with sleep disturbances.[2,4] In this way by taking each of the existing conditions into account, a multidimensional treatment plan can be devised.

The ICD-9-CM classifies sleep disturbances as nonorganic and organic disorders, whereas conditions that may occur during sleep and/or wakefulness are listed separately, eg, enuresis, bruxism, and head-banging. Narcolepsy is classified with disorders of the central nervous system. The ICD-9-CM "specific disorders of sleep of nonorganic origin" are listed in Table 7.4 (terms in parentheses are added).

This classification might be more useful for clinicians with minor modifications, such as retaining well-established and widely used terms

Table 7.4. Classification of Nonorganic Sleep Disorders Based on ICD-9-CM

307.40	Nonorganic sleep disorder, unspecified
307.41	Transient disorder of initiating or maintaining sleep (transient insomnia)
307.42	Persistent disorder of initiating or maintaining sleep (persistent insomnia)
307.43	Transient disorder of initiating or maintaining wakefulness (transient hypersomnia)
307.44	Persistent disorder of initiating or maintaining wakefulness (persistent hypersomnia)
307.45	Phase-shift disruption of 24-hour sleep-wake cycle
307.46	Somnambulism or night terrors
307.47	Other dysfunctions of sleep stages or arousal from sleep
307.48	Repetitive intrusions of sleep

(From Kales et al[4])

Table 7.5. Proposed Sleep Disorders Classification

Specific Disorders of Sleep of Nonorganic Origin	Specific Disorders of Sleep of Organic Origin
Nonorganic sleep disorder, unspecified	Organic sleep disorder, unspecified
Transient insomnia	Transient insomnia
Persistent insomnia	Persistent insomnia
Transient hypersomnia	Transient hypersomnia
Persistent hypersomnia	Persistent hypersomnia
Phase-shift disruption of 24-hour sleep-wake cycle	Sleep apnea
Somnambulism or night terrors	Somnambulism or night terrors
Other dysfunctions of sleep	Other dysfunctions of sleep

(From Kales et al[4])

like insomnia and hypersomnia, and excluding the diagnosis of "repetitive intrusions of sleep" because the latter diagnosis is unsubstantiated and not clinically relevant.[4] The portion of the ICD-9-CM dealing with sleep disturbances of organic origin could be altered to mirror the classification of the nonorganic sleep disorders. This would aid the physician's decision-making process and would be more clinically meaningful. The ICD-9-CM classification would be further improved by including a separate diagnosis for sleep apnea among the sleep disturbances of organic origin. Other disorders occurring in sleep and/or wakefulness, as well as narcolepsy, would continue to be classified separately, as in the current ICD-9-CM.

Based on the considerations just discussed, we envision an improved classification of sleep disorders, as shown in Table 7.5.

We are unable to recommend the Association of Sleep Disorders Centers' (ASDC) classification[88] to clinicians as practical for diagnosing insomnia and other clinically encountered sleep disorders.[2,4] Other investigators have reported difficulty utilizing the ASDC classification as well.[89,90] This classification system is not multiaxial and does not encourage the diagnosis of the multiple psychiatric, medical, or other conditions that may be causative or contributory to the insomnia, or simply associated with it.[2,4]

Importance of Evaluation for Treatment Outcome

As with any medical condition, insomnia can be treated properly only after a thorough evaluation has been conducted. An inadequate evaluation often results in superficial treatment of insomnia; the physician may minimize the problem, provide reassurance or counseling when it is inappropriate, or merely prescribe pharmacologic treatment. For example, a hypnotic drug might be prescribed as the sole pharmacologic treatment for endogenous depression in a suicidal patient, or, conversely, antidepressants might be given when a hypnotic drug would be more effective. Similarly, counseling would be inappropriate if it were directed toward a particular psychologic symptom when sleeplessness was directly caused by medication (eg, a stimulant, steroid, bronchodilator, or beta-adrenergic blocker) or by drug withdrawal (eg, relatively low dose of a benzodiazepine with a short elimination half-life or a high dose of a non-benzodiazepine hypnotic drug).

On the other hand, an overly extensive evaluation can be unnecessarily time consuming and even harmful in some cases of transient insomnia. For example, if a patient has transient sleep disturbance because of a change in work shift, the physician should not focus on the marital relationship or other emotional difficulties that might be present.

Advantages of Assessment in the Office Setting

Primary care physicians are in an excellent position to evaluate patients with insomnia. By taking histories that assess for drug, psychiatric, and general medical problems, performing a physical evaluation, and incorporating a prior knowledge of the patient and family, physicians can determine whether medical, psychiatric, or situational disturbances are contributing to insomnia. Where emotional difficulties are predominant, psychiatric referral may be indicated. Diagnostic recordings in the sleep laboratory are seldom required; suspicion of sleep apnea is the primary indication for such studies.[3,91-94] Although some investigators have stated or implied that laboratory diagnostic studies should be conducted in most, if not all, cases of chronic insomnia,[95-98] we have discussed in Chapter 3, Sleep Laboratory Studies of Insomnia, how an overemphasis on physiologic factors may lead to confusing causality with correlation.[42,99-101]

When evaluations for chronic insomnia are primarily based on physiologic assessment, an underemphasis of psychologic factors may result. For example, using a criterion for insomnia of obtaining less than six and a half hours of sleep in the laboratory, some investigators have reported that a high percentage of patients with chronic insomnia have a "diagnosis" of pseudoinsomnia, ie, a subjective complaint without objective findings.[16,96] Obviously, a criterion of insomnia that is based strictly on an arbitrary amount of sleep obtained in the sleep laboratory has many limitations: it provides no information on the quality of sleep, which is, in our current state of knowledge, essentially a subjective matter; it does not take into account the fact that patients' sleep difficulty may actually be less in the sleep laboratory as compared to their home environment;[17,102] and, most important of all, it neglects psychiatric factors, such as excessive somatization, hypochondriasis, obsessive-compulsiveness, hysteria, depression, and anxiety that usually predominate in patients whose clinical complaints appear to be disproportionate to laboratory data.

Physicians in the office setting, on the other hand, when well-informed about the evaluation and treatment of chronic insomnia, can provide evaluations that are highly personal, empathetic, and comprehensive, as well as cost-effective. The growing over-dependence on expensive clinical tests is a current and major problem in medicine.[50,103-106] To quote from a pertinent editorial: "It is time to reassess the value of clinical judgment. It is time for the pendulum to swing the other way, not only because of economic pressure but because of another lost art—common sense."[106] The personal physician, in the context of the office setting, is best able to assess all aspects of the patient's functioning (eg, physical health, emotional status, and life adjustment) to properly balance all the factors that contribute to an understanding of the patient's problems.

The family physician's skills in establishing rapport and meaningful communication with patients greatly enhance his ability to evaluate chronic insomnia. To begin with, patients are encouraged to volunteer relevant information about their sleep difficulties. Furthermore, the family physician is familiar with the patient's past and can identify important aspects of his or her life that may pertain to insomnia. In cases of transient insomnia, this familiarity enables physicians to identify precipitating life-stress events, and in cases of chronic insomnia, they will most likely be aware of any premorbid personality factors, any predisposition to chronic sleep difficulty, significant life-stress events, recent psychologic conflicts, and current and past medical conditions.

Because of these advantages, physicians in the office setting are best able to establish and implement therapeutic priorities for the patient. For example, when insomnia is secondary to depression, they can identify suicidal ideation and help to prevent an actual attempt at self-harm. Similarly, they can detect signs of organic mental disorder, which may be responsible for the patient's insomnia. They also will be able to intervene when a life-threatening medical disorder is at the root of insomnia, such as severe coronary artery insufficiency. In such cases as these, identification and treatment of the medical problem takes precedence over treating the patient's sleep disturbance, which will probably be alleviated when the medical problem is treated.

Summary

Evaluation of transient or situational insomnia centers on identifying stressful life events or other immediate causes, addressing these factors, and strengthening the patients' coping mechanisms. Evaluation of chronic insomnia needs to be more thorough and includes taking a sleep history, drug history, and psychiatric history, as well as a general medical history and physical examination.

When taking a sleep history, physicians begin by defining the specific sleep problem and assessing its clinical course. They are careful to differentiate sleep disorders, to evaluate sleep–wakefulness patterns and to question the bed partner. Also, they evaluate the impact of the disorder on the patient and his or her family and social network. In completing a thorough physical examination, physicians not only rule out certain physical conditions, but reassure the patient, relieving his or her preoccupation with sleeplessness and its possible health consequences.

The drug history includes assessment of the effects of prescribed drugs that may cause sleep disturbance, as well as the potential role of caffeine, nicotine, and alcohol. Drugs that may directly cause sleep difficulty include stimulants, bronchodilators, and beta blockers. Another type of drug-induced sleep difficulty is characteristically associated with short half-life benzodiazepines, which frequently cause early morning insomnia and rebound insomnia, as well as increases in levels of daytime anxiety.

The psychiatric history is often neglected in patients who have chronic insomnia. When properly taken, it includes assessment of life-stress events, coping patterns, and the premorbid personality and adjustment. Evaluation of the patient's mental status considers the presence of psychiatric symptomatology such as anxiety, obsessive-compulsiveness, rumination, depression, and hypochondriasis, and rules out the presence of organicity or suicidal ideation.

Two official diagnostic classification systems are recommended for diagnosing insomnia: the ICD-9-CM for diagnosing sleep disorders, and the DSM-III to diagnose psychiatric disorders that are frequently associated with sleep disturbances. Evaluation of insomnia can be conducted effectively by the physician in the office setting, utilizing interviewing skills to assess for sleep, drug, medical, and emotional problems. Additionally, familiarity with the patient enables the physician to complete an accurate, thorough, and cost-effective assessment of sleep difficulty that is balanced and integrated.

References

1. Kales A, Soldatos CR, Kales JD: Taking a sleep history. *Am Fam Physician* 22:101–108, 1980.
2. Kales A, Soldatos CR, Kales JD: Sleep disorders: evaluation and management in the office setting, in Arieti S, Brodie HKH (vol eds): *American Handbook of Psychiatry*, vol 7. New York, Basic Books Inc, 1981, ed 2, pp 423–454.
3. Soldatos CR, Kales A, Kales JD: Management of insomnia. *Annu Rev Med* 30:301–312, 1979.
4. Kales JD, Soldatos CR, Kales A: Diagnosis and treatment of sleep disorders, in Greist JH, Jefferson JW, Spitzer RL (eds): *Treatment of Mental Disorders*. New York: Oxford University Press, 1982, pp 473–500.
5. Bellak L, Small L: Basic principles (chapters 1–4), in *Emergency Psychotherapy and Brief Psychotherapy*. New York, Grune & Stratton, 1965, pp 2–86.
6. Greist JH: Adjustment disorders, in Greist JH, Jefferson JW, Spitzer RL (eds): *Treatment of Mental Disorders*. New York, Oxford University Press, 1982, pp 419–428.
7. Kales JD, Kales A: Managing the individual and family in crisis. *Am Fam Physician* 12:109–115, 1975.
8. Kales JD, Kales A, Bixler EO, Soldatos CR, Cadieux RJ, Kashurba GJ, Vela-Bueno A: Biopsychobehavioral correlates of insomnia, V: clinical characteristics and behavioral correlates. *Am J Psychiatry* (in press).
9. Kales A, Caldwell AB, Preston TA, Healey S, Kales JD: Personality patterns in insomnia: theoretical implications. *Arch Gen Psychiatry* 33:1128–1134, 1976.
10. Kales A, Caldwell AB, Soldatos CR, Bixler EO, Kales JD: Biopsychobehavioral correlates of insomnia, II: pattern specificity and consistency with the Minnesota Multiphasic Personality Inventory. *Psychosom Med* 45:341–356, 1983.

11. Healey ES, Kales A, Monroe LJ, Bixler EO, Chamberlin K, Soldatos CR: Onset of insomnia: role of life-stress events. *Psychosom Med 43*: 439–451, 1981.

12. Kales JD, Kales A: Rest and sleep, in Taylor RB (ed): *Health Promotion: Principles and Clinical Applications.* Norwalk, Conn, Appleton-Century-Crofts, 1982, pp 307–337.

13. Kales A, Kales JD, Bixler EO, Martin E: Common shortcomings in the evaluation and treatment of insomnia, in Kagan F, Harwood T, Rickels K, Rudzik A, Sorer H (eds): *Hypnotics: Methods of Development and Evaluation.* New York, Spectrum Publications Inc, 1975, pp 29–40.

14. Kales A, Kales JD, Bixler EO: Insomnia: an approach to management and treatment. *Psychiatr Ann 4*:28–44, 1974.

15. The Gallup Organization: *The Gallup Study of Sleeping Habits.* Princeton, NJ, 1979.

16. Carskadon MA, Dement WC, Mitler MM, Guilleminault C, Zarcone VP, Spiegel R: Self-reports versus sleep laboratory findings in 122 drug-free subjects with complaints of chronic insomnia. *Am J Psychiatry 133*:1382–1388, 1976.

17. Kales A, Bixler EO: Sleep profiles of insomnia and hypnotic drug effectiveness, in Burch N, Altshuler HL (eds): *Behavior and Brain Electrical Activity.* New York, Plenum, 1975, pp 81–91.

18. Kales A, Soldatos CR, Caldwell AB, Charney DS, Kales JD, Markel D, Cadieux R: Nightmares: clinical characteristics and personality patterns. *Am J Psychiatry 137*:1197–1201, 1980.

19. Kolb LC, Brodie HKH: *Modern Clinical Psychiatry.* Philadelphia, WB Saunders Co, 1982, ed 10.

20. Jones HS, Oswald I: Two cases of healthy insomnia. *Electroencephalogr Clin Neurophysiol 24*:378–380, 1968.

21. Meddis R, Pearson AJD, Langford G: An extreme case of healthy insomnia. *Electroencephalogr Clin Neurophysiol 35*:213–214, 1973.

22. Stuss D, Broughton R: Extreme short sleep: personality profiles and a case study of sleep requirement. *Waking and Sleeping 2*:101–105, 1978.

23. Regestein QR, Reich P: Current problems in the diagnosis and treatment of chronic insomnia. *Perspect Biol Med 21*:232–239, 1978.

24. Bixler EO, Kales A, Soldatos CR, Kales JD, Healey S: Prevalence of sleep disorders in the Los Angeles metropolitan area. *Am J Psychiatry 136*:1257–1262, 1979.

25. Dixon KN, Monroe LJ, Jakim S: Insomniac children. *Sleep 4*:313–318, 1981.

26. Hauri P, Olmstead E: Childhood-onset insomnia. *Sleep 3*:59–65, 1980.

27. Roth T, Kramer M, Lutz T: The nature of insomnia: a descriptive summary of a sleep clinic population. *Compr Psychiatry 17*:217–220, 1976.

28. Daly DD, Yoss RD: Narcolepsy, in Vinken PJ, Bruyn GW (eds): *The Epilepsies.* Amsterdam, North-Holland Publishing Co., 1974. (Handbook of Clinical Neurology: vol 15), pp 836–852.

29. Dement WC, Carskadon MA, Guilleminault C, Zarcone VP: Narcolepsy: diagnosis and treatment. *Primary Care* 3:609–623, 1976.

30. Guilleminault C, Dement WC, Passouant P: *Narcolepsy* (Weitzman ED [series ed]: *Advances in Sleep Research*, vol 3), New York, Spectrum Publications, 1976.

31. Kales A, Cadieux RJ, Soldatos CR, Bixler EO, Schweitzer PK, Prey WT, Vela-Bueno A: Narcolepsy-cataplexy, I: clinical and electrophysiologic characteristics. *Arch Neurol* 39:164–168, 1982.

32. Roth B: *Narcolepsy and Hypersomnia*. Prague, Avicenum-Czechoslovak Medical Press. Basel, S Karger, 1980. (Revised and edited by R Broughton.)

33. Block AJ: Respiratory disorders during sleep, Part I. *Heart Lung* 9: 1011–1024, 1980.

34. Guilleminault C, Tilkian A, Dement WC: The sleep apnea syndromes. *Annu Rev Med* 27:465–484, 1976.

35. Guilleminault C, van den Hoed J, Mitler MM: Clinical overview of the sleep apnea syndromes, in Guilleminault C, Dement WC (eds): *Sleep Apnea Syndromes*. New York, Alan R Liss Inc, 1978, pp 1–12.

36. Kales A, Cadieux RJ, Bixler EO, Soldatos CR, Vela-Bueno A, Misoul C, Locke TW: Obstructive sleep apnea, I: onset, clinical course, and characteristics (in preparation).

37. Lugaresi E, Coccagna G, Cirignotta F, Farneti P, Gallassi R, DiDonato G, Verucchi P: Breathing during sleep in man in normal and pathological conditions. *Adv Exp Med Biol* 99:35–45, 1977.

38. Lugaresi E, Coccagna G, Mantovani M: *Hypersomnia with Periodic Apneas* (Weitzman EH [series ed] *Advances in Sleep Research*, vol 4). New York, Spectrum Publications, 1978.

39. Hauri P: The influence of evening activity on the onset of sleep. *Psychophysiology* 5:426–430, 1969.

40. Bixler EO, Kales A, Vela-Bueno A, Jacoby JA, Scarone S, Soldatos CR: Nocturnal myoclonus and nocturnal myoclonic activity in a normal population. *Res Commun Chem Pathol Pharmacol* 36:129–140, 1982.

41. Guilleminault C, Raynal D, Weitzman ED, Dement WC: Sleep-related periodic myoclonus in patients complaining of insomnia. *Trans Am Neurol Assoc* 100:19–22, 1975.

42. Kales A, Bixler EO, Soldatos CR, Vela-Bueno A, Caldwell AB, Cadieux RJ: Biopsychobehavioral correlates of insomnia, I: role of sleep apnea and nocturnal myoclonus. *Psychosomatics* 23:589–600, 1982.

43. Lugaresi E, Coccagna G, Gambi D, Berti Ceroni G, Poppi M: Symond's nocturnal myoclonus. *Electroencephalogr Clin Neurophysiol* 23:289, 1967.

44. Symonds CP: Nocturnal myoclonus. *J Neurol Neurosurg Psychiatry* 16:166–171, 1953.

45. Kales A, Soldatos CR, Caldwell AB, Kales JD, Humphrey FJ II, Charney DS, Schweitzer PK: Somnambulism: clinical characteristics and personality patterns. *Arch Gen Psychiatry* 37:1406–1410, 1980.

46. Kales JD, Kales A, Soldatos CR, Caldwell AB, Charney DS, Martin ED: Night terrors: clinical characteristics and personality patterns. *Arch Gen Psychiatry* 37:1413–1417, 1980.

47. Feinberg I: Sleep in organic brain conditions, in Kales A (ed): *Sleep: Physiology and Pathology*. Philadelphia, Lippincott, 1969.

48. Tauber ES, Pavel M, Weitzman ED: Analysis of snoring patterns in obstructive sleep apnea (abstr). *Sleep Research* 7:250, 1978.

49. Cummiskey J, Williams TC, Krumpe PE, Guilleminault C: The detection and quantification of sleep apnea by tracheal sound recordings. *Am Rev Respir Dis* 126:221–224, 1982.

50. Petersdorf RG, Adams RD, Braunwald E, Isselbacher KJ, Martin JB, Wilson JD: The practice of medicine, in Petersdorf RG, Adams RD, Braunwald E, Isselbacher KJ, Martin JB, Wilson JD (eds): *Harrison's Principles of Internal Medicine*. New York, McGraw-Hill Book Company, 1983, ed 10, pp 1–5.

51. Rabkin JG, Klein DF: The biological therapies, in Lewis JM, Usdin G (eds): *Treatment Planning in Psychiatry*. Washington, DC, American Psychiatric Association, 1982.

52. Wyngaarden JB: The use and interpretation of laboratory-derived data, in Wyngaarden JB, Smith LH (eds): *Textbook of Medicine*. Philadelphia, WB Saunders Company, 1982, ed 16, pp 2317–2320.

53. Kales JK, Kales A: Nocturnal psychophysiological correlates of somatic conditions and sleep disorders. *Int J Psychiatry Med* 6:43–62, 1975.

54. Williams RL: Sleep disturbances in various medical and surgical conditions, in Williams RL, Karacan I, Frazier, SH (eds): *Sleep Disorders Diagnosis and Treatment*. New York, Wiley, 1978, pp. 285–301.

55. Dlin BM, Rosen H, Dickstein K, Lyons JW, Fischer HK: The problems of sleep and rest in the intensive care unit. *Psychosomatics* 12:155–163, 1971.

56. Murphy F, Bentley S, Ellis BW, Dudley H: Sleep deprivation in patients undergoing operation: a factor in the stress of surgery. *Br Med J* 2:1521–1522, 1977.

57. Walker BB: The postsurgery heart patient: amount of uninterrupted time for sleep and rest during the first, second, and third postoperative days in a teaching hospital. *Nurs Res* 21:164–169, 1972.

58. Hamilton M, Kopelman H: Treatment of severe hypertension with methyldopa. *Br Med J* 1:151–155, 1963.

59. Nicholson AN, Stone BM: Effect of some stimulants on sleep in man. *Br J Pharm* 66:476P, 1979.

60. Williams GH, Dluhy RG: Diseases of the adrenal cortex, in Petersdorf RG, Adams RD, Braunwald E, Isselbacher KJ, Martin JB, Wilson JD (eds): *Harrison's Principles of Internal Medicine*. New York, McGraw-Hill Book Company, 1983, ed 10, pp 634–657.

61. Karacan I, Thornby JI, Anch AM, Booth GH, Williams RL, Salis PJ: Dose-related sleep disturbances induced by coffee and caffeine. *Clin Pharmacol Ther* 20:682–689, 1976.

62. Soldatos CR, Kales JD, Scharf MB, Bixler EO, Kales A: Cigarette smoking associated with sleep difficulty. *Science* 207:551–553, 1980.
63. Yules RB, Lippman ME, Freedman DX: Alcohol administration prior to sleep. *Arch Gen Psych* 16:94–97, 1967.
64. Rundell OH, Lester BK, Griffiths WJ, Williams HL: Alcohol and sleep in young adults. *Psychopharmacologia* 26:201–218, 1972.
65. Kales A, Soldatos CR, Bixler EO, Kales JD: Early morning insomnia with rapidly eliminated benzodiazepines. *Science* 220:95–97, 1983.
66. Carskadon MA, Seidel WF, Greenblatt DJ, Dement WC: Daytime carryover of triazolam and flurazepam in elderly insomniacs. *Sleep* 5: 361–371, 1982.
67. Morgan K, Oswald I: Anxiety caused by a short-life hypnotic. *Br Med J* 284:942, 1968.
68. Kales A, Bixler EO, Tan TL, Scharf MB, Kales JD: Chronic hypnotic-drug use: ineffectiveness, drug-withdrawal insomnia, and dependence. *JAMA* 227:513–517, 1974.
69. Kales A, Scharf MB, Kales JD: Rebound insomnia: a new clinical syndrome. *Science* 201:1039–1041, 1978.
70. Kales A, Scharf MB, Kales JD, Soldatos CR: Rebound insomnia: a potential hazard following withdrawal of certain benzodiazepines. *JAMA* 241:1692–1695, 1979.
71. Kales A, Soldatos CR, Bixler EO, Kales JD: Rebound insomnia and rebound anxiety: a review. *Pharmacology* 26:121–137, 1983.
72. Essig CF: Addiction to nonbarbiturate sedative and tranquilizing drugs. *Clin Pharmacol Ther* 5:334–343, 1964.
73. Hollister LE: Pharmacology and pharmacokinetics of the minor tranquilizers. *Psychiatr Ann* 11:26–31, 1981 (Suppl).
74. Lader M: Dependence on benzodiazepines. *J Clin Psychiatry* 44:121–127, 1983.
75. Tyrer P, Rutherford D, Huggett T: Benzodiazepine withdrawal symptoms and propranolol. *Lancet* 1:520–522, 1981.
76. Winokur A, Rickels K, Greenblatt DJ, Snyder PJ, Schatz NJ: Withdrawal reaction from long-term, low-dosage administration of diazepam. *Arch Gen Psychiatry* 37:101–105, 1980.
77. Coursey RD, Buchsbaum M, Frankel BL: Personality measures and evoked responses in chronic insomniacs. *J Abnorm Psychol* 84:239–249, 1975.
78. Freedman RR, Sattler HL: Physiological and psychological factors in sleep-onset insomnia. *J Abnorm Psychol* 91:380–389, 1982.
79. Haynes SN, Follingstad DR, McGowan WT: Insomnia: sleep patterns and anxiety level. *J Psychosom Res* 18:69–74, 1974.
80. Lichstein KL, Rosenthal TL: Insomniacs' perceptions of cognitive versus somatic determinants of sleep disturbance. *J Abnorm Psychol* 89:105–107, 1980.
81. Monroe LJ: Psychological and physiological differences between good and poor sleepers. *J Abnorm Psychol* 72:255–264, 1967.

82. Haynes SN, Adams A, Franzen M: The effects of presleep stress on sleep-onset insomnia. *J Abnorm Psychol 90*:601–606, 1981.
83. American Psychiatric Association: *Diagnostic and Statistical Manual of Mental Disorders*, ed 3. Washington, DC, American Psychiatric Association, 1980.
84. Tan T-L, Kales JD, Kales A, Soldatos CR, Bixler EO: Biopsychobehavioral correlates of insomnia, IV: diagnosis based on the DSM-III. *Am J Psychiatry* (in press).
85. Langsley DG: The mental status examination, in Usdin G, Lewis JM (eds): *Psychiatry in General Medical Practice*. New York, McGraw-Hill Book Company, 1979, pp 22–38.
86. Lewis JM, Usdin G: Disease, illness, and the interview, in Usdin G, Lewis JM (eds): *Psychiatry in General Medical Practice*. New York, McGraw-Hill Book Company, 1979, pp 1–21.
87. WHO Center for Classification of Diseases for North America, National Center for Health Statistics: *International Classification of Diseases, 9th Revision, Clinical Modification (ICD-9-CM)*, Ann Arbor, Mich, Edwards Brothers, Inc, 1978.
88. Association of Sleep Disorders Centers: Diagnostic classification of sleep and arousal disorders. *Sleep 2* (1):1–137, 1979.
89. Reynolds CF III, Coble PA, Black RS, Holzer B, Carroll R, Kupfer DJ: Sleep disturbances in a series of elderly patients: polysomnographic findings. *J Am Geriatr Soc 28*:164–170, 1980.
90. Reynolds CF III, Shubin RS, Coble PA, Kupfer DJ: Diagnostic classification of sleep disorders: implications for psychiatric practice. *J Clin Psychiatry 42*:296–299, 1981.
91. Kales A, Kales JD: Sleep disorders: recent findings in the diagnosis and treatment of disturbed sleep. *N Engl J Med 290*:487–499, 1974.
92. Kales A, Kales JD, Soldatos CR: Insomnia and other sleep disorders. *Med Clin North Am 66*:971–991, 1982.
93. Kales JD, Kales A, Bixler EO, Soldatos CR: Resource for managing sleep disorders. *JAMA 241*:2413–2416, 1979.
94. Oswald I: Assessment of insomnia. *Br Med J 283*:874–875, 1981.
95. Coleman RM, Roffwarg HP, Kennedy SJ, Guilleminault C, Cinque J, Cohn MA, Karacan I, Kupfer DJ, Lemmi H, Miles LE, Orr WC, Phillips ER, Roth T, Sassin JF, Schmidt HS, Weitzman ED, Dement WC: Sleep-wake disorders based on a polysomnographic diagnosis. *JAMA 247*:997–1003, 1982.
96. Dement WC: *Some Must Watch While Some Must Sleep*. Stanford, Stanford Alumni Association, 1972.
97. Dement WC: Normal sleep and sleep disorders, in Usdin G, Lewis JM (eds): *Psychiatry in General Medical Practice*, New York, McGraw-Hill Book Company, 1979, pp 414–437.
98. Zorick FJ, Roth T, Hartze KM, Piccione PM, Stepanski EJ: Evaluation and diagnosis of persistent insomnia. *Am J Psychiatry 138*:769–773, 1981.
99. Coleman RM: Periodic movements in sleep (nocturnal myoclonus)

and restless legs syndrome, in Guilleminault C (ed): *Sleeping and Waking Disorders: Indications and Techniques.* Menlo Park, Calif, Addison-Wesley Publishing Company, 1982, pp 265–295.

100. Coleman RM, Pollak CP, Weitzman ED: Periodic movements in sleep (nocturnal myoclonus): relation to sleep disorders. *Ann Neurol 8*:416–421, 1980.
101. Lugaresi E, Cirignotta F, Montagna P, Coccagna G: Myoclonus and related phenomena during sleep, in Chase MH, Weitzman ED (eds): *Sleep Disorders: Basic and Clinical Research* (Weitzman ED [series ed]: *Advances in Sleep Research*, vol 8). New York, Spectrum Publications, Inc, 1983, pp 123–127.
102. Coates TJ, Killen JD, George J, Marchini E, Silverman S, Hamilton S, Thorensen C: Discriminating good sleepers from insomniacs using all-night polysomnograms conducted at home. *J Nerv Ment Dis 170*:224–230, 1982.
103. Eisenberg JM, Williams SV: Cost containment and changing physicians' practice behavior. *JAMA 246*:2195–2201, 1981.
104. Lundberg GD: Perseveration of laboratory test ordering: a syndrome affecting clinicians. *JAMA 249*:639, 1983.
105. Oldendorff WH: The quest for an image of brain: a brief historical and technical review of brain imaging techniques. *Neurology 28*:517–533, 1978.
106. Scott J: Why are we killing clinical medicine? *Med World News 20*:6, 1979.

8. General Measures for Treating Insomnia

This chapter is the first of four that discuss the treatment of insomnia. By way of introduction to this complex subject, it is worth repeating that the first step in the treatment of insomnia is to complete a comprehensive evaluation. This enables the physician to determine the duration and nature of the complaint, identify the problem as transient or chronic, delineate the biopsychobehavioral factors underlying the complaint and then, select the proper treatment from among the various therapeutic options available.

Because transient insomnia typically develops in reaction to physical, environmental, or psychologic stress, it can be expected to subside when the stress-generating factors are eliminated or minimized. Whether or not the cause of stress can be completely eliminated, the physician can best help patients by identifying and strengthening their adaptive coping mechanisms.[1-3]

The treatment of chronic insomnia, however, is a more complex undertaking. As a guiding principle, the physician should keep in mind that chronic insomnia is multidimensional in both its causes and effects,[4-7] and any treatment approach that addresses only one of the multiple factors involved will seldom meet with success. In general, the most effective treatment program selectively combines several elements from the following categories: (1) principles for improving general hygiene and modifying life-style patterns; (2) supportive, insight-oriented, and behavioral psychotherapeutic techniques; (3) adjunctive use of hypnotic medication; and (4) use of antidepressant medication. This chapter and chapters 9 through 11 explore these elements in detail and provide the information needed to design a balanced and effective treatment plan.

General measures for managing sleep difficulty by improving hygiene and modifying life-style patterns are to a large extent a matter of common sense. These principles are applicable in most cases of insomnia,[8] both transient and chronic, and also can be offered as suggestions for general health promotion or "preventive medicine" to most patients seen in the office setting. Too often, physicians are focused on diagnosing and treating illnesses rather than on strengthening patients' abilities to enhance their own health status. While American medicine has been slow to incorporate health promotion concepts, in the last several years there has been increasing emphasis on this topic.[9] Additionally, there is increasing public desire for health information, along with the greater recognition that living wisely is associated with a reduced incidence of many serious disorders. In fact, studies have demonstrated that certain health practices are favorably correlated with health status and longevity. Among these health practices, sleeping seven to eight hours per night was positively correlated with good health status in two separate series of prospective studies[10-13,14-16] (see also Chapter 2, Insomnia: Scope of the Problem).

When recommending the general measures presented in this chapter, the physician should neither underemphasize nor overstress their importance. Because chronic insomniacs often deny their psychologic conflicts and are usually obsessional, they tend to focus excessively on any external factor that might serve as a suitable scapegoat for their sleeplessness. It is therefore important to keep the patient from becoming preoccupied with an external factor, such as the sleep environment or daily schedule, as "the answer" to his or her sleep problem.

Nevertheless, patients with chronic insomnia can assume more responsibility for obtaining healthful sleep by identifying and maintaining habits and life-style patterns that are best for them.[8] Physicians' recommendations serve to structure and reinforce patients' efforts to modify their behavior. In general, physicians can help their patients by teaching them to develop positive attitudes, make common-sense changes in their environment, and practice desirable health habits.

Obtaining an Optimal Amount of Sleep

Most insomniac patients consider their health to be dependent upon a certain amount of sleep each night. While this is true to some extent, it should be impressed upon these patients that, unlike other health practices, such as eating properly or exercising, sleep cannot be "produced" or consciously made to happen. As the insomniac well knows, the harder a person "tries to fall asleep," the more tense and afraid of sleeplessness he or she is likely to become.[5,6] Thus, performance anxiety becomes another factor contributing to the continuation of sleep difficulty. Forced attempts to sleep often create longstanding and self-perpetuating problems by generating a vicious circle of sleeplessness—unsuccessful attempts to sleep, more anxiety, more intense sleeplessness, and eventually, chronic sleep difficulty.[17]

The optimum amount of sleep has not been specifically determined. We do know, however, that most adults consider the proper amount of sleep to be between seven and eight hours nightly,[18,19] and that this amount of sleep is positively correlated with good health and longevity. Sleeping less than six hours or more than nine hours has been associated with poorer health status.[10-16] Excessive sleep has also been reported to be associated with a worried outlook and a less confident personality.[20] Therefore, patients should establish bedtime habits that allow a sleep period of between seven and eight hours unless they know from past experience that their sleep needs are otherwise. Of course, one must keep in mind that either excessively long or short sleep periods may be a result, rather than a cause, of poor physical or mental health.

Establishing Regular Schedules

Patients should be encouraged to develop a routine of going to bed when they are sleepy and arising at a regular time each morning.[8] In particular, they should avoid sleeping excessively and "resting" in bed on weekends and holidays. Laboratory studies have shown that when persons sleep ten or more hours and are not making up a sleep deficit, they tend to feel tired, lethargic, and irritable the next morning.[21] The bedtime routine should be flexible, however, because anxiety over adhering tightly to a schedule can be as disruptive as an irregular schedule. Findings from studies of variable sleepers have demonstrated that more sleep is obtained during periods of increased stress[22] and suggest that having the ability to vary sleep duration is a useful mechanism for coping with stress.[22,23] Finally, there should be enough time to "wind down" from the day's activities, and the patient should avoid stress and mental stimulation just before bedtime.

As the following case history illustrates, patients' complaints of sleep disturbance may directly reflect markedly irregular schedules, which in turn are a result of patients' general life styles and psychologic and medical dysfunctions:

Case 1. An 18-year-old unemployed, single female consulted her family physician with the complaint of a sleep problem of two and a half years' duration. She indicated that she habitually went to bed in the early hours of the morning and then would sleep until about noon. With this sleep pattern, she had little difficulty falling or staying asleep and would awaken feeling refreshed. She claimed that if she attempted to go to bed at around 11:00 PM, she was unable to fall asleep and would remain awake for at least several hours.

The patient lived with her mother and had a three-year-old son out of wedlock. Because of her sleep problem, the patient was unable to work or care for her son, even though she felt able to go out socially in the evening. Her mother essentially took care of her responsibilities because of the sleep problem. On exploring the situation further, it was evident to the physician that this patient's sleep-wakefulness pattern was a consequence of being overwhelmed by the care of the infant and her mother's reinforcement of her avoidance of responsibility.

As this pattern was clarified, the physician was able to encourage the mother to expect more mature behavior from the daughter. He suggested placement of the toddler in a day nursery so that the patient would be free to obtain employment. He also outlined a program in which the patient would maintain a schedule of arising at the same time each morning and would assume responsibility for preparing her son for the day nursery. She was urged to remain up during the day and to avoid napping. With the physician's support, the patient's mother discontinued her role of assuming too much responsibility and thereby providing the patient with secondary gain. By the third week of waking herself with the alarm and arising at a regular time, the patient's sleeping problems were essentially eliminated.

Finally, the physician referred the young woman to the local mental health center for psychotherapy to allow the patient to become more mature and independent and to establish herself as a responsible adult.

Night-shift work and travel across time zones (jet lag) disturb biologic rhythms and often cause transient sleep loss. Numerous studies have shown that desynchronization of rhythms resulting from abrupt changes in sleep schedules, rapid crossing of time zones, and acute reversal of the sleep-wakefulness cycle affect a person both physically and mentally.[24-30] These abrupt environmental time changes place the individual's circadian rhythms in conflict with the new activity schedule, meal times, and social interactions. In addition to the direct effects of fatigue and sleep loss, the individual also may be internally out of synchrony with an external demand for maximum alertness and efficiency when functioning at minimum capability. An additional factor that further reduces performance capabilities is that the individual's inner "clocks," which regulate the various physiologic systems, are being reset to the new schedule at different rates, creating an internal lack of synchrony as well.[28] Although a shift in the sleep–wakefulness cycle may occur rapidly, other body rhythms take several days or even weeks to undergo the phase changes resulting from shifting the timing of sleep.[30]

The long-term effects of shift work and jet lag upon health and longevity are unknown. However, the question of performance decrements during the time the individual is internally out of phase with such external regulators as light, darkness, and meal times may have critical significance for workers who are responsible for safety-related operations, such as airline pilots, medical house staff, night-duty nurses, or nuclear power plant workers.[24,26,28] Studies have shown that shift workers often compensate for lost sleep by taking lengthy naps during off-duty hours or by repaying their sleep deficit on weekends or holidays. Thus, they never truly shift their circadian rhythms.[24]

Although flights from west to east may theoretically be more fatigue-producing because the time shifts ahead as one travels eastward and circadian rhythms lag behind, other factors enter into the effects of long-distance flights across time zones in either direction—these are the amount of fatigue caused by preflight rest–activity schedules, the stress of long-distance travel, the amount of sleep loss incurred, and the type of activity required on arrival.[26]

To lessen the effect of these disturbances upon performance resulting from shifts in the sleep–wakefulness cycle, it is possible to make several recommendations. The most important factor seems to be to reduce sleep loss as much as possible. For the traveler, whenever practical, a daytime flight should be chosen that will not eliminate the sleep period either at home or the destination.[28] For pilots, it should be taken into account that night flying is more fatiguing than the same routine during the day,[26,28] and for rest to be beneficial it should be scheduled at a time that is appropriate physiologically.[28,31]

Another helpful measure, when feasible, is to try to synchronize all environmental regulators maximally so that even though the individual is on a new shift schedule, social activities, lighting, temperature, and meal timing are synchronized to the new environment.[28] It has been reported that resynchronization of rhythms following transmeridian flights requires a more lengthy adjustment period for those who remain isolated in hotel rooms than for those who venture outdoors and resume social or work activities.[30] For those who must perform optimally in the new environment, it is recommended that, for at least

three days in the new time zone, activities should be planned at pre-
dicted times of high efficiency. In critical situations, preadjustment can
be made using artificial phase shift of synchronizers in an isolation
chamber.[26] If, however, the shift required is for a brief period of only
one to two days, the person may be better off maintaining synchrony
with home time, rather than attempting to shift.[28]

Improving the Sleep Environment

Although the environment can affect sleep, insomniacs tend to attribute to it more importance than it actually has. Anticipation of a certain environment's effects on sleep may have greater impact on sleep
quality than the environment itself.[8,32] In effect, if people expect to
sleep poorly in certain surroundings, they probably will. Of course, an
individual's expectations of sleep efficiency in a given situation depend
on previous experience sleeping in similar environments, as well as on
overall psychologic adjustment. Psychologic difficulties often lead to
poor sleep, which in turn conditions a person to expect poor sleep
regardless of the environment.[5,17]

Before concluding that a certain environment is disturbing or helpful to sleep, the sleeper needs to adapt to it completely.[8,32] Regardless
of preferences and expectations, most individuals encounter some sleep
difficulty in an unfamiliar environment. Laboratory studies have shown
that sleeping in a new environment results in the so-called "first-night
effect," which consists of changes in both REM and stage 4 sleep and
increased wakefulness.[33] Even after having adapted to the sleep laboratory, subjects often experience a readaptation effect upon returning to
the laboratory after a period of time.[34] This suggests that individuals
may have to readjust to a different sleep environment even if they previously had adapted to it. Although people generally need to adapt or
readapt to unfamiliar sleep environments, these adjustments are made
rather quickly, usually within one to several nights.

As with sleep-length requirements, personal preference governs an
individual's notion of "the best" sleep environment. Whether one
sleeps alone or with a partner, on a hard or soft mattress, in a cold
room or a warm one, or in darkness or light depends upon personal
preference and also on individual circumstances and means. Hauri has
provided a detailed review of how various personal, environmental,
and physical factors directly affect sleep and influence attitudes toward
sleep.[32]

Type of Bed

The type of bed one finds most restful seems to depend on both cultural custom and personal preference.[32] For the Japanese, the bed is simply a mat on the floor; most Americans seem to prefer flat, supportive mattresses, although some experiment with water beds, and some Europeans like to sleep in a reclining position rather than prone.

Although such differences do not appear to affect sleep once one is accustomed to them, excessively hard surfaces, such as wooden floors, are known to cause more body movements, more awakenings, and more stage 1 sleep than softer surfaces.[35] Compared with an ordinary bed, an air-fluidized bed does not appear to affect healthy persons' sleep, although it may be helpful for patients with certain medical conditions.[36] Interestingly, subjects in one study reported sleeping better on an air-fluidized bed than on an ordinary bed, even though there were no objective improvements in their sleep.[37] Water beds do not appear to improve sleep; in fact, one study showed a reduction in total sleep time compared with a night's sleep on a regular bed.[38] Because the subjects in this study were not allowed time to adapt to the water bed, however, the finding may not be valid.

Whether one sleeps alone or with a partner affects sleep to some extent. Monroe found that couples who were good sleepers and habitually slept in the same bed had more slow-wave (stages 3 and 4) sleep and slightly less REM sleep when they slept apart.[39] The loud snoring of a bed partner is a frequent cause of complaint; more women (18%) than men (7%) complain that their sleep is disturbed by their bed partner's snoring.[19] When a bed partner or roommate becomes a source of serious and unremitting sleep disturbance, moving to another bed or to another room may be advisable.

Noise

The effect of noise on sleep depends upon several factors that are related to both the characteristics of the sleeper and the nature of the noise.[32,40,41] A sleeper's response to noise depends partly on the stage he or she is in; based on auditory awakening thresholds, stage 2 and REM sleep are the lightest sleep stages and slow-wave sleep, the deepest.[40] Whether a person awakens to noise is also determined by accumulated sleep time, the time elapsed since the last sleep period, and the time of night.[40,41] Sex is another factor; women appear to be more sensitive to noise than men.[42] The age and health of the sleeper may also make a difference because ill persons and the elderly have less deep or slow-wave sleep and seem to be more sensitive to noise while sleeping.[41,43]

Whether noise will disturb sleep also depends upon characteristics of the noise.[44,45] For example, longer-lasting sounds are more likely to produce awakenings than are shorter but louder noises.[44] The social context of the noise affects its capacity to induce stress. For many urban residents, the noise of sirens, domestic squabbles, and other nighttime activity may influence sleep over a period of years and result in chronic sleep deprivation.[45] Finally, the specific meaning of a noise can affect sleep; for example, a mother may awaken to a baby's cry but sleep through a thunderstorm.[32,46]

Even though noise may not actually awaken some people, it can lighten their sleep and impair their performance the next day. Specifically, noise from simulated aircraft flyovers has been shown to cause a lightening of sleep in terms of desynchronization of the EEG (a shift toward lighter sleep stages), resulting in decrements in performance the next day.[47]

Blocking out excessive noise can improve sleep to some extent. The use of fiberglass earplugs (with about a 20 dB attenuation value) was shown to improve sleep disrupted by street-traffic noise; subjects had more stage 4 sleep and about half the number of awakenings that they had on baseline.[48] Earplugs are not without disadvantages, however, because they may eliminate noise that would alert the sleeper to danger. The use of "white noise" to mask disruptive sounds has not been proven effective. In one experiment, a constant "white noise" of 93 dB decreased REM sleep and increased stages 1 and 2 sleep, but did not reduce awakenings and had no effect on slow-wave sleep when compared with nights under normal, quiet conditions.[49]

Temperature and Other Environmental Conditions

Room temperature, particularly heat, can make a difference in how people sleep.[32,48,50] With a rise in room temperature to a maximum of 39.4°C (102.9°F), heart rate and body movements increase, and sleep becomes lighter.[48] Relatively cooler temperatures do not have as pronounced an effect on sleep, producing either little change[51] or somewhat more restful, longer sleep.[52] Time of night may interact with temperature to affect sleep. It appears that the body's thermoregulation changes during REM periods,[53-55] so that sleeping in extreme temperatures might have a greater effect in the later part of the night when REM periods are longer and sleep is lighter.[32,40] Also, Czeisler and Weitzman and their associates have demonstrated that both sleep duration and the propensity for REM sleep are correlated with changes in the body temperature cycle.[56,57]

Extremes of barometric pressure may be conducive to sleep, as shown by increases in sleepiness measured by clinical EEGs.[58,59] However, when the effects of low pressure were assessed in people who had recently arrived at the South Pole, the hypoxia caused by low pressure resulted in symptoms of dyspnea, nausea, loss of appetite, headache, palpitations, fatigue, and sleeplessness combined with loss of slow-wave sleep.[60,61] These symptoms usually improved after several days.[61] Sleep disruption has also been reported for persons sleeping at high altitude conditions.[62] The continual darkness of the Antarctic winter also appears to affect sleep. Investigators speculated that the subjects' apathy and periodic sleep disturbances were related to a depletion of serotonin (5-HT). Both the endogenous 5-HT and melatonin synthesis were seen as being altered by the continual darkness, so that melatonin synthesis became the primary metabolic pathway for the 5-HT produced.[61]

As with other environmental factors, the effects of weather conditions on sleep diminish as the sleeper adapts to them. If sleep is lost because of a move to a different climate, for example, the sleeper will gradually resume a normal sleep time while becoming accustomed to the new surroundings. Of course, if sleep disturbance persists, temperature, and humidity can be regulated through the use of air conditioning.

Table 8.1 summarizes our recommendations for obtaining an optimal amount of sleep, establishing regular schedules, and improving the sleep environment.

Exercising Properly

Contrary to popular belief, exercise does not always create a greater need for sleep, nor does it always produce more sound sleep. The effects of physical activity on sleep have been studied fairly extensively since 1962, when Oswald first proposed that exercise would increase slow-wave sleep.[63] This and other studies have produced conflicting results, however. The differences in findings may be related to varia-

Table 8.1. General Measures in Treating Insomnia
(Duration, Schedules, and Environment)

Recommendation	Implementation
Obtain an optimal amount of sleep	Seven to eight hours of sleep is usually adequate Generally avoid extremes in sleep duration Do not attempt to force sleep
Establish regular schedules	Develop flexible routine for retiring and arising Go to bed when sleepy "Wind down" before bedtime Avoid excessive sleep on weekends
Improve sleep environment	Expect an "adaptation effect" in new environment Minimize disruptive stimuli, eg, noise and light Regulate temperature and humidity

tions in the kinds of subjects studied (eg, in fitness levels and health habits); in experimental variables, such as types of exercise measured (strenuous or moderate); and in the time of day exercise was taken.

The effect of physical activity on sleep depends largely on what time of day a person exercises, as well as on whether he or she maintains physical activity over time. Sleep is minimally affected by morning exercise, possibly because there is enough time for physiologic recovery during the day. Afternoon exercise has been found to raise levels of stage 3 sleep for the first half of the night.[64] In other studies, however, strenuous exercise in the evening has not reduced the time needed to fall asleep, nor has it enhanced slow-wave sleep throughout the first three hours of the night.[65,66] Moreover, such exercise raised the levels of autonomic arousal at sleep onset. Another study showed that when persons unaccustomed to regular physical exertion exercised moderately in the afternoon, elevated heart rate was sustained during sleep.[67] Animal studies have shown that when the degree of exercise exceeds the metabolic and physiologic limits of fatigue, sleep disturbance results.[68] Thus, exercise performed just before sleep or by people unaccustomed to physical exertion may cause physiologic activation and increased arousal, which can interfere with the restful effects of sleep.[68]

To be beneficial for enhancing sleep, exercise should be consistent over time. Athletes have more slow-wave sleep than nonathletes, and

Table 8.2. General Measures in Treating Insomnia
(Activities, Exercise, and Nutrition)

Recommendation	Implementation
Plan activities and exercise properly	Plan activities, hobbies, and interesting diversion
	Gradually increase exercise levels
	Exercise regularly
	Avoid exercise close to bedtime
Regulate nutrition	Regularize eating habits
	Avoid extreme weight changes, which may produce sleep disruption
	Nighttime snack or milk may be relaxing
	No special foods have sleep-inducing properties

when their activity is restricted they experience more wakefulness during the night.[69] When nonathletes exercise for just one day, they have no greater amounts of slow-wave sleep on the following night.[70]

Thus, patients should be advised to increase their daily exercise gradually because regular exercise may promote deeper sleep, especially during the early part of the night. Physical activity just before bedtime should be avoided, however, as it may have an arousing effect (Table 8.2).

Regulating Nutrition

Most insomniacs want to know if there is some specific food or beverage they can eat or drink to help them fall asleep. Research evidence, which is extensive, indicates that for the most part, there is not. Instead, a person's changes in weight,[71-75] metabolic activity,[71,76,77] and total nutritional balance in terms of carbohydrates, fats, and protein are more likely to affect sleep.[78-81]

When body weight exceeds ideal weight, corresponding increases occur in total sleep time and sleep-cycle length.[71] REM sleep also increases with greater body weight. Less-than-normal body weight produces the opposite effects: patients with anorexia nervosa usually have difficulty falling asleep and staying asleep and are particularly troubled by early final awakening.[72,73] Although anorexia is associated with disturbances in mood and a general emotional state that might be considered responsible for these problems, these patients' sleep difficulty is more closely related to their nutritional deficiencies.

The type of food eaten can also affect sleep. High carbohydrate–

low fat intake, when compared with a balanced diet or a low carbohy-drate–high fat diet, is associated with a decrease in slow-wave sleep and an increase in REM sleep.[80-81] Some researchers claim that the amino acid L-tryptophan, which is present in milk, has considerable sleep-inducing properties,[82] but this assertion is debated. Thus Hart-mann has shown that 1 gm of L-tryptophan reduced sleep latency only slightly,[82] and when tryptophan was given to insomniacs in a sub-sequent study by Adam and Oswald, no hypnotic effect was measured.[83] Another study showed that sleep was improved by the ingestion of Horlicks, a milk-cereal drink.[84] In speculating on the possible mecha-nism of action, the investigators pointed to animal studies showing that introducing milk or corn oil into the cat's duodenum has a sedative effect which may have been mediated by the action of cholecystokinin-pan-creozymin.[85]

Thus, people should be advised to avoid nutritional fads and extreme changes in body weight not only because they are general health hazards, but also because they may interfere with sleep. In terms of suggestions for certain "sleep promoting" foods, no claims appear to be adequately substantiated at this time (Table 8.2).

Managing Stress

Transient Insomnia

Transient sleep difficulties often develop in response to stress created by job pressures, concern regarding examinations, and anticipation or reaction to life changes, such as marriage, divorce, or the loss of a loved one.[5-7] During transient periods of stress and emotional conflict, the body's systems become more aroused or even disrupted, often resulting in an inability to relax and transient sleep difficulty. During these times, the patient may sleep more readily by relying on environ-mental cues, such as a comfortable, quiet room or darkness. The pa-tient who feels especially tense and unprepared for sleep should not go to bed or stay in the bedroom but rather engage in a relaxing activ-ity.[86-88] In this way, the bedroom will be associated with sleep rather than with conflict and worry.

It is not uncommon to compensate for sleep lost during periods of stress by getting extra sleep on weekends and holiday periods. For example, students studying for examinations or physician-house staff frequently accumulate a "sleep debt," which they then attempt to make up during weekends or holidays.[89] This practice should not be allowed to become a habit because irregular sleep schedules, especially when coupled with stress, can predispose a patient to developing chronic insomnia.

People in the midst of unusual situations are often preoccupied and unable to recognize the connection between their insomnia and the stress they are experiencing. Once this association is clear, the physician can work with the patient in choosing ways to deal with the stress at hand. This can be a matter of addressing the specifics of the problem and discussing possible solutions or simply giving the patient an opportunity to "ventilate" about the situation.[1-3]

In these cases, physicians listen as helping, nonjudgmental, and compassionate persons. While they acknowledge the patient's feelings, they do not necessarily approve of the patient's actions. They can say, "That must have upset you" or "You must have been disappointed." It is vital to avoid quarreling with the patient, no matter how provocative he or she may be. When physicians do not agree with a patient, they should convey respect for the patient's right to express irritation and differing opinions. They can also help the patient through the process of identification, in which the patient does things as he or she thinks the physician would do them, borrowing effectively from the role model of the physician. Finally, physicians may, by verbal and nonverbal cues, signal confidence in their ability to help the patient without promising a cure. Physicians must have faith in the treatment and a conviction that most people, if given encouragement and an opportunity, have the capacity to problem-solve and to overcome life stress.[1-3]

Patients need to be assured that they can tolerate a certain degree of sleeplessness without serious consequences. Too often in our culture, individuals are conditioned to believe that they should seek relief for what may be both mild and transient disruptions in their lives.[90,91] Modern advertising, especially TV commercials for sedatives and tranquilizers, is quite persuasive in convincing individuals that it is acceptable, and even necessary, to use medication for disturbances of sleep, even if they are only minor or situational.

Chronic Insomnia

Compared to its role in transient insomnia, stress in chronic insomnia is more deeply rooted because it relates to basic emotional conflicts.[4-7,17,92] In this sense, the stress of patients with chronic insomnia is largely self-generated. These patients typically deny and repress their conflicts during the day, when events and circumstances occupy their attention. But at night, when external stimulation and distractions wane, attention is turned inward and the individual relaxes and begins to regress. As feelings of anger, aggression, and sadness threaten to break through into consciousness, the insomniac fights to suppress these feelings by maintaining vigilance, and sleeplessness worsens. This process soon leads to a fear of sleeplessness, and a chronic pattern of disturbed sleep eventually conditions the patient to expect insomnia. The ultimate result is a vicious circle of continued sleep disturbance, with an escalation of psychologic conflict, physiologic arousal, sleeplessness, fear of sleeplessness, further psychologic arousal, and still further sleep difficulty[5,17] (see also Chapter 5, Psychiatric Factors in Insomnia).

External sources of stress also can play a role in the development of chronic insomnia. Recent evidence has shown that in persons who are predisposed to handling stress in maladaptive ways, stressful life events can precipitate the onset of chronic insomia.[93,94] In a study evaluating the role of life events in the onset of insomnia, poor sleepers experienced a significantly greater number of stressful life events during the year their insomnia began, compared with previous and subsequent years and compared with good sleepers[93] (see also Chapter 4, Onset, Clinical Characteristics, and Behavioral Correlates).

Thus, patients' sleep problems and their characteristic ways of handling stress are usually related. Because insomniac patients tend to internalize stress,[4-7,17,92] the physician should help them to recognize and appropriately express their feelings. Mature expression of emotions, especially anger, is vital to avoiding a chronic "bottling up" of feelings. These stored-up, unacceptable feelings emerge as bedtime approaches, and they press for release, creating tension and making sleep difficult, if not impossible.[5] The patient should learn to express anger in an assertive but not overly aggressive manner[8]—a process that the physician can encourage by discussing anger-provoking incidents in the patient's life and by briefly role-playing various effective assertive responses with the patient. Problems of living that involve sadness, rejection, or disappointment should be discussed regularly with the spouse, a supportive friend, relative, or a trusted professional. It is also helpful for the patient to express physical closeness; sexual relations with the spouse are particularly important. Lovemaking should not be put off until the patient and spouse are exhausted at the end of a long day and sex becomes a chore. Also, sex should not be avoided or used as a weapon, means of punishment, or control because the continuous deprivation of physical closeness as a device for controlling or manipulating the spouse can lead not only to difficulties with sleep but also to sexual dysfunction.[8]

Relaxation with imagery can be helpful in managing bottled-up stress that the patient may experience at bedtime.[8,95] By visualizing a positive or neutral scene or by recalling a pleasant vacation spot or an enjoyable fantasy, the patient shifts attention from internal concerns to a neutral or pleasant topic, thus refocusing attention and interrupting habitual rumination that interferes with sleep.

More formal stress reduction techniques, including progressive relaxation training, meditation training, systematic desensitization accompanied by imagery, autogenic training, biofeedback, and stimulus control, have been studied in the treatment of insomnia.[86,87,96-100] These behavioral interventions are all based on evidence provided by several studies that insomniacs have higher levels of physiologic arousal prior to sleep.[101-105] Thus, the aim of behavioral therapy is to teach patients self-management techniques that will help them regulate the tension and accompanying emotional and physiologic arousal at bedtime that results in chronic sleep disturbance. In this way, patients gradually become reconditioned to a regularized physiologic pattern at bedtime.[8] Consequently, their anxiety may be reduced, owing to the fact that they have learned and practiced specific techniques that can be applied to deal with heightened tension level at bedtime.[95] Studies have suggested that for severe chronic insomniacs, simply being told to schedule time to relax is not adequate. Rather, systematic training in relaxation is required in order to obtain improvements. However, the effects of relaxation training are limited to some improvement in patients' sleep difficulties and usually do not extend to their psychologic and adjustment disorders.[86,97]

While physicians can recommend ways of eliminating day-to-day stress (Table 8.3), they need to remain aware that the maladaptive coping mechanisms typically associated with chronic insomnia will not automatically disappear. Furthermore, although management of stress is an important issue in the treatment of chronic insomnia, it usually does not produce changes in personality patterns that have been developed and ingrained over time. Consequently, referral to a psychiatrist should be considered when appropriate. A more comprehensive approach to supportive, insight-oriented, and behavioral psychotherapeu-

Table 8.3. General Measures in Treating Insomnia
(Stress and Drug-Induced Disturbances)

Recommendation	Implementation
Manage stress properly	Recognize association between stressful events and sleeplessness
	Ventilate conflicts and anger to avoid internalization
	Be tolerant of occasional sleeplessness
	Avoid rumination over sleep difficulty
	Relaxation exercises may be helpful
Avoid drug-induced sleep disturbances	Minimize use of caffeine and cigarettes
	Recognize that alcohol may cause fragmentation of sleep
	Be aware that stimulants and other medication may disturb sleep
	Recognize sleep disturbances following drug withdrawal

tic techniques in the management of insomniac patients is discussed in Chapter 9 (Psychodynamic Psychotherapy and Behavioral Treatment of Insomnia).

Avoiding Drug-Induced Sleep Disturbance

Patients with disturbed sleep should be informed about the arousing effects of certain pharmacologic agents such as amphetamines or other stimulants, steroids, central adrenergic blockers, and bronchodilators (see also Chapter 6, Medical and Other Pathophysiologic Factors in Insomnia). Cigarettes[106] and caffeine-containing beverages, such as colas and coffee,[107] can also contribute to difficulty falling asleep, while alcohol can cause awakenings during the night.[108]

The misuse of hypnotic drugs can be disruptive to sleep. Even though most sleep medications are not effective beyond two weeks,[109] prescriptions for hypnotics may be continued for months and even years.[110] In some of these cases, dosages may be increased gradually and sleep stages become notably altered, further disturbing sleep.[111] Withdrawal of benzodiazepine drugs with short-to-intermediate elimination half-lives can cause rebound insomnia (a considerable increase in wakefulness above baseline levels), even when such drugs have been taken in only single, nightly doses.[112-114] Ultrashort half-life drugs may also cause early morning insomnia by the end of the first or second week of drug administration, when tolerance has begun to develop.[115] These very rapidly eliminated drugs may additionally cause increases in daytime levels of anxiety and tension during drug administration.[115-117]

In general, abrupt withdrawal of any CNS depressant drug may result in sleep disturbance; the degree of potential disturbance is much greater for rapidly eliminated compounds, especially the ultrashort half-life benzodiazepine drugs.[114] For this reason, physicians should gradually withdraw these medications from patients. Additionally, they should inform the patient that changes in sleep and dream patterns may occur, including disrupted sleep, vivid dreams, and even nightmares.[111]

In summary, patients should know that sleep can be disrupted by certain prescription drugs, cigarette smoking, and excessive use of colas or coffee (Table 8.3). They should also avoid using alcohol as a sedative; although it may be relaxing at first, sleep during the night may be disturbed and fragmented. Similarly, over-the-counter sedatives are of little value.[118] They are ineffective at best, and at worst they may result in untoward side effects. Needless to say, the use of street drugs, such as marijuana, cocaine, "uppers," and "downers," is not conducive to sleep or to the promotion of general health.

Special Instructions for the Elderly

As people grow older, their sleep changes in terms of the length of the sleep period, the depth of sleep, and the timing of sleep.[119-126] In general, older people sleep less because their nighttime sleep is disrupted by more frequent and longer periods of wakefulness.[119-122,124,126] The comparatively deep slow-wave sleep of younger persons may diminish or disappear entirely as they age.[120-124,126] The percentage of REM or "dreaming" sleep, however, decreases only slightly.[123,126]

To offset these changes, older patients should plan a regular time of arising in the morning, followed by an activity or social event suited to their abilities. After lunch, an hour-long nap may be desirable. If naps are taken, they should be noted in the sleep history;[127] time asleep during the day should be added to the amount of nighttime sleep. Patients should not expect to sleep seven or eight hours at night in addition to taking naps. Multiple naps should be avoided because excessive daytime sleep may interfere with sleep onset at bedtime. Finally, a daily afternoon walk is beneficial and may improve sleep at night.

Elderly individuals' sleep–wakefulness schedules and patterns are often altered because of inactivity and boredom. As a result, they may develop feelings of uselessness, neglect exercise routines, become more withdrawn, and generally feel depressed. The physician additionally needs to be aware that the elderly are at risk for experiencing numerous unique stresses to a greater degree than younger individuals.[128] These stresses may include sharply reduced income and activity resulting from mandatory retirement, significant losses of family and friends due to illness and death, concern over personal health problems, and departure of children from home. Also, the elderly may live in crime-ridden areas and thus be at risk for robbery, muggings, or purse-snatchings that create a general atmosphere of anxiety, apprehension, and helplessness. Other stresses to aging persons include their need to eventually leave familiar surroundings to reside with a grown child or to live in a senior citizens' residence or nursing home. Lastly, the elderly are exposed to our society's rapid technological change, leading to feelings that the society they once knew is becoming strange and unfamiliar.

Considering these factors, it is not surprising that elderly individuals often develop patterns of rumination at bedtime regarding feelings of emptiness and despair. Existence of these stresses among the elderly requires that the physician who is providing holistic care for geriatric patients with sleep complaints be concerned about the total 24-hour period. In such cases, the physician should encourage the patient to become involved in various hobbies, special interests, and social groups, such as senior citizens' organizations and church groups, that will provide stimulation and a supportive social network (Table 8.4).

Of course, before making specific recommendations for elderly patients, the physician should carefully assess for the presence of medical and psychiatric disorders, such as organic brain syndrome or depression.[129,130] If such a condition is present, the recommendations need to be adjusted accordingly. For example, in the organically impaired el-

Table 8.4 General Measures in Treating Insomnia
(Special Instructions Regarding the Elderly)

Educate regarding changes in sleep patterns with age
Discourage multiple naps
If naps are taken, include in 24-hour sleep totals
Suggest activities, hobbies, and special interests
Rule out presence of depression or organicity

derly patient, arousal from sleep accompanied by wandering may occur as a manifestation of the "sundown" syndrome. This syndrome is generally the result of an accentuation of perceptual distortions, confusion, and the resultant disorientation that occurs with nightfall or when the patient sleeps in a totally darkened room.[129] The physician should advise families to keep a night light on in geriatric patients' rooms so that if they experience nocturnal awakenings, they will remain better oriented to their surroundings. If elderly patients are moved to a new environment, the bedroom should contain familiar objects, such as pictures and other personal articles, to further assist them in recognizing their surroundings.

In addition to these general measures for organically impaired elderly patients, when confusion is accompanied by agitation or hyperactive psychomotor activity, the use of an antipsychotic medication, such as haloperidol (Haldol) may be helpful in reducing confusion and agitation.[129,130] In patients suffering from this type of delirium, administration of barbiturate sedatives and hypnotics is inadvisable because patients may become even more disoriented and confused as a result of central nervous system depression. For the cognitively impaired elderly or debilitated patient often seen in extended-care facilities, caution should be exercised in avoiding excessive dosages of neuroleptic drugs[131] because drug metabolism and excretion are often reduced with advancing age.[132] Usually a low dosage once or twice per day will provide both daytime control and alleviation of nocturnal disturbances.

Summary

Hygienic principles and practical life-style changes recommended for managing sleep difficulty are to a large extent a matter of common sense. Extremes in sleep duration should be avoided; about seven to eight hours of sleep are usually adequate for most people. Schedules, including time to go to sleep and to arise, should be regularized but at the same time flexible.

Patients should arrange their sleep environment to meet their preferences but should allow time to fully adapt to any changes before deciding whether or not they are satisfactory. Of course, an effort should be made to eliminate any disruptive stimuli from the sleeping environment. For the most part, however, factors like the type of mattress used, ambient noise, and room temperature have variable effects on sleep, and they should be weighed in accordance with each individual's expectations and circumstances.

Exercise is beneficial for sleep when it is taken regularly over time; sporadic physical activity does not improve sleep. It is particularly important to avoid exercising immediately before bedtime since physiologic activation may interfere with sleep onset. Nutrition can affect sleep, but not in terms of specific foods having soporific properties. Rather, healthful eating habits and maintenance of normal body weight are most likely to aid restful sleep.

Effective management of stress is especially important for patients who have difficulty sleeping. In cases of transient insomnia, patients should first be made aware of the connection between sleeplessness and the stress they are experiencing and be encouraged to express their feelings about the situation. Stress-reduction techniques such as progressive relaxation may also be employed. Finally, it is also helpful for the physician to remind patients that everyone is capable of tolerating a certain amount of sleep loss without ill effects.

Appropriate expression of feelings is even more crucial for patients who have chronic insomnia. Because sleep difficulty is often worsened by their tendency to internalize negative feelings, these patients need to learn how to express anger and conflict in an assertive way. While stress-reduction techniques, such as progressive relaxation, can also be helpful to patients who have chronic sleep difficulty, these techniques do not usually effect changes in any underlying psychologic dysfunction.

The physician should educate patients with disturbed sleep regarding the adverse effects of stimulant pharmacologic agents, cigarette smoking, caffeinated beverages, and alcohol. Many hypnotic drugs are ineffective and may cause sleep alterations, especially if consumed in excessive doses over long periods. Withdrawal of relatively rapidly eliminated benzodiazepine hypnotics can lead to rebound insomnia, and with ultrashort half-life drugs, early morning insomnia, another withdrawal phenomenon, may occur even during administration. Over-the-counter sedatives are ineffective, and the use of street drugs is often disruptive to sleep.

The elderly suffer sleep difficulties as a result of normal age-related sleep changes that are both quantitative and qualitative. Excessive napping may interfere with nocturnal sleep; total sleep time needs to be determined on a 24-hour basis. Because the elderly experience unique stresses that may lead to disruptive feelings of apprehension and worry, the physician needs to encourage them to remain physically and psychologically active and maintain or establish a supportive social network. For the organically impaired elderly patient, a familiar structured environment will help to minimize disorientation and nocturnal disturbances.

References

1. Greist JH: Adjustment disorders, in Greist JH, Jefferson JW, Spitzer RL (eds): *Treatment of Mental Disorders*. New York, Oxford University Press, 1982, pp 419–428.
2. Kales JD, Kales A: Managing the individual and family in crisis. *Am Fam Physician 12*:109–115, 1975.
3. Kolb LC, Brodie HKH: Adaptive processes and mental mechanisms, in Kolb LC, Brodie HKH (ed): *Modern Clinical Psychiatry*, ed. 10. Philadelphia, WB Saunders Company, 1982, pp 80–111.
4. Kales A, Kales JD, Bixler EO: Insomnia: an approach to management and treatment. *Psychiatr Ann 4*:28–44, 1974.
5. Kales A, Soldatos CR, Kales JD: Sleep disorders: evaluation and management in the office setting, in Arieti S, Brodie HKH (eds): *American Handbook of Psychiatry*, ed 2. New York, Basic Books, Inc, 1981, vol 7, pp 423–454.
6. Kales JD, Soldatos CR, Kales A: Diagnosis and treatment of sleep disorders, in Greist JH, Jefferson JW, Spitzer RL (eds): *Treatment of Mental Disorders*. New York, Oxford University Press, 1982, pp 473–500.
7. Soldatos CR, Kales A, Kales JD: Management of insomnia. *Annu Rev Med 30*:301–312, 1979.
8. Kales JD, Kales A: Rest and sleep, in Taylor RB (ed): *Health Promotion: Principles and Clinical Applications*. Norwalk, Conn, Appleton-Century-Crofts, 1982, pp 307–337.
9. Taylor RB (ed): *Health Promotion: Principles and Clinical Applications*. Norwalk, Conn, Appleton-Century-Crofts, 1982.
10. Belloc NB, Breslow L: Relationship of physical health status and health practices. *Prev Med 1*:409–421, 1972.
11. Belloc NB: Relationship of health practices and mortality. *Prev Med 2*:67–81, 1973.
12. Wiley JA, Camacho TC: Life-style and future health: evidence from the Alameda County study. *Prev Med 9*:1–21, 1980.
13. Wingard DL, Berkman LF: Mortality risk associated with sleeping patterns among adults. *Sleep 6*:102–107, 1983.
14. Hammond EC: Some preliminary findings on physical complaints from a prospective study of 1,064,004 men and women. *Am J Public Health 54*:11–23, 1964.
15. Hammond EC, Garfinkel L: Coronary heart disease, stroke, and aortic

aneurysm: factors in the etiology. *Arch Environ Health* 19:167–182, 1969.

16. Kripke DF, Simons RN, Garfinkel L, Hammond EC: Short and long sleep and sleeping pills. *Arch Gen Psychiatry* 36:103–116, 1979.
17. Kales A, Caldwell AB, Preston TA, Healey S, Kales JD: Personality patterns in insomnia: theoretical implications. *Arch Gen Psychiatry* 33:1128–1134, 1976.
18. Lewis HE: Sleep patterns on polar expeditions, in *Ciba Foundation Symposium on the Nature of Sleep*. Boston, Little, Brown and Co, 1961, pp 322–328.
19. The Gallup Organization: *The Gallup Study of Sleeping Habits*. Princeton, NJ, 1979.
20. Hartmann E, Baekeland F, Zwilling GR: Psychological differences between long and short sleepers. *Arch Gen Psychiatry* 26:463–468, 1972.
21. Globus GG: A syndrome associated with sleeping late. *Psychosom Med* 31:528–535, 1969.
22. Hartmann E, Brewer J: When is more or less sleep required? A study of variable sleepers. *Comprehens Psychiatry* 17:275–284, 1976.
23. Hicks RA, Lingen S, Eastman PC: Habitual variable sleep and Type A behavior. *Bull Psychom Soc* 14:469–470, 1979.
24. Bryden G, Holdstock TL: Effects of night duty on sleep patterns of nurses. *Psychophysiology* 10:36–42, 1973.
25. Johnson LC, Tepas DI, Colquhoun WP, Colligan MJ: Biological rhythms, sleep and shift work, in Weitzman ED (ed): *Advances in Sleep Research*. New York, SP Medical and Scientific Books, 1981, vol 7.
26. Klein KE, Bruner H, Holtmann H, Rehme H, Stolze J, Steinhoff WD, Wegmann HM: Circadian rhythm of pilots' efficiency and effects of multiple time zone travel. *Aerospace Med* 41:125–132, 1970.
27. Kripke DF, Cook B, Lewis OF: Sleep of night workers: EEG recordings. *Psychophysiology* 7:377–384, 1970.
28. Moore-Ede MC, Sulzman FM, Fuller CA: *The Clocks That Time Us*. Cambridge, Harvard University Press, 1982.
29. Weitzman ED, Czeisler CA, Coleman RM, Spielman AJ, Zimmerman JC, Dement W, Richardson G, Pollak CP: Delayed sleep phase syndrome: a chronobiologic disorder with sleep–onset insomnia. *Arch Gen Psychiatry* 38:737–746, 1981.
30. Weitzman ED, Kripke DF: Experimental 12-hour shift of the sleep-wake cycle in man: effects on sleep and physiologic rhythms, in Johnson LC, Tepas DI, Colquhoun WP, Colligan MJ: *Biological Rhythms, Sleep and Shift Work* (Weitzman ED [series ed]: *Advances in Sleep Research*, vol 7). New York, SP Medical and Scientific Books, 1981, pp 93–110.
31. Gunby P: Piloting when you "should" be sleeping: what effects? *JAMA* 245:900–905, 1981.
32. Hauri P: *The Sleep Disorders*. Kalamazoo, The Upjohn Company, 1977.

33. Agnew HW Jr, Webb WB, Williams RL: The first night effect: an EEG study of sleep. *Psychophysiology* 2:263–266, 1966.
34. Scharf MB, Kales A, Bixler EO: Readaptation to the sleep laboratory in insomniac subjects. *Psychophysiology* 12:412–415, 1975.
35. Kinkel HJ, Maxion H: Schlafphysiologische Untersuchungen zur Beurteilung verschiedener Matratzen. *Int Zeit Angewand Physiolog* 28:247–262, 1970.
36. Dement WC, Kales A, Zarcone V, Scharf L, Smythe H, Kuch L: Effects of the fluidized bed on sleep patterns of normal subjects. *Psychophysiology* 9:144, 1972.
37. Shurley JT: Effect of the air-fluidized bed on sleep patterns in healthy human subjects, in Artz CP, Hargest TS (eds): *Air-Fluidized Bed Clinical and Research Symposium.* Charleston, SC, Medical University of South Carolina, 1971, pp 38–49.
38. Karacan I, Williams RL: The effect of floating on sleep patterns. *Psychophysiology* 7:357, 1970.
39. Monroe LJ: Transient changes in EEG sleep patterns of married good sleepers: the effects of altering sleeping arrangement. *Psychophysiology* 6:330–337, 1969.
40. Rechtschaffen A, Hauri P, Zeitlin M: Auditory awakening thresholds in REM and NREM sleep stages. *Percept Mot Skills* 22:927–942, 1966.
41. Williams HL: Auditory stimulation, sleep loss, and the EEG stages of sleep, in Welch BL, Welch AS (eds): *Physiological Effects of Noise.* New York, Plenum Press, 1970, pp 277–281.
42. Lukas JS, Dobbs ME, Kryter KD: Disturbance of human sleep by subsonic jet aircraft noise and simulated sonic booms. *NASA-CR-1780,* 1971, pp 1–68.
43. Townsend RE, Johnson LC, Muzet A: Effects of long term exposure to tone pulse noise on human sleep. *Psychophysiology* 10:369–376, 1973.
44. Berry B, Thiessen GJ: The effects of impulsive noise on sleep, in *(APS-478) NRC 1159.*7. Ottawa, The Acoustics Section of the Division of Physics, National Research Council of Canada, 1970.
45. Pierce CM: The ghetto: an extreme sleep environment. *J Natl Med Assoc* 67:162–166, 1975.
46. Oswald I: Discussion 1, in Kales A (ed): *Sleep Physiology and Pathology.* Philadelphia, JB Lippincott Company, 1969, p 106.
47. LeVere TE, Bartus RT, Hart FD: Electroencephalographic and behavioral effects of nocturnally occurring jet aircraft sounds. *Aerospace Med* 43:384–389, 1972.
48. Otto E: Physiological analysis of human sleep disturbances induced by noise and increased room temperature, in Koella WP, Levin P (eds): *Sleep: Physiology, Biochemistry, Psychology, Pharmacology, Clinical Implications.* Basel, S Karger, 1973, pp 414–418.
49. Scott TD: The effects of continuous, high intensity, white noise on the human sleep cycle. *Psychophysiology* 9:227–232, 1972.
50. Schmidt-Kessen W, Kendel K: Einfluss der Raumtemperatur auf den Nachtschlaf. *Res Exp Med (Berl.)* 160:220–233, 1973.

51. Presley JM, Ellen P, Foshee DP: Environmental temperature and sleep in psychiatric patients. *Newlett Res Ment Health Behav Sci I.B. 15-15, 15*:17–19, 1973.

52. Kendel K, Schmidt-Kessen W: The influence of room temperature on night-sleep in man (polygraphic night-sleep recordings in the climatic chamber), in Koella WP, Levin P (eds): *Sleep: Physiology, Biochemistry, Psychology, Pharmacology, Clinical Implications.* Basel, S Karger, 1973, pp 423–425.

53. Baker MA, Hayward JN: Autonomic basis for the rise in brain temperature during paradoxical sleep. *Science 157*:1586–1588, 1967.

54. Parmeggiani PL: Temperature regulation during sleep: a study in homeostasis, in Orem J, Barnes CD (eds): *Physiology in Sleep.* New York, Academic Press, 1980, pp 97–143.

55. Shapiro CM, Moore AT, Mitchell D, Yodaiken ML: How well does man thermoregulate during sleep? *Experientia 30*:1279–1280, 1974.

56. Czeisler CA, Weitzman ED, Moore-Ede MC, Zimmerman JC, Knauer RS: Human sleep: its duration and organization depend on its circadian phase. *Science 210*:1264–1267, 1980.

57. Czeisler CA, Zimmerman JC, Ronda J, Moore-Ede MC, Weitzman ED: Timing of REM sleep is coupled to the circadian rhythm of body temperature in man. *Sleep 2*:329–346, 1980.

58. Raboutet J, Lesevre N, Remond A: Involuntary sleeping during EEG research on promoting factors. *Rev Neurol 101*:404–408, 1959.

59. Webb WB, Ades H: Sleep tendencies: effects of barometric pressure. *Science 143*:263–264, 1964.

60. Joern AT, Shurley JT, Brooks RE, Guenter CA, Pierce CM: Short-term changes in sleep patterns on arrival at the south polar plateau. *Arch Intern Med 125*:649–654, 1970.

61. Natani K, Shurley JT: Disturbed sleep and effect in an extreme environment, in Koella WP, Levin P (eds): *Sleep: Physiology, Biochemistry, Psychology, Pharmacology, Clinical Implications.* Basel, S Karger, 1973, pp 426–430.

62. Reite M, Jackson D, Cahoon RL, Weil JV: Sleep physiology at high altitude. *Electroencephalogr Clin Neurophysiol 38*:463–471, 1975.

63. Oswald I: *Sleeping and Waking.* New York, Elsevier, 1962.

64. Horne JA, Porter JM: Time of day effects with standardized exercise upon subsequent sleep. *Electroencephalogr Clin Neurophysiol 40*:178–184, 1976.

65. Hauri P: Effects of evening activity on early night sleep. *Psychophysiology 4*:267–277, 1968.

66. Hauri P: The influence of evening activity on the onset of sleep. *Psychophysiology 5*:426–430, 1969.

67. Walker JM, Floyd TC, Fein G, Cavness C, Lualhati R, Feinberg I: Effects of exercise on sleep. *J Appl Physiol 44*:945–951, 1978.

68. Hobson JA: Sleep after exercise. *Science 162*:1503–1505, 1968.

69. Baekeland F: Exercise deprivation: sleep and psychological reactions. *Arch Gen Psychiatry 22*:365–369, 1970.

70. Zir, CM, Smith RA, Parker DC: Human growth hormone release in sleep: effect of daytime exercise. *J Clin Endocrinol Metab* 32:662–665, 1971.
71. Adam K: Brain rhythm that correlates with obesity. *Br Med J* 2:234–235, 1977.
72. Crisp AH: The possible significance of some behavioural correlates of weight and carbohydrate intake. *J Psychosom Res* 11:117–131, 1967.
73. Crisp AH: Sleep, activity, nutrition and mood. *Br J Psychiatry* 137: 1–7, 1980.
74. Crisp AH, Stonehill E: Sleep patterns, daytime activity, weight changes and psychiatric status: a study of three obese patients. *J Psychosom Res* 14:353–358, 1970.
75. Kalucy RS, Crisp AH, Chard T, McNeilly A, Chen CN, Lacey JH: Nocturnal hormonal profiles in massive obesity, anorexia nervosa and normal females. *J Psychosom Res* 20:595–604, 1976.
76. Dunleavy DLF, Oswald I, Brown P, Strong JA: Hyperthyroidism, sleep and growth hormone. *Electroencephalogr Clin Neurophysiol* 36: 259–263, 1974.
77. Kales A, Heuser G, Jacobson A, Kales JD, Hanley J, Zweizig JR, Paulson MJ: All-night sleep studies in hypothyroid patients before and after treatment. *J Clin Endocrinol Metab* 27:1593–1599, 1973.
78. Chen CN, Crisp AH, Hartmann MK: Carbohydrate-rich diet and nocturnal growth hormone secretion, in Koella WP, Levin P (eds): *Sleep: Third European Congress on Sleep Research*. Basel, S Karger, 1977, pp 264–265.
79. Chen CN, Kalucy RS, Hartmann MK, Lacey JH, Crisp AH, Bailey JE, Eccleston EG, Coppen A: Plasma tryptophan and sleep. *Br Med J* 4:564–566, 1974.
80. Philips F, Chen CN, Crisp AH, Koval J, McGuinness B, Kalucy RS, Kalucy EC, Lacey JH: Isocaloric diet changes and electroencephalographic sleep. *Lancet* 2:723–725, 1975.
81. Wurtman RJ, Fernstrom JD: Control of brain serotonin by the diet. *Adv Neurol* 5:19–29, 1974.
82. Hartmann E: L-tryptophan: a rational hypnotic with clinical potential. *Am J Psychiatry* 134:366–370, 1977.
83. Adam K, Oswald I: One gram of L-tryptophan fails to alter the time taken to fall asleep. *Neuropharmacology* 18:1025–1027, 1979.
84. Brezinova V, Oswald I: Sleep after a bedtime beverage. *Br Med J* 2: 431–433, 1972.
85. Fara JW, Rubinstein EH, Sonnenschein RR: Visceral and behavioral responses to intraduodenal fat. *Science* 166:110–111, 1969.
86. Bootzin RR, Nicassio PM: *Behavioral Treatments for Insomnia* (Progress in Behavior Modification, vol 6), New York, Academic Press, Inc, 1978, pp 1–45.
87. Haynes SN, Price MG, Simons JB: Stimulus control treatment of insomnia. *J Behav Ther Exp Psychiatry* 6:279–282, 1975.
88. Thoresen CE, Coates TJ, Zarcone VP, Kirmil-Gray K, Rosekind MR:

Treating the complaint of insomnia: self-management perspectives, in *The Comprehensive Handbook of Behavioral Medicine,* vol 1, New York, Spectrum Publications, Inc, 1980.

89. Masterton JP: Sleep of hospital medical staff. *Lancet 1*:41–42, 1965.

90. Cohen S: Methaqualone: a new twist. *Drug Abuse and Alcoholism Newsletter 11(1)*:1–4, 1982.

91. Cohen S: Pleasure and pain. *Drug Abuse and Alcoholism Newsletter 11(5)*:1–4, 1982.

92. Kales A, Caldwell AB, Soldatos CR, Bixler EO, Kales JD: Biopsycho-behavioral correlates of insomnia, II: MMPI pattern specificity and consistency. *Psychosom Med 45*:341–356, 1983.

93. Healey ES, Kales A, Monroe LJ, Bixler EO, Chamberlin K, Soldatos CR: Onset of insomnia: role of life-stress events. *Psychosom Med 43*: 439–451, 1981.

94. Kales JD, Kales A, Bixler EO, Soldatos CR, Cadieux RJ, Kashurba GJ, Vela-Bueno A: Biopsychobehavioral correlates of insomnia, V: clinical characteristics and behavioral correlates. *Am J Psychiatry* (in press).

95. Montgomery I, Perkin G, Wise D: A review of behavioral treatments for insomnia. *J Behav Ther Exp Psychiatry 6*:93–100, 1975.

96. Borkovec TD, Weerts TC: Effects of progressive relaxation on sleep disturbance: an electroencephalographic evaluation. *Psychosom Med 38*:173–180, 1976.

97. Nicassio P, Bootzin R: A comparison of progressive relaxation and autogenic training as treatments for insomnia. *J Abnorm Psychol 83*: 253–260. 1974.

98. Ribordy SC, Denney DR: The behavioral treatment of insomnia: an alternative to drug therapy. *Behav Res and Therapy 15*:39–50, 1977.

99. Thoresen CE, Coates TJ, Kirmil-Gray K, Rosekind MR: Behavioral self-management in treating sleep-maintenance insomnia. *J Behav Med 4*:41–52, 1981.

100. Woolfolk RL, Carr-Kaffashan L, McNulty TF, Lehrer PM: Meditation training as a treatment for insomnia. *Behav Ther 7*:359–365, 1976.

101. Coursey RD, Buchsbaum M, Frankel BL: Personality measures and evoked responses in chronic insomniacs. *J Abnorm Psychol 84*:239–249, 1975.

102. Freedman RR, Sattler HL: Physiological and psychological factors in sleep-onset insomnia. *J Abnorm Psychol 91*:380–389, 1982.

103. Haynes SN, Adams A, Franzen M: The effects of presleep stress on sleep-onset insomnia. *J Abnorm Psychol 90*:601–606, 1981.

104. Haynes SN, Follingstad DR, McGowan WT: Insomnia: sleep patterns and anxiety level. *J Psychosom Res 18*:69–74, 1974.

105. Monroe LJ: Psychological and physiological differences between good and poor sleepers. *J Abnorm Psychol 72*:255–264, 1967.

106. Soldatos CR, Kales JD, Scharf MB, Bixler EO, Kales A: Cigarette smoking associated with sleep difficulty. *Science 207*:551–553, 1980.

107. Karacan I, Thornby JI, Anch AM, Booth GH, Williams RL, Salis PJ:

Dose-related sleep disturbances induced by coffee and caffeine. *Clin Pharmacol Ther 20*:682–689, 1976.

108. Rundell OH, Lester BK, Griffiths WJ, Williams HL: Alcohol and sleep in young adults. *Psychopharmacologia 26*:201–218, 1972.

109. Kales A, Bixler EO, Kales JD, Scharf MB: Comparative effectiveness of nine hypnotic drugs: sleep laboratory studies. *J Clin Pharmacol 17*: 207–213, 1977.

110. Bixler EO, Kales JD, Kales A, Scharf MB, Leo LA: Hypnotic drug prescription patterns: two physician surveys. *Sleep Res 5*:62, 1976.

111. Kales A, Bixler EO, Tan TL, Scharf MB, Kales JD: Chronic hypnotic-drug use: ineffectiveness, drug-withdrawal insomnia and dependence. *JAMA 227*:513–517, 1974.

112. Kales A, Scharf MB, Kales JD: Rebound insomnia: a new clinical syndrome. *Science 201*:1039–1041, 1978.

113. Kales A, Scharf MB, Kales JD, Soldatos CR: Rebound insomnia: a potential hazard following withdrawal of certain benzodiazepines. *JAMA 241*:1692–1695, 1979.

114. Kales A, Soldatos CR, Bixler EO, Kales JD: Rebound insomnia and rebound anxiety: a review. *Pharmacology 26*:121–137, 1983.

115. Kales A, Soldatos CR, Bixler EO, Kales JD: Early morning insomnia with rapidly eliminated benzodiazepines. *Science 220*:95–97, 1983.

116. Carskadon MA, Seidel WF, Greenblatt DJ, Dement WC: Daytime carryover of triazolam and flurazepam in elderly insomniacs. *Sleep 5*: 361–371, 1982.

117. Morgan K, Oswald I: Anxiety caused by a short-life hypnotic. *Br Med J 284*:6320, 1982.

118. Kales J, Tan T-L, Swearingen C, Kales A: Are over-the-counter sleep medications effective? All-night EEG studies. *Curr Therap Res 13*: 143–151, 1971.

119. Bixler EO, Kales A, Jacoby JA, Soldatos CR, Vela-Bueno A: Nocturnal sleep and wakefulness: effects of age and sex in normal sleepers. *Int J Neurosci* (in press).

120. Feinberg I: Changes in sleep patterns with age. *J Psychiatr Res 10*:283–306, 1974.

121. Feinberg I, Koresko FL, Heller N: EEG sleep patterns as a function of normal and pathological aging in man. *J Psychiatr Res 5*:107–144, 1967.

122. Kales A, Wilson T, Kales JD, Jacobson A, Paulson MJ, Kollar E, Walter RD: Measurements of all-night sleep in normal elderly persons: effects of aging. *J Am Geriatr Soc 15*:405–414, 1967.

123. Roffwarg H, Muzio J, Dement W: Ontogenetic development of the human sleep-dream cycle. *Science 152*:604–619, 1966.

124. Webb WB: Sleep in older persons: sleep structure of 50- to 60-year-old men and women. *J Gerontology 37*:581–586, 1982.

125. Webb WB, Agnew HW Jr: Sleep cycling within twenty-four hour periods. *J Exp Psychol 74*:158–160, 1967.

126. Williams RL, Karacan I, Hursch CJ: *EEG of Human Sleep: Clinical Applications*. New York Wiley, 1974.
127. Kales A, Soldatos CR, Kales JD: Taking a sleep history. *Fam Physician* 22:101–108, 1980.
128. Finkel SI, Stein E, Miller N, Cameron I, Hontela S, Eisdorfer C: Special perspectives on treatment planning for the elderly, in Lewis JM, Usdin G (eds): *Treatment Planning in Psychiatry*. Washington, DC, American Psychiatric Association, 1982, pp 379–433.
129. Murray GB: Confusion, delirium, and dementia, in Hackett TP, Cassem NH (eds): *Massachusetts General Hospital Handbook of General Hospital Psychiatry*. St. Louis, CV Mosby Company, 1978, pp 93–116.
130. Wells CE, McEvoy JP: Organic mental disorders, in Greist JH, Jefferson JW, Spitzer RL (eds): *Treatment of Mental Disorders*. New York, Oxford University Press, 1982, pp 3–43.
131. Kales A, Kales JD, Soldatos CR: Insomnia and other sleep disorders. *Med Clinics N America* 66:971–991, 1982.
132. Shader RI, Greenblatt DJ: Management of anxiety in the elderly: the balance between therapeutic and adverse effects. *J Clin Psychiatry 43*: 8–18, 1982.

9. Psychotherapy and Behavior Therapy

One of the fundamental concepts repeated throughout this book is the association between insomnia and psychologic conflicts.[1-8] In the previous chapter on general measures for treating insomnia, non-pharmacologic ways to manage the minor emotional disturbances arising from day-to-day stress are offered. Here, we discuss the psychotherapeutic principles for the treatment of the longstanding psychopathology that is so commonly associated with the symptom of chronic insomnia. Many of these psychotherapeutic techniques are complex and time-consuming and require specialized training and expertise in psychiatry. Most physicians, though, by virtue of their general medical training, clinical experience, and sensitivity to patients, possess sufficient skill and confidence to provide supportive psychotherapeutic measures, as well as behavioral approaches.

Approaches to treating transient and chronic insomnia differ; these approaches are best understood within the context of the development and progression of each condition. In transient insomnia, the reactions of individuals to stressful life situations lead to emotional arousal.[9] This, in turn, leads to physiologic arousal and sleeplessness. If the stressful situation does not subside or the individual is unable to cope effectively, then a fear of sleeplessness itself may become a contributing factor in the development of chronic insomnia. As discussed in Chapter 5 (Psychiatric Factors in Insomnia), patients with chronic insomnia characteristically internalize their emotions instead of expressing them outwardly.[1-7] This internalization of psychologic conflicts may lead to chronic emotional arousal because conflicts that the insomniac typically tries to deny and repress during the day become a focus of attention and ruminative apprehension at night.[4] This rumination and apprehension in turn results in physiologic arousal, as evidenced by a number of studies showing that insomniacs have higher levels of autonomic activity at bedtime than good sleepers.[1,2,6,10,11] Soon, especially in individuals who have inadequate coping patterns,[12] a fear of sleeplessness and a conditioned pattern of disturbed sleep develops apart from the psychologic conflicts that first caused the insomnia, ultimately resulting in a vicious circle of chronic sleep disturbance.[3,5]

General Psychotherapeutic Considerations

Transient Insomnia

In transient insomnia, the physician's primary goal is to strengthen the patient's ego defenses and other adaptive mechanisms.[9,13,14] Depending on the nature of the patient's problem, the physician selects a form of brief psychotherapy that uses either supportive or insight-oriented techniques or a combination of both approaches. Supportive psychotherapy aims at restoring patients to their previous level of functioning. It emphasizes the role of the stressor in precipitating the symptoms, while providing strong reassurance that the patient's previous capacity to function will return.[13,15] Reassuring patients that their conditions are treatable helps to minimize the fear of sleeplessness that often leads to the development of chronic insomnia.[9] In addition, this strong emotional support assists patients in mastering stress and may reduce their vulnerability to mental or physical illness.[16,17]

Chronic Insomnia

The treatment of persistent insomnia is complicated by patients' denial of underlying psychologic conflicts—a characteristic that contributes to the impression that the symptom of insomnia is the only problem.[5,9,18,19] Patients also may be reluctant to give up the secondary gain afforded by incorporating insomnia into their life styles. Patients often employ the fatigue or irritation that results from insomnia as an excuse to withdraw from family, social, or occupational responsibilities. The use of denial, the presence of secondary gain, and the self-perpetuating nature of insomnia require that the physician initially be active and direct in exploring conflict areas, rather than using a gradual, uncovering approach.[5,9,19] Because insomniacs tend to focus on the somatic aspects of their problem, they are mainly interested in symptomatic relief. If areas of psychologic conflict are identified early in treatment, however, patients are more likely to commit themselves to therapy. In the early stages of psychotherapy, concurrent psychopharmacologic treatment can be useful. The pharmacologic agent provides immediate symptomatic relief and helps to break the vicious circle of insomnia, while the psychotherapeutic component allows the patient to become an active participant in working to master the problems underlying the chronic sleep disturbance.[9,18-21] Appropriate pharmacotherapy in the beginning phase of psychotherapy can encourage a patient's participation in psychotherapy because it reduces symptoms and fosters identification with the physician and the development of a positive transference.

Four basic therapeutic techniques are discussed in this chapter—supportive psychotherapy, psychodynamic therapy, interpersonal psychotherapy, and behavior therapy. Each method is useful for treating chronic insomnia and can be used by itself or in combination with the other techniques. Offenkrantz and Tobin have indicated that learning in therapy may occur through identification, conditioning, or insight,[22] and that these processes are in turn represented, respectively, by the psychodynamic, behavioral, and experiential schools of thought.[23] In psychodynamic therapy, insight is achieved through the basic techniques of clarification, confrontation, interpretation, and working through.[23] For this type of therapy, important issues are the patient's level of motivation, intelligence, and ability to communicate,[24] as well as the patient's ability to tolerate regression.[23] Several authors stress the importance of the therapist being active in the part of the therapeutic process that focuses on the "here and now" of the patient's daily life and interpersonal relationships, in addition to the uncovering and correcting of underlying causes.[23,25,26] Because it provides insight, psychodynamic therapy helps patients deal with the unexpressed psychologic conflicts and emotions that predispose them to emotional and physiologic arousal at night.[3-5,9,18,19] For example, a patient may fear going to bed because of repressed memories of traumatic events in childhood that were associated with sleep or bedtime. Or patients may feel that they will lose control of their feelings by going to sleep, and staying awake is a defense against this fear. Helping patients express their feelings and restore the balance of outwardly expressed, versus self-restrained, aggression during the day can be important tasks of treatment that will reduce nighttime emotional release and the resulting arousal at bedtime.[5]

When insomnia becomes chronic, patients' interpersonal relationships, particularly their interactions with those close to them, often change significantly. Interpersonal problems that arise are closely interwoven with patients' unresolved psychologic conflicts and in this way are intimately tied to both the development and persistence of insomnia. These problems may relate to fears of closeness or aggression, or they could represent manipulation of the spouse, for example, by being "too tired to have sex." In these cases, conjoint marital therapy along with sexual counseling is indicated.[5,9]

Behavioral therapy techniques are most useful as an adjunctive measure because they may be effective in treating the physiologic aspects of the symptom of insomnia, but they do not deal with the psychologic basis of the problem. As such, behavioral methods are best employed in the initial stages of therapy with patients who have difficulty falling asleep. Relaxation training combined with suggested, pleasant imagery focuses patients' thoughts on a positive or neutral theme, shifting attention from internal concerns to the external world.[27,28] Thus, patterned thinking replaces the ruminative concerns and apprehension that maintain the insomniac's high level of cognitive and autonomic arousal. Another advantage of behavioral therapy is that individuals' active participation in achieving therapeutic results gives them a sense of mastery, thereby reducing feelings of passivity and helplessness.

The types of psychotherapy to be used with the insomniac patient depend on the characteristics of the individual case and on the particular skills and expertise of the physician for any specific form of psychotherapy.[5,9,18,19] In general, however, certain therapeutic goals should be pursued regardless of the type of therapy used. These general therapeutic goals include: initial and gradual withdrawal of excessive or inappropriate medication (see also Chapter 8, General Measures for Treating Insomnia); education regarding basic sleep hygiene (see also Chapter 8); establishment of improved coping mechanisms for handling stress; improvement of ability to express emotions appropriately; relief of the symptom of insomnia by appropriate pharmacologic means, if necessary (see also Chapters 10 and 11 on hypnotic and antidepressant drugs, respectively); development of insight regarding personal vulnerability; improvement in the quality of the patient's interpersonal relationships; and restructuring of the patient's life style so that it does not revolve around the symptom of insomnia.

Certain therapeutic issues need to be dealt with in most cases of insomnia, again, independently of the type of therapy applied.[5,9,18,19] The issues that most commonly emerge during psychotherapy with insomniac patients include the following: denial of any problem areas other than insomnia; strong resistance to the physician's exploration of problem areas; need for control, as expressed in manipulation of medications and lack of compliance with general measures; reluctance to become an active participant in the therapeutic alliance, wishing instead to be overly dependent upon the physician; and an excessive need to please the physician, resulting in withholding direct expressions of negative feelings.

Another major issue in therapy relates to problems occurring within countertransference (the physician's unconscious or conscious reactions to the patient).[23,29] Physicians must be particularly sensitive to their reactions to the patient because some reactions may interfere with an effective therapeutic relationship. Initial problems with countertransference are usually associated with the insomniac patient's tendency to focus on the insomnia and minimize or completely deny any psychologic difficulties. Physicians may be misled into accepting the patient's rigid attitudes and may even join in the denial of significant psychopathology. On the other hand, if the physician tries to encourage the patient to discuss other conflicts and meets strong denial and resistance, the physician may become impatient and frustrated. Even if the patient can be engaged in a discussion of such issues, the physician may feel guilty, angry, or helpless because the therapy progresses slowly or reaches a stalemate. It is therefore crucial for therapists to maintain patience and a positive attitude and to be satisfied with gradual progress.

When pharmacologic and psychotherapeutic approaches are combined, a negative countertransference to the patient may lead physicians to reduce their psychotherapeutic involvement and to rely on the use of medication as a means of keeping emotional distance from the patient. The patient may then interpret the prescription of a drug as a form of hostility and rejection on the part of the physician and as a result may become more anxious.[21]

Effectiveness of Psychotherapy

As yet, no controlled studies have demonstrated the efficacy of psychotherapy in the treatment of insomnia. However, a number of recent reviews pertaining to the outcome of psychotherapy in general indicate that a high percentage of patients improve when treated by various psychotherapeutic methods.[30-35] A review of these controlled, comparative studies shows that all forms of psychotherapy tend to result in improvement for a substantial percentage of patients, as indicated by the reduction of specific symptoms and by improvement in global measures of general adjustment. The behavior therapies (and pharmacotherapies) tend to affect predominantly measures of symptom outcome, whereas psychotherapies that are long-term, intensive, and psychoanalytically oriented tend to have the greatest influence on general adjustment measures. Earlier effects are usually seen with therapies that are behaviorally oriented, time-limited, and directive, while slower but more lasting benefits are probably achieved with insight-oriented therapies and psychoanalysis.[32]

Smith, Glass, and Miller reviewed 475 studies of psychotherapy that included approximately 25,000 patients.[35] They found that persons who received therapy were better off in terms of symptom reduction and global improvement than 85 percent of persons who did not receive treatment. Other studies show that psychotherapy results in monetary savings in medical treatment for chronic diseases, as well as a decreased utilization of other medical services.[36-39]

A review of studies evaluating the predictors of psychotherapeutic outcome has shown that certain factors are associated with improvement.[31] Characteristics of the patient associated with improvement include adequacy of personality functioning, absence of psychotic trends, good motivation for treatment, a higher level of intelligence, high initial levels of anxiety or depression, and the presence of social achievements. Therapists' traits associated with improvement are level of experience, attitudes, interest patterns, empathy, and feeling of similarity between therapist and patient. When treatment factors are considered, the number of sessions is a more powerful predictor of improvement than the type of therapy, and a combination of individual and group psychotherapy is more effective than one or the other alone.

Specific Psychotherapeutic Approaches

The specific psychotherapeutic interventions discussed in this chapter are presented in relation to the psychiatric conditions most commonly associated with insomnia (see Tables 9.1 and 9.2).

Although a treatment approach involving multiple modalities is indicated in almost every case of insomnia, management of the patient's principal psychiatric difficulties is of primary importance. In our study of *Diagnostic and Statistical Manual of Mental Disorders*[40] (DSM-III) psychiatric diagnoses in 100 patients with chronic insomnia, the most prevalent principal diagnoses were affective disorders (mainly dysthy-

Table 9.1. Psychotherapeutic Approaches to Treating Insomnia
(Axis I Diagnoses in DSM-III)

Psychiatric Conditions	Treatment Recommendations
Affective Disorders	Identify and explain maladaptive patterns Carefully analyze transference Help modify harsh conscience Promote realistic self-perspective
Anxiety Disorders	Alleviate anxiety quickly Avoid premature optimism Gradually reduce support and promote insight Carefully analyze transference Elucidate dynamics of repressed conflicts
Somatoform Disorders	Emphasize psychologic causes of insomnia Educate and reassure Initially break vicious circle with hypnotics Reduce secondary gain Help reorganize interpersonal relationships
Substance Use Disorders	Start psychotherapy after withdrawal Use group psychotherapy Emphasize underlying psychopathology

mic disorder), anxiety disorders, and somatoform disorders on Axis I, and compulsive, borderline, and histrionic disorders on Axis II[41] (see also Chapter 5, Psychiatric Factors in Insomnia). Substance use disorder was the principal diagnosis in only one case, while it was an additional diagnosis in 16 cases. Because all 100 of our patients with chronic insomnia met the criteria for one or more DSM-III diagnoses on Axis I or II, and considering our experience in treating these patients, we believe that psychotherapy is often essential for treating the emotional disorders associated with the symptom of insomnia.

Affective Disorders

Before discussing the psychotherapy of affective disorders in patients with chronic insomnia, it should be pointed out that while the DSM-III apparently corrected for overdiagnosing schizophrenic disorders when the DSM-II had been used, it may have created a tendency for overdiagnosing affective disorders,[42] in particular, dysthymic disorder and atypical depression. This was certainly our impression in our DSM-III-based study of chronic insomnia.[41] Using DSM-III criteria, patients having a significant degree of anxiety in combination with depression are classified as having affective disorders rather than anxiety disorders. A relevant psychotherapeutic issue is that there does not seem to be a close affinity between major depression and dysthymic disorder.[42] In fact, psychotherapy of patients with dysthymic disorder focuses primarily on neurotic conflicts and personality disorders, in contrast to major depression or bipolar disorder, which are usually more responsive to pharmacologic treatment.[43,44] Furthermore, patients with dysthymic disorder who have a characterologic type of depression, without vegetative symptoms, have the poorest response to antidepressant medication.[42,45-47]

In our diagnostic study of patients with chronic insomnia, dysthymic disorder was the most common DSM-III diagnosis among patients who had affective disorders.[41] Thus, the following discussion focuses on psychotherapy for dysthymic disorder, which, as defined in DSM-III,[40] replaces the DSM-II category of depressive neurosis. It also applies to other types of depression, which are collectively referred to as characterologic depression.[48]

In individual psychodynamic psychotherapy of depressed patients, Jacobson has described several phases of treatment.[49] Once patients' initial resistance to treatment has been overcome, the therapist usually will be able to establish rapport quickly. Dramatic improvement may follow, but such progress can be deceptive.[49,50] After an initial tendency to idealize the therapist, patients soon enter a period of growing disappointment, in part because they are more able to identify their problems but see that they are essentially unchanged. Countertransference problems may become evident in this phase, requiring the physician to be more tolerant and positive.[29]

A third period follows, in which patients become more involved in therapy and withdraw from other interpersonal relationships.[49,50] This is when the physician needs to be most careful in handling patients' strong dependency needs, which prompt patients to be angry or accusatory because of the ambivalence over feeling dependent on the therapist. Therefore, a firm and careful analysis of transference conflicts is in order.

An important task in therapy is the identification of major maladaptive patterns, which are brought to light through the study of patients' histories of life events.[49,50] Such an inquiry demonstrates to patients that they do not react excessively to all situations, but that they respond selectively to certain events and experiences by becoming depressed. Patients will then understand their disturbance in terms of its relationship to specific problems and will begin to develop a sense of mastery.

We believe the following tasks of therapy described by Mendelson[50] for the treatment of depression are appropriate in managing chronic insomnia in depressed patients: 1) help patients identify their interpersonal and affectional needs; 2) evaluate defensive maneuvers that tend to isolate patients; 3) identify self-defeating patterns in relating to others, particularly members of the opposite sex; 4) help patients modify an unrealistically harsh conscience; and 5) help patients acquire a more realistic perspective of their abilities and talents.

Another approach to depressive disorders is cognitive therapy, which is designed to alleviate patients' negative self-perceptions, low self-esteem, and pessimism regarding the future.[51-53] In one study that compared cognitive therapy to treatment with imipramine (Tofranil), cognitive therapy produced a significant improvement in outlook and self-concept.[53] Thus, this approach may be indicated particularly for those patients with chronic insomnia whose self-esteem and general outlook are especially poor.

Interpersonal psychotherapy may be used when the focus of treatment is on improving a patient's social and interpersonal functioning.[29,49,54] In one study, social skills training plus placebo treatment resulted in more improvement in depressed patients than did treatment with amitriptyline (Elavil).[55] Also, the dropout rate for the amitriptyline group was extremely high (56%). Group psychotherapy is indicated for many depressed insomniacs because it can provide a corrective family type of experience and help with the development of more effective interpersonal skills.[56] Specifically, it gives patients a chance to discharge their emotions appropriately, rather than directing them inward. Attending a group in conjunction with individual psychotherapy is probably the best therapeutic option for most depressed patients with insomnia.

The need to explore the emotional dynamics of the family is particularly important for depressed patients because the members of such families characteristically avoid expressing affection and anger and handle these emotions inappropriately.[57,58] Therefore, the needs of each member for autonomy and intimacy may not be met in the family system because of an inability to tolerate the patient's emotional expression. Thus, the patient's depression may be the final common pathway for many repetitive and futile emotional encounters in the family. A corrective experience in family therapy may help the patient learn to express emotions appropriately,[29] which will reduce the tendency to internalize, and consequently lessen, emotional arousal and the symptom of insomnia.

Marital therapy[59] may be indicated in many cases because marital discord is known to be an important stressor among depressed patients.[29] This is particularly true for insomniac patients, who frequently develop unexpressed hostile feelings toward their spouses. Behavioral techniques can help to reduce the depressed insomniac patient's ruminations and complaints (see section in this chapter on Behavioral Treatment of Insomnia). These techniques, however, do not address issues of long-term personality change or global improvement of the patient's status.[9,60]

Anxiety Disorders

Most insomniac patients are quite anxious. Many of them are depressed and anxious at the same time; most of the depressed patients in our sample[41] showed considerable anxiety, apprehension, ruminative worrying, and phobicness. These patients were assigned a DSM-III diagnosis of dysthymic disorder because the DSM-III indicates that the diagnosis of anxiety disorder is not made in the presence of a depressive disorder.[40]

Anxiety disorders are best treated with individual psychodynamic psychotherapy;[61-65] this is also the case for patients with chronic insomnia who have anxiety disorders. For patients with intense, free-floating anxiety or with polymorphous, multiple symptoms, treatment should start with supportive psychotherapy (at times combined with anxiolytic or hypnotic medication), followed by psychodynamic psychotherapy.[65] Patients who are predominantly phobic or obsessive-compulsive may be more responsive to behavioral techniques.[66] Other psychotherapeutic modalities may be indicated, either by themselves or in combination with any of the above treatments, depending on the nature of the patient's problems and the skills of the therapist. For example, if the anxiety is focused and the precipitant is evident, short-term psychotherapy may be indicated.[67]

In the typical anxiety disorder, the anxiety is free-floating, ie, the patient is anxious without being aware of any apparent reason for it.[64,66] Thus, the psychotherapy of the anxiety-ridden insomniac patient should begin with a "decompression" phase to lower the patient's level of anxiety so that more in-depth therapeutic measures can be attempted.[64] The physician primarily provides support that favors the establishment of a solid therapeutic alliance; this can be done by providing education and reassurance and by allowing patients to ventilate their anxiety. When the anxiety is alleviated, the insomnia often subsides rapidly, particularly when medication is used as an adjunct. At this point, the physician should avoid premature enthusiasm over the patient's initial positive response to therapy. The physician should keep in mind that the patient still retains impaired coping mechanisms for dealing with problems in daily living.

When trust has been established and anxiety is lowered, the physician can gradually reduce the support provided during the initial phase, but only when the patient has developed stronger coping mechanisms. These strengths can be measured by the patient's reduced level of manifest anxiety and improved progress in adapting vocationally, socially, and sexually. Thus, therapy remains to a certain degree supportive, but the goal now becomes the development of insight.[64] The decision to employ psychodynamic psychotherapy is based not only on the patient's symptoms but also on a number of other factors, including the capacity to tolerate painful emotions and regression, the ability to express feelings openly and form meaningful relationships, good impulse control, and a relatively high level of intelligence.[23,24,65]

In psychodynamic therapy, the initial focus is to help patients become aware of areas in their current life situations that are causing anxiety.[63,64] Next, it is important to develop the common themes that exist in the different anxiety-producing situations. In this way, patients' core conflicts are identified and then understood from a historical perspective. For example, it may become apparent that a patient has repeated problems with authority figures. In turn, the therapeutic process reveals that this conflict area is a consequence of having had an overly critical parent, which resulted in excessive and unexpressed anger coupled with the fear of loss of control of this anger when interacting with authority figures.

As treatment becomes more insighted-oriented, patients may feel themselves becoming more dependent on the physician.[63,64] Out of a fear of losing the physician's support, they may withhold negative emotions. Because the development of a capacity for appropriate emotional expression is a goal of therapy, patients' needs to "please" the physician must be worked through early during this phase of treatment. Patients' suppression of unacceptable feelings is a threat to the resolution of the problem and may even lead to a reappearance of insomnia.

Eventually, the focus shifts to the essential work on the dynamics of the repressed psychologic conflicts[61,63] that led to the development of the insomnia. Many patients do not even mention their sleep difficulty after the initial stages of therapy, or if reminded, refer to it as a very remote experience, indicating the importance of conflictual life events in the development of insomnia.

Obsessive-compulsive personality components are common among insomniacs with anxiety disorders and dysthymic disorders, as well as in those in whom these disorders are not present. In our DSM-III diagnostic study of chronic insomniac patients, compulsive personality disorder or trait was the most frequent diagnosis on Axis II.[41] Both the psychotherapeutic and behavioral management of patients with obsessive-compulsive symptomatology are discussed in later sections of this chapter.

Somatoform Disorders

Patients with somatoform disorders complain of physical symptoms without organic findings, and it is presumed that their symptoms are linked to psychologic conflicts.[40] In this sense, almost every insomniac can be considered to have a somatoform disorder, although most insomniacs fall into other principal diagnostic categories, such as dysthymic disorder,[41] that preclude the diagnosis of a somatoform disorder. Further, most insomniacs are excessively concerned about their health, and especially about the effects of insomnia on both their physical and mental health. They may repeatedly undergo extensive medical and laboratory work-ups, a process that can exacerbate their hypochondriacal tendencies. Moreover, general physicians tend to focus on physical pathology and often ignore the patient's use of symptoms to cope with interpersonal conflict and stress in living.[68,69]

Patients with somatoform disorders are particularly resistant to formal psychotherapy, mainly because they fail to acknowledge any causal relationship between their emotions and their insomnia. The psychiatrist may repeatedly attempt to convince insomniacs that insomnia is not causing their poor emotional health (psychopathology), but rather, that the reverse is true. Initially, some type of supportive psychotherapy (education and reassurance) should be used. During this phase of the patient's treatment, the physician should also attempt to break the vicious circle of: insomnia → hypochondriacal concern → increased anxiety → more intense insomnia. This can be achieved through the adjunctive use of hypnotic medication for relatively short periods (a few weeks at most), with the main therapeutic endeavor being recognition and resolution of any underlying, masked conflicts and anxiety. Thus, psychotherapy changes gradually from a supportive to an insight-oriented approach and follows the same general principles as described in the previous two sections.[70]

Engaging insomniacs with a somatoform disorder in therapy is a difficult task. Patients usually are reluctant to relinquish their sick roles and the secondary gains they afford. In addition, a number of these patients have alexithymic characteristics, that is, difficulty describing their emotions verbally, and focus instead on external events.[71,72] Thus, an important goal in treating these patients is the gradual reorganization of their interpersonal relationships and the establishment of a life style that does not revolve around the symptom of insomnia.

Substance Use Disorders

Psychiatric diagnoses in insomniacs showed that most patients with substance use disorders had another Axis I diagnosis which was the principal one and often an additional Axis II diagnosis.[41] Only one of our patients had substance use disorder as a principal diagnosis. Thus, when no withdrawal symptoms are present, therapy should be directed toward the patient's anxiety and depression, which are most likely responsible for both the insomnia and substance use.

Treatment of drug-withdrawal symptoms should, of course, precede any other therapy.[73] Patients should be gradually withdrawn from drugs (see also Chapter 6, Medical and Other Pathophysiologic Factors). Although its effectiveness has been questioned, individual psychotherapy is important following detoxification and treatment of the withdrawal symptoms.[74] Group psychotherapy can be of particular therapeutic importance. Such treatment can be found in self-help groups based on the Alcoholics Anonymous (AA) model or in groups led by experienced drug-abuse counselors.[75]

Alcoholics probably are treated by non-psychiatric physicians more often than by psychiatrists, and evidence exists that general practitioners and internists are sometimes quite helpful.[76] This may be particularly true when the therapeutic approach is warm but authoritarian, with little stress on "insight" or "understanding." However, relapses are characteristic of alcoholism, and physicians should not feel frustrated or angry when such relapses occur.

The physician's support may be enhanced when the patient is willing to participate regularly in AA meetings. Attendance at AA has many therapeutic aspects: the assurance of a regular, sympathetic hearing, the feeling that somebody is taking one's condition seriously, and the discovery that others are in the same predicament.[75] Unlike most "talking" therapies, AA expends little effort trying to explain why anyone is an alcoholic and often discourages psychotherapy. AA does have a definite spiritual emphasis. Its "twelve steps," for example, stress a reliance on a higher power, the need for forgiveness, and making amends to others.[75] Nevertheless, AA has no formal doctrine; people of all religious persuasions, as well as atheists, can belong to AA with equal comfort. While we do not know how many alcoholics benefit from participating in AA, most clinicians would agree that alcoholics should be encouraged to attend AA meetings, at least on a trial basis.

Personality Disorders

Many insomniacs with personality disorders fall into the compulsive personality or borderline personality categories. Because both conditions are characterized by unique psychologic characteristics, special treatment strategies are in order when treating insomniacs with these conditions.

Compulsive Personality Because compulsive personality disorder is the most prevalent DSM-III diagnosis on Axis II among chronic insomniacs,[41] psychiatric treatment of these patients often involves specific psychotherapeutic strategies for the treatment of obsessive-compulsive symptomatology.[77,78] Such patients are characterized by their capacity to evade, distract, obfuscate, and displace in order to avoid confrontation and change. Although they are usually very astute intellectually and extremely capable of intellectual "understanding," they tend to remain totally unengaged emotionally for prolonged periods in therapy. This is mainly the result of the use of obsessive mechanisms to prevent any feelings or thoughts that might generate excessive shame, guilt, or loss of self-esteem, which in turn are ego-threatening. The major defenses involved include isolation, displacement, reaction formation, and undoing.

Because an in-depth approach may actually stimulate further obsessional thinking,[79,80] the therapist's emphasis should be placed on the "here and now," while carefully unraveling the intricate defenses.[77,80] An important task in treatment is to elucidate the patient's excessive feelings of insecurity, which cause a need for guarantees before taking almost any action. The physician should aim at demonstrating, by careful interpretation and encouragement to action, that such guarantees are not only unnecessary but actually very disruptive.[77,80] The obsessive-compulsive patient should also be encouraged to verbalize and work through his aggression and other emotions, which are generated but never appropriately discharged.[81] To facilitate this process, the physician should refrain from adopting a neutral attitude in the treatment. He or she should, thus, demonstrate to the patient that there is no real threat to self whenever displaying authentic emotions. In this regard, the therapist needs to be spontaneous during the therapeutic session in order to encourage more involvement and flexibility from the patient.[77,78] This is particularly useful for the insomniac patient, who typically tends to internalize emotions rather than expressing them appropriately.

With the obsessive-compulsive patient it is important, although difficult, to establish a trusting relationship. Suess suggests allowing the patient to "borrow" the therapist's less harsh superego in order to establish a self-criticizing identity more compatible with guilt-free

Table 9.2. Psychotherapeutic Approaches to Treating Insomnia (Axis II Diagnoses in DSM-III)

Psychiatric Conditions	Treatment Recommendations
Compulsive Personality	Emphasize "here and now"
	Elucidate excessive insecurity
	Encourage overcoming ambivalence
	Facilitate verbalization of emotions
	Allow patient to "borrow" therapist's less harsh superego
Borderline Personality	Use modified psychodynamic psychotherapy
	Use warmth and empathy
	Drastically limit therapist neutrality
	Focus on acting out and distorted perceptions
	Enhance patient's reality testing
	Structure patient's external life

living. In this way, the patient's abnormal guilt, resulting from an overpowering superego, can be reduced.[82]

Borderline Personality Borderline patients are characterized by impulsivity, and instability in interpersonal behavior, mood, and self-image. They display marked shifts in attitude, intense anger, and profound identity disturbances. Difficulty being alone and chronic feelings of emptiness and boredom are common.[40,83] The psychotherapeutic approach to the borderline patient varies considerably from a predominantly supportive[84-86] to a psychoanalytic approach,[87-89] or to one that employs a modified psychodynamic approach.[84,86,90-94]

Kernberg, who has written extensively on the topic of the treatment of borderline personality organization, states that the majority of patients with borderline personality disorders responds to a modified psychodynamic approach, which combines ego psychology and object relations theory.[92-94] As strong support for this position, Kernberg cites the Menninger Foundation report that indicates that borderline patients responded much better to an interpretive approach than to one which was essentially supportive.[95] An emphasis is placed on dealing with current issues, the "here and now." In particular, the patient needs to see how he or she misperceives current relationships and events, for example, how the patient tends to perceive people in extremes, as either all good or all bad, based on their responses to the patient's needs. Because of the extensive use of forms of projection, borderline patients characteristically misread the motives of others.

With time, a second focus in therapy is the patient–therapist relationship.[92-94,96] As patients get closer to the therapist, they begin to question the therapist's motives, becoming both more doubtful and demanding. Considerable anger toward the therapist becomes more manifest, and patients attempt to put more distance between themselves and the therapist, alternately idealizing and degrading him or her. The predominantly negative transference of these patients is examined primarily in the "here and now," rather than through reconstruction of the past history. At the same time, limits are set to minimize patients' likelihood for acting out. During this phase, the therapist must be especially patient and tolerant because patients are likely to have shifting moods and to be demanding, angry, and provocative.

In order to enhance the development of a therapeutic alliance, the less primitively determined aspects of the positive transference are not interpreted.[92-94] Concurrently, the splitting of object relations into "all good" or "all bad" is dealt with extensively, with the ultimate goal that the patient be able to see the therapist realistically, ie, as a complete person with a full spectrum of qualities and attributes.

Kohut developed another approach to treat narcissistic personality disorder,[97,98] a condition considered by some authors to be on a continuum with the borderline personality.[99] This psychoanalytic approach, based on the analysis of the self, emphasizes the development of a mature and realistic self through both interpretive and supportive techniques.[97,98] In general, the primitiveness of borderline patients' psychic structure and relations gives their emotions in therapy an intensity that is much more difficult to deal with than that of most other patients.[100]

The following case history illustrates many of the techniques described in this section on the psychotherapy of chronic insomnia:

Case 1. A 57-year-old married woman was referred by her physician to our Sleep Disorders Clinic for difficulty in both falling asleep and staying asleep of about two years' duration. In addition, she had a history of chronic anxiety, rumination, and depression for many years, for which she had been taking nortriptyline (Aventyl), 25 mg tid. A comprehensive psychiatric and psychometric assessment revealed that she was a rigid, perfectionistic, and emotionally suppressed woman with a strong tendency to exert excessive control on herself as well as on her family members. However, she was defensive and denied any areas of emotional conflict. Rather, she was almost entirely preoccupied with her sleeplessness and other persistent physical complaints, such as fatigue, dizziness, and headaches. Using DSM-III, the diagnoses were compulsive personality disorder and atypical depression. (Although the patient was hypochondriacal, the diagnosis of depression discourages an additional diagnosis of somatoform disorder.)[40]

Because the patient was becoming incapacitated by her preoccupation with her sleeplessness, she was admitted for inpatient psychiatric treatment. Following her admission, the antidepressant medication was gradually discontinued because it did not appear to have resulted in appreciable improvement. At the same time, she was involved in individual psychotherapy, as well as group therapy, activity therapy, milieu therapy, and conjoint marital therapy.

Initially the patient was very resistive and guarded during the daily individual psychotherapy sessions. She was reluctant to participate actively in her various treatments. She insisted that discussing her past would not be helpful to her. Her psychiatrist, however, was quite active and direct and repeatedly stressed the importance of verbalizing her feelings regarding recent and previous life experiences, and he encouraged her to talk openly. As the patient was able to discover a number of areas of distress in her life that she had not allowed herself to think about, she was able to appreciate the value of more freely expressing herself.

An area that became important in treatment was the patient's marriage. Her husband of 30 years was generally much more expressive and easygoing than she. The patient recalled that during her husband's service in World War II, he had several affairs while she remained faithful at home. She had many suppressed feelings of resentment about this. In addition, for about the last two years he had become more involved with local fraternal and service organizations and was away from home three or four evenings a week.

The patient had never acknowledged how frustrating it was to be left home alone so frequently. Also, she had suppressed concerns that her husband might again be unfaithful. Apparently, she attempted to manage her emotions by internalizing them and indirectly control him with her sleep problems and many somatic complaints. Also, she appeared to be punishing her husband through their sexual relationship by being generally uninterested and unresponsive.

With the active involvement of her psychiatrist and the unit staff, she became more engaged in her treatment and, within the first two weeks of hospitalization, it was noted that she discontinued her complaints regarding her somatic problems and insomnia. With the progress of psychotherapy, additional recollections of relevant life experiences emerged. Her previous defense of repression became even more apparent when she was able to relate childhood memories of locking herself in her bedroom to avoid her abusive alcoholic father and feeling isolated and socially inferior to her classmates at school.

In a similar manner, she made considerable progress in the other psychotherapeutic modalities that were applied. Gradually, the patient no longer considered herself an "insomniac," but rather, a person with chronic interpersonal difficulties that needed to be resolved in individual and conjoint marital therapy.

Behavioral Treatment of Insomnia

Behavior therapy attempts to alleviate specific behavioral problems by systematically altering the patient's learned behavior.[27,28,60,101,102] While traditional psychodynamic therapies attempt to resolve symptoms by understanding their psychologic origins, behavior therapy focuses directly on the symptom itself (eg, insomnia) by the application of general principles of conditioning and social learning theory.

Behavior therapy begins with a comprehensive analysis designed to identify the initial problem and related factors.[101,102] This analysis is made as much as possible through observation of the patient's behavior as it occurs naturally. The observer may be the physician, a relative or friend of the patient, or the patient himself.

This type of therapy is based on the principle that human behavior is learned and thus can be modified or controlled. First, behavior can be modified by altering the specific conditions that accompany or precipitate it. Second, the type of behavior that occurs in a particular situation can be changed or modified. Third, the consequences of the undesired behavior can be altered, thus modifying future behavior. Several of the techniques of behavior therapy to be described for the treatment of insomnia may be used by the physician in primary care practice.

Rationale for Behavior Therapy

Using principles of classical and operant conditioning, it is possible to develop various hypotheses regarding the antecedents, behavioral phenomena, and consequences that transform stress-induced transient insomnia into a chronic condition. We have stated that the chronic insomniac patient typically denies and internalizes emotions during the day, culminating in rumination and feelings of apprehension at bedtime.[3-5] In support of this hypothesis are several studies contrasting good and poor sleepers, which show that poor sleepers demonstrate heightened arousal on a number of physiologic parameters prior to sleep.[1,6,10,11]

Various learned behaviors have been identified as factors commonly reinforcing the maintenance of chronic insomnia. One observation has been that insomniacs may engage in many physiologically arousing behaviors at bedtime that are incompatible with sleep.[11,60] Hours are spent watching television, reading books, doing crossword puzzles, eating, or simply worrying about the day's events or future plans, all of which may condition insomniac patients to wakeful bedtime activity rather than to sleep.[60]

Furthermore, insomniacs' inconsistent sleep patterns may result from detrimental sleep-wake habits, such as sleeping late in the morning, taking daytime naps whenever they feel tired, and having an irregular schedule of activities. Adding to the inconsistency is the different sleep schedule a number of people follow on weekends, as compared to weekdays. Circadian rhythm disturbances, which can cause sleep difficulty, may result from this lack of consistency, with disrupted 24-hour bodily cycles involving temperature regulation and endocrine system functioning.[103-106]

Insomniacs' mistaken perceptions of the causes of their psychophysiologic state, often referred to as attribution or misattribution contribute to the perpetuation of their sleep difficulty.[27,60,107] Their belief that they do not have the ability to sleep without some external aid and their failure to recognize their capability in repatterning proper sleep hygiene have been proposed as factors leading to their overreliance on sleep medication.[107]

A final factor contributing to the maintenance of insomnia is the positive reinforcement resulting from the sympathy and attention given to the chronic insomniac patient by family members, friends, and employers.[60] Fordyce has shown that inadvertent reinforcement of illness behaviors plays a prominent role in the maintenance of various chronic disorders.[108]

Behavior Therapy Techniques

Behavioral techniques that have been studied for the treatment of insomnia can be classified into three general groups: relaxation procedures, stimulus control, and attribution techniques. These techniques and their clinical goals are summarized in Table 9.3. Relaxation techniques include such methods as hypnosis, progressive relaxation, autogenic training, systematic desensitization, meditation training, and biofeedback.[27,28,60,101,102] These methods are based upon the evidence that insomniacs are tense, anxious, and physiologically aroused at bedtime. The aim of relaxation is to achieve muscle relaxation in order to reduce autonomic parameters, such as heart rate and respiration. The second behavioral modality involves stimulus control measures. These are designed to maximize the association of the bedroom with sleep, rather than with behaviors unrelated to sleep, such as eating, reading, or watching TV.

The third behavioral technique relates to attribution theory.[27,60,107] Attribution therapies include source reattribution and control reattribution.[28] In source reattribution, the insomniac is encouraged to redefine the source of presleep autonomic arousal as some environmental factor that does not involve emotions, such as anger, fear, etc. In control reattribution, the patient is encouraged to see in him- or herself the ability to fall asleep and stay asleep. Another related behavioral strategy is cognitive restructuring, which attempts to correct the patient's misconceptions about the sleep process.[109,110]

Relaxation Techniques

Hypnosis   Early reports suggested some success in improving insomnia by using hypnotically-induced relaxation that included post-hypnotic suggestion and self-hypnosis.[27,111,112] However, several aspects of hypnotherapy render it generally inappropriate as a treatment for insomnia. It generally requires the presence of the therapist during initial hypnotic sessions, and not all subjects are easily hypnotizable. More important, sleep is generally not achieved during or following a hypnotic trance. Thus, it is the patient's voluntary mastery of relaxation that serves as a pre-induction to sleep.

Progressive Relaxation Training   Relaxation training, as developed by Jacobson, teaches the patient to relax systematically.[27,28,60,101,113] With relaxation, a lowered level of physiologic arousal and a feeling of calmness occur. The patient is asked to tense individual muscle groups voluntarily, beginning with the forearm. Muscles then are relaxed gradually while the patient breathes slowly and deeply. Instructions, such as, "All tension is leaving your arm; you are feeling very good, very relaxed," are given. Other muscle groups are systematically tensed and relaxed in the same manner. Imagery may be added to the exercises by asking the patient to fantasize a pleasant, calm scene. Practiced by the patient two or three times a day and at bedtime, progressive relaxation training can be a useful adjunct in the treatment of insomnia.[60,107]

Autogenic Training   Autogenic training is derived from the observation that hypnosis usually employs suggestions that the subject's arm is heavy in achieving relaxation.[28,60,107,114] Without hypnosis, Schultz and Luthe utilized language to elicit such changes by having the person systematically focus on the arms and legs in sequence to induce feelings of warmth or heaviness in their muscles. Instead of concentrating on relaxing various muscle groups, relaxation is induced by repeating, "My right arm is heavy . . . I am at peace," etc. One 20- to 30-minute session during the day and another while in bed preparing for sleep were prescribed for insomniac subjects. In a study of 30 insomniacs comparing progressive relaxation and autogenic training as treatments for insomnia, both resulted in equal improvement in reducing the time to fall asleep and in an initial overall improvement in sleep.[115] Six months later, the reduced sleep latency was maintained, but the overall improvement was not.

Systematic Desensitization The technique of systematic desensitization requires that insomniac patients first construct a hierarchy of anxiety-producing situations. Then, a counter conditioning program is established for each level of the hierarchy.[27,28,101,102] Insomniac patients may be asked to keep a behavioral log, noting the degree of anxiety induced by thoughts about each situation, then to rank the thoughts in order of their increasing anxiety-producing potentials.[116] With the physician's assistance, patients imagine the lowest ranked anxiety-producing situation, such as, "When I lie in bed, I just can't relax, fearing this will be another sleepless night." Patients are instructed to relax in the face of anxiety, repeating the scene until they can relax in the presence of each thought. An alternative method is to substitute a more positive thought in place of the negative one. Utilizing this technique, patients transfer the psychophysiologic responses that accompany relaxation to the real-life situation in which the anxiety occurs. Various studies comparing muscle relaxation alone to systematic desensitization have suggested that the two methods are similarly effective in alleviating insomnia.[27,28]

Meditation Training Various forms of meditation (Zen, Yoga, Transcendental Meditation) involve focusing attention on a repetitive stimulus or "mantra" with the aim of inducing inner calmness and tranquility,[117] reducing cortical excitation, and lowering metabolic rate. The meditation technique described by Woolfolk utilizes immobility, closed eyes, and restricted attention. The insomniac is instructed to maintain a passive focus on breathing-related physical sensations by silently repeating the mantra "in" and "out" while inhaling and exhaling. One of these words is constantly being subvocalized during the procedure, while the patient focuses on one specific image.[118] When this method was compared with progressive relaxation treatment, no differences were noted in effectiveness in reducing sleep latency; however, either method was better than no treatment.

Biofeedback In biofeedback treatment, information on physiologic activity of which the patient is usually unaware is transmitted to the patient via electronic instrumentation.[60,102] For example, frontalis muscle activity (EMG) associated with tension can be communicated back to the patient as a variably pitched tone or the deflection of a needle on a meter. Patients learn to reduce the tone or maintain the needle below a certain level by whatever means they can. As they learn to do this, they decrease the activity of the frontalis muscle, thereby learning to relax assisted by EMG feedback. Another form of biofeedback is the production of theta waves using electroencephalogram (EEG) feedback. There is some evidence that biofeedback may be useful in improving insomnia,[119,120] although it is not generally used in a private practice setting because of the special equipment required.

Stimulus Control

Whereas the previously discussed methods are designed to induce pre-sleep relaxation, stimulus control procedures are predicated upon the principle that the sleep of insomniacs is not appropriately associated with environmental stimuli (bed or bedroom).[121] Stimulus control treatments attempt to eliminate or reduce bedroom activities that are not compatible with sleep and to associate the bed and bedroom only with sleep.[60,122] The insomniac is given a set of rules to strengthen perception of the bed as a cue for sleep, with the intent of forming a basis for the development of improved and lasting sleep habits. Patients are instructed to go to bed and lie down for sleep only when drowsy. If they are unable to sleep, they must leave the bedroom. The bed may not be used for anything but sleep. The exception to the rule is sexual activity. Patients are encouraged to arise at the same time each morning and to avoid daytime naps, regardless of the number of hours slept at night.

Attribution Techniques

A clinical application of attribution theory in terms of source reattribution could involve suggesting to an insomniac patient that his or her sleep difficulty is related in great part to the patient's perception that some external factor, such as a sleeping pill, is a necessity for sleep.[27,28,60,107] Storms and Nisbett tested this type of attribution theory in insomniac patients by administering "stimulating" or "relaxing" placebo medication at bedtime.[123] The "arousal" pill group fell asleep more quickly, while the "relaxation" pill group remained awake longer than on their baseline. The results were interpreted as indicating that when the insomniacs attributed their arousal to a pill (external source) they could fall asleep sooner, while those who could not fall asleep despite a pill for "relaxation" viewed their internal arousal as being more intense, heightening their apprehension and decreasing their ability to sleep.

Because the results of the Storms and Nisbett study seemed to challenge the conventional wisdom of the "placebo effect" concept, two other studies attempted to replicate their findings, but they were unsuccessful.[124,125] Instead, they further strengthened the theory of the "placebo effect" because insomniacs in the two subsequent studies who received "arousal" pills took longer to fall asleep, while those receiving "relaxation" pills fell asleep more quickly. Thus, until reliable effects can be demonstrated in an experimental setting, the source reattribution technique cannot be recommended in the treatment of insomnia.

Control reattribution is involved when insomniacs are assisted in learning that they have the potential to control their ability to fall asleep. This type of therapy was assessed in a group of insomniac patients by first treating their sleep problem with an effective hypnotic drug along with a relaxation technique.[126] Half of these insomniacs were later told that they had received an optimal dosage of an effective drug while the other half were told they had received a minimal dosage of an ineffective drug. Following the discontinuation of the hypnotic, both groups continued to practice relaxation. Sleep worsened in the group that had been told they had received an effective hypnotic, while no change was seen in the group that was told they had received an ineffective drug. Thus, the latter group had reattributed the control of their sleep difficulty to themselves. These results support the importance of using hypnotics in an adjunctive context with other forms of therapy to prevent insomniacs from expecting that their sleep difficulties will return when the hypnotic is discontinued. A final point, which is relevant to attribution therapy, is that a "placebo effect" can best be obtained when the patient has a symptom that is only of mild to moderate severity.

Cognitive Restructuring

Cognitive restructuring is an attempt to enable patients to revise their personal beliefs about sleep by correcting misconceptions about basic sleep processes.[109,110] Negative thoughts about sleeplessness are replaced with more positive thoughts. For example, the patient may replace the detrimental thoughts, "I'll never get to sleep" and "I'll be exhausted tomorrow," with more positive thoughts regarding both getting to sleep and functioning with less than eight hours of sleep.

Table 9.3. Behavioral Approaches to Treating Insomnia

Specific Technique	Clinical Goals
Relaxation Procedures	Encourage muscle relaxation
	Reduce presleep autonomic arousal
Stimulus Control	Maximize association of bedroom with sleep
Attribution	Reinforce patient's ability to fall and stay asleep
Cognitive Restructuring	Correct patient's misconceptions about sleep
	Replace negative thoughts about insomnia with
	positive thoughts

Effectiveness of Behavior Therapy

Studies show that behavior therapy techniques can be effective in treating certain complaints of insomnia.[127,128] The effects, however, are beneficial principally in those who have mild to moderate, rather than severe and chronic, difficulties and those who have difficulty in falling asleep rather than staying asleep or early awakening.[122] Bootzin and Nicassio have summarized the results of behavioral therapy studies.[60] No improvement is shown in no-treatment control subjects. Placebo and self-relaxation are more effective in mild to moderate insomnia than in severe insomnia. Systematic relaxation approaches show significant but moderate improvement in both moderate and severe insomnia and are more effective than placebo and other control methods. Stimulus control management may be effective, especially when used in conjunction with relaxation training.

Several problems inherent in behavior therapy studies to date make comparison and evaluation of their results difficult. Selection of subjects is confounded by the difficulty in defining insomnia, the differences in type and degree of insomnia, and problems in controlling for variables known to affect sleep, such as age, sex, psychiatric disturbance and drug use.[129,130] Furthermore, because there is much variability in the selection of subjects, comparison between studies is less meaningful. For example, many studies recruit students from a university population who report some degree of difficulty sleeping, and others select subjects from the general population who have more severe sleep disturbances and greater degrees of psychopathology.[60,115,131]

While relaxation procedures and stimulus control appear to improve patients' ability to fall asleep, other manifestations of sleep difficulty, such as frequent and extended awakenings and early final awakenings, are less responsive to such treatments.[122] In general, it appears that all relaxation procedures, including biofeedback, produce only moderate improvement[60] specific to the subject's sleep difficulty, but not to other psychologic and adjustment problems that are associated with severe insomnia. It is for these problems that we feel the psychodynamic strategies described in this chapter are more applicable for the effective treatment of insomnia.

This case history describes the successful treatment of a drug-dependent insomniac patient, using a combination of appropriate behavior therapy techniques following supervised drug withdrawal:

Case 2. A 69-year-old widower and retired chemist who had once held a prestigious position with a university was referred to the Sleep Disorders Clinic for severe insomnia. He had been plagued with sleep difficulty since he had achieved what he described as a highly demanding and pressured administrative position 20 years earlier. He had taken multiple nightly doses of various hypnotics for years and was lately showing toxic effects of slurred speech and incoordination. For these reasons he was admitted to the inpatient psychiatric unit for drug withdrawal and a treatment regimen.

On admission, he was a surly, rather unkempt individual who responded to questions with sarcasm and disdain for the examining physician. His memory showed mild impairment, and the Bender Gestalt also indicated some signs of organicity felt to be the result of the drugs he was taking. The DSM-III diagnoses were substance use disorder, with passive-aggressive personality traits. A gradual withdrawal of his medications was instituted. Because of his age, and in particular, his general resistiveness and lack of psychologic mindedness, a behavior therapy treatment program was developed. It was felt that behavior therapy was more suitable for him because he would be able to see the treatment of his insomnia in terms of habit modification and could learn self-management strategies. In addition, he could reattribute the ability to sleep to himself once the drugs were withdrawn and relaxation techniques were learned.

To begin, the patient was instructed in progressive relaxation, utilizing taped instructions for 30 minutes twice a day. Additionally, the patient was provided with education regarding sleep hygiene and the negative effects of the chronic use of hypnotics upon sleep physiology. Stimulus-control methods were applied by prohibiting the patient from retiring to his bedroom during the day. He was advised not to read, smoke, listen to music, or visit in his bedroom. A regular time for retiring was instituted, which was flexible in that he was to leave the bedroom if he felt he could not sleep. A firm time of arising was designated and was not to vary regardless of how he had slept the night before. The patient kept a daily behavioral log, noting his daily activities, time of falling asleep, and waking up. Daily individual therapy sessions for about 30 minutes consisted of briefings about the patient's progress in relaxation training and utilized positive suggestion regarding re-establishment of the patient's ability to sleep without medication. The patient also participated in group therapy, where he was able to make incisive, intellectualized observations regarding the problems other patients were experiencing. However, he was adamantly disinclined to any self-disclosure. Nonetheless, he was able to accept the view that his sleep problem had been aggravated by a heightened physiologic arousal, which he had now learned to control himself by means of reducing muscle tension through relaxation methods and modification of ingrained sleep habits.

Summary

Because psychopathology reflecting unresolved emotional conflicts typically underlies chronic insomnia, psychotherapy has an important role in treatment. A psychiatric referral should be made when specialized psychotherapeutic techniques are required. However, the general physician should be familiar with basic psychotherapeutic principles useful in treating insomnia and incorporate them into an overall treatment strategy for approaching the insomniac patient in a supportive, holistic manner.

In treating transient insomnia, the physician should aim at strengthening the patient's ego defenses and adaptive mechanisms, utilizing techniques of brief supportive psychotherapy. In chronic insomnia, psychotherapy is more difficult because of the patient's frequent denial of emotional conflicts and the presence of secondary gain.

Review of numerous controlled studies indicates that psychotherapy is beneficial for alleviating many psychiatric conditions. Studies also show that behavioral therapies generally result in symptomatic improvement but are less effective in improving global measures of adjustment. Supportive, psychodynamic, interpersonal, and behavioral therapies often are used in combination, depending upon the patient's clinical features, underlying personality organization, and the multiaxial diagnoses, as well as the expertise of the physician. In this chapter we discussed the psychotherapy of the mental disorders that are most commonly associated with chronic insomnia. These disorders include: anxiety, affective, somatoform, and substance use disorders, as well as obsessive and borderline personality disorders.

The general therapeutic goals include: initial and gradual withdrawal of excessive or inappropriate medication; symptom relief by appropriate pharmacologic means if necessary; education regarding basic sleep hygiene; establishment of improved coping mechanisms for handling stress; improvement of the ability to express emotions appropriately; development of insight regarding personal vulnerability; improvement in the quality of interpersonal relationships; and restructuring the patient's life style so that it does not revolve around the symptom of insomnia.

The most common therapeutic issues are: denial of any problem areas other than insomnia; strong resistance to exploration of problem areas; need for control, as expressed by manipulation of medications and lack of compliance with general measures; reluctance to become an active participant in the therapeutic alliance, with excessive dependence upon the physician; and withholding of direct expression of negative feelings.

Behavior therapy techniques are often useful in the adjunctive treatment of chronic difficulty in falling asleep and are aimed directly at the elimination of the symptom itself. The usefulness of behavior therapy is based upon the observation that insomniacs have high levels of presleep muscle tension and autonomic arousal, they habitually associate the bedroom with sleep-incompatible behaviors, and they do not attribute to themselves the ability to sleep. They also hold many misconceptions and negative thoughts about sleep.

Behavior therapy techniques that are most applicable to treating insomnia are: relaxation procedures, stimulus control methods, attribution techniques, and cognitive restructuring. Behavior therapy techniques achieve the most favorable results when they are part of a comprehensive treatment plan and the primary complaint is difficulty falling asleep. Improvement is generally limited to the patient's sleep difficulty and does not extend to other psychologic and adjustment problems.

References

1. Coursey RD, Buchsbaum M, Frankel BL: Personality measures and evoked responses in chronic insomniacs. *J Abnorm Psychol 84*:239–249, 1975.
2. Haynes SN, Follingstad DR, McGowan WT: Insomnia: sleep patterns and anxiety level. *J Psychosom Res 18*:69–74, 1974.
3. Kales A, Caldwell AB, Preston TA, Healey S, Kales JD: Personality patterns in insomnia. *Arch Gen Psychiatry 33*:1128–1134, 1976.
4. Kales A, Caldwell AB, Soldatos CR, Bixler EO, Kales JD: Biopsychobehavioral correlates of insomnia, II: pattern specificity and consis-

tency with the Minnesota Multiphasic Personality Inventory. *Psychosom Med 45*:341–356, 1983.

 5. Kales A, Soldatos CR, Kales JD: Sleep disorders: evaluation and management in the office setting, in Arieti S, Brodie HKH (eds): *American Handbook of Psychiatry*, ed 2. New York, Basic Books, Inc, 1981, vol 7, pp 423–454.

 6. Monroe LJ: Psychological and physiological differences between good and poor sleepers. *J Abnorm Psychol 72*:255–264, 1967.

 7. Monroe LJ, Marks PA: Psychotherapists' descriptions of emotionally disturbed adolescent poor and good sleepers. *J Clin Psychol 33*:263–269, 1977.

 8. Roth T, Kramer M, Lutz T: The nature of insomnia: a descriptive summary of a sleep clinic population. *Compr Psychiatry 17*:217–220, 1976.

 9. Kales JD, Soldatos CR, Kales A: Diagnosis and treatment of sleep disorders, in Greist JH, Jefferson JW, Spitzer RL (eds): *Treatment of Mental Disorders*. New York, Oxford University Press, 1982, pp 473–500.

10. Freedman RR, Sattler HL: Physiological and psychological factors in sleep-onset insomnia. *J Abnorm Psychol 91*:380–389, 1982.

11. Haynes SN, Adams A, Franzen M: The effects of presleep stress on sleep-onset insomnia. *J Abnorm Psychol 90*:601–606, 1981.

12. Healey ES, Kales A, Monroe LJ, Bixler EO, Chamberlin K, Soldatos CR: Onset of insomnia: role of life-stress events. *Psychosom Med 43*:439–451, 1981.

13. Greist JH: Adjustment disorders, in Greist JH, Jefferson JW, Spitzer RL (eds): *Treatment of Mental Disorders*. New York, Oxford University Press, 1982, pp 419–428.

14. Kolb LC, Brodie HKH: Adaptive processes and mental mechanisms, in Kolb LC, Brodie HKH (ed): *Modern Clinical Psychiatry*. Philadelphia, W.B. Saunders Company, 1982, ed 10, pp 80–111.

15. Marks I: *Cure and Care of Neuroses*. New York, Wiley-Interscience, 1981.

16. Caplan G: Mastery of stress: psychosocial aspects. *Am J. Psychiatry 138*:413–420, 1981.

17. Kiritz S, Moos RH: Physiological effects of social environments. *Psychosom Med 36*:96–114, 1974.

18. Kales A, Kales JD, Bixler EO: Insomnia: an approach to management and treatment. *Psychiatr Ann 4*:28–44, 1974.

19. Soldatos CR, Kales A, Kales JD: Management of insomnia. *Ann Rev Med 30*:301–312, 1979.

20. Karasu TB: Psychotherapy and pharmacotherapy: toward an integrative model. *Am J Psychiatry 139*:1102–1113, 1982.

21. Sarwer-Foner GJ: Combined psychotherapy and pharmacotherapy, in Karasu TB, Bellak L (eds): *Specialized Techniques in Individual Psychotherapy*. New York, Brunner/Mazel, 1980, pp 479–490.

22. Offenkrantz W, Tobin A: Psychoanalytic psychotherapy. *Arch Gen Psychiatry* 30:593–606, 1974.
23. Karasu TB: Psychotherapies: an overview, in Karasu TB, Bellak L (eds): *Specialized Techniques in Individual Psychotherapy*. New York, Brunner/Mazel, 1980, pp 3–32.
24. Nemiah JC: Anxiety: signal, symptom, and syndrome, in Arieti S (ed): *American Handbook of Psychiatry*. New York, Basic Books, 1974, vol 3, pp 91–109.
25. Bruch H: *Learning Psychotherapy: Rationale and Ground Rules*. Cambridge, Harvard University Press, 1974.
26. Schafer R: Talking to patients in psychotherapy. *Bull Menninger Clinic* 38:503–515, 1974.
27. Montgomery I, Perkin G, Wise D: A review of behavioral treatments for insomnia. *J Behav Ther Exp Psychiatry* 6:93–100, 1975.
28. Ribordy SC, Denney DR: The behavioral treatment of insomnia: an alternative to drug therapy. *Behav Res Ther* 15:39–50, 1977.
29. Jacobson A, McKinney WT: Affective disorders, in Greist JH, Jefferson JW, Spitzer RL: *Treatment of Mental Disorders*. New York, Oxford University Press, 1982, pp 184–233.
30. Karasu TB: Proving the efficacy of psychotherapy to government: a bureaucratic solution? (editorial). *Am Psychiatry* 139:789–790, 1982.
31. Luborsky L, Chandler M, Auerbach AH, Cohen J, Bachrach HM: Factors influencing the outcome of psychotherapy: a review of quantitative research. *Psychol Bull* 75:145–185, 1971.
32. Luborsky L, Singer B, Luborsky L: Comparative studies of psychotherapies. *Arch Gen Psychiatry* 32:955–1008, 1975.
33. Parloff MB: Can psychotherapy research guide the policymaker? *Am Psycho* 34:296–306, 1979.
34. Parloff MB: Psychotherapy and research: an anaclitic depression. *Psychiatry* 43:279–293, 1980.
35. Smith ML, Glass GV, Miller TI: *The Benefits of Psychotherapy*. Baltimore, Johns Hopkins University Press, 1980.
36. Gruen W: Effects of brief psychotherapy during the hospitalization period on the recovery process in heart attacks. *J Consult Clin Psychol* 43:223–232, 1975.
37. Jameson J, Shuman LJ, Young WW: The effects of outpatient psychiatric utilization on the costs of providing third-party coverage. *Med Care* 16:383–399, 1978.
38. Mumford E, Schlesinger HJ, Glass GV: The effects of psychological intervention on recovery from surgery and heart attacks: an analysis of the literature. *Am J Public Health* 72:141–151, 1982.
39. Schlesinger HJ, Mumford E, Glass GV, Patrick C, Sharfstein S: Mental health treatment and medical care utilization in a fee-for-service system: outpatient mental health treatment following the onset of a chronic disease. *Am J Public Health* 73:422–429, 1983.
40. American Psychiatric Association: *Diagnostic and Statistical Manual of Mental Disorders* (*DSM-III*), ed 3. Washington, DC, American Psychiatric Association, 1980.

41. Tan TL, Kales JD, Kales A, Soldatos CR, Bixler EO: Biopsychobe-havioral correlates of insomnia, IV: diagnosis based on the DSM-III. *Am J Psychiatry* (in press).
42. Frances A, Cooper AM: Descriptive and dynamic psychiatry: a per-spective on DSM-III. *Am J Psychiatry 138*:1198–1202, 1981.
43. Hollister LE: Tricyclic antidepressants (Part 1). *N Engl J Med 299*: 1106–1109, 1978.
44. Hollister LE: Tricyclic antidepressants (Part 2). *N Engl J Med 299*: 1168–1172, 1978.
45. Akiskal HS: Dysthymic disorder: psychopathology of proposed chronic depressive subtypes. *Am J Psychiatry 140*:11–20, 1983.
46. Akiskal HS, Rosenthal TL, Haykal RF, Lemmi H, Rosenthal RH, Scott-Strauss A: Characterological depressions. *Arch Gen Psychiatry 37*:777–783, 1980.
47. Raskin A, Crook TH: The endogenous and neurotic distinction as a prediction of response to antidepressant drugs. *Psychol Med 6*:59–70, 1976.
48. Yerevanian BI, Akiskal HS: "Neurotic," characterological, and dys-thymic depressions. *Psychiatr Clinics N Am 2*:595–618, 1979.
49. Jacobson E: *Depression*. New York, International Universities Press, 1971.
50. Mendelson M: The psychotherapy of the depressed patient, in Karasu TB, Bellak L (eds): *Specialized Techniques in Individual Psycho-therapy*. New York, Brunner/Mazel, 1980, pp 143–161.
51. Beck AT: *Depression: Clinical, Experimental and Theoretical Aspects*. New York, Paul B Hoeber, 1967.
52. Beck AT: *The Diagnosis and Management of Depression*. Philadelphia, University of Pennsylvania Press, 1973.
53. Rush AJ, Beck AT, Kovacs M, Weissenburger J, Hollon SD: Com-parison of the effects of cognitive therapy and pharmacotherapy on hopelessness and self-concept. *Am J Psychiatry 139*:862–866, 1982.
54. Weissman MM, Klerman GL, Paykel ES, Prusoff B, Hanson B: Treat-ment effects on the social adjustment of depressed patients. *Arch Gen Psychiatry 30*:771–778, 1974.
55. Bellack AS, Hersen M, Himmelhoch J: Social skills training com-pared with pharmacotherapy and psychotherapy in the treatment of unipolar depression. *Am J Psychiatry 138*:1562–1567, 1981.
56. Yalom I: *Theory and Practice of Group Psychotherapy*. New York, Basic Books, 1975.
57. Hogan P, Hogan BK: The family treatment of depression, in Flach FF, Draghi SC (eds): *The Nature and Treatment of Depression*. New York, Wiley, 1975.
58. Slipp S: An intrapsychic-interpersonal theory of depression. *J Am Acad Psychoanalysis 4*:389–409, 1976.
59. Paolino TJ, McCrady BS: *Marriage and Marital Therapy*. New York, Brunner/Mazel, 1978.
60. Bootzin RR, Nicassio PM: *Behavioral Treatments for Insomnia* (Prog-

ress in Behavior Modification, vol 6). New York, Academic Press, Inc, 1978, pp 1–45.

61. Fenichel O: *The Psychoanalytic Theory of Neurosis.* New York, WW Norton and Company, Inc, 1945.

62. Freud S: *Inhibition, Symptom and Anxiety.* London, Hogarth Press, 1959.

63. Greenson RR: *The Technique and Practice of Psychoanalysis.* New York, International Universities Press, Inc, 1967, vol 1.

64. Lesse S: Psychotherapy of ambulatory patients with severe anxiety, in Karasu TB, Bellak L (eds): *Specialized Techniques in Individual Psychotherapy.* New York, Brunner/Mazel, 1980, pp 220–235.

65. Nemiah J: *Foundations of Psychopathology.* New York, Jason Aronson, Inc, 1973.

66. Marks I: Anxiety disorders, in Greist JH, Jefferson JW, Spitzer RL (eds): *Treatment of Mental Disorders.* New York, Oxford University Press, 1982, pp 234–265.

67. Sifneos PE: *Short-Term Psychotherapy and Emotional Crisis.* Cambridge, Harvard University Press, 1972.

68. Barsky AJ, Klerman GL: Overview: hypochondriasis, bodily complaints, and somatic styles. *Am J Psychiatry 140*:273–283, 1983.

69. Kleinman A, Eisenberg L, Good B: Culture, illness, and care: clinical lessons from anthropologic and cross-cultural research. *Ann Intern Med 88*:251–258, 1978.

70. Ochitill H: Somatoform disorder, in Greist JH, Jefferson JW, Spitzer RL (eds): *Treatment of Mental Disorders.* New York, Oxford University Press, 1982, pp 266–308.

71. Nemiah JC: Alexithymia. *Psychother Psychosom 28*:199–206, 1977.

72. Sifneos PE, Apfel-Saxitz R, Frankel FH: The phenomenon of 'Alexithymia': observations in neurotic and psychosomatic patients. *Psychother Psychosom 28*:47–57, 1977.

73. Lewis DC, Senay EC: *Treatment of Drug and Alcohol Abuse* (Buchwald C, Katz D, Callahan JF, eds, Medical Monograph Series, vol 2, no 2). New York, State University of New York Career Teacher Center, 1981.

74. Zimberg S: Psychotherapy with alcoholics, in Karasu TB, Bellak L (eds): *Specialized Techniques in Individual Psychotherapy.* New York, Brunner/Mazel, 1980, pp 382–399.

75. Goodwin DW: Substance induced and substance use disorders: alcohol, in Greist JH, Jefferson JW, Spitzer RL (eds): *Treatment of Mental Disorders.* New York, Oxford University Press, 1982, pp 44–61.

76. Gerard DL, Saenger G: *Outpatient Treatment of Alcoholism.* Toronto, University of Toronto Press, 1966.

77. Salzman L: *Psychotherapy of the Obsessive Personality.* New York, Jason Aronson, 1980.

78. Salzman L: Psychotherapy with the obsessive personality, in Karasu TB, Bellak L (eds): *Specialized Techniques in Individual Psychotherapy.* New York, Brunner/Mazel, 1980, pp 184–198.

79. Noonan JR: An obsessive-compulsive reaction treated by induced anxiety. *Am J Psychotherapy* 25:293–299, 1971.
80. Salzman L, Thaler FH: Obsessive-compulsive disorders: a review of the literature. *Am J Psychiatry* 138:286–296, 1981.
81. Gutheil E: Problems of therapy in obsessive-compulsive neurosis. *Am J Psychotherapy* 13:793–808, 1959.
82. Suess JF: Short-term psychotherapy with the compulsive personality and the obsessive-compulsive neurotic. *Am J Psychiatry* 129:270–275, 1972.
83. Gunderson JG, Kolb JE: Discriminating features of borderline patients. *Am J Psychiatry* 135:792–796, 1978.
84. Gordon C, Beresin E: Conflicting treatment models for the inpatient management of borderline patients. *Am J Psychiatry* 140:979–983, 1983.
85. Knight RP: Management and psychotherapy of the borderline schizophrenic patient, in Knight RP, Friedman CR (eds): *Psychoanalytic Psychiatry and Psychology*. New York, International Universities Press, 1954, pp 110–122.
86. Masterson JF: *The Narcissistic and Borderline Disorders*. New York, Brunner/Mazel Publishers, 1981.
87. Bion WR: *Second Thoughts: Selected Papers on Psychoanalysis*. London, Heinemann, 1967, pp 86–109.
88. Fairbairn WRD: *An Object Relations Theory of the Personality*. New York, Basic Books, 1954.
89. Winnicott DW: *The Maturational Process and the Facilitating Environment*. New York, International Universities Press, 1965.
90. Frosch J: Technique in regard to some specific ego defects in the treatment of borderline patients. *Psychiatr Q* 45:216–220, 1971.
91. Greenson RR: The struggle against identification. *J Am Psychoanal Assoc* 2:200–217, 1954.
92. Kernberg O: *Borderline Conditions and Pathological Narcissism*. New York, Jason Aronson, 1975.
93. Kernberg O: *Object Relations Theory and Clinical Psychoanalysis*. New York, Jason Aronson, 1976.
94. Kernberg OF: Psychotherapy with borderline patients: an overview, in Karasu TB, Bellak L (eds): *Specialized Techniques in Individual Psychotherapy*. New York, Brunner/Mazel, 1980, pp 85–117.
95. Kernberg O, Burnstein E, Coyne L, Appelbaum A, Horwitz L, Voth H: Psychotherapy and psychoanalysis: final report of the Menninger Foundation's psychotherapy research project. *Bull Menninger Clin* 36:1–275, 1972.
96. Grinker RR Sr: Neurosis, psychosis, and the borderline states, in Freedman AM, Kaplan HI, Sadock BJ (eds): *Comprehensive Textbook of Psychiatry, II*. Baltimore, Williams & Wilkins, 1975, pp 845–850.
97. Kohut H: *The Restoration of the Self*. New York, International Universities Press, Inc, 1977.

98. Kohut H, Wolf ES: The disorders of the self and their treatment, in Slipp S (ed): *Curative Factors in Dynamic Psychotherapy.* New York, McGraw-Hill Book Company, 1981, pp 44–59.

99. Adler G: The borderline-narcissistic personality disorder continuum. *Am J Psychiatry 138:*46–50, 1981.

100. Giovacchini P: *Psychoanalysis of Character Disorders.* New York, Jason Aronson, 1975.

101. Lazarus AA: *Multimodal Behavior Therapy.* New York, Springer Publishing Company, 1976.

102. O'Leary KD, Wilson GT: *Behavior Therapy: Application and Outcome.* Englewood Cliffs, Prentice-Hall, Inc, 1975.

103. Johnson LC, Tepas DI, Colquhoun WP, Colligan MJ: *Biological Rhythms, Sleep and Shift Work* (Weitzman ED [series ed]: *Advances in Sleep Research,* vol 7). New York, SP Medical and Scientific Books, 1981.

104. Kripke DF, Cook B, Lewis OF: Sleep of night workers: EEG recordings. *Psychophysiology 7:*377–384, 1971.

105. Moore-Ede MC, Sulzman FM, Fuller CA: *The Clocks that Time Us.* Cambridge, Harvard University Press, 1982.

106. Weitzman ED, Kripke DF: Experimental 12-hour shift of the sleep-wake cycle in man: effects on sleep and physiologic rhythms, in Johnson LC, Tepas DI, Colquhoun WP, Colligan MJ (eds): *Biological Rhythms, Sleep and Shift Work* (Weitzman ED [series ed]: *Advances in Sleep Research,* vol 7). New York, SP Medical and Scientific Books, 1981, pp 93–110.

107. Bootzin RR: Effects of self-control procedures for insomnia, in Stuart RB (ed): *Behavioral Self-Management: Strategies, Techniques and Outcomes.* New York, Brunner/Mazel, pp 176–195.

108. Fordyce WE: *Behavioral Methods for Chronic Pain and Illness.* St Louis, Mosby, 1976.

109. Goldfried M, Goldfried A: Cognitive change methods, in Kanfer F, Goldstein A (eds): *Helping People Change.* New York, Pergamon, 1975.

110. Thoresen CE, Coates TJ, Kirmil-Gray K, Rosekind MR: Behavioral self-management in treating sleep-maintenance insomnia. *J Behav Med 4:*41–52, 1981.

111. Fry A: Hypnosis in the treatment of insomnia. *Med World 99:*194–199, 1963.

112. Hanley FW: Modern hypnotherapy. *Appl Therapeutics 7:*625–628, 1965.

113. Jacobson E: *Progressive Relaxation.* Chicago, University of Chicago Press, 1938.

114. Schultz JH, Luthe W: *Autogenic Training.* New York, Grune & Stratton, 1959.

115. Nicassio P, Bootzin R: A comparison of progressive relaxation and autogenic training as treatments for insomnia. *J Abnorm Psychol 83:*253–260, 1974.

116. Tan T-L, Pertschuk M: Behavior therapy in primary care practice. *Pennsylvania Medicine 81*:27–28, 56–57, 1978.
117. Woolfolk RL: Psychophysiological correlates of meditation. *Arch Gen Psychiatry 32*:1326–1333, 1975.
118. Woolfolk RL, Carr-Kaffashan L, McNulty TF, Lehrer PM: Meditation training as a treatment for insomnia. *Behav Ther 7*:359–365, 1976.
119. Raskin M, Johnson G, Rondestvedt JW: Chronic anxiety treated by feedback-induced muscle relaxation. A pilot study. *Arch Gen Psychiatry 28*:263–267, 1973.
120. Budzynski TH: Biofeedback procedures in the clinic. *Semin Psychiatry 5*:537–548, 1973.
121. Haynes SN, Price MG, Simons JB: Stimulus control treatment of insomnia. *J Behav Ther Exp Psychiatry 6*:279–282, 1975.
122. Thoresen CE, Coates TJ, Zarcone VP, Kirmil-Gray K, Rosekind MR: Treating the complaint of insomnia: self-management perspectives, in Ferguson JM, Taylor CB (eds): *The Comprehensive Handbook of Behavioral Medicine*. New York, Spectrum Publications, Inc, 1980, vol 1.
123. Storms MD, Nisbett RE: Insomnia and the attribution process. *J Pers Social Psychol 16*:319–328, 1970.
124. Bootzin RR, Herman CP, Nicassio P: The power of suggestion: another examination of misattribution and insomnia. *J Person Soc Psychol 34*:673–679, 1976.
125. Kellogg R, Baron RS: Attribution theory, insomnia, and the reverse placebo effect: a reversal of Storms and Nisbett's findings. *J Person Soc Psychol 32*:231–256, 1975.
126. Davison GC, Tsujimoto RN, Glaros AG: Attribution and the maintenance of behavior change in falling asleep. *J Abnorm Psychol 82*:124–133, 1973.
127. Hauri P, Cohen S: The treatment of insomnia with biofeedback: final report of study I. *Sleep Res 6*:136, 1977.
128. Traub AC, Jencks B, Bliss EL: Effects of relaxation training on chronic insomnia. *Sleep Res 2*:164, 1973.
129. McGhie A: The subjective assessment of sleep patterns in psychiatric illness. *Br J Med Psychol 39*:221–230, 1966.
130. McGhie A, Russell SM: The subjective assessment of normal sleep patterns. *J Ment Sci 108*:642–654, 1962.
131. Borkovec TD, Weerts TC: Effects of progressive relaxation on sleep disturbance: an electroencephalographic evaluation. *Psychosom Med 38*:173–180, 1976.

10. Adjunctive Treatment of Insomnia with Hypnotic Drugs

In the multidimensional treatment of insomnia, hypnotic medication has an important but adjunctive role. Simply prescribing a hypnotic drug will seldom be of lasting benefit to the patient if the problem is not thoroughly evaluated and the underlying causes identified and treated. In fact, such an approach may create additional serious problems, such as an undue reliance on hypnotic drugs or even drug dependence.

Over the last several years, articles in both the medical literature[1] and the popular press have stressed the negative consequences of taking hypnotic medication. In particular, such articles have emphasized that sleeping pills are prescribed too often and for too long. The facts indicate, however, that these concerns may be overstated. Actually, only a small percentage of the population takes prescribed hypnotic medication nightly for more than a few weeks, as shown by the following summary of the results of several epidemiologic studies.[2-6]

About one-third of the general population has some type of complaint of disturbed sleep[3] and half of these individuals, approximately 15 percent of the population, go to a physician seeking help for the problem.[6] Those seeking treatment probably represent, for the most part, patients with complaints of severe insomnia.[2,5,7] About half of the patients seen by physicians for a complaint of insomnia are prescribed a hypnotic drug (approximately 7.5% of the population).[4] Of this group, 60 percent (5% of the population) take the drug for longer than a month, but only about 20 percent of these (1% of the general population) take the medication each night.[4] This latter estimate is supported by other survey data, which show that approximately one percent of the general population uses hypnotic drugs nightly for longer than a two-month period.[2,5]

Whereas the problems associated with hypnotic drugs have been portrayed largely as a matter of overprescription, the real difficulties, in our opinion, lie with the attitude that hypnotic drugs alone can cure insomnia. In fact, the usefulness of these drugs usually depends upon the ways they are used in conjunction with other treatments.

To use hypnotic drugs properly in the treatment of insomnia, physicians must first determine if their use is indicated and will complement the overall therapeutic approach. Having decided that the use of hypnotic medication could be beneficial for a given patient, they should be thoroughly knowledgeable regarding drug profiles for efficacy and safety[8] in order to select the appropriate hypnotic agent. Because such profiles are established by clinical trials and sleep laboratory evaluations,[9-11] these assessment methods are described in this chapter, and their advantages and shortcomings are compared. Then, the efficacy, side effects, and withdrawal findings are discussed for both non-benzodiazepine and benzodiazepine hypnotic drugs. The chapter concludes with general guidelines for prescribing hypnotic medications.

Clinical Trials and Sleep Laboratory Evaluations

Clinical Trials

Until the 1960s, when investigators began to use sleep laboratory studies to assess the effectiveness and withdrawal effects of hypnotic drugs,[12-15] clinical trials were the only means of evaluating their safety and efficacy. The primary advantages of clinical trials are: (1) hypnotic drugs can be evaluated in large groups of subjects, (2) effects of these drugs on special patient populations can be studied, and (3) types and frequency of a drug's side effects can be thoroughly assessed.[10,11]

Because clinical trials can be conducted in almost any setting, a drug's efficacy and side effects can be assessed in such varied populations as geriatric patients or individuals suffering from chronic cardiovascular or respiratory conditions.[10] The indications and contraindications for using the drug in special populations need to be assessed, mainly because hypnotic drugs are often prescribed for patients with medical conditions.[16] Also, certain patient groups are known to use hypnotics extensively; for example, 76 percent of geriatric patients taking psychotropic drugs were found to use hypnotics.[17]

Because clinical trials permit evaluation of both large samples of subjects and special target groups, they also allow for an accurate assessment of the severity and frequency of drug side effects.[10] Thus, clinical trials are an important part of the early stages of evaluating investigational hypnotic drugs because the decision to continue or terminate the evaluation of a drug largely depends on the presence of adverse reactions and other side effects.

Clinical trials have several serious shortcomings, however, some inherent in the clinical trial format and others stemming from certain methodologic problems.[10,11] This type of drug trial format does not include the use of objective and precise measurements, which are characteristic of sleep laboratory studies. Further, subjects cannot be monitored closely, and experimental variables are difficult to control. Perhaps the most common methodologic shortcomings of clinical trials are a failure to evaluate a drug's effectiveness with continued use and a lack of attention to potential drug interaction and withdrawal effects.

Sleep Laboratory Evaluations

When compared with clinical trials, sleep laboratory studies have certain advantages.[9-11] Most important is the objective, second-by-second monitoring of sleep throughout the night, which allows for precise quantification of a drug's efficacy. This precision is enhanced by the rigorous control of experimental variables; while the sleep laboratory provides a sound-attenuated, temperature-controlled environment that is free of noise or interruption, clinical trials often are conducted in hospital wards or at home, where disturbances may be frequent. Moreover, introduction of a standardized system for scoring sleep[18] has strengthened the interlaboratory reliability in analyzing data and replicating findings. Finally, because of the more precise control of experimental variables, the subjective sleep estimates obtained in laboratory studies are probably more accurate than those obtained in clinical trials.

The use of the sleep laboratory has enabled investigators to assess certain clinically important drug properties, such as efficacy with continued administration and withdrawal, that are not evaluated in clinical trials.[9-11] In 1965, Oswald and Priest published their classic study introducing an innovative design that included three successive study conditions: placebo baseline, drug administration, and placebo withdrawal.[15] They found that a rebound increase in REM sleep following drug withdrawal was correlated with the increased incidence of unpleasant dreams and nightmares. In 1969, we published the first report of sleep laboratory evaluations of hypnotic drug effectiveness.[13,14] These and later studies, in which we used an original approach for evaluating initial, short-term, and continued drug administration (from two to four weeks) showed that most hypnotic drugs lose their effectiveness within two weeks.[13,14,19,20] Subsequently, we discovered two withdrawal phenomena that may have contrasting implications for the development of drug dependence:[19-25] carry-over effectiveness, wherein long-acting benzodiazepines remain effective for one to several nights after their abrupt withdrawal;[19-21,25] and rebound insomnia, a marked increase in total wake time above baseline levels following the abrupt withdrawal of benzodiazepines with short and intermediate half-lives.[22-24]

Although there are clear advantages in sleep laboratory studies, they do have certain shortcomings. Inherent disadvantages stem from the limited number of subjects that can be evaluated and the high cost per subject for each night of recording.[9-11] Because only a few subjects can be evaluated at the same time, it is difficult to conduct sleep laboratory studies in special patient groups and adequately assess side effects.

Methodologic inadequacies occasionally found in sleep laboratory studies of hypnotic drugs include using normal subjects rather than insomniacs and emphasizing a drug's effects on sleep stages rather than its efficacy. Sleep laboratory studies may also share some of the problems associated with clinical trials whenever investigators fail to evaluate effectiveness with continued use, to assess drug interactions, or to determine withdrawal effects.

A hypnotic drug's profile is not complete unless it combines findings from both sleep laboratory studies and clinical trials. For this reason, both assessment methods are included in the Food and Drug Administration's *Guidelines for the Clinical Evaluation of Hypnotic Drugs*, published in 1977.[10,26,27] The guidelines do not emphasize either clinical trials or sleep laboratory studies at the expense of the other, but rather stress their complementary utilization.

Since the late 1960s, we have evaluated the efficacy and withdrawal effects of 15 hypnotic drugs in 25 sleep laboratory studies; nine of these drugs are commercially available in the United States and six are investigational hypnotics or available in other countries. The commercially available drugs included chloral hydrate (Noctec), 1000 mg;[19] ethchlorvynol (Placidyl), 500 mg;[28] flurazepam (Dalmane), 15 and 30 mg;[19,20,25,29,30] glutethimide (Doriden), 500 mg;[19] methaqualone (Parest), 250 and 400 mg;[28] pentobarbital (Nembutal), 100 mg;[20] secobarbital (Seconal), 100 mg;[31] temazepam (Restoril), 30 mg; [32] and triazolam (Halcion), 0.5 mg.[33] The six investigational drugs were flunitrazepam, 0.25, 1 and 2 mg;[30,34-36] GP 41299, 100 mg, (a dibenzo-thiepine);[28] lormetazepam, 0.5, 1.0, 1.5, and 2.0 mg;[37] midazolam, 10, 20, and 30 mg;[38] nitrazepam, 10 mg;[22,36] and quazepam, 7.5, 15, and 30 mg.[29,39,40] In addition to the individual studies cited, comparisons among these drugs have been described previously in detail.[28,41,42]

Methodology

In each of the 25 studies, a standard protocol[9-11] was used, consisting of three days,[19-21,25,28,40] or one,[34,36-38] two,[19-21,28,29,31-33,35,40] or four[20,21,29,32,35] weeks of nightly drug administration preceded by four placebo nights and followed by at least three placebo nights. During the first placebo period, subjects adapted to the sleep laboratory (night one) and baseline measurements were obtained (nights 2–4). On nights when the drugs were administered, they were evaluated for effectiveness in inducing and maintaining sleep over periods of short-, inter-mediate-, and long-term use. The final placebo nights were used to evaluate the effects of withdrawing the drug. All effectiveness and withdrawal data were then compared with their respective baseline values.

Non-Benzodiazepine Hypnotic Drugs

The six non-benzodiazepine drugs that we evaluated included: chloral hydrate,[19] ethchlorvynol,[28] glutethimide,[19] methaqualone in two doses (250 and 400 mg),[28] pentobarbital,[20] and secobarbital.[31] Each drug ex-cept pentobarbital, was evaluated separately using a 22-night protocol design, which consisted of four nights of placebo, two weeks of drug, and four nights of placebo administration. With pentobarbital, a 47-night protocol was employed, which included four nights of placebo, 28 nights of drug, and 15 nights of placebo administration. Table 10.1 lists for each drug the values for the percentage of change in total wake time from baseline for each of the two drug conditions evaluated (short-term and intermediate-term).[20,28] With short-term administra-tion (nights 5–7), the decreases in total wake time ranged from 22 to 55 percent, with the largest decreases produced by secobarbital (55%) and methaqualone, 250 mg (48%). The decreases in total wake time produced by secobarbital, both doses of methaqualone, and pento-barbital were statistically significant as compared with their respective baseline values. Thus, all of the drugs studied showed some degree of

Table 10.1. Non-benzodiazepine Hypnotics: Efficacy and Withdrawal Effects

Drug	Percent Change of Total Wake Time from Baseline		
	Short-term Drug	Intermediate-Term Drug	Drug Withdrawal
Chloral hydrate (Noctec), 1000 mg	−25	−17	−5
Ethchlorvynol (Placidyl), 500 mg	−22	−7	−4
Glutethimide (Doriden), 500 mg	−32	+19	+10
Methaqualone (Parest), 250 mg	−48	−33	−2
Methaqualone (Parest), 400 mg	−36	−25	+6
Pentobarbital (Nembutal), 100 mg	−33	−2	−2
Secobarbital (Seconal), 100 mg	−55	−21	0

(Modified from Kales et al[20,28])

efficacy, although it was somewhat limited for ethchlorvynol and chloral hydrate.

However, when the drugs were studied during intermediate-term drug administration (nights 16–18, the last three nights of a two-week period of drug administration), very little efficacy was demonstrated for these non-benzodiazepine hypnotics.[28] Methaqualone, 250 mg, produced the greatest decrease in total wake time (33%). The remaining drugs showed decreases in total wake time of 25 percent or less, with glutethimide producing a worsening of sleep as compared to the placebo-baseline value.

With none of the drugs studied, did withdrawal result in a marked or significant increase in total wake time above the respective baseline value.[20,28] Table 10.1 lists the percentage of change in total wake time in comparing the mean value for the first three withdrawal nights combined to the respective baseline value. None of the drugs showed an increase in total wake time that was greater than 10 percent over the baseline value. The greatest increase in mean total wake time for an individual withdrawal night occurred with secobarbital on the third night of withdrawal (38%). As will be shown in our discussion of benzodiazepines, the degree of sleep disturbance following abrupt withdrawal of single, nightly clinical doses of a drug is much greater for benzodiazepine drugs with short and intermediate half-lives than for non-benzodiazepine drugs with similar rates of elimination. However, non-benzodiazepine drugs are often taken in high doses for prolonged periods because of rapid development of tolerance and loss of effectiveness. Abrupt withdrawal under these conditions often produces severe abstinence symptoms.[43-52]

The following case history illustrates the withdrawal difficulties that may be encountered with non-benzodiazepine hypnotic drugs:

Case 1. A 44-year-old woman had been hospitalized for elective surgery two years prior to coming to our Sleep Disorders Clinic for evaluation and treatment.[50] While in the hospital, her physician had prescribed 100 mg of pentobarbital at bedtime, and she continued to take the pentobarbital following discharge because of pain and discomfort. Over time she gradually increased the nightly dosage to 200 and then to 300 mg. On several occasions, on the advice of her physician, she attempted to abruptly stop taking the medication, but was totally unsuccessful because of extreme insomnia and nightmares. As a result of these difficulties, she would resume taking the drug after one or two nights.

The patient was eager to be withdrawn from her medication, and we proceeded with a gradual withdrawal schedule. Each night the patient was given the same number of identically matching capsules, with the drug dosage decreasing at a rate of 50 mg every three days, or one clinical dose every six days. One of the matching capsules contained flurazepam, 15 mg, and this was continued for ten days following complete withdrawal of the pentobarbital. In addition, supportive psychotherapy was provided as well as recommendation of several changes regarding sleep hygiene. Clinically, she reported sleep as slightly improved both during the last period of withdrawal and after she had attained a totally drug-free condition. At no time did she experience the withdrawal symptoms she had previously reported.

Benzodiazepine Hypnotic Drugs

In this section we discuss our findings from studies of benzodiazepine hypnotic drugs, as well as the related findings of other investigators. The topic areas in this section include clinically relevant pharmacokinetic issues, the efficacy and side effects of benzodiazepine hypnotics, and withdrawal effects seen with these drugs. In each area, we first detail findings relating to the three benzodiazepine hypnotic drugs that are currently commercially available in the United States and then discuss data pertaining to other investigational drugs and drugs currently used in Europe.

Pharmacokinetic Issues

The rapidity of a hypnotic drug's effectiveness for inducing sleep is a critical issue in treating patients with insomnia because complaints of sleep induction difficulty are most prevalent among patients with chronic insomnia.[53] In turn, the rate of absorption of a hypnotic drug is the most important factor determining onset of action. Of the three hypnotics commercially available in the United States, flurazepam is most quickly absorbed.[54] It has an intermediate rate of absorption, followed by triazolam, and finally by temazepam, which has an extremely slow rate of absorption. Peak concentrations of temazepam are not reached until two to three hours after administration. Thus, one would predict from the pharmacokinetic data that flurazepam and triazolam are effective for inducing sleep, while temazepam would have little efficacy for this type of insomnia complaint unless taken an hour or two before bedtime. Temazepam's slow absorption is apparently the result of the particular formulation available in this country: the hard gelatin capsule available in the United States has a much slower rate of absorption than the soft capsule formulation used in Europe.[55-57]

Drug accumulation and the consequent potential for producing carry-over effectiveness and daytime sedative effects are determined primarily by the drug's elimination half-life and total metabolic clearance.[54,58] Obviously, the rate of elimination of a given drug is affected by the presence of active metabolites and their rates of elimination. If the elimination half-life of the parent compound and any active metabolites is short, a minimum of drug accumulation will occur. Thus, there is less potential for such a drug to produce daytime sedation and performance decrements,[59-61] but a greater potential for producing early morning insomnia[62] and daytime anxiety[62-64] during drug administration, as well as rebound insomnia and rebound anxiety following abrupt drug withdrawal.[22-24] On the other hand, drugs with long elimination half-lives will accumulate and consequently have less potential for producing early morning insomnia, rebound insomnia, and increases in daytime levels of anxiety and a greater potential for producing carry-over effectiveness and daytime sedation.

Three different components contribute to the activity of flurazepam;[57,58,65-68] both the parent compound and the hydroxyethyl flurazepam metabolite contribute to the drug's efficacy for sleep induction, then are eliminated rapidly. The desalkylflurazepam metabolite, however, is eliminated very slowly (half-life of 50 to 100 hours) and accumulates with nightly drug administration. Temazepam has an intermediate elimination half-life, with a mean of about 15 hours,[55,57] producing an intermediate degree of accumulation. Finally, for triazolam, with an ultrashort elimination half-life (2 to 4 hours), there is essentially no accumulation with consecutive nights of drug administration.[58,69,70]

Hypnotic Efficacy

Flurazepam, the most thoroughly studied of all hypnotic drugs, has consistently shown efficacy, both initially and with continued use. Our studies demonstrated that with short-term drug administration, sleep is significantly improved on the first night of drug administration.[19-21,29] Because of the carry-over effect of the desalkylflurazepam metabolite, effectiveness is further increased to a slight degree with continued drug administration so that peak effectiveness of the drug occurs on the second and third consecutive nights of drug use. In contrast to the non-benzodiazepines and most other benzodiazepines, however, flurazepam continues to be effective both for inducing and maintaining sleep not only with intermediate-term use[19] but also with long-term use (one month of consecutive nightly drug administration[20,21,29]). Sleep laboratory studies of flurazepam, 30 mg, subsequent to our own, have produced results similar to our findings of the drug's initial effectiveness,[61,71-73] as well as its intermediate and long-term efficacy.[61,71] There is also agreement regarding the effectiveness of the 15-mg dose of flurazepam.[30,74-77]

Because temazepam is prepared in a hard gelatin capsule (the only formulation available in the United States), it is absorbed slowly from the gastrointestinal tract so that peak concentrations are reached an average of 2.8 hours after oral ingestion.[54,55] The drug's slow absorption accounts for its ineffectiveness for inducing sleep in our own study,[32] as well as in other sleep laboratory studies.[78,79] Data from clinical trials support this conclusion. For example, temazepam has not been effective for inducing sleep in hospitalized patients awaiting surgery or in adolescent patients with disturbed sleep.[78] In both groups of patients, one would expect complaints primarily of difficulty in falling asleep. In terms of sleep maintenance, temazepam has produced only a mild to moderate effect.[32,79] Although the soft gelatin formulation of temazepam available in Europe is reported to be absorbed more rapidly than the United States formulation, comprehensive sleep laboratory assessment of its efficacy is lacking.

In general, sleep laboratory studies of triazolam have shown that it is effective with short-term use.[33,73,80-83] Our study, however, showed that this efficacy was not maintained with intermediate-term use; there was a considerable loss of efficacy at the end of two weeks of drug administration.[33] Although the findings from two other studies[80,82] appear to be at variance with ours, this is not actually the case. In both of these studies, the subjects were allowed to sleep "ad lib" (without being awakened at a set time each morning). When we calculated values for total sleep time from the data reported in the latter study,[82] the percentage of total sleep time after two weeks of drug administration was the same as during baseline. In the other study, total sleep time was reported to be only slightly increased (from 5 to 15 minutes more than baseline) with drug administration.[80]

Based on our studies of flurazepam, we expected to find that other benzodiazepine hypnotics would also show a relatively slow development of tolerance in terms of their efficacy. Our studies, however, have shown that this is not the case and that benzodiazepine hypnotics with relatively short elimination half-lives show a rather rapid development of tolerance and loss of efficacy. In separate sleep laboratory studies, we evaluated the efficacy of seven other benzodiazepine hypnotic drugs, including temazepam and triazolam. With initial and short-term drug administration (first three nights), each of the benzodiazepine hypnotics (with the exception of midazolam and temazepam) showed a statistically significant or at least moderate improvement of sleep when values for total wake time were compared with the respective placebo-baseline values[28,36,41,42] (Table 10.2).

Each of the benzodiazepine hypnotics was given on consecutive nights for at least a one- or two-week period of time; for three of the drugs the administration period lasted four weeks. Efficacy at the end of one week of drug administration was assessed for flunitrazepam, lormetazepam, midazolam, and nitrazepam; flunitrazepam and nitrazepam showed no loss of efficacy, lormetazepam was moderately effective, and midazolam only slightly effective.[36-38] The values shown in Table 10.2 illustrate that, at the end of two weeks of nightly administration, the two benzodiazepine hypnotics with long elimination half-lives (flurazepam and quazepam) showed the least degree of loss of efficacy with continued use;[28,41,42] the other drugs had lost most of their effectiveness. Except for flurazepam 30 mg and quazepam 15 mg, no drug produced a significant decrease in total wake time as compared to baseline with either intermediate- or long-term drug administration. Our data clearly demonstrate that benzodiazepine hypnotics with relatively short elimination half-lives rapidly lose their effectiveness, but to a somewhat lesser degree than previously demonstrated

Table 10.2. Efficacy and Withdrawal Effects of Benzodiazepine Hypnotics[a]

	Percent Change of Total Wake Time from Baseline				
	Drug Administration				Drug Withdrawal
	1st 3 nights	1 wk	2 wks	4 wks	
Triazolam, 0.50 mg	−45	*	−17	*	+60
Midazolam, 30.0 mg	−28	−8	*	*	+88
Lormetazepam, 2.0 mg	−47	−28	*	*	+73
Temazepam, 30.0 mg	−12	*	−2	+3	+12
Flunitrazepam, 2.0 mg	−57	−50	*	*	+25
Flunitrazepam, 2.0 mg	−39	*	−17	−9	+35
Nitrazepam, 10.0 mg	−36	−43	*	*	+40
Flurazepam, 30.0 mg	−51	*	−60	*	−34
Flurazepam, 30.0 mg	−48	*	−56	−43	−10
Flurazepam, 30.0 mg	−51	*	−43	−35	−13
Quazepam, 30.0 mg	−57	*	−30	−23	−30

a For each drug listed in order of approximate elimination half-life, data are presented from those studies in which the highest dose of the drug was evaluated. Thus, data are not presented for midazolam, 10 and 20 mg, lormetazepam, 0.5, 1.0, and 1.5 mg, flunitrazepam, 0.25 and 1.0 mg, and quazepam, 7.5 and 15.0 mg. With midazolam, lormetazepam, and flunitrazepam, the lower doses were generally less effective, while with quazepam the 15-mg dose was similar in efficacy to flurazepam, as was the case for quazepam, 30 mg, when one subject, an outlier, was excluded.

* Time not recorded in sleep laboratory.

for most non-benzodiazepine hypnotic drugs. In contrast, the long elimination half-life benzodiazepine drugs, particularly flurazepam, produce a much slower development of tolerance. Other studies by Oswald and his associates have shown that nitrazepam[84,85] and lormetazepam[61,85] maintain their effectiveness with continued use. Our findings on nitrazepam[36] are consistent with their reports; however, we did find evidence of tolerance developing with several of the doses of lormetazepam that we studied.[37]

Side Effects

Daytime Sedation   Daytime sedation is not an unexpected side effect with hypnotic drugs; it represents a direct extension of the drugs' therapeutic effects. Because benzodiazepine hypnotics such as flurazepam accumulate with consecutive nightly drug administration, these drugs present a greater potential for producing excessive daytime sedation and decrements in performance.[59-61] In 1976, when we summarized and reviewed a number of our studies with flurazepam, we alerted physicians to both the potential advantages and disadvantages of the drug's accumulation and carry-over effectiveness;[21] we also emphasized that use of the 15-mg dose for most patients, not just for the elderly, would maintain the many advantages of the drug while greatly minimizing any daytime sedation.[21,86,87] More recently, in separate long-term evaluations of flurazepam, 30 mg, and quazepam, 30 and 15 mg, we found that quazepam, 30 mg, produced considerably more frequent and severe daytime sedation than flurazepam, 30 mg.[29] This is not surprising because quazepam has three components with relatively long elimination half-lives (the parent compound and two active metabolites, 2-oxoquazepam and alkylflurazepam).*

It is surprising that in clinical use the three hypnotic drugs that are available commercially (each with a different elimination half-life) do not appear to differ markedly from each other in terms of adverse side effects, of which daytime sedation is one of the most common. For example, the overall prevalence of drowsiness was found to be 11.4 percent with flurazepam,[88] 17.0 percent with temazepam,[89] and 14.0 percent with triazolam.[90] Thus, daytime sedation may be related more to dose than to a drug's rate of elimination.[86]

Most of the studies of temazepam's effects on performance were conducted in Europe with a soft gelatin capsule preparation, usually in doses of 10 or 20 mg, rather than the hard-capsule, 30-mg dose available in the U.S.[57] Compared with the European formulation, the higher dose and slower absorption rate of the U.S. preparation would be expected to produce more residual drowsiness and daytime sedation and an increased potential for performance decrements.

Memory Impairment   Compared with flurazepam and temazepam, triazolam produces, by far, the greatest degree of memory impairment.[33,91-94] There are now a number of studies of triazolam that report varying degrees of memory impairment extending to lengthy episodes of anterograde amnesia. In one study comparing the degree of memory impairment caused by triazolam, flurazepam, and lorazepam, both triazolam and lorazepam (a benzodiazepine with a relatively short elimination half-life) produced significantly greater memory impairment than flurazepam.[92] In our sleep laboratory evaluation of triazolam, two patients reported episodes of anterograde amnesia while taking the drug.[33] The occurrence of anterograde amnesia has also been noted during the administration of midazolam,[38,95] another benzo-

* Schering Corporation: data on file.

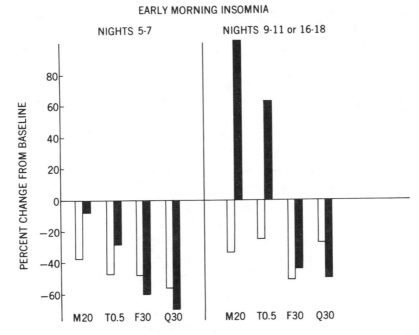

Fig. 10.1. Early morning insomnia with rapidly eliminated benzodiazepine hypnotics. For each drug, the mean wake time for the first six hours of sleep is represented by the first vertical bar (clear) and the mean wake time for the last two hours by the second vertical bar (shaded). On the first set of drug nights (5–7), the two drugs with short elimination half-lives (midazolam and triazolam) show a considerable loss of effectiveness in the last two hours of the night. On the second set of drug nights (9–11 for midazolam and 16–18 for triazolam), early morning insomnia occurs, as evidenced by a marked increase in wake time above the baseline value. (From Kales et al[62])

diazepine drug with an ultrashort elimination half-life,[96,97] and flunitrazepam,[98] a drug with an intermediate elimination half-life.[58]

Early Morning Insomnia and Daytime Anxiety   More recently, several studies have reported the occurrence of early morning insomnia[62] and daytime anxiety[62-64] during administration of triazolam, 0.5 mg (Fig. 10-1). We also have noted the occurrence of early morning insomnia and increases in the levels of daytime anxiety with the administration of midazolam.[38,62] To us, an important aspect of the side effects of early morning insomnia and daytime anxiety is that because they are the opposite of the drug's therapeutic effects, they are entirely unexpected by the patient and for that reason most disturbing.

In contrast to these changes seen with administration of benzodiazepine hypnotics with short elimination half-lives, drugs that are slowly eliminated produce a carry-over effect, and do not cause early morning insomnia or increases in daytime levels of anxiety and tension. The potential that triazolam has for producing daytime anxiety was clearly demonstrated in one study comparing this drug with flurazepam.[63] Triazolam produced a 70 percent increase in the levels of daytime anxiety and tension, while flurazepam resulted in a significant improvement in most daytime mood factors. In the same study, the authors reported that neither flurazepam nor triazolam produced increases in daytime sedation as measured by the Stanford Sleepiness Scale (SSS). Yet, the authors concluded that flurazepam produced more daytime sedation than triazolam because flurazepam subjects had shorter sleep latencies when allowed to sleep during the day as assessed by the Multiple Sleep Latency Test.[63] Our interpretation of these findings, however, is quite different and, we believe, more consistent with the actual data. The lack of daytime sedation with flurazepam as measured by the SSS and the general improvement in daytime mood factors, indicates that the flurazepam subjects were able to fall asleep quickly because they were less dysphoric, not because they were overly sedated. In contrast, the mood data suggest that triazolam subjects had more difficulty trying to sleep during the daytime tests because they were experiencing a marked increase in levels of tension and anxiety.

Other Behavioral Changes In a controversy regarding triazolam and its side effects,[99-106] a Dutch physician reported the occurrence of a number of serious behavioral side effects including psychotic-like reactions with triazolam administration.[106] These findings led to the suspension of the drug's license in the Netherlands[101] and to the drug company's voluntary withdrawal of the 1-mg tablet from the world market.[105] Hallucinations with triazolam use have been reported in case reports from Canada.[107,108] Some of the side effects reported for triazolam may have been the result of excessively high doses of the drug (1 to 2 mg).[99,103] We feel, however, that some of these adverse psychologic effects can be explained by the phenomena of amnesia, early morning insomnia, daytime anxiety, and rebound insomnia occurring in patients with various personality patterns and life stresses, who, therefore, have certain psychologic vulnerabilities and reactions. In the package insert for triazolam, the FDA indicates that the drug may have a narrow margin of safety between therapeutic dose levels (0.5

mg) and levels only several times higher (1–2 mg), which are associated with serious behavioral changes.[90]

Withdrawal Effects

Withdrawal of flurazepam in most studies has demonstrated the presence of a carry-over effectiveness for one to several nights; rebound insomnia has not been reported following abrupt withdrawal of flurazepam.[19-21,25,28-30,61,71,73] Some studies assessed only the first three or four nights after withdrawal of flurazepam, whereas others included lengthy withdrawal periods of seven[61] or eight[25] nights, and in four studies, 14 nights.[20,29,71] In one of the latter studies, subjects were recorded in the laboratory for each of the 14 withdrawal nights and only slight increases in total wake time were noted (a 22% increase on the fourth and fourteenth nights of withdrawal).[29] Our finding of a delayed and slight increase in total wake time following withdrawal of flurazepam is similar to the findings of two other studies;[67,109] one study reported only an eight-minute increase in sleep latency,[67] and the other only a five-minute increase.[109]

Only three sleep laboratory studies have assessed the withdrawal of temazepam; two showed rebound insomnia, while one did not. In our study of temazepam, rebound insomnia did not occur.[32] In another study,[79] however, mean total wake time for the three nights of withdrawal combined increased about 50 percent above baseline, while in the third study,[78] total wake time rose sharply on the first night after withdrawal.

There is considerable agreement that withdrawal of triazolam consistently produces rebound insomnia.[33,73,81-83] Rebound insomnia was present in two studies conducted by Vogel and associates, one with three doses of triazolam (0.25, 0.5, and 1.0 mg),[83] and another with triazolam, 0.5 mg.[73] Also, Mamelak and his colleagues observed a marked increase in total wake time on the first withdrawal night compared to baseline.[81] When we calculated total sleep time from the data of Roth, et al,[82] rebound insomnia was clearly present. In his study, total sleep time for the entire four nights of withdrawal averaged 60 minutes less than the baseline value for total sleep time. This increase in sleep difficulty is considerable in itself and would be expected to be much greater on one or more of the individual withdrawal nights.

Table 10.3 compares the efficacy, side effects, and withdrawal effects of flurazepam, temazepam, and triazolam.

Table 10.3. Comparison of Temazepam, Triazolam, and Flurazepam

	Short-Term Effectiveness	Effectiveness with Continued Administration	Side Effects
Temazepam 30 mg (Restoril)	Ineffective for induction	Ineffective for induction	Morning sleepiness
	Slight to moderate effectiveness for maintenance	Slight effectiveness for maintenance	Rebound insomnia
Triazolam 0.5 mg (Halcion)	Effective for induction and maintenance	Considerable loss of effectiveness with intermediate-term use	Amnesia Early morning insomnia Daytime anxiety Rebound insomnia
Flurazepam 30 mg (Dalmane)	Effective for induction and maintenance	Some loss of effectiveness only with long-term use	Daytime sleepiness

(From Kales et al[41])

We also obtained withdrawal data for all the benzodiazepine drugs studied in our sleep laboratory; this is summarized in Table 10.2. Withdrawal of those drugs with rapid or intermediate elimination rates resulted in rebound insomnia.[24,28,41,42] Rebound insomnia occurred with five of the drugs even when the mean values for the first three withdrawal nights were combined. Each of these drugs produced either a 40 percent or statistically significant increase in total wake time compared to its respective baseline value. The drugs and their doses in order of decreasing degree of rebound insomnia were midazolam, 30 mg; lormetazepam, 2 mg; triazolam, 0.5 mg; nitrazepam, 10 mg; and flunitrazepam, 2 mg, with the increase in total wake time above baseline ranging from 88 percent for midazolam to 35 percent for flunitrazepam. In contrast, the values for total wake time for flurazepam and quazepam were below baseline levels, ie, sleep was still slightly to moderately improved following withdrawal.

We also assessed the values for total wake time for the single withdrawal night within each drug study that showed the greatest percentage of increase over baseline.[24] Striking increases were shown by the five benzodiazepine drugs with short or intermediate elimination half-lives; triazolam produced the greatest increase in total wake time over baseline (130%).[33] In the flurazepam and quazepam studies, the withdrawal period extended for 15 consecutive nights, yet increases in total wake time were slight for both drugs; the greatest change for flurazepam (22%) occurred on nights 4 and 14 of the withdrawal period and the greatest change for quazepam (8%), on the eighth withdrawal night.[29]

In summary, our findings indicate that following withdrawal of a benzodiazepine with a short half-life, rebound insomnia and rebound anxiety usually occur and are of an intense degree; with a benzodiazepine with an intermediate half-life, they frequently occur and are of a moderate degree; and with a long half-life benzodiazepine, they may occur infrequently and be of a mild degree.[24,41,42] In our studies, the greatest increases in total wake time produced by abrupt withdrawal were caused by the short half-life drugs, triazolam, midazolam, and lormetazepam. Additionally, other studies have shown that a marked worsening of sleep occurs following the abrupt withdrawal of midazolam,[110] lormetazepam,[85] and nitrazepam.[84]

For three of the 8 drugs evaluated (lormetazepam,[37] midazolam,[38] and quazepam[39]), at least three different doses were studied, thus enabling us to correlate dose-response data with the effects of drug withdrawal. Two of these benzodiazepine drugs, one with a short elimination half-life (midazolam) and one with a short-to-intermediate elimination half-life (lormetazepam), showed a clear dose-response effect for rebound insomnia;[37,38] this was true for the entire withdrawal period, as well as for the highest value of total wake time for a single withdrawal night across doses. In the quazepam study, none of the doses showed rebound insomnia following drug withdrawal; in fact, there was clear-cut carry-over effectiveness.[39]

Drug Tolerance

Tolerance is now known to develop more quickly with benzodiazepines that have a rapid elimination rate than with those that are slowly eliminated.[22-24] It has been well-recognized that tolerance with continued use of large doses of non-benzodiazepine sedative-hypnotics for prolonged periods of time leads to dependence and withdrawal syndromes characterized by symptoms opposite to those for which drug treatment was intended (agitation, tremulousness, insomnia, hyperpyrexia, and even convulsive seizures).[43-52] Furthermore, the syndrome of drug withdrawal insomnia may occur, which consists of severe difficulty in falling asleep, and, once the patient is asleep, fragmentation and disruption of sleep associated with a marked increase in REM sleep above baseline levels.[50]

For benzodiazepine anxiolytics and hypnotics, there have been fewer reports of withdrawal reactions,[111-121] and their dependence liability has generally been considered to be lower than that of non-benzodiazepine sedative-hypnotics.[115] In most cases, withdrawal reactions reported for benzodiazepines have followed their prolonged use in high doses. More recently, withdrawal symptoms also have been noted following the use of relatively low doses of benzodiazepines for prolonged periods.[111,117,121] In either case, it is recognized that short half-life benzodiazepine drugs induce more abrupt and severe withdrawal reactions than benzodiazepines that are slowly eliminated. Hollister, in a recent review, indicated that severe withdrawal reactions have been reported frequently following discontinuation of short half-life benzodiazepines such as lorazepam and oxazepam;[114] in 1980-81, there were at least 48 such reports, including the occurrence of seizures.[122-125]

Our findings from a number of controlled clinical studies have demonstrated clear differences in withdrawal reactions between benzodiazepines with short and long elimination half-lives.[22-24,62] Further, we have shown that definite withdrawal syndromes can occur not only with discontinuation of a low daily dose of a drug but also after it has been administered for only a short period. Benzodiazepines with relatively short elimination half-lives, even when used in only single nightly doses for relatively short periods of time, appear to have a greater potential than previously thought for development of dependence through a combination of several properties: tolerance, early morning insomnia, daytime anxiety, and rebound insomnia and anxiety. In most circumstances, rebound insomnia and anxiety represent a relatively limited withdrawal reaction. However, when definite drug dependence occurs and withdrawal is followed by a full-blown abstinence syndrome, rebound insomnia and anxiety are expected to be more intense and prolonged.[24]

Mechanism of Rebound Insomnia and Rebound Anxiety

Elimination rate appears to be a critical factor that determines whether a benzodiazepine produces rebound insomnia. Following the discovery of benzodiazepine receptors in the brain,[126,127] we suggested that rebound insomnia may be linked to changes at benzodiazepine receptor sites and corresponding fluctuations in the production of endogenous benzodiazepine-like ligands.[22] We hypothesized that abrupt withdrawal of a benzodiazepine with a relatively short duration of action may result in more intense rebound insomnia due to a postulated lag in production and replacement of endogenous benzodiazepine-like compounds that had been suppressed while the exogenous drug was present. When benzodiazepines with a long duration of action are withdrawn, effects on benzodiazepine receptors may be less evident because endogenous benzodiazepine-like compounds may be partially restored before active metabolites of the exogenously administered drugs are completely eliminated.[22] It appears that as long as a benzodiazepine is present at receptor sites, the intrinsic inhibitory neuronal mechanisms function at reduced levels, with excitatory mechanisms tending to compensate for exogenous inhibition.[22,128] Snyder has postulated a similar mechanism, primarily involving GABA.[128] Benzodiazepine receptors interact with GABA receptors, thereby enhancing GABA's inhibitory effects.[129,130]

Although the duration of drug action is important in determining its potential for producing rebound insomnia and/or rebound anxiety, other factors are also involved. The drug's dose and length of administration, as well as tolerance of its effects, may also be important considerations along with the functional state of the receptor, ie, change in the number of benzodiazepine receptors in response to drug administration,[131] affinity of drug for receptor, and the possibility that benzodiazepines may selectively attach to subclasses of benzodiazepine receptors.[132]

Guidelines for Prescribing Hypnotic Drugs

The Sleep History and Overall Evaluation

A complete history as described in Chapter 7 (Evaluation of Insomnia) is necessary whenever a patient presents with a complaint of insomnia, particularly when the condition is chronic and hypnotic medication is to be considered as an adjunctive treatment.[8,133] The sleep history, drug history (including prior use of hypnotic medication), and psychiatric history should be obtained before treatment is selected.

The high prevalence of significant psychologic conflicts in patients with chronic insomnia necessitates a psychiatric history.[134] The extent and severity of these conflicts are important factors in considering hypnotic medication in the multidimensional treatment. Of course, the physician should not hesitate to refer the patient for a thorough and careful psychiatric evaluation.

The drug history may indicate that the use of pharmacologic agents, for treating either medical illness or sleep difficulty, has complicated the clinical picture of insomnia.[134] Some drugs may directly cause or exacerbate the symptom of insomnia, while on the other hand, the ineffectiveness of most sleep medications may cause the patient to increase the dosage, leading to drug dependence. Similarly, the effects of alcohol use and high caffeine intake should be taken into account.

The sleep history can also help to determine whether hypnotic medication is necessary[133] by characterizing patients' sleep-wakefulness patterns on a 24-hour basis throughout the week. In this way, the physician can properly assess the effects of naps, prolonged sleeping on the weekend, or other alterations in schedules, habits, or life style.

Indications for Use

It is important to ask the question, "Under what circumstances are hypnotic drugs indicated?" In certain cases of transient insomnia, hypnotic medication may be used selectively. However, the primary focus in transient insomnia is to remove or relieve the stress-generating situation that precipitated the onset of sleeplessness. In some cases, short-term use of hypnotic medication may be helpful. If the stressful situation cannot be eliminated, the physician is best able to help the patient by identifying and strengthening adaptive coping mechanisms.[135-137] In the case of chronic insomnia, however, the adjunctive use of hypnotic medication is often indicated.

In chronic insomnia, the internalization of emotions experienced by patients leads to emotional arousal that, in turn, results in physiologic activation and insomnia. Before long, the fear of sleeplessness and its consequences develops, leading to a vicious circle of physiologic activation, sleeplessness, more fear of sleeplessness, further emotional arousal and still further sleeplessness.[138] Only a small percentage of patients with chronic insomnia have major (endogenous) depression[139] for which the tricyclic antidepressants would be the drug of choice. Thus, for the majority of patients with chronic insomnia, hypnotic medication is indicated if the physician desires to use pharmacologic therapy as an adjunct to the overall therapeutic approach.

The primary goal of using hypnotic medication in the treatment of chronic insomnia is to alleviate the symptom of sleeplessness so that psychotherapy can proceed effectively. A brief trial of hypnotic medication in the initial phases of psychotherapy will encourage patients to remain in treatment at a time when their motivation for therapy is low or they are overly preoccupied with sleeplessness and consequently cannot effectively participate in the psychotherapeutic process.[86,134] This permits the physician to explore areas of psychologic conflict while a meaningful doctor-patient relationship is developing. With delineation of conflict areas early in treatment, patients will more likely become actively involved in therapy. Providing symptomatic relief for insomnia in the first stages of psychotherapy also helps to alleviate the patient's preoccupation with the symptom. Because many patients fear that continued sleep loss may be harmful to their health, they are very reluctant to wait until psychotherapy results in improved sleep, which is often a matter of weeks or months.

The following case history illustrates one example of the adjunctive use of a hypnotic drug in the treatment of insomnia.

Case 2. A 38-year-old married man employed as a computer technician complained of persistent insomnia of 16 years' duration. This chronic sleep disturbance began when he was a college student experiencing stress and anxiety over his mediocre academic performance. He described himself as a perfectionistic person who spent much of his time ruminating over his perceived shortcomings. He had tried many different prescribed hypnotics and over-the-counter medications, as well as various self-help measures, such as transcendental meditation, to help himself get to sleep. Currently, he was experiencing considerable apprehension about a possible layoff and financial concerns, and while trying to fall asleep was obsessed over these problems. Recently, he had begun to use alcohol in an effort to sleep.

When seen for evaluation, he was a large, perspiring anxious-appearing man who seemed to be pressured and rigid and overly focused on his sleep difficulty. The *Diagnostic and Statistical Manual of Mental Disorders* (DSM-III)[140] diagnoses were: generalized anxiety disorder (Axis I) and compulsive personality disorder (Axis II).

Psychotherapy was recommended and readily accepted. However, on beginning therapy, the patient was excessively preoccupied with his sleeplessness and its possible consequences. Accordingly, the psychiatrist elected to prescribe a hypnotic medication as an adjunct to his psychotherapy. Although flurazepam, 15 mg, is recommended for most patients, a 30 mg dose was prescribed for this patient because of the severity and chronicity of his problem, and previous history of using sleep medication.

After three weeks of psychotherapy and hypnotic medication, his insomnia had improved and the nightly dosage was reduced to 15 mg. After one week the drug was completely withdrawn with the recommendation that it be used only on a prn basis. This adjunctive use of a hypnotic drug helped to break the vicious circle of insomnia and enabled the psychiatrist to focus the patient on his problem areas without dwelling on the symptom of insomnia.

Safety Issues

Benzodiazepines are preferable to the barbiturates and other non-benzodiazepine hypnotics that have a narrow margin of safety; in cases of overdose, the barbiturate drugs in particular can cause severe respiratory compromise and death.[141] Although patients develop considerable tolerance to these drugs' therapeutic effects with chronic administration, minimal tolerance occurs for the drugs' lethal effects. Benzodiazepines, in contrast, provide a wide margin of safety between the therapeutic dose and serious overdose or lethal dose. While benzodiazepine overdose has seldom been the cause of death, suicide by means of mixed-drug overdose has become more common.[141] Therefore, patients should be cautioned about the dangers of combining these drugs with other CNS depressants, particularly alcohol.

To prescribe hypnotic drugs appropriately, physicians also need to be familiar with potential drug interactions.[142] Interactions that may occur with hypnotic medication include: additive effects to other CNS-depressant drugs; the induction of enzymes that stimulate the metabolism of other drugs, thereby decreasing their clinical effects; and protein binding accompanied by displacement of other protein-bound drugs, leading to a potentiation of the displaced drugs' clinical effects. Also, the metabolism of benzodiazepine hypnotics may be delayed by concomitant administration of commonly used drugs such as cimetidine[143] or oral contraceptives.[144]

Whenever possible, the lowest effective dose of a hypnotic drug should be used.[1,21,86,87] With any hypnotic drug, particularly those that may accumulate, patients should be cautioned regarding the drug's potential for producing daytime sedation and decrements in performance. In particular, patients should be advised to avoid driving or operating machinery if they feel excessively drowsy during the day. Certainly, patients suspected of having sleep apnea or other hypoventilatory conditions should not be prescribed hypnotic medication, as well as any CNS-depressant drug.

In the elderly, drugs tend to remain in the body and are biologically active for longer periods, resulting in more potent therapeutic and toxic effects.[145] For these reasons, the history, physical examination, and laboratory tests for the elderly patient should be particularly thorough. Generally, the initial dose and maintenance dose for the older patient is about half that for young adults. Also, changes in dosage should be more gradual than those for other patients, and the course of drug therapy should be carefully monitored for side effects.

By being aware of the efficacy and the side effects of the benzodiazepine hypnotics, physicians can maximize their benefit-to-risk ratio and utilize these medications judiciously in the adjunctive treatment of insomnia. In order to accomplish this task, physicians' education regarding sleep disorders and their evaluation and treatment needs to be comprehensive[146,147] so that physicians can rely on the scientific data available regarding a hypnotic drug's complete profile, rather than to simply be guided in their choice by the most persuasive promotional material.[148,149] Such information will also permit physicians to consider the overall benefits of using a hypnotic agent, not just its potential for abuse or misuse, to determine whether or not to prescribe.[150]

Summary

Prescribing hypnotic medication is an important adjunct in the multidimensional treatment of insomnia. Contrary to the popular impression that hypnotics are often abused, surveys show that only a small percentage of insomniacs use hypnotics nightly for more than eight weeks. A greater misuse of hypnotic drugs results from considering them as the sole treatment for chronic insomnia, a disorder that is usually induced by psychologic and physiologic arousal, stemming from longstanding internalized emotional conflicts and stress.

To properly select a hypnotic drug, the physician needs to be familiar with the drug's profile of efficacy and safety, as well as its side effects and withdrawal characteristics. These drug profiles have now been established through a combination of extensive clinical trials and sleep laboratory studies for numerous non-benzodiazepines and benzodiazepine hypnotic drugs. Clinical trials are useful in studying drug effects in large numbers of patients and in varied subpopulations; they are especially useful in assessing severity and frequency of drug side effects. Clinical trials have the disadvantage of lacking the objective and precise measurements of the laboratory. Sleep laboratory evaluations permit a precise and rigorous examination of the drug's efficacy during short-, intermediate-, and long-term drug administration, as well as following its withdrawal. The limitations of sleep laboratory studies, however, are their high cost and the small number of subjects who can be evaluated.

Non-benzodiazepine drugs are relatively effective with short-term administration but lose most of their effectiveness after about two weeks of drug administration. Because of this, non-benzodiazepine hypnotics are often taken in multiple doses for long periods, and with abrupt withdrawal a severe abstinence syndrome may occur. Because of its greater margin of safety and degree of effectiveness, the benzodiazepine class of hypnotic drugs has largely replaced other types of hypnotics in the adjunctive treatment of insomnia.

A hypnotic drug's onset of action in inducing sleep depends on how rapidly it is absorbed. Because of its delayed absorption, temazepam has little efficacy for sleep induction. Carry-over sedative effects, as well as side effects such as early morning insomnia and daytime anxiety, are determined by a drug's elimination half-life. Ultrashort elimination half-life drugs such as triazolam are more likely to produce early morning insomnia and daytime anxiety, whereas long half-life drugs have carry-over sedative effects. In terms of continued efficacy or development of tolerance, the long elimination half-life drug, flurazepam, maintains its effectiveness for as long as four weeks of nightly administration, whereas the shorter elimination half-life drugs rapidly lose much of their effectiveness. Following withdrawal, those benzodiazepine hypnotics with short half-lives are generally associated with a frequent, immediate, and intense degree of rebound insomnia. With the longer half-life benzodiazepines, withdrawal sleep disturbance occurs infrequently, is delayed in its appearance, and is of a milder degree.

In prescribing a hypnotic drug, a complete evaluation of the patient's complaint is necessary. Prior use of hypnotic drugs, alcohol, caffeine, or other drugs prescribed for medical conditions should be taken into account. A hypnotic drug should not be the sole treatment but rather an adjunct to break the vicious circle of insomnia. Special caution is needed for those who drive or use machinery and for the elderly, who are especially sensitive to the effects of drug therapy.

References

1. Institute of Medicine: *Sleeping Pills, Insomnia, and Medical Practice.* Washington, DC, National Academy of Sciences, 1979.

2. Balter MB, Bauer ML: Patterns of prescribing and use of hypnotic drugs in the United States, in Clift AD (ed): *Sleep Disturbance and Hypnotic Drug Dependence*. New York, Excerpta Medica, 1975, pp 261–293.

3. Bixler EO, Kales A, Soldatos CR, Kales JD, Healey S: Prevalence of sleep disorders in the Los Angeles metropolitan area. *Am J Psychiatry 136*:1257–1262.

4. Bixler EO, Kales JD, Kales A, Scharf MB, Leo L: Hypnotic drug prescription patterns: two physician surveys. *Sleep Res 5*:62, 1976.

5. Mellinger GD, Balter MB: Prevalence and patterns of use of psychotherapeutic drugs: Results from a 1979 national survey of American adults, in Pognoni G, Bellantuoano C, Lader M (eds): *Epidemiological Impact of Psychotropic Drugs*. Amsterdam, Elsevier/North-Holland Biomedical Press, 1981.

6. The Gallup Organization: *The Gallup Study of Sleeping Habits*. Princeton, NJ, 1979.

7. Kales A, Caldwell AB, Soldatos CR, Bixler EO, Kales JD: Biopsychobehavioral correlates of insomnia. II. Pattern specificity and consistency with the Minnesota Multiphasic Personality Inventory. *Psychosom Med 45*:341–356, 1983.

8. Kales A, Kales JD, Scharf MB, Soldatos CR: The prescription of hypnotic drugs, in Buchwald C, Cohen S, Katz D, Solomon J (eds): *Frequently Prescribed and Abused Drugs: Their Indications, Efficacy, and Rational Prescribing*, NTS Medical Monograph Series, vol 1, no 1. New York, Career Teacher Center, 1980, pp 57–75.

9. Kales A, Kales JD, Bixler EO, Scharf MB: Methodology of sleep laboratory drug evaluations: further considerations, in Kagan F, Harwood T, Rickels K, Rudzik A, Sorer H (eds): *Hypnotics: Methods of Development and Evaluation*. New York, Spectrum Publications, 1975, pp 109–126.

10. Kales A, Scharf MB, Soldatos CR, Bixler EO: Clinical evaluation of hypnotic drugs: contributions from sleep laboratory studies. *J Clin Pharmacol 19*:329–336, 1979.

11. Soldatos CR, Kales A: Role of the sleep laboratory in the evaluation of hypnotic drugs, in Priest RG, Pletscher A, Ward J (eds): *Sleep Research* (Proceedings of the Northern European Symposium on Sleep Research). England, MTP Press Ltd, 1979, pp 181–195.

12. Kales A, Malmstrom EJ, Scharf MB, Rubin RT: Psychophysiological and biochemical changes following use and withdrawal of hypnotics, in Kales A (ed): *Sleep: Physiology and Pathology*. Philadelphia, JB Lippincott Company, 1969, pp 331–343.

13. Kales A, Scharf M, Tan T-L, Kales J, Allen C, Malmstrom E: Sleep patterns with short-term drug use. *Psychophysiology 6*:262, 1969.

14. Kales A, Tan T, Scharf M, Kales J, Malmstrom E: Effects of long- and short-term administration of flurazepam (Dalmane) in subjects with insomnia. *Psychophysiology 6*:260, 1969.

15. Oswald I, Priest RG: Five weeks to escape the sleeping-pill habit. *Br Med J* 2:1093–1095, 1965.
16. Hollister LE: Antianxiety drugs in clinical practice, in Garattini S, Mussini E, Randall LO (eds): *The Benzodiazepines*. New York, Raven Press, 1973, pp 367–377.
17. Achong MR, Bayne JR, Gerson LW, Golshani S: Prescribing of psychoactive drug for chronically ill patients. *Canad Med Assoc J 118*: 1503–1508, 1978.
18. Rechtschaffen A, Kales ·A (eds): *A Manual of Standardized Terminology, Techniques and Scoring System for Sleep Stages of Human Subjects*, no 204. National Institutes of Health, 1968.
19. Kales A, Allen C, Scharf MB, Kales JD: Hypnotic drugs and their effectiveness. *Arch Gen Psychiatry 23*:226–232, 1970.
20. Kales A, Kales JD, Bixler EO, Scharf MB: Effectiveness of hypnotic drugs with prolonged use: flurazepam and pentobarbital. *Clin Pharmacol Ther 18*:356–363, 1975.
21. Kales A, Bixler EO, Scharf MB, Kales JD: Sleep laboratory studies of flurazepam: a model for evaluating hypnotic drugs. *Clin Pharmacol Ther 19*:576–583, 1976.
22. Kales A, Scharf MB, Kales JD: Rebound insomnia: a new clinical syndrome. *Science 201*:1039–1041, 1978.
23. Kales A, Scharf MB, Kales JD, Soldatos CR: Rebound insomnia: a potential hazard following withdrawal of certain benzodiazepines. *JAMA 241*:1692–1695, 1979.
24. Kales A, Soldatos CR, Bixler EO, Kales JD: Rebound insomnia and rebound anxiety: a review. *Pharmacology 26*:121–137, 1983.
25. Kales J, Kales A, Bixler EO, Slye ES: Effects of placebo and flurazepam on sleep patterns in insomniac subjects: *Clin Pharmacol Ther 12*: 691–697, 1971.
26. Finkel MJ: Historical development of FDA's clinical guidelines, in Williams RL, Karacan I (eds): *Pharmacology of Sleep*. New York, John Wiley & Sons, 1976, pp 339–341.
27. U.S. Department of Health, Education and Welfare: *Guidelines for the Clinical Evaluation of Hypnotic Drugs*. Washington, DC, U.S. Government Printing Office, 1977.
28. Kales A, Bixler EO, Kales JD, Scharf MB: Comparative effectiveness of nine hypnotic drugs: sleep laboratory studies. *J Clin Pharmacol 17*: 207–213, 1977.
29. Kales A, Bixler EO, Soldatos CR, Vela-Bueno A, Jacoby J, Kales JD: Quazepam and flurazepam: long-term use and extended withdrawal. *Clin Pharmacol Ther 32*:781–788, 1982.
30. Kales A, Scharf MB: Sleep laboratory and clinical studies of the effects of benzodiazepines on sleep: flurazepam, diazepam, chlordiazepoxide, and RO 5–4200, in Garattini S, Mussini E, Randall LO (eds): *The Benzodiazepines*. New York, Raven Press, 1973.
31. Kales A, Hauri P, Bixler EO, Silberfarb P: Effectiveness of intermediate-term use of secobarbital. *Clin Pharmacol Ther 20*:541–545, 1976.

32. Bixler EO, Kales A, Soldatos CR, Scharf MB, Kales JD: Effectiveness of temazepam with short-, intermediate-, and long-term use: sleep laboratory evaluation. *J Clin Pharmacol 18*:110–118, 1978.

33. Kales A, Kales JD, Bixler EO, Scharf MB, Russek E: Hypnotic efficacy of triazolam: sleep laboratory evaluation of intermediate-term effectiveness. *J Clin Pharmacol 16*:399–406, 1976.

34. Bixler EO, Kales A, Soldatos CR, and Kales JD: Flunitrazepam, an investigational hypnotic drug: sleep laboratory evaluations. *J Clin Pharmacol 17*:569–578, 1977.

35. Scharf MB, Bixler EO, Kales A, Soldatos CR: Long-term sleep laboratory evaluation of flunitrazepam. *Pharmacology 19*:173–181, 1979.

36. Soldatos CR, Kales A, Bixler EO: Effectiveness of flunitrazepam and nitrazepam. *Pharmacology* (in press).

37. Kales A, Bixler EO, Soldatos CR, Mitsky DJ, Kales JD: Dose-response studies of lormetazepam: efficacy, side effects, and rebound insomnia. *J Clin Pharmacol 22*:520–530, 1982.

38. Kales A, Soldatos CR, Bixler EO, Goff PJ, Vela-Bueno A: Midazolam: dose-response studies of effectiveness and rebound insomnia. *Pharmacology 26*:138–149, 1983.

39. Kales A, Scharf MB, Bixler EO, Schweitzer PK, Jacoby JA, Soldatos CR: Dose-response studies of quazepam. *Clin Pharmacol Ther 30*: 194–200, 1981.

40. Kales A, Scharf MB, Soldatos CR, Bixler EO, Bianchi SB, Schweitzer PK: Quazepam: a new benzodiazepine hypnotic: intermediate-term sleep laboratory evaluation. *J Clin Pharmacol 20*:184–192, 1980.

41. Kales A: Benzodiazepines in the treatment of insomnia, in Usdin E, Skolnick P, Tallman J, Greenblatt D, Paul SM (eds): *Pharmacology of Benzodiazepines*. London, The Macmillan Press, Ltd, Scientific and Medical Division, 1982, pp 199–217.

42. Kales A, Kales JD: Sleep laboratory studies of hypnotic drugs: efficacy and withdrawal effects. *J Clin Psychopharmacol 3*:140–150, 1983.

43. Essig CF: Addiction to nonbarbiturate sedative and tranquilizing drugs. *Clin Pharmacol Ther 5*:334–343, 1964.

44. Fraser HF, Isbell H, Eisenman AJ, Wikler A, Pescor FT: Chronic barbiturate intoxication. *Arch Intern Med 94*:34–41, 1954.

45. Fraser HF, Shaver MR, Maxwell ES, Isbell H: Death due to withdrawal of barbiturates. *Ann Intern Med 38*:1319–1325, 1953.

46. Fraser HF, Wikler A, Essig CF, Isbell H: Degree of physical dependence induced by secobarbital or pentobarbital. *JAMA 166*:126–129, 1958.

47. Isbell H: Addiction to barbiturates and the barbiturate abstinence syndrome. *Ann Intern Med 33*:108–121, 1950.

48. Isbell H, Altschul S, Kornetsky CH, Eisenman AJ, Flanary HC, Fraser HF: Chronic barbiturate intoxication. An experimental study. *AMA Arch Neurol and Psychiat 64*:1–28, 1950.

49. Johnson FA, Van Buren HC: Abstinence syndrome following glutethimide intoxication. *JAMA 180*:1024–1027, 1962.

50. Kales A, Bixler EO, Tan T-L, Scharf MB, Kales JD: Chronic hypnotic-drug use: ineffectiveness, drug-withdrawal insomnia, and dependence. *JAMA* 227:513–517, 1974.
51. Lloyd EA, Clark LD: Convulsions and delirium incident to glutethimide (Doriden) withdrawal. *Dis Nerv System* 20:524–526, 1959.
52. Swanson LA, Okada T: Death after withdrawal of meprobamate. *JAMA* 184:780–781, 1963.
53. Kales JD, Kales A, Bixler EO, Soldatos CR, Cadieux RJ, Kashurba GJ, Vela-Bueno A: Biopsychobehavioral correlates of insomnia, V: clinical characteristics and behavioral correlates. *Am J Psychiatry* (in press).
54. Greenblatt DJ, Shader RI, Abernethy DR, Ochs HR, Divoll M, Sellers EM: Benzodiazepines and the challenge of pharmacokinetic taxonomy, in Usdin E, Skolnick P, Tallman JF Jr, Greenblatt D, Paul SM (eds): *Pharmacology of Benzodiazepines.* London, The Macmillan Press, Ltd, Scientific and Medical Division, 1982, pp 257–269.
55. Divoll M, Greenblatt DJ, Harmatz JS, Shader RI: Effect of age and gender on disposition of temazepam. *J Pharm Sci* 70:1104–1107, 1981.
56. Fuccella LM, Bolcioni G, Tamassia V, Ferrario L, Tognoni G: Human pharmacokinetics and bioavailability of temazepam administered in soft gelatin capsules. *Europ J Clin Pharmacol* 12:383–386, 1977.
57. Greenblatt DJ, Divoll M, Abernethy DR, Shader RI: Benzodiazepine hypnotics: kinetic and therapeutic options. *Sleep* 5:S18–S27, 1982.
58. Breimer DD, Jochemsen R: Pharmacokinetics of hypnotic drugs, in Wheatley D (ed): *Psychopharmacology of Sleep.* New York, Raven Press, 1981, pp 135–152.
59. Church MW, Johnson LC: Mood and performance of poor sleepers during repeated use with flurazepam. *Psychopharmacology* 61:309–316, 1979.
60. Johnson LC, Chernik DA: Sedative-hypnotics and human performance. *Psychopharmacology* 76:101–113, 1982.
61. Oswald I, Adam K, Borrow S, Idzikowski C: The effects of two hypnotics on sleep, subjective feelings and skilled performance, in Passouant P, Oswald I (eds): *Pharmacology of the States of Alertness.* New York, Pergamon Press, 1979, pp 51–63.
62. Kales A, Soldatos CR, Bixler EO, Kales JD: Early morning insomnia with rapidly eliminated benzodiazepines. *Science* 220:95–97, 1983.
63. Carskadon MA, Seidel WF, Greenblatt DJ, Dement WC: Daytime carry-over of triazolam and flurazepam in elderly insomniacs. *Sleep* 5:361–371, 1982.
64. Morgan K, Oswald I: Anxiety caused by a short-life hypnotic. *Br Med J* 284:942, 1982.
65. Amrein R, Bovey F, Cano JP, Eckert M, Ziegler WH, Coassolo PH, Schalch E, Burckhardt J: Pharmacokinetics and pharmacodynamics of flurazepam in man, part II. *Drugs Exper Clin Res* 9:85–99, 1983.
66. Eckert M, Ziegler WH, Cano JP, Bovey F, Amrein R, Coassolo PH, Schalch E, Burckhardt J: Pharmacokinetics and pharmacodynamics of flurazepam in man, part I. *Drugs Exper Clin Res* 9:77–84, 1983.

67. Greenblatt DJ, Divoll M, Harmatz JS, MacLaughlin DS, Shader RI: Kinetics and clinical effects of flurazepam in young and elderly non-insomniacs. *Clin Pharmacol Ther* 30:475–486, 1981.

68. Kaplan SA, de Silva JAF, Jack ML, Alexander K, Strojny N, Weinfeld RE, Puglisi CV, Weissman L: Blood level profile in man following chronic oral administration of flurazepam hydrochloride. *J Pharm Sci* 62:1932–1935, 1973.

69. Eberts FS, Philopolous Y, Reineke LM: Triazolam disposition. *Clin Pharmacol Ther* 29:81–93, 1981.

70. Greenblatt DJ, Divoll M, Moschitto LJ, Shader RI: Electron-capture gas chromatographic analysis of the triazolobenzodiazepine alprazolam and triazolam. *J Chromatogr* 225:202–207, 1981.

71. Dement WC, Carskadon MA, Mitler MM, Phillips RL, Zarcone VP: Prolonged use of flurazepam: a sleep laboratory study. *Behav Med* 5: 25–31, 1978.

72. Snyder J, Thomas GB: Interlaboratory reliability in testing a new hypnotic. *Sleep Res* 1:73, 1972.

73. Vogel GW, Barker K, Gibbons P, Thurmond A: A comparison of the effects of flurazepam 30 mg and triazolam 0.5 mg on the sleep of insomniacs. *Psychopharmacology* 47:81–86, 1976.

74. Dement WC, Zarcone VP, Hoddes E, Smythe H, Carskadon M: Sleep laboratory and clinical studies with flurazepam, in Garattini S, Mussini E, Randall LO (eds): *The Benzodiazepines*. New York, Raven Press, 1973.

75. Frost JD, DeLucchi MR: Insomnia in the elderly: treatment with flurazepam hydrochloride. *J Am Geriatr Soc* 27:541–546, 1979.

76. Johns MW, Masterton JP: Effect of flurazepam on sleep in the laboratory. *Pharmacology* 11:358–363, 1974.

77. Roehrs T, Zorick F, Kaffeman M, Sicklesteel J, Roth T: Flurazepam for short-term treatment of complaints of insomnia. *J Clin Pharmacol* 22:290–296, 1982.

78. Food and Drug Administration (FDA): Psychopharmacologic Drugs Advisory Meeting Minutes on Evaluation of Temazepam, Washington DC, 1978 and 1980.

79. Mitler MM, Carskadon MA, Phillips RL, Sterling WR, Zarcone VP Jr, Spiegel R, Guilleminault C, Dement WC: Hypnotic efficacy of temazepam: a long-term sleep laboratory evaluation. *Br J Clin Pharmacol* 8:63S–68S, 1979.

80. Pegram V, Hyde P, Linton P: Chronic use of triazolam: the effects on the sleep patterns of insomniacs. *J Int Med Res* 8:224–231, 1980.

81. Mamelak M, Csima A, Price V: A comparative 25-night sleep laboratory study on the effects of quazepam and triazolam on the sleep of chronic insomniacs. *J Clin Pharmacol* (in press).

82. Roth T, Kramer M, Lutz T: Intermediate use of triazolam: a sleep laboratory study. *J Int Med Res* 4:59–62, 1976.

83. Vogel G, Thurmond A, Gibbons P, Edwards K, Sloan KB, Sexton K:

The effect of triazolam on the sleep of insomniacs. *Psychopharmacology* 41:65–69, 1975.

84. Adam K, Adamson L, Brezinova V, Hunter WM, Oswald I: Nitrazepam: lastingly effective but trouble on withdrawal. *Br Med J* 1:1558–1560, 1976.

85. Oswald I, French C, Adam K, Gilham J: Benzodiazepine hypnotics remain effective for 24 weeks. *Br Med J* 284:860–864, 1982.

86. Kales A, Soldatos CR, Kales JD: Sleep disorders: evaluation and management in the office setting, in Arieti S, Brodie HKH (eds): *American Handbook of Psychiatry*. New York, Basic Books Inc., 1981, ed 2, pp 423–454.

87. Kales JD, Soldatos CR, Kales A: Diagnosis and treatment of sleep disorders, in Greist JH, Jefferson JW, Spitzer RL (eds): *Treatment of Mental Disorders*. New York, Oxford University Press, 1982, pp 473–500.

88. Flurazepam, new drug application submission.

89. Food and Drug Administration (FDA): Package insert for temazepam (Restoril).

90. Food and Drug Administration (FDA): Package insert for triazolam (Halcion).

91. Poitras R: A propos d'episodes d'amnesies anterogrades associes a l'utilisation du triazolam. *Union Med Can* 109:427–429, 1980.

92. Roth T, Hartse KM, Saab PG, Piccione PM, Kramer M: The effects of flurazepam, lorazepam, triazolam on sleep and memory. *Psychopharmacology* 70:231–237, 1980.

93. Shader RI, Greenblatt DJ: Triazolam and anterograde amnesia: all is not well in the Z-zone (editorial). *J Clin Psychopharmacol* 3:272, 1983.

94. Spinweber CL, Johnson LC: Effects of triazolam (0.5 mg) on sleep, performance, memory, and arousal threshold. *Psychopharmacology* 76:5–12, 1982.

95. Vogel GW, Vogel F: Effect of midazolam on sleep of insomniacs. *Br J Clin Pharmacol* 16 (*Suppl 1*):103S–108S, 1983.

96. Brown CR, Sarnquist FH, Canup CA, Pedley TA: Clinical, electroencephalographic, and pharmacokinetic studies of a water-soluble benzodiazepine, midazolam maleate. *Anesthesiology* 50:467–470, 1979.

97. Smith MT, Eadie MJ, Brophy TO: The pharmacokinetics of midazolam in man. *Eur J Clin Pharmacol* 19:271–278, 1981.

98. Bixler EO, Scharf MB, Soldatos CR, Mitsky DJ, Kales A: Effects of hypnotic drugs on memory. *Life Sci* 25:1379–1388, 1979.

99. Ayd FJ Jr, Barclay WR, Curran WJ, Greenblatt DJ, Lapierre Y, O'Donnell TJ, Callan JP, Garner EA, Ladimer I, Lehmann HE, Van Praag HM, Shader RI: Behavioral reactions to triazolam (letter to editor). *Lancet* 2:1018, 1979.

100. Drost RA: The Halcion story (letter to editor). *Lancet* 1:1027–1028, 1980.

101. Dukes MNG: The Van der Kroef syndrome, in Dukes MNG (ed), *Side Effects of Drugs Annual IV*. Amsterdam, Excerpta Medicine, 1980.

102. Ladimir I: Trials and tribulations of triazolam (commentary). *J Clin Pharmacol 20*:159–161, 1980.
103. Lasagna L: The Halcion story: trial by media. *Lancet 1*:815–816, 1980.
104. MacLeod N, Kratochvil CH: Behavioural reactions to triazolam. *Lancet 2*:638–639, 1979.
105. Offerhaus L: Trials and tribulations of triazolam. *J Clin Pharmacol 20*: 700–701, 1980.
106. Van der Kroef C: Reactions to triazolam (letter to editor). *Lancet 2*: 526, 1979.
107. Einarson TR: Hallucinations from triazolam. *Drug Intell Clin Pharm 14*:714, 1980.
108. Einarson TR, Yoder ES: Triazolam psychosis—a syndrome? *Drug Intell Clin Pharmacol 16*:330, 1982.
109. Mendelson WB, Weingartner H, Greenblatt DJ, Garnett D, Gillin JC: A clinical study of flurazepam. *Sleep 5*:350–360, 1982.
110. Monti JM, Debellis J, Gratadoux E, Alterwain P, Altier H, D'Angelo L: Sleep laboratory study of the effects of midazolam in insomniac patients. *Eur J Clin Pharmacol 21*:479–484, 1982.
111. Berlin RM, Conell LJ: Withdrawal symptoms after long-term treatment with therapeutic doses of flurazepam: a case report. *Am J Psychiatry 140*:488–490, 1983.
112. Hanna SM: A case of oxazepam (Serenid D) dependence. *Br J Psychiatry 120*:443–445, 1972.
113. Hollister LE: Withdrawal from benzodiazepine therapy. *JAMA 237*: 1432, 1977.
114. Hollister LE: Pharmacology and pharmacokinetics of the minor tranquilizers. *Psych Ann 11*:26–31, 1981 (Suppl).
115. Jacob MS, Sellers EM: Use of drugs with dependence liability. *CMA Journal 121*:717–724, 1979.
116. Khan A, Joyce P, Jones AV: Benzodiazepine withdrawal syndromes. *NZ Med J 92*:94–96, 1980.
117. Lader M: Dependence on benzodiazepines. *J Clin Psychiatry 44*:121–127, 1983.
118. Preskorn SH, Denner LJ: Benzodiazepines and withdrawal psychosis. *JAMA 237*:36–38, 1977.
119. Rickels K, Case WG, Downing RW, Winokur A: Long-term diazepam therapy and clinical outcome. *JAMA 250*:767–771, 1983.
120. Tyrer P, Rutherford D, Huggett T: Benzodiazepine withdrawal symptoms and propranolol. *Lancet 1*:520–522, 1981.
121. Winokur A, Rickels K, Greenblatt DJ, Snyder PJ, Schatz NJ: Withdrawal reaction from long-term, low-dosage administration of diazepam. *Arch Gen Psychiatry 37*:101–105, 1980.
122. De la Fuente JR, Rosenbaum AH, Martin HR, Niven RG: Lorazepam-related withdrawal seizures. *Mayo Clin Proc 55*:190, 1980.
123. Einarson TR: Lorazepam withdrawal seizures. *Lancet 1*:151, 1980.
124. Howe JG: Lorazepam withdrawal seizures. *Br Med J 280*:1163, 1980.

125. Steward RB, Salem RB, Springer PK: A case report of lorazepam withdrawal. *Am J Psychiatry* 137:1113, 1980.
126. Mohler H, Okada T: Benzodiazepine receptor: demonstration in the central nervous system. *Science 198*:849–851, 1977.
127. Squires RF, Braestrup C: Benzodiazepine receptors in rat brain. *Nature 266*:732–734, 1977.
128. Snyder SH: Opiate and benzodiazepine receptors. *Psychosomatics 22*: 986–989, 1981.
129. Muller WE: The benzodiazepine receptor: an update. *Pharmacology 22*:153–161, 1981.
130. Tallman JF, Paul SM, Skolnick P, Gallager DW: Receptors for the age of anxiety: pharmacology of the benzodiazepines. *Science 207*: 274–281, 1980.
131. Speth RC, Besolin N, Yamamura HI: Acute diazepam administration produces rapid increases in brain benzodiazepine receptor density. *Eur J Pharmacol 59*:159–160, 1979.
132. Braestrup C, Nielsen M: Benzodiazepine receptors. *Arzneimittelforsch 30*:852–857, 1980.
133. Kales A, Soldatos CR, Kales JD: Taking a sleep history. *Am Fam Physician 22*:101–108, 1980.
134. Soldatos CR, Kales A, Kales JD: Management of insomnia. *Annu Rev Med 30*:301–312, 1979.
135. Greist JH: Adjustment disorders, in Greist JH, Jefferson JW, Spitzer RL (eds): *Treatment of Mental Disorders*. New York, Oxford University Press, 1982, pp 419–428.
136. Kales JD, Kales A: Managing the individual and family in crisis. *Am Fam Physician 12*:109–115, 1975.
137. Kolb LC: Adaptive processes and mental mechanisms, in Kolb LC (ed): *Modern Clinical Psychiatry*. Philadelphia, WB Saunders Company, 1977, ed 9, pp 85–116.
138. Kales A, Caldwell AB, Preston TA, Healey S, Kales JD: Personality patterns in insomnia. *Arch Gen Psychiatry 33*:1128–1134, 1976.
139. Tan T-L, Kales JD, Kales A, Soldatos CR, Bixler EO: Biopsychobehavioral correlates of insomnia, IV: diagnosis based on the DSM-III. *Am J Psychiatry* (in press).
140. American Psychiatric Association: *Diagnostic and Statistical Manual of Mental Disorders (DSM-III)*, ed 3. Washington, DC, American Psychiatric Association, 1980.
141. Cooper JR (ed): Sedative-hypnotic drugs: risks and benefits. *National Institute on Drug Abuse Report*, US Department of Health, Education and Welfare Publication No. [ADM] 79–592, Washington, DC, US Government Printing Office, 1977.
142. Greenblatt DJ, Shader RI: Drug interactions in psychopharmacology, in Shader RI (ed): *Manual of Psychiatric Therapeutics: Practical Psychopharmacology and Psychiatry*. Boston, Little, Brown, 1975, pp 269–279.

143. Klotz U, Anttila V-J, Reimann I: Cimetidine/diazepam interaction. *Lancet 2*:699, 1979.
144. Abernethy DR, Greenblatt DJ, Divoll M, Arendt R, Ochs HR, Shader RI: Impairment of diazepam metabolism by low-dose estrogen-containing oral-contraceptive steroids. *N Engl J Med 306*:791–792, 1982.
145. Greenblatt DJ, Sellers EM, Shader RI: Drug disposition in old age. *N Engl J Med 306*:1081–1088, 1982.
146. Kales JD, Kales A, Bixler EO, Soldatos CR: Resource for managing sleep disorders. *JAMA 241*:2413–2416, 1979.
147. Kales JD, Kales A, Bixler EO, Soldatos CR: Sleep disorders: what the primary care physician needs to know. *Postgrad Med 67*:213–220, 1980.
148. Kales A, Kales JD: Shortcomings in the evaluation and promotion of hypnotic drugs. *N Engl J Med 293*:826–827, 1975.
149. Williams RL, Karacan I: Prescription practices, problems, solutions? in Williams RL, Karacan I (eds): *Pharmacology of Sleep*. New York, John Wiley & Sons, 1976, pp 343–347.
150. Council on Scientific Affairs, Smith RJ (Chairman): Hypnotic drugs and treatment of insomnia. *JAMA 245*:749–750, 1981.

11. Use of Antidepressants in Treating Insomnia

In the multidimensional treatment of insomnia, adjunctive pharmacologic therapy is an important parameter. When the patient has chronic insomnia resulting from a major depression, a serious and potentially life-threatening condition, the use of antidepressant medication is essential.[1-7] A common shortcoming in the use of antidepressant medication in chronic insomnia, however, is that sedative-antidepressants are often prescribed during the day, a practice that causes patients to have excessive daytime sedation and leads to their prematurely discontinuing drug treatment or maintaining their total daily dosage at a subtherapeutic and, therefore, ineffective level.[8-10]

Antidepressants are generally not indicated for the majority of patients with chronic insomnia because their side effects are frequent and because most insomniacs do not have major (endogenous) depression,[11] which is the primary indication for the use of these drugs.[3,6] We have found that the most common depressive pattern among patients with chronic insomnia is that of dysthymic disorder[11] (neurotic and characterological depressions), which, for the most part, is not the primary indication for antidepressant medication.[3,6,12-15] Thus, the physician evaluating and treating patients with chronic insomnia needs to be aware of when to employ antidepressant drugs, as well as to be knowledgeable concerning their relative efficacy and tendency for certain side effects.

Relation of Insomnia to Depression

Sleep disturbance is an extremely common complaint of patients with psychiatric disorders. Studies have suggested that the majority of any given outpatient or inpatient psychiatric population demonstrates some type of sleep problem.[16-19] Specifically, sleep disturbance is one of the most consistent symptoms of depressive illness.[3,20] Moreover, the type of sleep disturbance has often been considered diagnostic of the type of depression; endogenous depressives have been characterized as having more frequent early awakenings, and reactive depressives as having more frequent difficulty falling asleep.[20] Conversely, depression appears to be very prevalent among insomniacs. MMPI studies show that the depression scale is elevated in over half the patients with a primary complaint of insomnia.[21,22]

In a diagnostic study of 100 patients with chronic insomnia, about two-thirds had a DSM-III diagnosis of some type of affective disorder.[11] Within this diagnostic class, five individual diagnoses were made: dysthymic disorder, atypical depression, major depression, cyclothymic disorder, and bipolar disorder. Dysthymic disorder was by far the most frequent diagnosis; in the total sample, 45 percent of the patients had this diagnosis, either as the principal (34%) or as an additional (11%) diagnosis. The next most frequent affective disorder was atypical depression, which was the principal diagnosis in 11 percent and an additional one in three percent of the sample. Although major depression was the principal diagnosis in only four percent, it was present as an additional diagnosis in another eight percent of the sample. Finally, only three percent of the insomniacs had a diagnosis of cyclothymic disorder or bipolar disorder.[11]

These findings indicate a major role for depression in the pathogenesis and maintenance of insomnia. Thus, treating depression appropriately is one crucial aspect in the overall management of insomnia.[23] On the other hand, alleviation of insomnia has a high priority in the treatment of depressed patients with complaints of disturbed sleep. When the symptom of insomnia is effectively treated early in the course of depression, the patient feels less helpless and hopeless and therefore is more likely to comply with the overall treatment approach. This chapter discusses the pharmacologic and clinical issues related to the use of antidepressants in the treatment of patients with chronic insomnia in whom depression is the major feature.

Tricyclic Antidepressants

Pharmacologic Considerations

Tricyclic antidepressants, which have a characteristic three-ring nucleus, are divided into two groups: tertiary [eg, imipramine (Tofranil), amitriptyline (Elavil), doxepin (Sinequan)], and secondary [eg, desipramine (Norpramin, Pertofrane), nortriptyline (Aventyl, Pamelor), protriptyline (Vivactil)].[1,24] Metabolism of the tertiary compounds produces their corresponding secondary amines through demethylation. Therefore, patients taking imipramine or amitriptyline receive the therapeutic benefits of both the parent compound and the active metabolite, desipramine or nortriptyline, respectively.

Tricyclic antidepressants possess three major pharmacologic actions: they may be sedating; they may have both peripheral and central anticholinergic action; and they may block the re-uptake of amine neurotransmitters (Table 11.1).[1,5] The sedative effect varies among tricyclics and its quality resembles that produced by the phenothiazines more than that produced by the benzodiazepines. Some tricyclic antidepressants are highly sedating, for example, amitriptyline, whereas others, such as protriptyline and imipramine, have more of an energizing effect.[6,25] Although this difference in drug properties does not appear to relate to antidepressant efficacy, it is very pertinent when treating depressed insomniacs; most often, a sedating tricyclic is the drug of choice. The anticholinergic action of tricyclic antidepressants produces their most common side effects; amitriptyline has the strongest anticholinergic action, and desipramine the weakest.[1]

Tricyclics' effects are thought to be mediated through serotonin and norepinephrine, and probably other neurotransmitters as well.[1,3,26-28] By blocking the re-uptake of neurotransmitters to the presynaptic neuron, tricyclics increase the quantity of the neurotransmitters in the synaptic cleft, making them more available to the postsynaptic receptors. It has been hypothesized that tricyclics that block serotonin re-uptake, such as amitriptyline, are more efficacious in patients with low pretreatment levels of serotonin metabolites;[26] and that noradrenergic tricyclics, such as desipramine, are more efficacious in patients with low pretreatment levels of norepinephrine metabolites.[29,30] Some studies support this hypothesis, while others do not;[26-31] the reliability of biochemical predictors in the therapeutic response to tricyclic antidepressants appears to be limited by methodologic inconsistencies.[32]

Following oral administration, tricyclics are absorbed relatively rapidly, with peak plasma levels occurring within two to four hours,[24] even though their elimination half-lives are 24 hours or more.[1] Thus, it is not surprising that steady-state plasma levels of tricyclic antidepressants are reached within 7 to 21 days.[24]

Clinical Considerations

Tricyclic agents have been the drugs of choice for the treatment of most patients with major depression. Numerous double-blind, placebo-controlled studies demonstrate the efficacy of tricyclics in depression.[5,33] However, these studies have certain limitations.[3] Various subtypes of depression have sometimes been grouped together, and depression was not always the primary diagnosis. Furthermore, diagnostic criteria were often not stated. Thus, at present, it is impossible to know what percentage of patients with major depression, as defined by the DSM-III, can be expected to respond to tricyclic antidepressants. Recently, identification of biologic markers of various subtypes of depression that respond to different treatments has been receiving much attention[34,35] and may prove helpful in clinical research and practice in the future.

There are numerous tricyclic drugs on the market. However, none has been shown to be clearly superior to the others in terms of efficacy. Most often, the physician chooses among tricyclics based on the degree of their general adverse effects or on the basis of their specific sedative side effect. Another important consideration is the patient's past response or lack of response to a particular tricyclic.[1,3,5] In the case of a lack of response, it is important to know whether the dose and length of administration was adequate to attain a response.

Attaining a sufficient dosage level is critical to the effectiveness of antidepressant medications; the effective dosage of tricyclics may range from 50 to 600 mg daily.[2,3] For most depressed patients, a daily maintenance dosage of about 150 mg is effective. Treatment may begin with a daily dosage of 50 mg, which should be increased by 25 mg every two to three days until a dosage of about 150 mg has been reached. At the end of two weeks of treatment with this approximate dosage level, the outcome should be assessed. If response is not adequate and there are no considerable side effects, further gradual increments of 25 mg every two to three days should be added until either improvement begins to occur, side effects become intolerable, or a maximum dose of 300 mg is reached. Such dosage levels do not apply to protriptyline, which is administered in amounts of 10 to 60 mg daily.

Specific symptoms of depression that improve with tricyclic antidepressant treatment deserve special attention, eg, early improvement of sleep difficulty has been reported with amitriptyline.[2,36] After such changes, the patient may appear to the observer to be generally relieved, but in reality, he or she continues to feel quite depressed. In most cases, a marked effect on mood is not seen before two to four weeks of treatment with tricyclics.[2,3,5]

According to the Boston Collaborative Drug Surveillance Program, 15.4 percent of patients treated with tricyclic antidepressants show side effects ranging from drowsiness and mild symptoms of autonomic overactivity (anticholinergic) to severe reactions, such as confusional states and psychotic episodes.[37] Dry mouth, sweating, constipation, and urinary hesitancy are some of the more frequent anticholinergic side effects.[2] In extreme cases, adynamic ileus or urinary retention may occur. Such anticholinergic effects can be treated with a peripherally acting cholinomimetic, bethanechol. Precipitation of narrow-angle glaucoma, however, is a less frequent anticholinergic side effect of tricyclic antidepressants than it was originally thought to be. Also, erectile dysfunction and ejaculatory problems are not infrequent side effects.[38]

The side effect of greatest concern with tricyclics is cardiotoxicity.[2,3,39] Low doses of these drugs may have an antiarrhythmic action on the heart, but higher doses may cause arrhythmias.[2] The anticholinergic action of tricyclics results in an increase in heart rate, depression of cardiac conduction, adrenergic potentiation through inhibition of neuronal uptake of norepinephrine, and prolongation of cardiac repolarization. Patients with pre-existing cardiac arrhythmias or conduction defects are not good candidates for treatment with tricyclics, nor are those who are still in an unstable cardiac state after acute myocardial infarction. Sudden death resulting from ventricular fibrillation has been linked to tricyclic use.[39]

Amitriptyline and imipramine are the best known tricyclics; both drugs have undergone many clinical studies as well as lengthy clinical experience. Amitriptyline has the greatest sedative and anticholinergic side effects.[1,3,5] Doxepin, another sedating tricyclic, may have less anticholinergic effect than amitriptyline, and thus somewhat less cardiotoxicity, but this is not well established.[3] Generally, the secondary tricyclics (desipramine, nortriptyline, and protriptyline) have less sedative and anticholinergic side effects than tertiary tricyclics.

Confusional episodes may at times occur as a side effect, particularly in older patients. These episodes can be more intense if the patient is concomitantly taking other anticholinergic drugs, such as antipsychotics or anti-Parkinsonism drugs.[40] An infrequent neurologic side effect is tremor; seizures have occasionally been reported.[41] Although insomnia is generally improved when sedating antidepressant drugs are used,[3,6] sleeplessness may occur initially as a side effect of those tricyclic antidepressant drugs that have energizing qualities.[6,25]

Sedating effects of tricyclics may be additive to those of other sedatives, especially alcoholic beverages.[2] Patients taking tricyclic medication should be warned that concomitant use of alcohol may lead to impairment of their ability to drive a car and operate machinery. When barbiturate drugs are administered concomitantly with tricyclic drugs, liver microsomal enzymes are stimulated, increasing the metabolism of the tricyclics and reducing their plasma levels.[42] Benzodiazepine anxiolytics, however, do not appear to alter the metabolism of tricyclic antidepressants to any appreciable extent[43] and are probably the best drugs to employ in conjunction with tricyclics, whenever both antidepressant and anti-anxiety effects are desirable.

Of particular clinical importance is the interaction of tricyclics with antihypertensive drugs such as guanethidine.[44] In the presence of tricyclics, guanethidine is prevented from reaching its site of action. The elevated blood pressure of hypertensive patients treated with guanethidine quickly returns and may even exceed the elevated pretreatment levels when tricyclics are concomitantly administered. A similar reversal of action of other antihypertensives, such as clonidine, has been described.[45]

"Second Generation" Antidepressants

Newer, or "second generation," antidepressant drugs have recently become available in the United States.[46-49] These new agents have not been proven more effective than the established tricyclics. However, several advantages are claimed for them: more rapid onset of antidepressant action, less sedative and anticholinergic side effects, and less cardiotoxicity (Table 11.1). Some of these drugs have been used in Europe for some time; others are new worldwide. Thus, their safety and efficacy are issues that remain to be more thoroughly assessed.

Other Tricyclic Agents

Amoxapine (Asendin) is the main representative in this category and is chemically related to loxapine (Loxitane), an effective antipsy-

Table 11.1. Comparison of Antidepressants

Antidepressants (Generic Names)	Amine Uptake Inhibition			Side Effects		
				Sedative (S) vs Energizing (E)	Anti-cholinergic and Cardiotoxic	Dose Range (mg)
	NE	5-HT	DA			
Tricyclics						
Amitriptyline	+	+++	0	S+++	+++	75-300
Imipramine	++	+++	0	S+ or E+	+++	75-300
Doxepin	++	++	0	S+++	+++	75-300
Desipramine	++++	+	0	E+	+	75-300
Nortriptyline	+++	+	0	S+ or E+	++	75-300
Protriptyline	+++	+	0	E++	++	10-60
2nd Generation Drugs						
Amoxapine	++	+	0	S+	+	150-600
Maprotiline	+++	0	0	S++	+	75-300
Mianserin	0	0	0	0	0	30-120
Viloxazine	++	0	0	S+	+	150-300
Zimelidine	+	+++	0	E++	+	50-300
Trazodone	±	++	0	S++	+	50-600
Nomifensine	+++	+	+++	E+++	+	50-200

chotic.[50] Although amoxapine has some of the dopamine receptor-blocking action of the neuroleptics, it also has a number of the pharmacologic properties of antidepressants.[51] Thus, it blocks both the re-uptake of norepinephrine and serotonin, but serotonin blockage is relatively low.[52] Amoxapine has been reported to possess antidepressant effects comparable to those of the traditional tricyclics, although usual doses are about twice those of conventional tricyclics. Its antipsychotic effects have not been demonstrated.[48,50] Treatment is initiated with 50 mg bid and continued with gradual increases to a maximum dosage of 400 mg or even 600 mg, if necessary.[50] The drug is claimed to have a faster onset of action and fewer side effects when compared to amitriptyline.[48,50] Nevertheless, amoxapine is similar to amitriptyline in the types of anticholinergic and sedative side effects; moreover, recent reports of sexual dysfunction and neurotoxicity,[49] such as akathisia,[53] tardive dyskinesia,[54] and seizure activity,[55] indicate potential disadvantages related to the drug's similarity to antipsychotic medication.

Tetracyclics

Two tetracyclic compounds with antidepressant properties are currently in use: maprotiline (Ludiomil)[46-48,56,57] and mianserin.[47,48,58] The action of maprotiline on a synaptic level is mediated mainly through blocking the re-uptake of norepinephrine, with no appreciable effects on the serotonin or dopamine systems. In a study of 75 mg of maprotiline taken at bedtime, 85 percent of 5,000 patients showed marked or moderate improvement at the end of 11 days.[59] Of these 5,000 patients, 28 percent were considered endogenous depressives, 42 percent reactive, and 30 percent mixed. The therapeutic dose of maprotiline is 100 to 300 mg daily.[56] Although no clear-cut difference in antidepressant efficacy was found when this drug was compared to amitriptyline and imipramine, a more rapid onset of action has been suggested.[48] Also, an antianxiety effect comparable to that of diazepam has been reported.[60] Its sedative side effects, as well as cardiotoxicity and general anticholinergic effects, have been claimed to be less than those of amitriptyline.[56] Finally, maprotiline shows a propensity to precipitate seizure activity, mainly in predisposed individuals.[61,62]

The pharmacologic effects of mianserin appear to be limited to presynaptic alpha-receptor blocking as well as antihistamine activity.[48,58] This drug exhibits few of the pharmacologic characteristics of the antidepressants. Nevertheless, clinical trials have suggested that mianserin may have comparable efficacy to that of standard tricyclics. Few anticholinergic side effects, including cardiotoxicity, have been noted even in cases of overdose; however, there have been reports of agranulocytosis with this drug.[49]

Bicyclics

Viloxazine and zimelidine, two bicyclic compounds, have been found to have antidepressant properties.[48,63] Viloxazine blocks the uptake of norepinephrine in a fashion similar to the tricyclics.[64] It also has been reported to have some amphetamine-like effects, but little peripheral anticholinergic action, while it blocks central muscarinic receptors.[48] Viloxazine is considered as efficacious as the tricyclics in a dose range of 100–300 mg daily. Side effects are generally fewer, particularly those of sedative and anticholinergic types. However, this drug is reported to cause nausea and vomiting.

Zimelidine is specific in blocking the uptake of serotonin.[65] It seems to be as effective as the tricyclic antidepressants,[48,63] with fewer subjective side effects[66] and fewer cardiotoxic effects.[67] It should be considered an energizing antidepressant because it causes little sedation and may induce paradoxical excitement and sleep disturbances.[49] Its recommended daily dose ranges between 50 mg and 300 mg.[66]

Other Chemical Structures

Trazodone (Desyrel), a phenylpiperazine derivative of triazolopyridine, inhibits synaptic serotonin re-uptake. Its serotonergic activity is weaker than that of clomipramine; however, it is more specific and selective because it only minimally affects norepinephrine re-uptake.[68] There are data supporting the claim that trazodone is of equal antidepressant efficacy to tricyclics.[47,69] Similar to other second-generation antidepressant drugs, this drug has less anticholinergic action and less cardiotoxicity;[68] although it has been reported to aggravate preexisting ventricular arrhythmias.[70] It does, however, produce sedation comparable to that of the tricyclics.[68,69] Also, trazodone has been reported to have considerable anxiolytic effects and to be beneficial for patients with "neurotic depression."[71] Trazodone appears to have a wide dose range between 50–600 mg;[49] most often, a dosage of 150–300 mg is adequate.[68]

Nomifensine, a tetrahydroisoquinoline compound, has the effect of blocking uptake of norepinephrine and dopamine[72] and has been found to be similar in its therapeutic effects to imipramine.[63] This drug has fewer anticholinergic side effects, less cardiotoxicity, and possibly a more rapid onset of antidepressant effect.[48,73] Nomifensine has been shown to be an efficacious antidepressant in doses ranging from 50–200 mg. However, insomnia, restlessness, paranoid ideas, nausea, and tachycardia have been reported as side effects.[74]

Monoamine Oxidase Inhibitors (MAOIs)

MAO inhibitors are often effective in treating affective disorders.[75] Phenelzine is a relatively effective MAOI.[76] Many patients require 60–90 mg per day for good effect. Treatment with MAOIs requires dietary restrictions, particularly of certain foods containing large quantities of tyramine.[77] Use of MAOIs has been suggested for the treatment of "atypical depression." Patients with atypical depression usually present with more anxiety, various somatic complaints, phobias, and hysterical manifestations.[78] With MAOIs, psychophysiologic symptoms (anxiety, somatic complaints) and psychomotor symptoms (retardation, agitation, irritability) tend to show greater improvement than depressed mood and depressive ideas (guilt, suicide ideation, and nihilistic ideation).[3,76] The combined use of MAOIs and tricyclics is reported to be effective[79] but others report toxicity.

Special Clinical Issues in Using Antidepressants for Insomnia

Type of Depression and Pharmacologic Treatment

Because the vast majority of antidepressant drug studies include patients having different types of depression, it is difficult to specify the indications for each individual antidepressant as well as to decide which drug treatment is the most advantageous for a specific type of depression. Moreover, as yet, no studies have dealt with the treatment of different types of depression based specifically on the new DSM-III classification.[3] Some previous studies, however, have described the effects of various antidepressants on special target symptoms,[80] such as sleep difficulty, retardation, agitation, and somatic complaints, and have reported on overall diagnostic impressions. Also, for the various antidepressants, certain side effects, such as sedation, can be utilized to treat target symptoms, whereas anticholinergic side effects impose clear therapeutic restrictions whenever certain symptoms are present (eg, urinary retention in a patient with prostatic hypertrophy).[1-3,48,80] Thus, based on the existing clinical evidence, the indications of certain antidepressants for specific DSM-III diagnoses can be extrapolated.

Dysthymic Disorder   For the treatment of some insomniacs with dysthymic disorder, a trial of tricyclic antidepressants may be beneficial.[81] While certain studies show that these drugs have greater efficacy in endogenous depression than in reactive or neurotic depression,[3,6,12-15] there is some evidence that they are effective in both general categories.[24,82-84] Moreover, dysthymic disorder has most features[85] of what previously had been called neurotic depression, but it also includes or overlaps with other depressive spectrum disorders.[86] Thus, one might expect tricyclics to have some therapeutic effect on dysthymic disorder.[81] The sedating tricyclic agents (eg, amitriptyline), in addition to improving the underlying depression and thus indirectly, the symptom of insomnia, can be beneficial for sleep difficulty soon after administration begins. The side effects of tricyclics, however, often limit their use considerably. Because insomniacs tend to be older and often have medical problems,[87,88] the cardiotoxicity of tricyclics[2,3,39] often makes their use inadvisable.

Among the second generation antidepressants, trazodone[68] and maprotiline[57] appear to be the most sedating and therefore may prove to be more effective in treating insomniacs with dysthymic disorder. In addition, there is evidence that each of these drugs can improve neurotic depression,[59,71] with a reduced risk of anticholinergic side effects and cardiovascular disturbance.

Another therapeutic option in the treatment of the insomniac patient with dysthymic disorder is the adjunctive use of benzodiazepine anxiolytics. By decreasing the patient's anxiety, these drugs may facilitate the basic antidepressive treatment (psychotherapy and/or use of antidepressants). Physicians' preference for benzodiazepines in treating neurotic depression recently has been defended; it is claimed that the benzodiazepine anxiolytics are both safer and of comparable efficacy to the tricyclic antidepressants.[10] Benzodiazepines' lack of anticholinergic effects, particularly cardiotoxicity, is indeed a major advantage when compared to the tricyclics. However, it is very difficult to ascribe a definite antidepressant effect to this drug class. Regardless of whether this is the case, the anxiolytic effect of the benzodiazepine itself can be essentially beneficial in anxiety-ridden individuals, as is the case for most patients with dysthymic disorder. Another potentially beneficial effect of a benzodiazepine drug may be on the insomniac's obsessive ruminations, which are particularly intense and disturbing at bedtime and a major factor in the vicious circle of emotional arousal, physiologic activation, sleeplessness, fear of sleeplessness and further insomnia.[21,22]

Atypical Depression   Atypical depression is a residual diagnostic category that may include patients with symptoms resembling, but not fulfilling, the criteria of other better-defined types of depression.[85] Thus, the treatment plan takes into account the type of depression to which a patient's condition conforms.[3] In the past, the term atypical depression was used to describe conditions with neurotic and phobic components lacking some of the typical depressive symptomatology. Such patients are irritable, hypochondriacal and agitated, and frequently present with complaints of sleeplessness. For this type of "atypical depression" a course of a MAOI may be particularly helpful.[78] However, MAOIs should be administered with extreme caution because of potential toxic effects;[76] they interact with other drugs (sympathomimetics), as well as foods containing large amounts of tyramine, causing severe hypertensive crises that may be fatal.[77] Another side effect of MAOIs is the recently described occurrence of hypomanic behavior during drug administration and, to a lesser degree, following withdrawal.[89] Thus, patients on MAOIs should be closely monitored by physicians who are thoroughly familiar with their side effects and contraindications.

Major Depression   It is well established that tricyclic antidepressants are effective in treating major depression.[24] The second generation antidepressants are claimed to be at least as effective as the tricyclics, to have a lower incidence of side effects, and probably to have a somewhat earlier onset of antidepressant effects.[46-48] Thus, in the treatment of insomniacs with major depression, a sedating antidepressant from either drug group should preferably be used, depending on the patient's age, physical condition, prior history, level of functioning, and individual sensitivity, all of which may indicate unwanted side effects and consequently exclude certain drugs. MAOIs should generally be avoided for major depression because of their poor benefit-to-risk ratio. However, they can be considered for carefully monitored use when two or three adequate trials with tricyclics or other antidepressants have proven to be ineffective.[3]

The following case history illustrates the preclinical workup, gradual incrementing of dosage to a therapeutic level, and monitoring of side effects involved in treating a patient with major depression using a tricyclic antidepressant:

Case 1. A 68-year-old married, retired social worker sought help from her physician because of severe sleeping difficulty. For the past three months she had experienced difficulty falling asleep as well as nocturnal awakenings. She described a "drastic change" in herself over a six-month period and had lost interest in housework and social activities. Her husband, who accompanied her, reported that there was no affection between them; she had lost any desire for sexual relations and had moved to another bedroom. Because of her difficulty sleeping, she would pace the bedroom and hallway. She stated that she had been treated for a "severe case of the blues" ten years previously and responded to amitriptyline.

During the examination the physician observed a tense, tearful elderly woman who described her need to sleep better with some hostility and

agitation. Her mood was depressed, but there was no evidence of suicidal thoughts. She was fully oriented with no organicity evident.

For this patient, the physician's impression was that her insomnia was
the result of a recurrence of a major depression, and in view of her
symptoms and previous response, he considered placing her again on
amitriptyline. The physical examination, routine blood work, urinalysis,
and chest x-ray were within normal limits. An EKG showed no irreg-
ularities or cardiac difficulty. The patient was started on 25 mg of
amitriptyline at bedtime. Her dosage was gradually increased in 25-mg
increments every few days. The patient's insomnia improved rapidly
as a result of the drug's sedative effects, but she began to experience dry
mouth and difficulty with constipation and wanted to stop the medication. Her physician reassured her that these side effects were expected
and that as she became adjusted to her medication, they would be less
bothersome.

Sugarless chewing gum was recommended to relieve the dry mouth.
Increasing her dietary roughage, drinking an adequate supply of fluids,
and taking a stool softener resulted in improved bowel function. With
this symptomatic treatment, and the physician's firm reassurance, the
patient reached a dose of 150 mg of amitriptyline at bedtime. Within
three weeks she was feeling better and beginning to resume interest in
her former activities. After three months on the therapeutic dose of
amitriptyline, the physician began to gradually reduce the patient's dose
to a lower maintenance level.

In a study of 316 patients with major depressive disorder, approximately 25 percent were reported to have a pre-existing chronic "minor"
depression (dysthymic disorder) of at least two years' duration.[90] The
DSM-III encourages recording a diagnosis of both dysthymic disorder
and major depressive episode when a patient with pre-existing dysthymic disorder develops a major depressive episode. This so-called
"double depression" leaves the patient at risk for further recurrent episodes of major depressive disorder when pharmacologic treatment is
discontinued.[90,91] It appears that patients with acute major depressive
episodes (major depression) superimposed on chronic minor depressive
disorders (dysthymic disorders) should receive continued intensive
treatment with both pharmacologic agents and concurrent psychotherapy aimed at alleviating the chronic minor depression that predis-
poses them to episodes of major depression.[90]

When a major depressive episode includes, in addition to the affective disturbance, a gross impairment in reality testing with psychotic
features, such as hallucinations or delusions, the use of both an antidepressant agent and an antipsychotic drug may be indicated. In this

situation it should be noted that the plasma level of an antidepressant may be increased when an antipsychotic drug is concomitantly administered and, therefore, a lower dose of antidepressant drug may be required.[92]

Other combinations of drugs can be tried in the treatment of depression that is refractory to an adequate dose level of a single antidepressant. Although the safety and efficacy of these combinations has not been thoroughly evaluated in controlled studies, there are reports of the usefulness of tricyclic antidepressants combined with MAOIs, L-triiodothyronine, methylphenidate, lithium carbonate, L-tryptophan, reserpine and neuroleptics; MAOIs with lithium and L-tryptophan; and L-tryptophan with allopurinol.[93] However, a small proportion of severely depressed patients (about 5%) exists for whom no pharmacologic treatment or psychotherapy has any significant benefit. A recent well-controlled study suggests that clinical data do not adequately predict therapeutic response to pharmacologic treatment.[94] Thus, for those patients who do not respond, electroconvulsive therapy (ECT) should be tried. When effective, ECT acts more rapidly than drugs and is most valuable for actively suicidal patients, the profoundly depressed, and those patients whose medical conditions contraindicate the use of medication.[95]

Cyclothymic and Bipolar Disorders   Only a few insomniacs have been diagnosed as having cyclothymic or bipolar disorders. In patients with bipolar illness and, presumably, those with cyclothymic disorder, prophylactic treatment using lithium carbonate is indicated.[3] The dosage of the drug should be maintained within the therapeutic range, while monitoring lithium plasma levels. Also, lithium's side effects and contraindications are important considerations for the clinician, who should be familiar with its use before prescribing it.[96]

Independent of the use of lithium, when depression occurs in patients with bipolar disorder, the use of effective antidepressants may be indicated. Tricyclic antidepressants are not only effective in improving the symptoms of patients while they are depressed, they also help in the prevention of relapses of unipolar and, perhaps, bipolar disorder.[97,98] However, the use of imipramine in the prevention of bipolar disorder is not indicated due to the relatively frequent triggering of manic episodes by the drug.[97] Second generation antidepressants have been shown to be as effective as tricyclics,[48] but there is no information on their prophylactic efficacy. If the bipolar patient develops manic symptomatology, neuroleptic drugs, such as haloperidol or chlorpromazine, are indicated to control excitement or agitation.

Depression in the Elderly

Depression is commonly seen in the elderly,[99-101] in whom the prevalence of insomnia increases with age,[87] as does the use of drugs to treat sleeplessness.[102,103] Thus, treatment of the elderly insomniac-depressed patient is of particular clinical importance.

Along with elderly patients' intolerance for most medications, they frequently show higher plasma levels than younger individuals with any given oral dose of antidepressant.[104] They generally show less protein binding of tricyclics than younger adults and metabolize and excrete these drugs more slowly. Moreover, they have greater vulnerability to cardiotoxic substances because their cardiovascular function is often already compromised. Another special consideration in treating the depressed elderly patient is urinary retention with antidepressants,[2] which may occur more readily in males with a hypertrophied prostate gland. Thus, special caution is needed when prescribing antidepressants for the elderly insomniac. If tricyclics are well tolerated by an otherwise healthy elderly person, they can be administered in relatively low doses, which may be carefully increased if there is no therapeutic response in two to three weeks.

Maprotiline and trazodone are the two second generation antidepressants reported to have minimal anticholinergic side effects and cardiotoxicity.[56,68] Because they are claimed to have antidepressant efficacy equivalent to that of tricyclics, as well as sedative properties,[56,71] they may prove to be especially helpful in treating depressed elderly insomniacs. A problem with these two drugs, and particularly with trazodone, however, is daytime drowsiness and, more important, the impairment of performance they may cause. Also, maprotiline has been reported to lower the seizure threshold in predisposed individuals,[56,61,62] which may be particularly hazardous for the elderly. Thus, with the elderly, higher doses of any antidepressant drug should be avoided, as well as unnecessarily complex drug regimens, including using several drugs in various combinations.

Sedating vs Energizing Antidepressants

Sedating antidepressants are generally preferred over the energizing when treating the depressed insomniac patient, particularly if the patient is agitated.[8,23,80,105] The more sedating tricyclics (amitriptyline and doxepin) and the second generation antidepressants with sedative side effects (trazodone) can be prescribed for depressed insomniacs with all or most of the daily dose given at bedtime. Sedative effect, however, is not the only issue to consider when selecting an antidepressant drug for the depressed insomniac. The basic antidepressant effect should be the main factor influencing a physician's choice because insomnia usually subsides when depression improves. A reasonable drug choice should take into account many factors pertaining to the drug's effects and side effects, as well as the individual patient's characteristics.[80]

A common problem with sedating antidepressants, such as amitriptyline and doxepin, is that patients receive too much of their medication during the day rather than at bedtime.[9] Thus, instead of receiving the benefit of the sedative side effects at bedtime, when they are most needed, the patient must cope with the sedative side effects during the day, when they are very discomforting and may present a hazard in performing critical tasks, such as driving an automobile. The sedative side effects of the tricyclic antidepressants are immediate, while the antidepressant effect is more likely to occur after seven to ten days. Confusing the side effects of these drugs with their basic action may account for much of the difficulty in attaining a sufficient total daily dosage, and also in appropriately adjusting the daytime-to-bedtime dosage ratio.[8,23,80,105]

The second generation antidepressants have been claimed to have less side effects than the tricyclics.[46-48] However, clinical experience is, as yet, very limited with these compounds and physicians should be particularly cautious when prescribing them because they may prove to have more side effects than originally reported or some type of toxicity as yet undetected. Although it is claimed that these drugs have fewer anticholinergic and sedative effects, reports of a lowering of seizure threshold[55,61,62] and the occurrence of akathisia[53] and tardive dyskinesia[54] indicate that the physician should be cautious in prescribing them.

In treating sleep disturbances associated with major depression and motor retardation, an energizing antidepressant, such as protriptyline or nomifensine, should be used in divided doses during the day.[8,23, 80,105] When the therapeutic effects of the antidepressant drug have been well established, which takes about two to three weeks for the tricyclics and one to two weeks for the second generation antidepressants, there also should be improvement in terms of the symptom of insomnia. The following case history is an example of the daytime use of an energizing antidepressant in the treatment of a depressed insomniac with motor retardation.

> *Case 2.* A 50-year-old, widowed dairy farmer was brought to the local physician by his son. The son stated that, since midwinter, his father had become "all played out" because of poor sleep. He not only had trouble sleeping throughout the night but had begun to consistently awaken two to three hours before his usual time of rising at dawn. He had become increasingly inactive, withdrawn, and, although never very talkative, was almost totally uncommunicative. The son indicated he had been concerned about his father's loss of appetite and noticeable weight loss. He stated his father had spoken of guilt in regard to the death of his mother from cancer three years previously, and had mentioned the wish to die, quoting his father's statement, "I'm no good for nothing anymore."
>
> The physician recognized that this man's fatigue and sleep loss was secondary to a major depression with psychomotor retardation and that the man also represented a suicidal risk because of his hopelessness and wish to be dead. Immediate psychiatric hospitalization was recommended.
>
> While in the hospital, a medical workup was negative. The patient was treated with imipramine in two daily doses, one in the early morning and one before 4:00 PM. Some initial improvement in sleep was obtained in about a week and within 10 days some antidepressant effect was observed with an improved appetite and an increase in the patient's participation in hospital activities. Within two and a half weeks of hospitalization, the patient had reached a dosage level of 200 mg per day. He was more hopeful and no longer was expressing suicidal wishes.

Safety Considerations

In prescribing antidepressant medication, physicians need to be aware of their potential for cardiotoxic and general anticholinergic side effects. The anticholinergic action of tricyclics may result in increases in heart rate, abnormalities in cardiac conduction, and arrhythmias. Although it has been suggested that doxepin has fewer cardiovascular effects than other tricyclics, a recent review indicates that the drugs' cardiac effects are similar.[106] Tricyclics should be prescribed with caution in patients suspected of having cardiac abnormalities. Tricyclic

Table 11.2. Guidelines for Using Antidepressants in Insomnia

1. Antidepressants should be prescribed only when the type of depression present is treatable with this drug class.
2. Dosage should be gradually increased to therapeutic levels.
3. Sedative antidepressants are usually preferred with all or most of the daily dose given at bedtime.
4. When energizing antidepressants are necessary, daytime doses should be used to avoid nocturnal sleep disturbance.
5. Patients need to be reassured that insomnia eventually subsides with remission of depression.
6. Patients should be advised on the general anticholinergic effects of most antidepressants.
7. Patients should be carefully monitored for potential cardiotoxicity.
8. Side effects of antidepressants should be avoided through the use of other drug classes or treatment modalities whenever possible, eg, using psychotherapy and/or tranquilizers in certain cases of dysthymic disorder.
9. Drug interactions should be avoided or kept to a minimum.
10. Elderly patients necessitate extreme caution because they are most vulnerable in terms of side effects, especially cardiotoxicity.
11. Second generation antidepressants should be used cautiously because both their efficacy and profiles of side effects have not been well established.
12. Limited amounts of medication should be prescribed at each office visit, especially in the presence of suicidal ideation.

use has been associated with sudden death resulting from ventricular fibrillation.[39] In the elderly, a limitation of tricyclic administration exists when there is prostatic hypertrophy.[2] Glaucoma and renal or hepatic insufficiency are also possible contraindications.[2] A decrease in the convulsive threshold has been reported to occur with both the tricyclic antidepressants[41,44] and the newer "second generation" antidepressants.[55,61,62,107] Although a wider margin of safety is claimed, in general, for the newer antidepressants, there have been reports of movement disorders,[53,108,109] including tardive dyskinesia.[54] Additionally, with all of the antidepressants concomitant use of alcohol or barbiturates may lead to excessive sedation.[2] For the tricyclics there is a relatively narrow range between the therapeutic dose and the potentially lethal overdose;[110] a dose of 2.5 g of tricyclics may be fatal.[2] A recent report suggests that the mortality and seizure rates associated with overdose of one of the new generation antidepressants (amoxapine) exceeds that associated with overdose with other tricyclic antidepressants.[107] Thus, physicians should prescribe a limited amount of antidepressant medication, especially for patients who have suicide ideation.

Table 11.2 summarizes the general guidelines for using antidepressant medication in treating patients with chronic insomnia.

Summary

Depression frequently underlies the complaint of chronic insomnia. The physician needs to be knowledgeable concerning the efficacy, indications, and side effects of antidepressants in the treatment of insomniac patients with depressive disorders. Our diagnostic study of a group of 100 insomniac patients showed that two-thirds had affective disorders, either dysthymic disorder, atypical depression, major depression, cyclothymic disorder or bipolar disorder, in order of decreasing frequency. Major depression, although infrequent in our study, is the main indication for antidepressant drug therapy.

Tricyclic antidepressant drugs have sedative and anticholinergic effects and block the re-uptake of amine neurotransmitters to the presynaptic neuron, making them more available to postsynaptic receptors. Sedative effects are obtained almost immediately after beginning administration, but the antidepressant effects are generally not reached before 7 to 21 days. Often, treatment is prematurely discontinued before benefit is achieved because of uncomfortable sedative or anticholinergic side effects, such as dry mouth, sweating, constipation, urinary hesitancy or retention, delayed ejaculation, cardiotoxicity, and toxic confusional states. To minimize unwanted daytime sedation, the larger dose of the drug should be given at bedtime. The sedative side effects require that the physician warn the patient about the potentiating effect of alcohol or other depressant drugs. Further, the tricyclics interact with antihypertensive drugs such as guanethidine, reducing their effectiveness. Sleeplessness may be a side effect of energizing tricyclics, particularly if these drugs are administered in bedtime doses; this can be avoided by using the antidepressant drug in divided daytime doses.

The newer "second generation" antidepressant drugs have not been proven to be more effective than the older tricyclics. Their claimed advantages are a more rapid onset of action, fewer sedative and anticholinergic side effects, and less cardiotoxicity. However, serious side effects, such as a lowering of seizure threshold, akathisia, and tardive dyskinesia, have been reported with some of these drugs.

Major depression is a clear-cut indication for the use of antidepressant medication. The selection should depend on the patient's age, physical condition, level of functioning, prior history, and individual sensitivity. Special caution should be observed when treating elderly patients with antidepressants; their tolerance for medication is lower, they achieve higher plasma levels more quickly, and they are more vulnerable to the serious side effects of these drugs such as cardiotoxicity and acute urinary retention. Thus, treatment should be initiated in low doses and cautiously increased until a therapeutic effect is obtained.

Sedative antidepressants are generally preferred over energizing ones when treating depressed insomniac patients. The larger dosage should be given at night when the need for sedation is greatest. When the patient has insomnia and a retarded depression, an energizing antidepressant may be used during the day in divided doses.

References

1. Hollister LE: Tricyclic antidepressants (Part 1). *N Engl J Med 229*: 1106–1109, 1978.
2. Hollister LE: Tricyclic antidepressants (Part 2). *N Engl J Med 229*: 1168–1172, 1978.
3. Jacobson A, McKinney WT: Affective disorders, in Greist JH, Jefferson JW, Spitzer RL (eds): *Treatment of Mental Disorders*. New York, Oxford University Press, 1982, pp 184–233.
4. Keller MB, Klerman GL, Lavori PW, Fawcett JA, Coryell W, Endicott J: Treatment received by depressed patients. *JAMA 248*:1848–1855, 1982.
5. Kessler A: Tricyclic antidepressants: mode of action and clinical use, in Lipton MA, DiMascio A, Killiam KF (eds): *Psychopharmacology: A Generation of Progress*. New York, Raven Press, 1978, pp 1289–1302.
6. Kolb LC, Brodie HKH: Pharmacological therapy, in Kolb LC, Brodie HKH: *Modern Clinical Psychiatry*, ed 10. Philadelphia, W. B. Saunders Company, 1982, pp 809–834.
7. Usdin G, Lewis JM: *Psychiatry in General Medical Practice*. New York, McGraw-Hill Book Co, 1979.
8. Kales A, Kales JD, Bixler EO: Insomnia: an approach to management and treatment. *Psychiatr Ann 4*:28–44, 1974.
9. Kales A, Kales JD, Bixler EO, Martin EO: Common shortcomings in the evaluation and treatment of insomnia, in Kagan F, Harwood T, Rickels K, Rudzik A, Sorer H (eds): *Hypnotics: Methods of Development and Evaluation*. New York: Spectrum Publications Inc, 1975, pp 29–40.
10. Uhlenhuth EH: Depressives, doctors, and antidepressants. *JAMA 248*: 1879–1880, 1982.
11. Tan TL, Kales JD, Kales A, Soldatos CR, Bixler EO: Biopsychobehavioral correlates of insomnia, IV: diagnosis based on the DSM-III. *Am J Psychiatry* (in press).
12. Akiskal HS, Rosenthal RL, Haykal RF, Lemmi H, Rosenthal RH,

Scott-Strauss A: Characterological depressions. *Arch Gen Psychiatry* 37:777–783, 1980.

13. Deykin EY, DiMascio A: Relationship of patient background characteristics to efficacy of pharmacotherapy of depression. *J Nerv Ment Dis* 155:209–215, 1972.

14. Frances A, Cooper AM: Descriptive and dynamic psychiatry: a perspective on DSM-III. *Am J Psychiatry* 138:1198–1202, 1981.

15. Raskin A, Crook TH: The endogenous and neurotic distinction as a prediction of response to antidepressant drugs. *Psychol Med* 6:59–70, 1976.

16. Detre T: Sleep disorders and psychosis. *Canad Psychiatr Assoc J* 11 Suppl:169–177, 1966.

17. Sweetwood H, Grant I, Kripke DF, Gerst MS, Yager J: Sleep disorder over time: psychiatric correlates among males. *Br J Psychiatry* 136:456–462, 1980.

18. Sweetwood HL, Kripke DF, Grant I, Yager J, Gerst MS: Sleep disorder and psychobiological symptomatology in male psychiatric outpatients and male nonpatients. *Psychosom Med* 38:373–378, 1976.

19. Weiss HR, Kasinoff BH, Bailey MA: An exploration of reported sleep disturbance. *J Nerv Ment Dis* 134:528–534, 1962.

20. Kiloh LG, Garside RF: The independence of neurotic depression and endogenous depression. *Br J Psychiatry* 109:451–463, 1963.

21. Kales A, Caldwell AB, Preston TA, Healy S, Kales JD: Personality patterns in insomnia: theoretical implications. *Arch Gen Psychiatry* 33:1128–1134, 1976.

22. Kales A, Caldwell AB, Soldatos CR, Bixler EO, Kales JD: Biopsychobehavioral correlates of insomnia, II: pattern specificity and consistency with the Minnesota Multiphasic Personality Inventory. *Psychosom Med* 45:341–356, 1983.

23. Soldatos CR, Kales A, Kales JD: Management of insomnia. *Annu Rev Med* 30:301–312, 1979.

24. Amsterdam J, Brunswick D, Mendels J: The clinical application of tricyclic antidepressant pharmacokinetics and plasma levels. *Am J Psychiatry* 137:653–662, 1980.

25. Kales A, Kales JD, Jacobson A, Humphrey FJ II, Soldatos CR: Effects of imipramine on enuretic frequency and sleep stages. *Pediatrics* 60:431–436, 1977.

26. Goodwin FK, Cowdry RW, Webster MH: Predictors of drug response in the affective disorders: toward an integrated approach, in Lipton MA, DiMascio A, Killam KF (eds): *Psychopharmacology: A Generation of Progress.* New York, Raven Press, 1978, pp 1277–1288.

27. Murphy DL, Campbell I, Costa JL: Current status of indoleamine hypothesis of the affective disorders, in Lipton MA, DiMascio A, Killam KF (eds): *Psychopharmacology: A Generation of Progress.* New York, Raven Press, 1978, pp. 1235–1247.

28. Schildkraut JJ: Current status of the catecholamine hypothesis of affective disorders, in Lipton MA, DiMascio A, Killam KF (eds): *Psy-*

chopharmacology: A Generation of Progress. New York, Raven Press, 1978, pp 1223–1234.

29. Beckmann H, Goodwin FK: Antidepressant response to tricyclics and urinary MHPG in unipolar patients. *Arch Gen Phychiatry* 32:17–21, 1975.
30. Maas JW, Fawcett JA, Dekirmenjian H: Catecholamine metabolism, depressive illness, and drug response. *Arch Gen Psychiatry* 26:252–262, 1972.
31. Coppen A, Rao VAR, Ruthven CRJ, Goodwin BL, Sandler M: Urinary 4-hydroxy-3-methoxyphenylglycol is not a predictor for clinical response to amitriptyline in depressive illness. *Psychopharmacology* 64: 95–97, 1979.
32. Veith RC, Bielski RJ, Bloom V, Fawcett JA, Narasimhachari N, Friedel RO: Urinary MHPG excretion and treatment with desipramine or amitriptyline: prediction of response, effect of treatment, and methodological hazards. *J Clin Psychopharmacol* 3:18–27, 1983.
33. Klerman GL, Cole JO: Clinical pharmacology of imipramine and related antidepressant compounds. *Pharmacol Rev* 17:100–141, 1965.
34. Brown WA, Haier RJ, Qualls CB: Dexamethasone suppression test identifies subtypes of depression which respond to different antidepressants. *Lancet* 1:928–929, 1980.
35. Carroll BJ, Curtis GC, Mendels J: Neuroendocrine regulation in depression, II: discrimination of depressed from non-depressed patients. *Arch Gen Psychiatry* 33:1051–1058, 1976.
36. Haskell DS, DiMascio A, Prusoff B: Rapidity of symptom reduction in depression treated with amitriptyline. *J Nerv Ment Dis* 160:24–33, 1975.
37. Boston Collaborative Drug Surveillance Program (BCDSP): Adverse reactions to the tricyclic-antidepressant drugs. *Lancet* 1:522–531, 1972.
38. Mitchell JE, Popkin MK: Antidepressant drug therapy and sexual dysfunction in men: a review. *J Clin Psychopharmacol* 3:76–79, 1983.
39. Moir DC, Cornwell WB, Dingwall-Fordyce I, Crooks J, O'Malley K, Turnbull MJ: Cardiotoxicity of amitriptyline. *Lancet* 2:561–564, 1972.
40. Davies RK, Tucker GJ, Harrow M, Detre TP: Confusional episodes and antidepressant medication. *Am J Psychiatry* 128:95–99, 1971.
41. Jick H, Dinan BJ, Hunter JR, Stergachis A, Ronning A, Perera DR, Madsen S, Nudelman PM: Tricyclic antidepressants and convulsions. *J Clin Psychopharmacol* 3:182–185, 1983.
42. Alexanderson B, Evans DAP, Sjoqvist F: Steady-state plasma levels of nortriptyline in twins: influence of genetic factors and drug therapy. *Br Med J* 4:764–768, 1969.
43. Gram LF, Overo KF, Kirk L: Influence of neuroleptics and benzodiazepines on metabolism of tricyclic antidepressants in man. *Am J Psychiatry* 131:863–866, 1974.
44. Baldessarini RJ, Lipinski JF: Toxicity and side effects of antipsychotic, antimanic, and antidepressant medications: *Psychiatr Ann* 6:484–493, 1976.

45. van Spanning HW, van Zwieten PA: The interference of tricyclic antidepressants with the central hypotensive effect of clonidine. *Eur J Pharmacol* 24:402–404, 1973.
46. Ayd FJ: New antidepressant drugs. *Psychiatr Ann* 11:11–17, 1981.
47. Feighner JP: Clinical efficacy of the newer antidepressants. *J Clin Psychopharmacol* 1:23S–26S, 1981.
48. Hollister LE: "Second generation" antidepressant drugs. *Psychosomatics* 22:872–879, 1981.
49. Hollister LE: Second-generation antidepressants. *Ration Drug Ther* 16:1–5, 1982.
50. Donlon PT: Amoxapine: a newly marketed tricyclic antidepressant. *Psychiatr Ann* 11:23–27, 1981.
51. Greenblatt EN, Kippa AS, Osterberg AC: The neuropharmacological actions of amoxapine. *Arch Int Pharmacodyn Ther* 233:107–135, 1978.
52. Coupet J, Rauh CE, Szues-Myers VA, Yunger LM: 2-chloro-11 (1-piperazinyl) dibenz (b,f) (1-4) oxazepine (amoxapine), an antidepressant with antipsychotic properties—a possible role for 7-hydroxyamoxapine. *Biochem Pharmacol* 28:2514–2515, 1979.
53. Ross DR, Walker JI, Peterson J: Akathisia induced by amoxapine. *Am J Psychiatr* 140:115–116, 1983.
54. Lapierre YD, Anderson K: Dyskinesia associated with amoxapine antidepressant therapy: a case report. *Am J Psychiatr* 140:493–494, 1983.
55. Koval G, VanNuis C, Davis TD: Seizures associated with amoxapine. *Am J Psychiatr* 139:845, 1982.
56. Settle, EC Jr: Maprotiline: update 1981. *Psychiatr Ann* 11:384–390, 1981.
57. Gruter W, Poldinger W: Maprotiline. *Mod Probl Pharmacopsychiatry* 18:17–48, 1982.
58. Brogden RN, Heel RC, Speight TM, Avery GS: Mianserin: a review of its pharmacological properties and therapeutic efficacy in depressive illness. *Drugs* 16:273–301, 1978.
59. Forrest WA: A report on a general practice-monitored release study, in Murphy ED (ed): *Research and Clinical Investigation in Depression*. Northampton, Cambridge Medical Publications, 1976, pp 90–94.
60. Selvini A, Rossi C, Belli C, Corallo S, Lucchelli PE: Antidepressant treatment with maprotiline in the management of emotional disturbances in patients with acute myocardial infarction: a controlled study. *J Int Med Res* 4:42–49, 1976.
61. Burley D, Jukes A, Steen J: Maprotiline hydrochloride and grand-mal seizures. *Br Med J* 2:1230, 1978.
62. Kim WY: Seizures associated with maprotiline. *Am J Psychiatr* 139:845–846, 1982.
63. Ban TA: Monoamine uptake inhibitors. *Mod Probl Pharmacopsychiatry* 18:1–16, 1982.
64. Ban TA, McEvoy JP, Wilson WH: Viloxazine: a review of the literature. *Int Pharmacopsychiatry* 15:118–123, 1980.

65. Ross SB, Renyi AL: Inhibition of the neuronal uptake of 5-hydroxytryptamine and noradrenaline in rat brain by (Z)- and (E)-3-(4-bromophenyl)-N, N-dimethyl-3-(3'-pyridyl) allylamines and their secondary analogues. *Neuropharmacology 16*:57–63, 1977.

66. Coppen A, Rama Rao VA, Swade C, Wood K: Zimelidine: a therapeutic and pharmacokinetic study in depression. *Psychopharmacology 63*:199–202, 1979.

67. Burgess CD, Montgomery SA, Montgomery DB, Wadsworth J: Cardiovascular effects of amitriptyline, mianserin and zimelidine in depressive patients. *Prog Neuropsychopharmacol 4*:523–526, 1980.

68. Risch SC, Janowsky DS: Trazodone. *Psychiatr Ann 11*:396–401, 1981.

69. Kellams JJ, Klapper MH, Small JG: Trazodone, a new antidepressant: efficacy and safety of endogenous depression. *J Clin Psychiatry 40*: 390–395, 1979.

70. Janowsky D, Curtis G, Zisook S, Kuhn K, Resovsky K, Le Winter M: Ventricular arrhythmias possibly aggravated by trazodone. *Am J Psychiatry 140*:796–797, 1983.

71. Goldberg HL, Finnerty RJ: Trazodone in the treatment of neurotic depression. *J Clin Psych 41*:430:434, 1980.

72. Hunt P, Kannengiesser MH, Raynaud JP: Nomifensine: a new potent inhibitor of dopamine uptake into synaptosomes from rat brain corpus striatum. *J Pharm Pharmac 26*:370–371, 1974.

73. Pohl R, Gershon S: Nomifensine: a new antidepressant. *Psychiatr Ann 11*:391–395, 1981.

74. Brogden RN, Heel RC, Speight TM, Avery GS: Nomifensine: A review of its pharmacological properties and therapeutic efficacy in depressive illness. *Drugs 18*:1–24, 1979.

75. Tollefson GD: Monoamine oxidase inhibitors: a review. *J Clin Psychiatry 44*:280–288, 1983.

76. Robinson DS, Nies A, Ravaris CL, Lamborn KR: The monoamine oxidase inhibitor phenelzine in the treatment of depressive-anxiety states. *Arch Gen Psychiatry 29*:407–413, 1973.

77. Folks, DG: Monoamine oxidase inhibitors: reappraisal of dietary considerations. *J Clin Psychopharmacol 3*:249–252, 1983.

78. Robinson DS, Nies A, Ravaris CL, Ives JO, Bartlett D: Clinical psychopharmacology of phenelzine: MAO activity and clinical response, in Lipton MA, DiMascio A, Killam KF (eds): *Psychopharmacology: A Generation of Progress*. New York: Raven Press, 1978, pp 961–973.

79. White K, Simpson G: Combined MAOI-tricyclic antidepressant treatment: a reevaluation. *J Clin Psychopharmacol 1*:264–282, 1981.

80. Stern SL, Rush AJ, Mendels J: Toward a rational pharmacotherapy of depression. *Am J Psychiatry 137*:545–552, 1980.

81. Kales JD, Soldatos CR, Kales A: Diagnosis and treatment of sleep disorders, in Greist JH, Jefferson JW, Spitzer RL (eds): *Treatment of Mental Disorders*. New York: Oxford University Press, 1982.

82. Kuhn R: The treatment of depressive states with G22355 (imipramine hydrochloride). *Am J Psychiatry 115*:459–464, 1958.

83. Morris JB, Beck AT: The efficacy of antidepressant drugs. A review of research (1958 to 1972). *Arch Gen Psychiatry 30*:667–674, 1974.

84. Paykel ES: Depressive typologies and response to amitriptyline. *Br J Psychiatry 120*:147–156, 1972.

85. American Psychiatric Association: *Diagnostic and Statistical Manual of Mental Disorders (DSM-III)*, ed 3. Washington, D.C., American Psychiatric Association, 1981.

86. Akiskal HS: Dysthymic disorder: psychopathology of proposed chronic depressive subtypes. *Am J Psychiatry 140*:11–20, 1983.

87. Bixler EO, Kales A, Soldatos CR, Kales JD, Healey S: Prevalence of sleep disorders in the Los Angeles metropolitan area. *Am J Psychiatry 136*:1257–1262, 1979.

88. Kales JD, Kales A, Bixler EO, Soldatos CR, Cadieux RJ, Kashurba GJ, Vela-Bueno A: Biopsychobehavioral correlates of insomnia, V: clinical characteristics and behavioral correlates. *Am J Psychiatry* (in press).

89. Pickar D, Murphy DL, Cohen RM, Campbell IC, Lipper S: Selective and nonselective monoamine oxidase inhibitors: behavioral disturbances during their administration to depressed patients. *Arch Gen Psychiatry 39*:535–540, 1982.

90. Keller MB, Lavori PW, Endicott J, Coryell W, Klerman GL: "Double depression": two-year follow-up. *Am J Psychiatry 140*:689–694, 1983.

91. Keller MB, Shapiro RW: "Double depression": superimposition of acute depressive episodes on chronic depressive disorders. *Am J Psychiatry 139*:438–442, 1982.

92. Ayd FJ (ed): Plasma levels of psychopharmaceuticals. *International Drug Therapy Newsletter 9*:1–4, 1974.

93. Stern SL, Mendels J: Drug combinations in the treatment of refractory depression: a review. *J Clin Psychiatry 42*:368–373, 1981.

94. Kupfer DJ, Spiker DG: Refractory depression: prediction of non-response by clinical indicators. *J Clin Psychiatry 42*:307–312, 1981.

95. Bernstein JG: *Clinical Psychopharmacology.* Littleton, PSG Publishing Company, 1978.

96. Jefferson JW, Greist JH: *Primer of Lithium Therapy.* Baltimore, Williams & Wilkins, 1977.

97. Prien RF, Klett CJ, Caffey EM Jr: Lithium carbonate and imipramine in prevention of affective episodes: a comparison in recurrent affective illness. *Arch Gen Psychiatry 29*:420–425, 1973.

98. Freyhan FA: On the controversy of prophylactic antidepressants. *Compr Psychiatry 16*:1–5, 1975.

99. Blazer D: The diagnosis of depression in the elderly. *J Am Geriatr Soc 28*:52–58, 1980.

100. Gurland BJ: The comparative frequency of depression in various adult age groups. *J Gerontol 31*:283–292, 1976.

101. Weissman MM, Myers JK: Affective disorders in a U.S. urban community: the use of research diagnostic criteria in an epidemiologic survey. *Arch Gen Psychiatry 35*:1304–1311, 1978.

102. Balter MB, Bauer ML: Patterns of prescribing and use of hypnotic drugs in the United States, in Clift AD (ed): *Sleep Disturbance and Hypnotic Drug Dependence.* New York: Excerpta Medica, 1975, pp 261–293.

103. Mellinger GD, Balter MB: Prevalence and patterns of use of psychotherapeutic drugs: results from a 1979 national survey of American adults, in Pognoni G, Bellantuoano C, Lader M (eds): *Epidemiological Impact of Psychotropic Drugs.* Amsterdam, Elsevier/North-Holland Biomedical Press, 1981.

104. Nies A, Robinson DS, Friedman MJ, Green R, Cooper TB, Ravaris CL, Ives JO: Relationship between age and tricyclic antidepressant plasma levels. *Am J Psychiatry* 134:790–793, 1977.

105. Kales A, Soldatos CR, Kales JD: Sleep disorders: evaluation and management in the office setting, in Arieti S (ed): *American Handbook of Psychiatry,* ed 2. New York, Basic Books Inc, 1981, vol 7, pp 423–454.

106. Luchins DJ: Review of clinical and animal studies comparing the cardiovascular effects of doxepin and other tricyclic antidepressants. *Am J Psychiatry* 140:1006–1009, 1983.

107. Litovitz TL, Troutman WG: Amoxapine overdose: seizures and fatalities. *JAMA* 250:1069–1071, 1983.

108. Steele TE: Adverse reactions suggesting amoxapine-induced dopamine blockade. *Am J Psychiatry* 139:1500–1501, 1982.

109. Sunderland T, Orsulak PJ, Cohen BM: Amoxapine and neuroleptic side effects: a case report. *Am J Psychiatry* 140:1233–1235, 1983.

110. Lundberg GD: Antidepressant drugs as a cause of death: a call for caution and data. *JAMA* 248:1879, 1982.

Author Index

Abernethy DR, 270
Achong MR, 250
Adam K, 22, 196, 197, 259, 265
Adler G, 230
Agnew HW, 6, 20, 39, 61, 62, 72, 135, 191
Ague C, 149
Akerstedt T, 97
Akiskal HS, 123, 221, 282, 291
Alexanderson B, 287
Allison T, 21
American Psychiatric Association, 43, 99, 111, 122–24, 126, 128, 170, 174, 219, 221, 223, 225, 229, 230, 269, 291, 292
Amrein R, 256
Amsterdam J, 284, 291, 293
Anch M, 12, 14
Ancoli-Israel S, 76, 79
Andersson KE, 149
Antrobus JS, 6
Arduini A, 12
Armstrong RH, 140, 141
Aschoff J, 14
Aserinsky E, 3, 4, 12, 14
Association of Sleep Disorders Centers, 79, 120, 126, 175
Ayd FJ, 262, 287, 289, 293, 295, 297

Baekeland F, 196
Baker MA, 194
Baldessarini RJ, 287, 299
Balter MB, 249, 296
Ban TA, 289, 290
Barsky AJ, 225
Bateman JRM, 12, 14
Batini CF, 145
Beck AT, 222
Beckmann H, 284

Bellack AS, 222
Bellak L, 162
Belloc NB, 39–42, 187, 188
Bergamasco B, 145, 146
Berger H, 3
Berger RJ, 4, 11, 12, 14, 19, 39
Berlin RM, 266
Bernstein JG, 295
Berry B, 193
Better SR, 47
Beutler LE, 68, 78, 101, 102, 111, 120
Bing R, 144
Bion WR, 229
Bixler EO, 11, 36–38, 43, 61–64, 68, 69, 72, 74–79, 88, 89, 93, 99, 100, 127, 135, 140, 165–67, 201, 202, 249, 252, 253, 257, 261, 263, 292, 296
Blazer D, 296
Block AJ, 76, 79, 166
Bonica JJ, 43
Bootzin RR, 127, 197, 200, 223, 231–39
Borbely AA, 15
Borkovec TD, 71, 200, 238
Boston Collaborative Drug Surveillance Program, 286
Boyar RM, 17
Braestrup C, 267
Brazier MAB, 3
Brebbia RD, 12, 14
Breimer DD, 256, 257, 261
Brezinova V, 69, 197
Bricolo A, 145, 146
Brierley J, 145, 146
Brogden RN, 289, 290
Broughton RJ, 12, 23, 138, 145, 146
Brown CR, 261
Brown WA, 285
Bruch, H, 216
Bryden G, 189, 190
Budzynski TH, 236
Bulow K, 12, 14

Burgess CD, 290
Burley D, 289, 296, 297, 299
Bursten B, 44, 46, 47
Byrne D, 121

Callahan EM, 44, 87
Caplan G, 215
Carroll BJ, 285
Carskadon MA, 43, 68, 71, 76, 79, 150, 164, 169, 177, 202, 256, 261, 262
Chen CN, 196
Church MW, 256, 257, 259
Clemente CD, 145
Cluff LE, 47
Coates TJ, 67–69, 73, 177
Coccagna G, 12, 14, 138, 139
Cohen J, 123
Cohen S, 47, 198
Coleman RM, 75, 76, 78, 79, 111, 120, 126, 127, 176
Colquhoun WP, 136, 137
Cooper JR, 51, 270
Coppen A, 284, 290
Coupet J, 288
Coursey RD, 46, 78, 93, 94, 101, 111, 120–22, 170, 200, 214, 215, 232
Crick F, 22
Crisp AH, 142, 143, 196
Cryer PE, 149
Cummiskey J, 167
Czeisler CA, 14, 15, 194

Dahlstrom WG, 113, 114, 119
Daitz BD, 45
Daly DD, 165
Daly RJ, 142
Davies RK, 286
Davison GC, 237
De la Fuente JR, 266
Deamer RM, 138
Dement WC, 3, 4, 9, 11, 12, 14, 20, 39, 62, 75, 78, 79, 111, 139, 165, 176, 177, 192, 257, 263
Detre T, 283
Dewan EM, 21
Dexter JD, 144
Deykin EY, 282, 291
Divoll M, 256, 257
Dixon KN, 165
Dlin BM, 148, 169
Dohrenwend BS, 37, 89
Donlon PT, 288
Dragstedt LR, 141
Drake LE, 113
Drost RA, 262
Drucker-Colin R, 21

Dukes MNG, 262
Dunleavy DLF, 143, 144, 196
Duron B, 12, 14

Eberts FS, 257
Eckert M, 256
Economo von C, 145, 146
Einarson TR, 262, 266
Eisenberg JM, 177
Elenewski JJ, 111, 120
Elliott GR, 87
Ellis BW, 146, 147
Ephron HS, 21
Essig CF, 169, 255, 265
Evarts EV, 12

Fairbairn WRD, 229
Fara JW, 197
Feighner JP, 287, 289, 290, 293, 297
Feinberg I, 11, 12, 22, 61, 62, 69, 72, 135, 166, 202
Fenichel O, 223, 225
Finkel MJ, 252
Finkel SI, 203
Fisher C, 12, 14, 23
Fleetham J, 138
Fleiss JL, 123
Flick MR, 138
Folks DG, 290, 293
Food and Drug Administration, 257, 260, 263
Fordyce WE, 44, 45, 87, 233
Forrest WA, 289, 292
Frances A, 124, 221, 282, 291
Frankel BL, 43, 67, 71, 73
Fraser HF, 255, 265
Freedman RR, 73, 74, 111, 120, 170, 200, 215, 232
Freemon FR, 145
Freud S, 4, 223
Freyhan FA, 295
Frosch J, 229
Frost JD, 257
Fry A, 234
Fuccella LM, 256

Gaillard JM, 67–69, 73
Gallup, 37, 39, 40, 88, 89, 94, 95, 163, 188, 192, 249
Gastaut H, 3, 7, 139, 140
Gerard DL, 226
Giblin E, 138
Gilberstadt H, 113
Gillin JC, 67, 68, 73
Giovacchini P, 230

Globus GG, 188
Goldberg HL, 290, 292, 296
Goldfried M, 233, 237
Goldman R, 48
Goodwin DW, 226, 227
Goodwin FK, 284
Gordon C, 229
Gough H, 113
Graham JR, 145, 149
Gram LF, 287
Greenberg R, 21, 22
Greenblatt DJ, 256, 257, 260, 263, 270, 271
Greenblatt EN, 288
Greenson RR, 223, 224, 229
Greist JH, 162, 186, 198, 215, 268
Griesinger W, 4
Grinker RR Sr, 229
Gruen W, 219
Gruter W, 289, 292
Gucer G, 12, 14
Guilleminault, 23, 75, 78, 79, 139, 140, 165–67
Gunby P, 190
Gunderson JG, 229
Gurland BJ, 296
Gutheil E, 228
Gynther MD, 119

Haber LD, 45
Halberg F, 14
Hamilton M, 148, 169
Hammond EC, 36–42, 93, 187, 188
Hanley FW, 234
Hanna SM, 266
Hartmann EL, 18, 21, 39, 66, 188, 197
Haskell DS, 286
Hathaway SR, 113, 119
Hauri P, 39, 74, 90, 120, 165, 166, 191–95, 238
Hauty GT, 136
Hawkins DR, 23
Hayashi Y, 11, 12, 61, 72, 135
Haynes SN, 46, 71, 73, 74, 78, 93, 94, 120, 121, 170, 197, 200, 214, 215, 232, 236
Healey ES, 46, 78, 88, 90–92, 99–101, 111–13, 163, 165, 171–73, 199, 215
Henane R, 12, 14
Hicks RA, 66, 188
Hinkle LE, 44, 45, 87, 119
Hobson JA, 16, 195
Hoddes E, 43, 71
Hogan P, 222
Hollingshead A, 37, 89
Hollister LE, 169, 221, 250, 266, 282, 284–93, 295–97, 299

Holmes TH, 88
Hopfield JJ, 22
Horne JA, 23, 97, 195
Howe JG, 266
Howell WH, 4
Hunt P, 290
Huttenlocher PR, 12, 14

Institute of Medicine, 51, 249, 270
Isbell H, 255, 265

Jacob SM, 266
Jacobson A, 4, 11, 14
Jacobson A, 218, 221–23, 282–87, 291–93, 295
Jacobson E, 221, 222, 234
Jameson J, 219
Janowsky D, 290
Jefferson G, 145, 146
Jefferson JW, 295
Jick H, 287, 299
Joern AT, 194
Johns MW, 36, 37, 146–48, 257
Johnson FA, 255, 265
Johnson LC, 14, 18, 19, 39, 136, 137, 189, 232, 256, 259
Jones HS, 39, 66, 67, 165
Jouvet M, 4, 11, 12, 14–17, 145, 146

Kahn E, 61, 72, 135
Kales A, 3, 5–13, 19, 20, 23, 39, 43–46, 48, 51, 53, 61, 65, 67–69, 71–79, 91, 93, 102, 104, 111, 113–21, 124, 127, 135–37, 139, 140, 143, 145, 148–51, 162–71, 174–77, 186, 188, 191, 196–99, 201, 202, 204, 214–17, 232, 249–61, 263–71, 282–84, 287, 292, 297, 298
Kales JD, 3, 8, 9, 23, 39, 45, 48, 52, 53, 79, 88–91, 93–96, 98–105, 111, 113, 119, 126, 127, 137, 138, 162–68, 170–76, 186–88, 191, 197–200, 202, 214–17, 223, 252, 253, 256, 260, 263, 268, 270, 271, 291, 292
Kalucy RS, 196
Kaplan SA, 256
Karacan I, 12, 14, 17, 36–38, 67–69, 73, 89, 93, 100, 138, 142, 144, 149, 169, 192, 201
Karasu TB, 216, 218, 224
Kawamura H, 12
Kellams JJ, 290
Keller MB, 282, 294
Kellogg R, 237
Kendel K, 193
Kernberg OF, 229

Kessler A, 282, 284–86
Khan A, 266
Kiloh LG, 283
Kim WY, 289, 296, 297, 299
Kinkel HJ, 192
Kiritz S, 215
Klein KE, 136, 137, 189–91
Kleinman A, 225
Kleitman N, 3, 4, 11, 14, 36
Klerman GL, 285
Klotz U, 270
Knight RP, 229
Koella WP, 16
Kohut H, 230
Kolb LC, 164, 186, 198, 215, 268, 282, 284, 287, 291
Koval G, 288, 297, 299
Krieger J, 76, 79
Kripke DF, 39–43, 136, 137, 187–89, 232
Krueger JM, 22
Kudrow L, 120
Kuhn R, 291
Kupfer DJ, 23, 295

Lacey JH, 142, 143
Lader M, 169, 266
Ladimir I, 262
Langsley DG, 172
Lapierre YD, 288, 297, 299
Lasagna L, 262
Lazarus AA, 231, 233–35
LeVere TE, 193
Legendre R, 22
Lesse S, 223–25
Levi L, 45, 119
Levin E, 141
Levy M, 149
Lewis DC, 226
Lewis HE, 39, 188
Lewis JM, 172
Lewis SA, 71, 143
Lichstein KL, 120–22, 170
Litovitz, TL, 299
Littler WA, 12, 14
Lloyd EA, 255, 265
Loomis AL, 3
Luborsky L, 218, 219
Luchins DJ, 298
Lugaresi E, 79, 139, 140, 166, 167, 176
Lukas JS, 193
Lundberg GD, 177, 299
Lundberg U, 88

Maas JW, 284
MacAndrew C, 104, 118

MacLeod N, 262
MacWilliam JA, 4
Mamelak M, 151, 257, 263
Mandell AJ, 17
Marchini EJ, 97
Markand ON, 145, 146
Marks I, 223
Marks PA, 46, 113, 120
Masterson JF, 229
Masterton JP, 197
McCarley RW, 16
McFarland RA, 136
McGhie A, 36–38, 89, 238
McGinty DJ, 16, 23
Mechanic D, 45
Meddis R, 39, 66, 67, 165
Mellinger GD, 249, 296
Mendelson M, 221
Mendelson WB, 3, 4, 7, 263
Mills JN, 136
Mitchell JE, 286
Mitler MM, 257, 263
Mohler H, 266
Moir DC, 286, 292, 299
Monnier M, 22
Monroe LJ, 43, 46, 67–69, 71, 73, 78, 93, 94, 99, 101, 120, 121, 170, 192, 200, 214, 215, 232
Montgomery I, 200, 217, 231, 233–36
Monti JM, 265
Montplaisir J, 139
Moore T, 11
Moore-Ede MC, 14, 136, 137, 189–91, 232
Morgan K, 150, 169, 202, 256, 261
Morgane PJ, 15, 17
Morris JB, 291
Moruzzi G, 145
Muller JC, 148
Muller WE, 267
Mumford E, 219
Murphy DL, 284
Murphy F, 146, 148, 169
Murray GB, 203, 204

Naitoh P, 18, 39
Natani K, 194
Neil JF, 142
Nemiah JC, 216, 223, 224, 226
Nicassio P, 200, 234, 238
Nicholson AN, 148, 169
Nies A, 296
Noonan JR, 227, 228

O'Leary KD, 231, 233, 235
Ochitill H, 226

Offenkrantz W, 216
Offerhaus L, 262
Ohlmeyer P, 4
Oldendorff WH, 177
Ord WM, 143
Orem J, 12
Orr WC, 79, 141, 146, 148
Oswald I, 22, 53, 127, 176, 193, 194,
    250, 251, 256, 257, 259, 263, 265
Otto E, 193

Palmore E, 41
Paolino TJ, 223
Parker DC, 17, 142
Parloff MB, 218
Parmeggiani PL, 12, 14, 194
Parmelee AH, 11
Parson T, 45, 46
Passouant P, 142, 145, 146
Paykel ES, 291
Pegram V, 257, 258
Petersdorf RG, 168, 177
Petre-Quadens O, 22, 144
Petrie WM, 148
Phillips F, 196, 197
Phillipson EA, 12, 14
Piccione P, 111, 120
Pickar D, 293
Pierce AK, 138
Pierce CM, 37, 193
Plum F, 145, 146
Pohl R, 149, 290
Poitras R, 260
Pompeiano O, 12, 14, 16
Pratt L, 41
Preskorn SH, 266
Presley JM, 193
Price VA, 37, 94
Prien RF, 295
Prinz PN, 61, 72, 135
Puca F, 145, 146

Rabkin JG, 88, 168
Raboutet J, 194
Rahe RH, 88
Raskin A, 221, 282, 291
Raskin M, 236
Rechtschaffen A, 4–7, 9–12, 14, 15, 17,
    21, 62, 73, 74, 135, 192, 194, 251
Regelsberger H, 4
Regestein QR, 53, 127, 165
Reite M, 194
Reynolds CF III, 79, 127, 136, 137, 175
Ribordy SC, 200, 217, 231, 233–36
Rice DP, 43
Rickels K, 266
Risch SC, 290, 292, 296

Robin ED, 138
Robinson DS, 290, 291, 293
Roehrs T, 257
Roffwarg H, 11, 12, 21, 61, 72, 135, 202
Rogers DE, 45, 47, 87
Ross DR, 288, 297, 299
Ross JJ, 143
Ross SB, 290
Rossi GF, 145
Roth B, 23, 165
Roth T, 93, 99, 104, 105, 111, 120, 151,
    165, 214, 257, 258, 260, 263
Rubin RT, 16, 17
Rundell OH, 150, 169, 201
Rush AJ, 222

Sakai K, 16
Sallanon M, 16
Salzman L, 227, 228
Sampson H, 20
Sarwer-Foner GJ, 216, 218
Sassin JF, 17
Schafer R, 216
Scharf MB, 62, 191, 253
Schildkraut JJ, 284
Schlesinger HJ, 219
Schmidt-Kessen, 193
Schneider D, 66, 67
Schoonover SC, 149
Schultz JH, 234
Schultz MA, 143
Schwartz BA, 43, 71
Schweiger MS, 144
Scott J, 177
Scott TD, 193
Selvini A, 289
Settle EC, 289, 296
Shader RI, 204, 260
Shapiro CM, 194
Shurley JT, 192
Sifneos PE, 223, 226
Simonds JF, 37, 88, 96
Simpson RG, 138, 142
Slipp S, 222
Smirk H, 148
Smith DE, 148
Smith ML, 218, 219
Smith MT, 261
Smith RJ, 271
Snyder F, 12, 14, 21, 23
Snyder J, 257
Snyder SH, 267
Soldatos CR, 3, 5, 7, 8, 44, 46, 48, 51,
    53, 68, 74, 93, 100, 111, 119, 120, 127,
    136, 137, 149, 162, 163, 166, 168–71,
    176, 186, 197–99, 201, 215–17, 250–53,
    258, 259, 267–69, 283, 297, 298

Speth RC, 267
Spiegel R, 11, 12, 61
Spinweber CL, 260
Spitzer RL, 122, 123
Squires RF, 266
Srole L, 37, 89
Stacher G, 141
Steele TE, 299
Stephen S, 148
Stern SL, 291, 295, 297, 298
Steward RB, 266
Storms MD, 236
Strassberg DS, 120
Stunkard AJ, 143
Stuss D, 18, 39, 66, 67, 165
Suess JF, 228, 229
Sunderland T, 299
Suwa N, 45, 119
Swanson LA, 255, 265
Sweetwood HL, 37, 39, 93, 283
Swenson WM, 113, 119
Symonds CP, 166, 167

Tallman JF, 267
Tan TL, 44, 45, 99, 111, 122–25, 170,
    173, 220, 223, 225, 226, 228, 235, 268,
    282, 283
Taub JM, 18
Tauber ES, 167
Taylor RB, 187
Thoresen CE, 197, 200, 233, 236–39
Tollefson GD, 290
Townsend RE, 12, 14, 193
Traub AC, 238
Tune GS, 36–39, 135
Tyrer P, 169, 266

Uhlenhuth EH, 282, 292
United States Department of Health,
    Education and Welfare, 36–38, 93,
    252
Usdin G, 282

van der Kroef C, 262
van Spanning HW, 287
Veith RC, 284

Velok G, 66, 67
Vogel GW, 20, 39, 151, 257, 260, 263

Walker BB, 146–148, 169
Walker JM, 195
Webb P, 76, 79
Webb WB, 11, 18, 21, 61–64, 66, 67,
    72, 135, 137, 194, 202
Weiss HR, 36, 37, 283
Weiss T, 21
Weissman MM, 222, 296
Weitzman ED, 14, 16, 17, 136, 137,
    189, 190, 232
Wells CE, 203, 204
Wever RA, 14
White K, 291
Wiley JA, 39, 40, 42, 187, 188
Williams GH, 148, 169
Williams HL, 19, 39, 192, 193
Williams RL, 3, 7, 11, 12, 17, 61–64,
    72, 73, 135, 137, 138, 168, 202, 271
Wingard DL, 39, 40, 42, 187, 188
Winnicott DW, 229
Winokur A, 169, 266
Wolff P, 141
Wolpert EA, 12, 14
Woods NF, 146–48
Woolfolk RL, 200, 235
World Health Organization Center
    for Classification of Diseases, 128,
    174
Wurtman RJ, 196, 197
Wyngaarden JB, 168
Wynne JW, 138, 139

Yalom I, 222
Yerevanian BI, 221
Yules RB, 150, 169

Zepelin H, 74, 135
Zimberg S, 226
Zimmerman WB, 73, 74
Zir CM, 196
Zorick FJ, 75, 78, 79, 111, 127, 139, 176
Zung WW, 121

Subject Index

Adaptation
  to environment, 191–95
  to sleep laboratory, 6, 61–63
Addiction, drug. *See* Drug
  dependency
Adjective Checklist, 113
Adjustment disorder and insomnia,
  123
Affective disorder and insomnia
  atypical depression, 123, 220, 230,
    283, 292, 293
  bipolar disorder, 221, 283, 295
  cyclothymic disorder, 221, 283, 295,
    296
  dysthymic disorder, 123–26, 219–23,
    225, 282, 283, 291–94
  major depression, 221, 268, 282–85,
    289, 291–98
Age, insomnia and
  distribution of wakefulness, 69, 70
  nightly awakenings, 65, 68, 135
  onset of insomnia, 89, 90
  personality patterns, 114, 117, 135,
    136
  prevalence of insomnia, 36–38
  sleep latency, 65, 68
  sleep stage patterns, 73
  total wake time, 65, 69
  wake time after sleep onset, 65, 68,
    69
Age, normal sleep patterns and
  auditory awakening threshold, 74,
    135, 193
  distribution of wakefulness, 13, 64,
    66
  naps, 11, 12, 38, 135
  nightly awakenings, 11, 13, 63–65,
    135
  sleep distribution, 11, 135
  sleep latency, 11, 63, 65
  sleep stage patterns, 11–13, 62, 72, 73
  sleep time, 11, 39, 40, 135

  total wake time, 64, 65
  wake time after sleep onset, 63–65
Alachua County survey, 36–38, 89, 93
Alameda County survey, 39–42, 187,
  188
Alcohol, 150, 226, 227, 270
Alcohol use
  drug history for, 169, 170, 201, 268
  health correlates and, 105, 106
  sleep disturbance and, 102–5, 201
Alcoholics Anonymous, 226, 227
Allopurinol (Lopurin, Zyloprim), 295
American Cancer Society survey, 39–
  43, 187, 188
Amines, biogenic
  effects of antidepressants on, 284,
    286, 288–90
  hormonal secretion and, 17
  role in depression, 284
  role in sleep, 15, 16
  sleep stages and, 15–17
Amitriptyline (Elavil), 223, 284, 286,
  288, 289, 291, 293, 294, 297
Amnesia, 151, 260–63
Amoxapine (Asendin), 287, 288, 299
Amphetamines, 148, 149, 201
Anorexia nervosa and sleep, 142, 143,
  196
Antidepressant drugs
  anticholinergic effects, 284, 286–93,
  cardiotoxicity, 286–90, 292, 296–
    99
    296–99
  clinical considerations, 285–87
  effectiveness, 221, 285, 289
  indications for use, 282, 283
  movement disorders, 288, 297, 299
  safety, 287, 289, 298, 299
  second generation, 287–90, 292, 293,
    295–99
  sedating vs energizing, 284–93, 296–
    98

Antidepressant drugs (*Cont.*)
  seizures, 287–90, 296, 297, 299
  side effects, 284–99
  tricyclics, 283–88, 291–99
Anxiety
  drug-induced, 150, 151, 169, 201,
    202, 256, 261–66
  insomnia and, 200, 223–25
  rebound, 151, 202, 256, 262, 265–67
Anxiety disorder and insomnia, 123,
    124, 220, 223–25, 269, 270
Apnea. *See* Sleep apnea
Association of Sleep Disorders Cen-
    ters Classification, 79, 126, 127,
    175
Asthma and sleep, 139
Attribution techniques, 233, 236–39
Atypical depression and insomnia,
    123, 220, 230, 283, 292, 293
Auditory arousal threshold
  age and, 74, 135, 193
  sleep stages and, 192, 193
  time of night and, 192
Autogenic training, 200, 233, 234
Avoidant personality and insomnia,
    125

Barbiturates
  comparison, 253–55
  efficacy, 253, 254
  REM rebound, 251, 266
  safety issues, 270, 271
  withdrawal of, 149, 150, 251, 254,
    255, 265, 266
Basic rest-activity cycle, 4, 190, 191
Bed partner, history from, 140, 164,
    166, 167
Bedtime routines, 94–96, 188
Behavior therapy, 216, 223
  effectiveness, 219, 223, 238, 239
  rationale for, 223, 232, 233
  types of, 233–40
Behavioral correlates of insomnia
  daytime behavior, 94, 96, 97
  nighttime behavior, 94–96
  post-sleep behavior, 96
  pre-sleep behavior, 93–95
Benzodiazepine anxiolytics
  treatment of affective disorder, 287,
    292
  treatment of anxiety disorder, 223
  withdrawal from, 266
Benzodiazepine hypnotics
  absorption rate, 256, 257, 260
  adjunctive use, 226, 237, 249, 269,
    270, 282
  behavioral changes, 262, 263

carryover effectiveness, 252, 256,
    257, 260, 262–65
  comparison, 256–66
  daytime anxiety, 150, 151, 169, 202,
    256, 261–66
  daytime sedation, 256, 259, 260, 262,
    264, 282
  early morning insomnia, 150, 151,
    201, 256, 261, 262, 264, 266
  efficacy, 255–59, 263–65
  elimination half-life, 252, 256–67
  memory impairment, 151, 260–63
  rebound anxiety, 151, 202, 256, 262,
    265–67
  rebound insomnia, 151, 201, 252,
    256, 263–67
  receptors for, 266, 267
  side effects, 255, 256, 259–66
  tolerance, 265, 266
Biofeedback, 200, 233, 235, 236, 239
Biologic rhythms
  body temperature cycle, 14, 15, 136,
    137
  REM-NREM cycle, 14, 15, 22
  sleep disturbances and, 136, 137,
    189–91
  sleep-wakefulness cycle, 14, 15,
    189–91
Biopsychosocial factors in insomnia
  family, 44, 46, 47, 49, 167, 168
  illness, 44, 45, 49, 163
  patient, 44–46, 49, 163
  physician, 44, 48, 49, 186, 271
  society, 44, 47, 49
Bipolar disorder and insomnia, 221,
    283, 295
Blood pressure, 4, 12
Body temperature
  circadian rhythms and, 14, 15
  in insomnia, 73, 74
  in normal sleep, 12, 14, 15, 73–75,
    136
Borderline personality and insomnia,
    124, 125, 227–30
Boston Collaborative Drug Surveil-
    lance Program, 286
Brain
  biogenic amine localization in, 15–17
  lesions of, effects on sleep, 15, 146
  temperature, in REM sleep, 12, 14

Caffeine and sleep disturbance, 100,
    149, 169, 170, 201, 202, 268
Cardiovascular disorders and sleep,
    138
Carryover effectiveness of hypnotics,
    252, 256, 257, 260, 262–65

Catecholamines. *See* Amines, biogenic
Central adrenergic blockers and sleep
  disturbance, 148, 149, 169, 170, 201
Characterologic depression, 123, 221,
  282
Children, sleep patterns in, 11, 12
Chloral hydrate (Noctec), 252–54
Chlorpromazine (Thorazine), 296
Chronic obstructive pulmonary disease and sleep, 138, 139
Cimetidine (Tagamet), 270
Circadian rhythms. *See* Biologic
  rhythms
Clinical characteristics of insomnia
  age at onset, 89, 90, 103
  behavioral correlates, 93–97
  clinical course, 93
  duration, 89, 93
  general health correlates, 97–100,
    105, 106
  in drug or alcohol use, 102–6
  mental health correlates, 100–2
  subjective estimates, 70, 71, 104, 105
  type of complaint, 89, 93
Clinical trials of hypnotics, 9, 250–52,
  257
Clonidine (Catapres), 287
Cognitive restructuring, 237, 238
Cognitive therapy in depression, 222
Compulsive personality and insomnia,
  124–26, 223, 225, 227–31, 269, 270
Conversion hysteria and MMPI, 114–
  17, 120
Coping mechanisms in insomnia, 47,
  112, 113, 172, 173
Cornell Medical Index, 99, 101
Cortisol secretion and sleep, 17, 22, 23,
  137
Cyclothymic disorder and insomnia,
  221, 283, 295, 296

Daytime anxiety, 150, 151, 169, 202,
  256, 261–66
Daytime sedation, 256, 259, 260, 262,
  264, 282
Depression and MMPI, 114–17, 120.
  See also Affective disorder and
  insomnia
Desipramine (Norpramin, Perto-
  frane), 284, 286, 288
Diagnostic and Statistical Manual of
  Mental Disorders (DSM-III), 99,
  122–28, 170, 174, 219–21, 223, 227,
  230, 239, 269, 283, 285, 291, 294
Dialysis, effects on sleep, 142
Dopamine (DA), 17, 288–90
Double depression, 294

Doxepin (Adapin, Sinequan), 284,
  286, 288, 297
Drug dependency. *See also* Substance
  use disorder
  barbiturates and, 254, 255, 265, 266
  elimination half-life and, 252
  tolerance and, 239, 254, 255, 265,
    266, 268
Drug evaluation studies
  clinical trials, 9, 250–52, 257
  sleep laboratory, 251–71
Drug history, insomnia
  alcohol use, 169, 170, 201, 268
  caffeine, 170, 201, 268
  clinical characteristics of, 102–5
  correlates of psychopathology and,
    118
  early morning insomnia and, 149–
    51, 169, 170, 201, 202
  nicotine, 149, 170, 201
  prescribed medication, 148–51, 169,
    170, 201, 202
  rebound insomnia and, 149–51, 169,
    170, 201, 202
Drug interactions
  barbiturates, 287
  hypnotics, 251, 252, 270, 287
  tricyclic antidepressants, 287
Drug-induced sleep disturbance
  alcohol, 169, 170, 201, 268
  antihypertensives, 148, 149
  bronchodilators, 149, 201
  caffeine, 100, 149, 169, 170, 201, 202,
    268
  central adrenergic blockers, 148,
    149, 169, 170, 201
  cigarette smoking, 149, 170, 201
  CNS stimulants, 148, 149, 169, 170,
    201, 202
  drug withdrawal insomnia, 149, 150,
    169, 254, 255, 265, 266
  early morning insomnia, 150, 151,
    169, 201, 256, 261, 262, 264, 266
  monoamine oxidase inhibitors, 149
  rebound anxiety, 151, 202, 256, 262,
    265–67
  rebound insomnia, 149–51, 201, 252,
    263–67
  second generation antidepressants,
    149
  steroids, 148, 149, 201
  tolerance and withdrawal, 201, 202,
    239, 254, 255, 265, 266
  tricyclic antidepressants, 149
Drug withdrawal insomnia, 149, 150,
  169, 254, 255, 265, 266
DSM-III. *See* Diagnostic and Statistical
  Manual of Mental Disorders

Duodenal ulcer and sleep, 140–42
Dysthymic disorder and insomnia,
    123–26, 219–23, 225, 282, 283, 291–
    94

Early morning insomnia, 150, 151, 169,
    201, 256, 261, 262, 266
Eating disorders and insomnia, 142,
    143
Elderly, insomnia in
    antipsychotic medication, 204
    depression, 203, 296
    hypnotic drug use, 204, 270, 271
    naps, 202, 203
    organic brain syndrome, 203, 204
    social interaction, 202, 203
Electroconvulsive therapy (ECT), 295
Electroencephalogram (EEG), 3–6, 9,
    10, 12, 15
Electromyogram (EMG), 4–6, 9–11,
    14, 16
Electro-oculogram (EOG), 5, 6, 9, 10
Elimination half-life, hypnotics. See
    Benzodiazepine hypnotics
Emotions, internalization of. See
    Internalization hypothesis
Endocrine conditions and sleep, 143,
    144
Endogenous depression. See Major
    depression
Enuresis, 174
Environment and sleep
    adaptation to, 191, 195
    barometric pressure, 194
    noise, 192, 193, 195
    temperature, 193–95
    type of bed, 192
    weather, 194
Epidemiologic surveys of
    health status and sleep length, 40–43
    insomnia, 36–39, 88, 89
    sleep quality and quantity, 39–43
Ethchlorvynol (Placidyl), 252–54
Etiology of insomnia
    biopsychosocial factors in, 43–50
    conditioning in, 49, 119, 120, 163,
        215, 231
    drugs, 148–51, 169, 170, 201, 202,
        261–68
    hospital environment in, 146–48
    internalization hypothesis in, 115,
        116, 118–22, 124, 125, 163, 199
    jet travel, 136, 137, 189–91
    life-stress events in, 89–93, 100,
        111–13, 177, 199, 201
    maladaptive coping mechanisms in,
        111–13, 124, 172, 186, 200

medical conditions, 137–47
predisposing factors in, 44–46, 49,
    111–13, 119, 173, 177
psychologic distress and, 98, 112–14,
    198, 199
shift work, 136, 137
situational disturbances, 136, 137,
    186, 214
Evaluation of insomnia
    bed partner history, 140, 164, 166,
        167
    clinical course in, 165
    common shortcomings, 51–53
    definition of sleep problem, 164, 165
    differentiating sleep disorders in,
        165, 166
    drug history, 169, 170, 201, 202, 267,
        268
    DSM-III/ICD-9-CM diagnosis in,
        127, 128, 174–77
    impact of disorder and, 167, 168
    interviewing principles, 172
    medical assessment in, 127, 168, 169
    psychiatric assessment in, 127, 170–
        74, 267, 268
    sleep history, 127, 163–68, 267, 268
    sleep laboratory studies in, 48, 53,
        67–71, 73–79
    treatment outcome and, 175, 176
Excessive daytime sleepiness, 165–67
Exercise and sleep, 194–96

Factor S and sleep. See Sleep factors
Fenfluramine (Pondimin), 143
First-night effect. See Adaptation to
    sleep laboratory
Flunitrazepam, 253, 258, 259, 264
Flurazepam (Dalmane), 252, 255–64,
    269

GABA, 267
Gallup survey, 37, 39, 40, 88, 89, 94,
    95, 163, 188, 192, 249
Gastric acid, nocturnal secretion
    in duodenal ulcer patients, 140, 141
    in healthy controls, 141
Gastrointestinal disorders and sleep,
    141, 142
General measures, treatment of in-
    somnia
    activities, 196
    avoidance of certain drugs, 201, 202
    exercise, 194–96
    in the elderly, 202–4
    nutrition, 196, 197
    schedules, 188–91, 195

sleep amount, 187, 188, 195
sleep environment, 191–95
stress management, 197–201
Glutethimide (Doriden), 252–54
Guanethidine (Ismelin), 287

Haloperidol (Haldol), 296
Headaches and sleep, 144, 145
Health correlates of insomnia
drug and alcohol use, 102–6
mental health, 100–2, 225
physical health, 97–100, 225
Health status and sleep length, 39–43
Heart rate
in insomnia, 73, 74
in normal sleep, 12, 14, 73–75
HEW psychologic health survey,
36–38, 93, 252
Hormonal secretion and sleep, 16, 17,
22, 23
Hospital environment and sleep, 146–
48
Human Population Laboratory, 40–42
Hypersomnia, 23, 39, 165, 175
Hypnosis, 233, 234
Hypnotic drugs
absorption rate, 256, 257, 260
adjunctive use, 226, 237, 249, 269, 270
carryover effectiveness, 252, 256,
257, 260, 262–65
clinical trials, 9, 250–52, 257
continued use, 251, 252, 257–60
dependency on, 151, 249, 252, 266
early morning insomnia, 150, 151,
201, 256, 261, 262, 264, 266
efficacy, 252–59, 263–65
indications for, 250, 268, 269
intermediate-term use, 253, 254,
257–59
long elimination half-life, 252, 256–
60, 265
long-term use, 253, 254, 257–60
rebound insomnia, 151, 201, 252,
256, 263–67
REM rebound, 202, 251, 266
short elimination half-life, 256–58,
260–62, 264–66
short-term use, 226, 253, 254, 257–59
side effects, 252, 255, 256, 259–66
sleep laboratory evaluations, 251–71
tolerance, 254, 255, 258, 259, 265, 266
withdrawal of, 149–51, 169, 201, 202,
227, 239, 251–56, 261–67
Hypochondriasis and MMPI, 114, 115,
120
Hypomania and MMPI, 114–16, 120
Hypothyroidism and sleep, 143, 144

ICD-9-CM, 127, 128, 174, 175
Iatrogenic factors in insomnia, 48–50
Imipramine (Tofranil), 149, 222, 283,
284, 286, 288–90, 295, 298
Insomnia
affective disorders and, 123, 124,
219–23
age factors in, 65, 68–70, 89, 90, 134,
135
anorexia nervosa, 142, 143, 196
antidepressants and, 149, 221, 282–99
anti-hypertensives and, 148, 149
anxiety disorders and, 123, 124, 220,
223–25
asthma and, 139
barometric pressure and, 194
behavioral correlates of, 93–97
behavioral treatment of, 216, 223,
231–40
biopsychosocial factors in, 43–50
borderline personality disorder and,
124, 125, 227–30
caffeine and, 100, 149, 169, 170, 201,
202, 268
cardiovascular disorders and, 138
childhood experiences and, 112
chronic obstructive pulmonary disease and, 138, 139
cigarette smoking and, 99, 100, 149,
170, 201
clinical characteristics, 89, 90, 93,
102–5
CNS stimulants and, 148, 149, 169,
170, 201, 202
compulsive personality disorder
and, 124–26, 225, 227–31
diagnosis and, 99, 122–27, 174, 175
diagnostic variability in, 126, 127
distribution of wakefulness in, 69,
70
drug and alcohol use, correlates of,
102–7, 118
drug history for, 149–51, 169, 170,
201, 202, 267, 268
drug-induced, 148–57, 169, 201, 202,
261–67
duodenal ulcer and, 140–42
duration of, 89, 93, 103
dysthymic disorder and, 123–26,
219–23, 291–94
eating disorders and, 142, 143
economic impact of, 43, 47, 48
endocrine conditions, 143, 144
environmental factors in, 191–95
epidemiological surveys of, 36–39,
88, 89
gastrointestinal disorders and, 141,
142

Insomnia (*Cont.*)
  general measures in treatment, 186–204
  headaches and, 144, 145
  health status and, 37, 38, 40, 97–100, 105, 106, 225
  home vs sleep lab recordings in, 71
  hospital environment and, 146–48
  hypnotic drugs and, 149–51, 201, 202, 226, 237, 239, 249–72
  in elderly, 135, 136, 202–4, 296
  internalization of emotions in, 115, 116, 118–22, 124, 125, 199
  jet travel and, 136, 137, 189–91
  marital status and, 37, 38, 89
  medical assessment for, 8, 168, 169
  medical conditions and, 137–47
  mental health and, 37–39, 98, 100–2, 111–28
  MMPI studies in, 77, 78, 81, 93, 94, 96, 97, 101, 102, 104, 113–17, 120
  multidimensional treatment of, 186, 249, 282
  neurologic conditions and, 144–46
  neuropathologic states, 145, 146
  night-to-night variability in, 69
  nocturnal myoclonus and, 75–79, 166, 167
  noise and, 192, 193
  obesity, 143
  Parkinson's disease and, 145
  personality trait or disorder in, 124–26, 227–31
  physician education on, 8, 9, 50–53, 271
  physiologic activation in, 45, 119–21, 125, 170, 199, 232–38
  physiologic correlates of, 73–80
  predisposing factors in, 44–46, 49, 111–13, 163, 173, 177
  pregnancy and, 144
  prevalence of, 36–39
  psychiatric assessment of, 8, 122–28, 170–75, 219–21, 267, 268
  psychiatric disorders in, 122–25, 170, 219–21
  psychiatric factors in, 45, 46, 93, 111–28, 170–73, 199, 214–18, 268, 269
  psychosocial correlates, 94–102
  psychotherapy and, 214–31
  pulmonary disorders and, 138–40
  renal insufficiency and, 142
  shift work and, 136, 137, 189–91
  situational disturbances, 136, 137, 186, 214
  sleep apnea and, 75–79, 139, 140, 165–67
  sleep efficiency in, 65, 68, 69
  sleep history for, 8, 162–68, 267, 268
  sleep laboratory evaluation of, 48, 53, 67–71, 73–79, 166, 167
  sleep stages in, 73
  socioeconomic status and, 37, 88, 89
  somatoform disorder and, 99, 123, 124, 220, 225, 226
  stress and, 197–201, 205
  stressful life events in, 89–93, 100, 111–13, 214
  subjective estimates of, 70, 71, 102–5
  substance use disorder and, 123, 124, 220, 226, 227, 239, 240
  suicidal ideation and, 98, 100
  thyroid dysfunction and, 143, 144
  total wake time in, 65, 69
  transient vs chronic, 134, 162, 163, 169, 174, 175, 177, 186, 187, 197–201, 214, 215
  type of complaint in, 37, 38, 89, 93, 102
  vicious circle in, 188, 199, 215, 216, 225, 226, 268, 292
  wake time after sleep onset in, 65, 68, 69
Institute of Medicine (IOM) report, 51, 249, 270
Internalization hypothesis
  personality patterns in, 114–16, 118–20, 125, 214–16, 228, 268
  physiologic activation in, 119–21, 125, 199, 214, 268, 292
  predisposing factors, 119, 121, 173, 177, 215
  psychiatric conflicts and, 124, 214, 215, 267, 269
  role of conditioning, 49, 119, 120, 163, 215, 231
Interpersonal relationships, 44–48, 96, 97, 112, 113, 167, 168, 216, 217, 221
Interviewing principles, 172

Jet lag and sleep, 136, 137, 189–91

Levodopa (Laradopa, Sinemet), 145
Life-stress events and insomnia, 89–93, 100, 111–13, 214
Lithium carbonate (Eskalith, Lithane), 295
Long sleepers, 17, 18, 66, 67
Lorazepam (Ativan), 260, 266
Lormetazepam, 253, 258, 259, 265
Los Angeles Metropolitan Area Survey (LAMAS), 36–38, 89, 90, 99, 100
Loxapine (Loxitane), 287

MacAndrew Alcoholism Scale and MMPI, 104, 118
Major depression and insomnia, 221, 268, 282–85, 289, 291–98
Maprotiline (Ludiomil), 164, 288, 289, 292, 296
Marital therapy in insomnia, 223, 230
Medical assessment, insomnia, 8, 168, 169
Medical conditions and sleep, 137–47
Meditation training, 200, 233, 235
Memory impairment, 151, 260–63
Mental health in insomnia, 37, 38, 98, 100–2, 111–28
Methaqualone (Parest, Quaalude), 252–54
Methyldopa (Aldomet), 148, 149, 287
Methylphenidate (Ritalin), 295
Methysergide (Sansert), 145, 148, 149
Mianserin, 288, 289
Midazolam, 151, 253, 258–61, 264, 265
MMPI findings in insomnia
  age factors, 114, 117, 135
  clinical scales, 114–18
  code patterns, 116–18
  consistency of, 114
  drug and alcohol use and, 114, 118
  internalization hypothesis and, 114–16, 118–20
Monoamine oxidase inhibitors
  atypical depression and, 290–93
  dietary restrictions, 290, 293
  insomnia induced by, 149
  toxicity, 290, 291, 293
Monoamines. *See* Amines, biogenic
Muscle tonus during sleep, 4, 6, 9–11, 14, 16

Naps, 166, 190, 202, 268
Narcolepsy/cataplexy, 23, 91, 119, 120, 148, 165, 174, 175
National Institute of Drug Abuse (NIDA), 51, 270
Network for Continuing Medical Education (NCME), 52, 53, 271
Neurologic conditions and sleep, 144–46
Neuropathologic states and sleep, 145, 146
Neurotic depression, 123, 290–92
Neurotransmitters and sleep. *See* Amines, biogenic
Night terrors, 23, 39, 91, 119, 166, 174, 175
Nightmares, 39, 91, 95, 119, 164, 169
Nitrazepam, 253, 258, 259, 264, 265

Nocturnal myoclonus
  in insomniacs, 75–79, 166, 176
  in normal sleepers, 75–79
Nocturnal wandering, 166, 167
Nomifensine, 149, 288, 290, 298
Norepinephrine (NE), 15–17, 149, 288–90
Nortriptyline (Aventyl, Pamelor), 230, 284, 286, 288
NREM sleep
  age effects on, 72
  cycle, 11, 22, 23
  slow-wave, 9, 10, 72, 73
  stage 1, 9, 10, 72
  stage 2, 9, 10, 72
Nutrition and sleep, 142, 143, 196, 197

Obesity and sleep, 143
Onset of insomnia
  age, 89, 90, 103, 165, 171
  sex, 89, 90, 103
  stressful life events, role of, 89–93, 111–13, 165, 171
  type of complaint and, 89, 93
Over-the-counter sedatives, 202
Oxazepam (Serax), 266

Paranoia and MMPI, 114–16
Parkinson's disease and sleep, 145
Penile erections in sleep, 12–14, 17
Pentobarbital (Nembutal), 252–55
Performance decrements
  drug-induced, 256, 259, 260, 270, 296
  sleep deprivation and, 19
  sleep duration and, 18
Peripheral vasoconstriction, 73, 74
Personality disorder and insomnia, 124–26, 227–31
Personality patterns in insomnia
  age factors, 114, 117, 135
  geographic region and, 114
  internalization hypothesis and, 114–16, 118–20, 125, 214–16, 228, 268
  MMPI code patterns, 116–18
  MMPI scale elevations, 114, 115
  presleep emotional arousal and, 121, 214–16, 268
Personality trait and insomnia, 124–26
Pharmacologic therapy, adjunctive use in insomnia, 226, 237, 249, 269, 270, 282
Phasic events in sleep, 12, 14, 16
Phenelzine (Nardil), 290
Physical health and insomnia, 46, 47, 97–100

Physician education on insomnia, 8,
    9, 50–53, 249, 250, 271
Physiologic arousal in insomnia, 74,
    75, 121, 125, 170, 214–16, 232–38
Pregnancy and insomnia, 144
Prevalence of insomnia
    age, 36–38, 89, 90
    hypnotic drug use, 37, 38
    marital status, 37, 38
    medical patients and, 38, 39
    physical health, 37, 38, 99
    psychiatric patients and, 38, 39
    psychologic disturbances, 37–39, 89,
        100–3
    public surveys of, 36–39, 88, 89
    sex, 36–38, 90
    socioeconomic status, 37, 88, 89
    type of complaint, 37, 38, 93
Progressive relaxation, 200, 233–35,
    238–40
Project Sleep, 51
Prolactin, 17
Propranolol (Inderal), 148
Protein synthesis hypothesis, 22, 23
Protocol, ad-lib vs fixed, 61, 62
Protriptyline (Vivactil), 149, 284–86,
    288, 297
Psychasthenia and MMPI, 114, 115
Psychiatric assessment, insomnia, 122–
    28, 170–75, 219–21, 267, 268
    mental status in, 173, 174
Psychiatric diagnoses and insomnia
    affective disorders, 123, 124, 219–23
    anxiety disorder, 123, 124, 220, 223–
        25
    borderline personality, 124, 125,
        227–30
    compulsive personality, 124–26, 225,
        227–31
    dysthymic disorder, 123–26, 219–23,
        225
    somatoform disorder, 99, 123, 124,
        220, 225, 226
    substance use disorder, 123, 124, 220,
        226, 227, 239, 240
Psychopathic deviate and MMPI,
    114–16
Psychotherapy in insomnia
    cognitive therapy, 222
    countertransference in, 218, 221
    effectiveness of, 218, 219, 224, 238, 239
    group, 222, 226, 230
    individual, 226
    insight-oriented, 224–26, 230, 231
    interpersonal, 216, 222
    marital, 223, 230
    psychodynamic, 216, 221, 223, 224,
        229–31

    supportive, 216, 223–26, 230, 255
    transference in, 221, 229

Quazepam, 253, 258–61, 264, 265

Rauwolfia (Raudixin), 148, 149
Rebound anxiety, 151, 202, 256, 262,
    265–67
Rebound insomnia, 151, 201, 252, 256,
    263–67
    brain receptors in, 266, 267
    dose response, 265
    role of half-life, 201, 252
    tolerance and, 266
Relaxation training, 200, 234, 238–40
REM sleep, 4, 11, 12, 14–16, 20, 22, 23,
    72, 73, 251, 266
Renal insufficiency and sleep, 142
Reserpine (Serpasil), 295

Schedule of Recent Experience, 90–93
Schedules and sleep, 188–91, 195
Schizophrenia and MMPI, 114, 115
Secobarbital (Seconal), 252–54
Second generation antidepressants,
    287–90, 292, 293, 295–99. *See also*
    Antidepressant drugs
Secondary gain in insomnia, 44–46, 48,
    167, 215, 226
Serotonin (5-HT), 15–17, 284, 288–90
Shift work
    body temperature, 136
    cortisol levels, 137
    effects on sleep, 136, 137, 189–91
Short sleepers, 17, 18, 66, 67
Situational insomnia, 136, 137, 214, 215
Sleep apnea, 91, 119
    age factors in, 75–77, 140
    bed partner history in, 140, 164, 166,
        167
    cardiovascular sequelae of, 175, 176
    classification of, 140
    hypnotic drugs and, 270
    obesity and, 140
    prevalence in insomniacs, 76–79
    prevalence in normals, 75–79
    sex and, 75–77, 140
    types, 139, 140, 166, 167
Sleep attacks, 140, 165–67
Sleep cycle, 11, 13
Sleep deprivation, 18–20
Sleep disturbances
    age, 62–70, 134, 135

drug withdrawal and, 149–51, 169, 201, 202, 227, 239, 251–56, 261–67
drug-induced, 150, 151, 169, 202, 256, 261, 262, 264, 266
jet lag and, 136, 137, 189–91
medical conditions, 137–47
psychologic factors, 45, 46, 93, 111–28, 170–73, 199, 214–18, 268, 269
shift work and, 136, 137, 189–91
situational disturbances, 136, 137, 186, 214
Sleep duration
circadian rhythm, 15, 136, 137
long and short sleepers, 17, 18, 66, 67
normal sleepers, 11, 40, 135
optimal, 39–43, 195
type A behavior, 66
Sleep efficiency in insomnia
sleep latency, 65, 68
total wake time, 65, 69
variability in, 69
wake time after sleep onset, 65, 68, 69
Sleep efficiency-in normals
sleep latency, 63, 65
total wake time, 64–66
unusual sleep length, 66, 67
wake time after sleep onset, 63, 65
Sleep environment. *See* Environment and sleep
Sleep factors, 16, 22
Sleep function hypotheses
cortical homeostasis, 21
dreaming, 22
ethological, 21
hypnotoxin dissipation, 22
learning, 21
memory consolidation, 21, 22
ontogenetic, 21
organizational, 23
phylogenetic, 21
protein synthesis, 22
psychoanalytic, 23
reverse learning, 22
sleep factors, 16, 22
Sleep history, 8, 267, 268
bed partner and, 140, 164, 166, 167
clinical course, 165
differential diagnosis, 165, 166
impact of disorder, 167, 168
interviewing techniques, 163
sleep-wakefulness patterns, 166
specific sleep problem, 164, 165
Sleep laboratory evaluations
ad-lib sleep length, 62, 258
adaptation, 6, 61–63
definition of sleep stages, 6, 9–11

diagnostic studies, 48, 53, 166, 167, 176, 177
fixed sleep length, 62, 63
hypnotic drugs, 9, 251, 271
recording techniques, 4–6, 9
standardized scoring system, 5, 6, 9–11, 251
study conditions, 62, 251, 253
Sleep patterns in insomniacs
age effects on, 65, 67–70, 73, 134, 135
methods of study of, 7–9, 61, 62
naps, 166, 190, 202, 268
nocturnal myoclonus in, 75–79
physiologic correlates of, 73–80
sleep apnea in, 75–79, 139, 140, 165–67
sleep efficiency of, 65, 68, 69
sleep stages, 73
subjective estimates and, 70, 71, 102–5
variability of, 69
Sleep patterns in normals
age effects on, 11–13, 62–66, 72, 73, 135
cycle of young adult, 11
hormonal secretion and, 16, 17, 22, 23
methods of study, 5, 6, 9–11, 62, 63
naps, 11, 12, 38, 135
neurotransmitters and, 15, 16
nocturnal myoclonus, 75–79
physiologic correlates of, 9–17
sex effects on, 62–64
sleep apnea in, 75–79, 139, 140
sleep duration and, 11, 15, 18, 40, 66, 67
sleep efficiency of, 63–67
sleep stages, 9–17, 72
subjective estimates and, 70, 71
total sleep deprivation, effects on, 18, 19
Sleep physiology, 7, 9–17
Sleep Research and Treatment Center, 8
Sleep stages
definition, 4, 9–11
insomniacs vs controls, 73
normal sleepers, 5, 6, 11, 12, 72, 73, 135
short vs long sleepers, 66, 67
Sleepiness, daytime. *See* Excessive daytime sleepiness
Sleepwalking, 23, 91, 119, 166, 174, 175
Slow-wave sleep. *See* NREM sleep
Smoking and sleep disturbance, 99, 100, 149, 170, 201
Snoring, 140, 166, 167

Somatoform disorder and insomnia, 99, 123, 124, 220, 225, 226
Steroid preparations, 148
Stimulus control, 200, 233, 236, 238, 239
Stress management
    chronic insomnia, 197–201
    maladaptive coping mechanisms, 200, 201
    transient insomnia, 186, 187, 197, 198, 201
Stressful life events, 89–93, 100, 111–13, 171, 199, 214
Subjective estimates, sleep/wake-fulness
    accuracy, 70, 71
    drug and alcohol use, 102–5
    home vs laboratory sleep, 71
Substance use disorder and insomnia, 123, 124, 220, 226, 227, 239, 240
Suicidal ideation, 98, 100, 164, 173, 178, 295, 299
"Sundown syndrome," 204
Systematic desensitization, 200, 233, 235

Taylor Manifest Anxiety Scale and MMPI, 121
Temazepam (Restoril), 252, 256–60, 263, 264
Temperature regulation in sleep, 12, 14, 15, 136, 137
Testosterone, 17
Thyroid dysfunction and sleep, 143, 144
Tolerance, hypnotic drugs, 254, 255, 258, 259, 265–68
Tonic events in sleep, 12, 14, 16

Transient insomnia
    evaluation of, 162, 163, 169, 174, 175, 177
    hypnotic drug treatment in, 268
    psychotherapy in, 214, 215
    stress management in, 186, 187, 197, 198, 201
Trazodone (Desyrel), 288, 290, 292, 296, 297
Treatment of insomnia
    antidepressants, 282–99
    behavior therapy, 231–40
    benzodiazepine hypnotics, 255–71
    clinical issues in the elderly, 270, 271, 296, 299
    common shortcomings in, 51–53
    general recommendations, 187–204
    monoamine oxidase inhibitors, 290–93
    nonbenzodiazepine hypnotics, 253–55
    psychotherapy, 214–31
Triazolam (Halcion), 151, 252, 256–65
Tricyclic antidepressants, 222, 223, 268, 283–87
Triiodothyronine (Cytomel), 295
Tryptophan (Trofan, Tryptacin), 197, 295
Tyramine, 293

Vicious circle, insomnia, 188, 199, 215, 216, 225, 226, 268, 292
Viloxazine, 288, 289

Zimelidine, 288, 289
Zung Depression Scale, 121